Why Machines Learn

ANIL ANANTHASWAMY

Why Machines Learn

The Elegant Maths Behind Modern AI

ALLEN LANE

an imprint of

PENGUIN BOOKS

ALLEN LANE

UK | USA | Canada | Ireland | Australia
India | New Zealand | South Africa

Penguin Books is part of the Penguin Random House group of companies
whose addresses can be found at global.penguinrandomhouse.com.

First published in the United States of America by Dutton 2024
First published in Great Britain by Allen Lane 2024
002

Portions of chapter 12 and the epilogue appeared in *Quanta Magazine*.
The illustration in chapter 6 on PCA done on EEG data adapted with permission
from John Abel. The illustrations in chapter 12 on the bias-variance and double descent
curves adapted with permission from Mikhail Belkin. Illustrations about properties
of penguins in chapter 4 created courtesy of data made freely available by Kristen Gorman,
Allison Horst, and Alison Hill. The illustrations of biological neuron (p. 14),
paddy fields (p. 68), and the map of Manhattan (p. 147) by Roshan Shakeel.

The moral right of the author has been asserted

Printed and bound in Great Britain by Clays Ltd, Elcograf S.p.A.

The authorized representative in the EEA is Penguin Random House Ireland,
Morrison Chambers, 32 Nassau Street, Dublin D02 YH68

A CIP catalogue record for this book is available from the British Library

ISBN: 978–0–241–58648–8

www.greenpenguin.co.uk

to teachers everywhere, sung and unsung

Whatever we do, we have to make our life vectors.
Lines with force and direction.

—LIAM NEESON AS FBI AGENT MARK FELT
IN THE 2017 MOVIE OF THE SAME NAME

The author acknowledges with gratitude the support
of the Alfred P. Sloan Foundation in the
research and writing of this book.

CONTENTS

Prologue

Buried on page 25 of the July 8, 1958, issue of *The New York Times* was a rather extraordinary story. The headline read, "New Navy Device Learns by Doing: Psychologist Shows Embryo of Computer Designed to Read and Grow Wiser." The opening paragraph raised the stakes: "The Navy revealed the embryo of an electronic computer today that it expects will be able to walk, talk, see, write, reproduce itself and be conscious of its existence."

With hindsight, the hyperbole is obvious and embarrassing. But *The New York Times* wasn't entirely at fault. Some of the over-the-top talk also came from Frank Rosenblatt, a Cornell University psychologist and project engineer. Rosenblatt, with funding from the U.S. Office of Naval Research, had invented the perceptron, a version of which was presented at a press conference the day before the *New York Times* story about it appeared in print. According to Rosenblatt, the perceptron would be the "first device to think as the human brain" and such machines might even be sent to other planets as "mechanical space explorers."

None of this happened. The perceptron never lived up to the hype. Nonetheless, Rosenblatt's work was seminal. Almost every lecturer on artificial intelligence (AI) today will harken back to the perceptron. And that's justified. This moment in history—the arrival of large language models (LLMs) such as ChatGPT and its ilk and our response to it—which some have likened to what it must have felt like in the 1910s and '20s, when physicists were confronted with the craziness of quantum mechanics, has its roots in research initiated by Rosenblatt. There's a line in the *New York Times* story that only hints at the revolution the perceptron set in motion: "Dr. Rosenblatt said he could explain *why the machine learned* only in highly technical terms" (italics mine). The story, however, had none of the "highly technical" details.

This book does. It tackles the technical details. It explains the elegant mathematics and algorithms that have, for decades, energized and excited researchers in "machine learning," a type of AI that involves building machines that can learn to discern patterns in data without being explicitly programmed to do so. Trained machines can then detect similar patterns in new, previously unseen data, making possible applications that range from recognizing pictures of cats and dogs to creating, potentially, autonomous cars and other technology. Machines can learn because of the extraordinary confluence of math and computer science, with more than a dash of physics and neuroscience added to the mix.

Machine learning (ML) is a vast field populated by algorithms that leverage relatively simple math that goes back centuries, math one learns in high school or early in college. There's, of course, elementary algebra. Another extremely important cornerstone of machine learning is calculus, co-invented by no less a polymath than Isaac Newton. The field also relies heavily on the work of Thomas Bayes, the eighteenth-century English statistician and minister who gave us the eponymous Bayes's theorem, a key contribution to the field of probability and statistics. The work of German mathematician Carl Friedrich Gauss on the Gaussian distribution (and the bell-shaped curve) also permeates machine learning. Then there's linear algebra, which forms the backbone of machine learning. The earliest exposition of this branch of mathematics appears in a two-thousand-year-old Chinese text, *Nine Chapters on the Mathematical Art*. The modern version of linear algebra has its roots in the work of many mathematicians, but mainly Gauss, Gottfried Wilhelm Leibniz, Wilhelm Jordan, Gabriel Cramer, Hermann Günther Grassmann, James Joseph Sylvester, and Arthur Cayley.

By the mid-1850s, some of the basic math that would prove necessary to building learning machines was in place, even as other mathematicians continued developing more relevant mathematics and birthed and advanced the field of computer science. Yet, few could have dreamed that such early mathematical work would be the basis for the astounding developments in AI over the past half century, particularly over the last decade, some of which may legitimately allow us to envision a semblance of the kind of future Rosenblatt was overoptimistically foreshadowing in the 1950s.

This book tells the story of this journey, from Rosenblatt's perceptron to modern-day deep neural networks, elaborate networks of computational units called artificial neurons, through the lens of key mathematical ideas underpinning the field of machine learning. It eases gently into the math and then, ever so slowly, ratchets up the difficulty, as we go from the relatively simple ideas of the 1950s to the somewhat more involved math and algorithms that power today's machine learning systems.

Hence, we will unabashedly embrace equations and concepts from at least four major fields of mathematics—linear algebra, calculus, probability and statistics, and optimization theory—to acquire the minimum theoretical and conceptual knowledge necessary to appreciate the awesome power we are bestowing on machines. It is only when we understand the inevitability of learning machines that we will be prepared to tackle a future in which AI is ubiquitous, for good and for bad.

Getting under the mathematical skin of machine learning is crucial to our understanding of not just the power of the technology, but also its limitations. Machine learning systems are already making life-altering decisions for us: approving credit card applications and mortgage loans, determining whether a tumor is cancerous, predicting the prognosis for someone in cognitive decline (will they go on to get Alzheimer's?), and deciding whether to grant someone bail. Machine learning has permeated science, too: It is influencing chemistry, biology, physics, and everything in between. It's being used in the study of genomes, extrasolar planets, the intricacies of quantum systems, and much more. And as of this writing, the world of AI is abuzz with the advent of large language models such as ChatGPT. The ball has only just gotten rolling.

We cannot leave decisions about how AI will be built and deployed solely to its practitioners. If we are to effectively regulate this extremely useful, but disruptive and potentially threatening, technology, another layer of society—educators, politicians, policymakers, science communicators, or even interested consumers of AI—must come to grips with the basics of the mathematics of machine learning.

In her book *Is Math Real?*, mathematician Eugenia Cheng writes about the gradual process of learning mathematics: "It can . . . seem like we're taking very small steps and not getting anywhere, before suddenly we look behind us and discover we've climbed a giant mountain. All these things can be disconcerting, but accepting a little intellectual discomfort (or sometimes a lot of it) is an important part of making progress in math."

Fortunately, the "intellectual discomfort" in store for us is eminently endurable and more than assuaged by the intellectual payoff, because underlying modern ML is some relatively simple and elegant math—a notion that's best illustrated with an anecdote about Ilya

Sutskever. Today, Sutskever is best known as the co-founder of OpenAI, the company behind ChatGPT. More than a decade ago, as a young undergraduate student looking for an academic advisor at the University of Toronto, Sutskever knocked on Geoffrey Hinton's door. Hinton was already a well-known name in the field of "deep learning," a form of machine learning, and Sutskever wanted to work with him. Hinton gave Sutskever some papers to read, which he devoured. He remembers being perplexed by the simplicity of the math, compared to the math and physics of his regular undergrad coursework. He could read these papers on deep learning and understand powerful concepts. "How can it be that it's so simple . . . so simple that you can explain it to high school students without too much effort?" he told me. "I think that's actually miraculous. This is also, to me, an indication that we are probably on the right track. [It can't] be a coincidence that such simple concepts go so far."

Of course, Sutskever already had sophisticated mathematical chops, so what seemed simple to him may not be so for most of us, including me. But let's see.

This book aims to communicate the conceptual simplicity underlying ML and deep learning. This is not to say that everything we are witnessing in AI now—in particular, the behavior of deep neural networks and large language models—is amenable to being analyzed using simple math. In fact, the denouement of this book leads us to a place that some might find disconcerting, though others will find it exhilarating: These networks and AIs seem to flout some of the fundamental ideas that have, for decades, underpinned machine learning. It's as if empirical evidence has broken the theoretical camel's back in the same way experimental observations of the material world in the early twentieth century broke classical physics; we need something new to make sense of the brave new world awaiting us.

As I did the research for this book, I observed a pattern to my learning that reminded me of the way modern artificial neural networks learn: With each pass the algorithm makes through data, it learns more about the patterns that exist in that data. One pass may not be enough; nor ten; nor a hundred. Sometimes, neural networks learn over tens of thousands of iterations through the data. This is indeed the way I grokked the subject in order to write about it. Each pass through some corner of this vast base of knowledge caused some neurons in my brain to make connections, literally and metaphorically. Things that didn't make sense the first or second time around eventually did upon later passes.

I have used this technique to help readers make similar connections: I found myself repeating ideas and concepts over the course of writing this book, sometimes using the same phrasing or, at times, a different take on the same concept. These repetitions and rephrasings are intentional: They are one way that most of us who are not mathematicians or practitioners of ML can come to grips with a paradoxically simple yet complex subject. Once an idea is exposed, our brains might see patterns and make connections when encountering that idea elsewhere, making more sense of it than would have been possible at first blush.

I hope your neurons enjoy this process as much as mine did.

CHAPTER 1

Desperately Seeking Patterns

W hen he was a child, the Austrian scientist Konrad Lorenz, enamored by tales from a book called *The Wonderful Adventures of Nils*—the story of a boy's adventures with wild geese written by the Swedish novelist and winner of the Nobel Prize for Literature, Selma Lagerlöf—"yearned to become a wild goose." Unable to indulge his fantasy, the young Lorenz settled for taking care of a day-old duckling his neighbor gave him. To the boy's delight, the duckling began following him around: It had imprinted on him. "Imprinting" refers to the ability of many animals, including baby ducks and geese (goslings), to form bonds with the first moving thing they see upon hatching. Lorenz would go on to become an ethologist and would pioneer studies in the field of animal behavior, particularly imprinting. (He got ducklings to imprint on him; they followed him around as he walked, ran, swam, and even paddled away in a canoe.) He won the Nobel Prize for Physiology or Medicine in 1973, jointly with fellow ethologists Karl von Frisch and Nikolaas Tinbergen. The three were celebrated "for their discoveries concerning organization and elicitation of individual and social behavior *patterns*."

Patterns. While the ethologists were discerning them in the behavior of animals, the animals were detecting patterns of their own. Newly hatched ducklings must have the ability to make out or tell apart the properties of things they see moving around them. It turns out that ducklings can imprint not just on the first living creature they see moving, but on inanimate things as well. Mallard ducklings, for example, can imprint on a pair of moving objects that are similar in shape or color. Specifically, they imprint on the relational concept embodied by the objects. So, if upon birth the ducklings see two moving red objects, they will later follow two objects of the same color (even if those latter objects are blue, not red), but not two objects of different colors. In this case, the ducklings imprint on the *idea* of similarity. They also show the ability to discern *dis*similarity. If the first moving objects the ducklings see are, for example, a cube and a rectangular prism, they will recognize that the objects have different shapes and will later follow two objects that are different in shape (a pyramid and a cone, for example), but they will ignore two objects that have the same shape.

Ponder this for a moment. Newborn ducklings, with the briefest of exposure to sensory stimuli, detect patterns in what they see, form abstract notions of similarity/dissimilarity, and then will recognize those abstractions in stimuli they see later and act upon them. Artificial intelligence researchers would offer an arm and a leg to know just how the ducklings pull this off.

While today's AI is far from being able to perform such tasks with the ease and efficiency of ducklings, it does have something in common with the ducklings, and that's the ability to pick out and learn about patterns in data. When Frank Rosenblatt invented the perceptron in the late 1950s, one reason it made such a splash was because it was the first formidable "brain-inspired" algorithm that could learn about patterns in data simply by examining the data. Most important, given certain assumptions about the data, researchers proved that Rosenblatt's perceptron will always find the pattern hidden in the data in a finite amount of time; or, put differently, the perceptron will converge upon a solution without fail. Such certainties in computing are like gold dust. No wonder the perceptron learning algorithm created such a fuss.

But what do these terms mean? What are "patterns" in data? What does "learning about these patterns" imply? Let's start by examining this table:

x1	x2	y
4	2	8
1	2	5
0	5	10
2	1	4

Each row in the table is a triplet of values for variables $x1$, $x2$, and y. There's a simple pattern hidden in this data: In each row, the value of y is related to the corresponding values of $x1$ and $x2$. See if you can spot it before reading further.

In this case, with a pencil, paper, and a little effort one can figure out that y equals $x1$ plus two times $x2$.

$$y = x1 + 2x2$$

A small point about notation: We are going to dispense with the multiplication sign ("×") between two variables or between a constant and a variable. For example, we'll write

$$2 \times x2 \text{ as } 2x2 \text{ and } x1 \times x2 \text{ as } x1x2$$

Ideally, we should write $2x2$ as $2x_2$ and $x1x2$ as $x_1 x_2$, with the variables subscripted. But we'll dispense with the subscripts, too, unless it becomes absolutely necessary to use them. (Purists will cringe, but this method helps keep our text less cluttered and easy on the eye;

when we do encounter subscripts, read x_i as "x sub-i.") So, keep this in mind: If there's a symbol such as "x" followed by a digit such as "2," giving us $x2$, take the entire symbol to mean one thing. If a symbol (say, x or $x2$) is preceded by a number (say, 9), or by another symbol (say, $w1$), then the number and the symbol, or the two symbols, are being multiplied. So:

$$2x2 = 2 \times x2$$

$$x1x2 = x1 \times x2$$

$$w2x1 = w2 \times x1$$

Getting back to our equation $y = x1 + 2x2$, more generally, we can write this as:

$$y = w1x1 + w2x2, \text{ where } w1 = 1 \text{ and } w2 = 2$$

To be clear, we have found one of the many possible relationships between y and $x1$ and $x2$. There can be others. And indeed, for this example, there are, but we don't need to worry about them for our purposes here. Finding patterns is nowhere near as simple as this example is suggesting, but it gets us going.

We identified what's called a linear relationship between y, on the one hand, and $x1$ and $x2$, on the other. ("Linear" means that y depends only on $x1$ and $x2$, and not on $x1$ or $x2$ raised to some power, or on any product of $x1$ and $x2$.) Also, I'm using the words "equation" and "relationship" interchangeably here.

The relationship between y, $x1$, and $x2$ is defined by the constants $w1$ and $w2$. These constants are called the coefficients, or weights, of the linear equation connecting y to $x1$ and $x2$. In this simple case, assuming such a linear relationship exists, we figured out the values for $w1$ and $w2$ after inspecting the data. But often, the relationship between y and $(x1, x2, \ldots)$ is not so straightforward, especially when it extends to more values on the right side of the equation.

For example, consider:

$$y = w1x1 + w2x2 + w3x3 + \cdots + w9x9$$

Or, more generally, for a set of n weights, and using formal mathematical notation:

$$y = w1x1 + w2x2 + w3x3 + \cdots + wnxn = \sum_{i=1}^{n} wixi$$

The expression on the right, using the sigma notation, is shorthand for summing all $wixi$, where i takes on values from 1 to n.

In the case of 9 inputs, you'd be hard-pressed to extract the values of $w1$ to $w9$ just by visually inspecting the data and doing some mental arithmetic. That's where learning comes in. If there's a way to algorithmically figure out the weights, then the algorithm is "learning" the weights. But what's the point of doing that?

Well, once you have learned the weights—say, $w1$ and $w2$ in our simple, toy example—then given some value of $x1$ and $x2$ that wasn't in our initial dataset, we can calculate the value of y. Say, $x1 = 5$ and $x2 = 2$. Plug these values into the equation $y = x1 + 2x2$ and you get a value of $y = 9$.

What's all this got to do with real life? Take a very simple, practical, and some would say utterly boring problem. Let's say $x1$ represents the number of bedrooms in a house, and $x2$ represents the total square footage, and y represents the price of the house. Let's assume that there exists a linear relationship between $(x1, x2)$ and y. Then, by learning the weights of the linear equation from some existing data about houses and their prices, we have essentially built a very simple model with which to predict the price of a house, given the number of bedrooms and the square footage.

The above example—a teeny, tiny baby step, really—is the beginning of machine learning. What we just did is a simplistic form of something called supervised learning. We were given samples of data that had hidden in them some correlation between a set of inputs and a set of outputs. Such data are said to be annotated, or labeled; they are also called the training data. Each input $(x1, x2, \ldots, xn)$ has a label y attached to it. So, in our earlier numerical table, the pair of numbers $(4, 2)$ is labeled with $y = 8$, the pair $(1, 2)$ with 5, and so on. We figured out the correlation. Once it is learned, we can use it to make predictions about new inputs that weren't part of the training data.

Also, we did a very particular kind of problem solving called regression, where given some independent variables $(x1, x2)$, we built a model (or equation) to predict the value of a dependent variable (y). There are many other types of models we could have built, and we'll come to them in due course.

In this case, the correlation, or pattern, was so simple that we needed only a small amount of labeled data. But modern ML requires orders of magnitude more—and the availability of such data has been one of the factors fueling the AI revolution. (The ducklings, for their part, likely indulge in a more sophisticated form of learning. No parent duck sits around labeling the data for its ducklings, and yet the babies learn. How do they do it? Spoiler alert: We don't know, but maybe by understanding *why* machines learn, we can one day fully understand how ducklings and, indeed, humans learn.)

It may seem implausible, but this first step we took using a laughably simple example of supervised learning sets us on a path toward understanding modern deep neural networks—one step at a time, of course (with small, gentle, and occasionally maybe not so gentle dollops of vectors, matrices, linear algebra, calculus, probability and statistics, and optimization theory served, as needed, along the way).

Rosenblatt's perceptron, which we briefly encountered in the prologue, was for its time an astonishing example of one such learning algorithm. And because it was modeled on how neuroscientists thought human neurons worked, it came imbued with mystique and the promise that, one day, perceptrons would indeed make good on the promise of AI.

THE FIRST ARTIFICIAL NEURON

The perceptron's roots lie in a 1943 paper by an unlikely combination of a philosophically minded neuroscientist in his mid-forties and a homeless teenager. Warren McCulloch was an American neurophysiologist trained in philosophy, psychology, and medicine. During the 1930s, he worked on neuroanatomy, creating maps of the connectivity of parts of monkey brains. While doing so, he also obsessed over the "logic of the brain." By then, the work of mathematicians and philosophers like Alan Turing, Alfred North Whitehead, and Bertrand Russell was suggesting a deep connection between computation and logic. The statement "If P is true AND Q is true, then S is true" is an example of a logical proposition. The assertion was that all computation could be reduced to such logic. Given this way of thinking about computation, the question bothering McCulloch was this: If the brain is a computational device, as many think it is, how does it implement such logic?

With these questions in mind, McCulloch moved in 1941 from Yale University to the University of Illinois, where he met a prodigiously talented teenager named Walter Pitts. The youngster, already an accomplished logician ("a protégé of the eminent mathematical logician Rudolf Carnap"), was attending seminars run by Ukrainian mathematical physicist Nicolas Rashevsky in Chicago. Pitts, however, was a "mixed-up adolescent, essentially a runaway from a family that could not appreciate his genius." McCulloch and his wife, Rook, gave Walter a home. "There followed endless evenings sitting around the McCulloch kitchen table trying to sort out how the brain worked, with the McCullochs' daughter Taffy sketching little pictures," wrote computer scientist Michael Arbib. Taffy's drawings would later illustrate McCulloch and Pitts's 1943 paper, "A Logical Calculus of the Ideas Immanent in Nervous Activity."

In that work, McCulloch and Pitts proposed a simple model of a biological neuron. First, here's an illustration of a generic biological neuron:

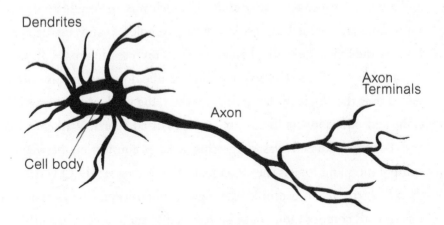

The neuron's cell body receives inputs via its treelike projections, called dendrites. The cell body performs some computation on these inputs. Then, based on the results of that computation, it may send an electrical signal spiking along another, longer projection, called the axon. That signal travels along the axon and reaches its branching terminals, where it's communicated to the dendrites of neighboring neurons. And so it goes. Neurons interconnected in this manner form a biological neural network.

McCulloch and Pitts turned this into a simple computational model, an artificial neuron. They showed how by using one such artificial neuron, or neurode (for "neuron" + "node"), one could implement certain basic Boolean logical operations such as AND, OR, NOT, and so on, which are the building blocks of digital computation. (For some Boolean operations, such as exclusive-OR, or XOR, you need more than one neurode, but more on this later.) What follows is an image of a single neurode. (Ignore the "*g*" and "*f*" inside the neuron for now; we'll come to those in a moment.)

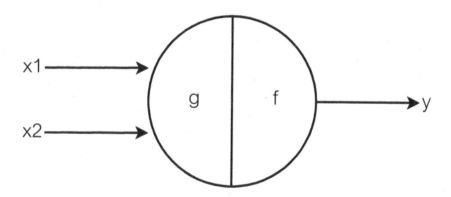

In this simple version of the McCulloch-Pitts model, *x1* and *x2* can be either 0 or 1. In formal notation, we can say:

$$x1, x2 \in \{0,1\}$$

That should be read as *x1* is an element of the set $\{0, 1\}$ and *x2* is an element of the set $\{0, 1\}$; *x1* and *x2* can take on only values 0 or 1 and nothing else. The neurode's output *y* is calculated by first summing the inputs and then checking to see if that sum is greater than or equal to some threshold, *theta* (θ). If so, *y* equals 1; if not, *y* equals 0.

$$sum = x1 + x2$$

$$If\ sum \geq \theta: y = 1$$

$$Else: y = 0$$

Generalizing this to an arbitrary sequence of inputs, $x1$, $x2$, $x3, \ldots, xn$, one can write down the formal mathematical description of the simple neurode. First, we define the function $g(x)$—read that as "g of x," where x here is the set of inputs $(x1, x2, x3, \ldots, xn)$—which sums up the inputs. Then we define the function $f(g(x))$—again, read that as "f of g of x"—which takes the summation and performs the thresholding to generate the output, y: It is zero if $g(x)$ is less than some θ and 1 if $g(x)$ is greater than or equal to θ.

$$g(x) = x1 + x2 + x3 + \cdots + xn = \sum_{i=1}^{n} xi$$

$$f(z) = \begin{cases} 0, & z < \theta \\ 1, & z \geq \theta \end{cases}$$

$$y = f(g(x)) = \begin{cases} 0, & g(x) < \theta \\ 1, & g(x) \geq \theta \end{cases}$$

With one artificial neuron as described, we can design some of the basic Boolean logic gates (AND & OR, for example). In an AND logic gate, the output y should be 1 if both $x1$ and $x2$ are equal to 1; otherwise, the output should be 0. In this case, $\theta = 2$ does the trick. Now, the output y will be 1 only when $x1$ and $x2$ are both 1 (only then will $x1 + x2$ be greater than or equal to 2). You can play with the value of θ to design the other logic gates. For example, in an OR gate, the output should be 1 if either $x1$ or $x2$ is 1; otherwise, the output should be 0. What should θ be?

The simple MCP model can be extended. You can increase the number of inputs. You can let inputs be "inhibitory," meaning $x1$ or $x2$ can be multiplied by -1. If one of the inputs to the neurode is inhibitory and you set the threshold appropriately, then the neurode will always output a 0, regardless of the value of all the other inputs. This allows you to build more complex logic. As does interconnecting multiple neurodes such that the output of one neurode serves as the input to another.

All this was amazing, and yet limited. The McCulloch-Pitts (MCP) neuron is a unit of computation, and you can use combinations of it to create any type of Boolean logic. Given that all digital computation at its most basic is a sequence of such logical operations, you can essentially mix and match MCP neurons to carry out any computation. This was an extraordinary statement to make in 1943. The mathematical roots of McCulloch and Pitts's paper were apparent. The paper had only three references—Carnap's *The Logical Syntax of Language;* David Hilbert and Wilhelm Ackermann's *Foundations of Theoretical Logic;* and Whitehead and Russell's *Principia Mathematica*—and none of them had to do with biology. There was no doubting the rigorous results derived in the McCulloch-Pitts paper. And yet, the upshot was simply a machine that could compute, not learn. In particular, the value of θ had to be hand-engineered; the neuron couldn't examine the data and figure out θ.

It's no wonder Rosenblatt's perceptron made such a splash. It could learn its weights from data. The weights encoded some knowledge, however minimal, about patterns in the data and remembered them, in a manner of speaking.

LEARNING FROM MISTAKES

Rosenblatt's scholarship often left his students floored. George Nagy, who came to Cornell University in Ithaca, New York, in 1960 to do his Ph.D. with Rosenblatt, recalled a walk the two of them took, during which they talked about stereo vision. Rosenblatt blew Nagy away with his mastery of the topic. "It was difficult not to feel naïve talking to him in general," said Nagy, now professor emeritus at Rensselaer Polytechnic Institute in Troy, New York; Rosenblatt's evident erudition was accentuated by his relative youth. (He was barely ten years older than Nagy.)

Rosenblatt's youthfulness almost got the two of them into trouble during a road trip. He and Nagy had to go from Ithaca to Chicago for a conference. Rosenblatt hadn't yet written the paper he wanted to present, so he asked Nagy to drive while he worked. Nagy had never owned a car and barely knew how to drive, but he agreed nonetheless. "Unfortunately, I drove in several lanes at once, and a policeman stopped us," Nagy said. Rosenblatt told the cop that he was a professor and had asked his student to drive. "The cop laughed and said, 'You are not a professor, you are a student.'" Fortunately, Rosenblatt had enough papers on him to convince the cop of his credentials, and the cop let the two go. Rosenblatt drove the rest of the way to Chicago, where he stayed up all night typing his paper, which he presented the next day. "He was able to do these things," Nagy told me.

By the time Nagy arrived at Cornell, Rosenblatt had already built the Mark I Perceptron; we saw in the prologue that Rosenblatt had done so in 1958, leading to the coverage in *The New York Times*. Nagy began working on the next machine, called Tobermory (named after the talking cat created by H. H. Munro, aka Saki), a hardware neural network designed for speech recognition. Meanwhile, the Mark I Perceptron and Rosenblatt's ideas had already garnered plenty of attention.

In the summer of 1958, the editor of the Cornell Aeronautical Laboratory's *Research Trends* magazine had devoted an entire issue to Rosenblatt ("because of the unusual significance of Dr. Rosenblatt's article," according to the editor). The article was titled "The Design of an Intelligent Automaton: Introducing the Perceptron—A Machine that Senses, Recognizes, Remembers, and Responds Like the Human Mind." Rosenblatt would eventually rue choosing the term "perceptron" to describe his work. "It became one of Rosenblatt's great regrets that he used a word that sounds like a machine," Nagy told me. By "perceptron," Rosenblatt really meant a class of models of the nervous system for perception and cognition.

His emphasis on the brain wasn't a surprise. Rosenblatt had studied with James Gibson, one of the giants in the field of visual perception. He also looked up to McCulloch and Pitts and to Donald Hebb, a Canadian psychologist who in 1949 introduced a model for how biological neurons learn—to be clear, "learning" here refers to learning about patterns in data and not to the kind of learning we usually associate with high-level human cognition. "He'd always talk highly of them," Nagy said.

While McCulloch and Pitts had developed models of the neuron, networks of these artificial neurons could not learn. In the context of biological neurons, Hebb had proposed a mechanism for learning that is often succinctly, but somewhat erroneously, put as "Neurons that fire together wire together." More precisely, according to this way of thinking, our brains learn because connections between neurons strengthen when one neuron's output is consistently involved in the firing of another, and they weaken when this is not so. The process is called Hebbian learning. It was Rosenblatt who took the work of these pioneers and synthesized it into a new idea:

artificial neurons that reconfigure as they learn, embodying information in the strengths of their connections.

As a psychologist, Rosenblatt didn't have access to the kind of computer power he needed to simulate his ideas in hardware or software. So, he borrowed time on the Cornell Aeronautical Laboratory's IBM 704, a five-ton, room-size behemoth. The collaboration proved fruitful when Rosenblatt's work caught the attention of physicists, resulting in papers in journals of psychology and of the American Physical Society. Rosenblatt eventually built the Mark I Perceptron. The device had a camera that produced a 20x20-pixel image. The Mark I, when shown these images, could recognize letters of the alphabet. But saying that the Mark I "recognized" characters is missing the point, Nagy said. After all, optical character recognition systems, which had the same abilities, were commercially available by the mid-1950s. "The point is that Mark I *learned* to recognize letters by being zapped when it made a mistake!" Nagy would say in his talks.

But what exactly is a perceptron, and how does it learn? In its simplest form, a perceptron is an augmented McCulloch-Pitts neuron imbued with a learning algorithm. What follows is an example with two inputs. Note that each input is being multiplied by its corresponding weight. (There is also an extra input, *b*, the reason for which will soon become clear.)

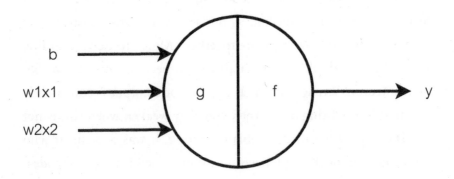

The computation carried out by the perceptron goes like this:

$$sum = w1x1 + w2x2 + b$$

$$If\ sum > 0: y = 1$$

$$Else: y = -1$$

More generally and in mathematical notation:

$$g(x) = w1x1 + w2x2 + \cdots + wnxn + b = \sum_{i=1}^{n} wixi + b$$

$$f(z) = \begin{cases} -1, z \leq 0 \\ 1, z > 0 \end{cases}$$

$$y = f(g(x)) = \begin{cases} -1, g(x) \leq 0 \\ 1, g(x) > 0 \end{cases}$$

The main difference from the MCP model presented earlier is that the perceptron's inputs don't have to be binary (0 or 1), but can take on any value. Also, these inputs are multiplied by their corresponding weights, so we now have a weighted sum. Added to that is an additional term b, the bias. The output, y, is either -1 or $+1$ (instead of 0 or 1, as in the MCP neuron). Crucially, unlike with the MCP neuron, the perceptron can learn the correct value for the weights and the bias for solving some problem.

To understand how this works, consider a perceptron that seeks to classify someone as obese, $y = +1$, or not-obese, $y = -1$. The inputs are a person's body weight, $x1$, and height, $x2$. Let's say that the dataset contains a hundred entries, with each entry comprising a person's body weight and height and a label saying whether a doctor thinks the person is obese according to guidelines set by the National Heart, Lung, and Blood Institute. A perceptron's task is to learn the values for $w1$ and $w2$ and the value of the bias term b, such that it correctly classifies each person in the dataset as "obese" or "not-obese." Note: We are analyzing a person's body weight and height while also talking about the perceptron's weights ($w1$ and $w2$); keep in mind these two different meanings of the word "weight" while reading further.

Once the perceptron has learned the correct values for $w1$ and $w2$ and the bias term, it's ready to make predictions. Given another person's body weight and height—this person was not in the original dataset, so it's not a simple matter of consulting a table of entries—the perceptron can classify the person as obese or not-obese. Of course, a few assumptions underlie this model, many of them to do with probability distributions, which we'll come to in subsequent chapters. But the perceptron makes one basic assumption: It assumes that there exists a clear, linear divide between the categories of people classified as obese and those classified as not-obese.

In the context of this simple example, if you were to plot the body weights and heights of people on an xy graph, with weights on the x-axis and heights on the y-axis, such that each person was a point on the graph, then the "clear divide" assumption states that there would exist a straight line separating the points representing the obese from the points representing the not-obese. If so, the dataset is said to be linearly separable.

Here's a graphical look at what happens as the perceptron learns. We start with two sets of data points, one characterized by black circles ($y = +1$, obese) and another by black triangles ($y = -1$, not-obese). Each data point is characterized by a pair of values ($x1$, $x2$), where $x1$ is the body weight of the person in kilograms, plotted along the x-axis, and $x2$ is the height in centimeters, plotted along the y-axis.

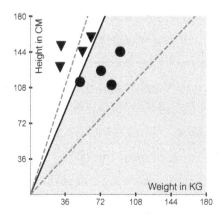

The perceptron starts with its weights, *w1* and *w2,* and the bias initialized to zero. The weights and bias represent a line in the xy plane. The perceptron then tries to find a separating line, defined by some set of values for its weights and bias, that attempts to classify the points. In the beginning, it classifies some points correctly and others incorrectly. Two of the incorrect attempts are shown as the gray dashed lines. In this case, you can see that in one attempt, all the points lie to one side of the dashed line, so the triangles are classified correctly, but the circles are not; and in another attempt, it gets the circles correct but some of the triangles wrong. The perceptron learns from its mistakes and adjusts its weights and bias. After numerous passes through the data, the perceptron eventually discovers at least one set of correct values of its weights and its bias term. It finds a line that delineates the clusters: The circles and the triangles lie on opposite sides. This is shown as a solid black line separating the coordinate space into two regions (one of which is shaded gray). The weights learned by the perceptron dictate the slope of the line; the bias determines the distance, or offset, of the line from the origin.

Once the perceptron has learned the correlation between the physical characteristics of a person (body weight and height) and whether that person is obese ($y = +1$ or -1), you can give it the body weight

23

and height of a person whose data weren't used during training, and the perceptron can tell you whether that person should be classified as obese. Of course, now the perceptron is making its best prediction, having learned its weights and bias, but the prediction can be wrong. Can you figure out why? See if you can spot the problem just by looking at the graph. (Hint: How many different lines can you draw that succeed in separating the circles from the triangles?) As we'll see, much of machine learning comes down to minimizing prediction error.

What's described above is a single perceptron unit, or one artificial neuron. It seems simple, and you may wonder what all the fuss is about. Well, imagine if the number of inputs to the perceptron went beyond two: ($x1$, $x2$, $x3$, $x4$, and so on), with each input (xi) getting its own axis. You can no longer do simple mental arithmetic and solve the problem. A line is no longer sufficient to separate the two clusters, which now exist in much higher dimensions than just two. For example, when you have three points ($x1$, $x2$, $x3$), the data is three-dimensional: you need a 2D plane to separate the data points. In dimensions of four or more, you need a hyperplane (which we cannot visualize with our 3D minds). In general, this higher-dimensional equivalent of a 1D straight line or a 2D plane is called a hyperplane.

Now think back to 1958. Rosenblatt built his Mark I Perceptron with numerous such units. It could process a 20x20-pixel image—for a total of 400 pixels, with each pixel corresponding to an x input value. So, the Mark I took as input a long row of values: $x1$, $x2$, $x3$, . . . , $x400$. A complex arrangement of artificial neurons, both with fixed, random weights and weights that could be learned, turned this vector of 400 values into an output signal that could be used to discern the pattern in the image. (This is an oversimplified description. Some of the computing was complex enough that it needed an IBM 704. We'll get a glimpse of the architectural details in chapter 10.) The Mark I could learn to categorize the letters of the alphabet encoded in those pixel values. All the logic just described, scaled up to handle 400 inputs, was built-in hardware. The machine, once it had learned (we'll see how in the next chapter), contained knowledge in the strengths (weights) of its connections. It's little wonder that everyone let their imagination run wild.

But if you closely examine what the perceptron learns, its limitations—in hindsight, of course—become obvious. The algorithm is helping the perceptron learn about correlations between values of $(x1, x2, \ldots, x400)$ and the corresponding value of y, if such correlations exist in the data. Sure, it learns the correlations without being explicitly told what they are, but these are correlations nonetheless. Is identifying correlations the same thing as thinking and reasoning? Surely, if the Mark I distinguished the letter "B" from the letter "G," it was simply going by the patterns and did not attach any meaning to those letters that would engender further reasoning. Such questions are at the heart of the modern debate over the limits of deep neural networks, the astonishing descendants of perceptrons. There is a path connecting these early perceptrons to the technology of large language models or the AI being developed for, say, self-driving cars. That path is not a straight one; rather, it's long and winding, with false turns and dead ends. But it's a fascinating, intriguing path nonetheless, and we are setting off on it now.

Building the perceptron device was a major accomplishment. An even bigger achievement was the mathematical proof that a single layer of perceptrons will always find a linearly separating hyperplane, *if* the data are linearly separable. Understanding this proof will require us to get our first taste of vectors and how they form the backbone of methods used to represent data in machine learning. It's our first mathematical pit stop.

CHAPTER 2

We Are All Just Numbers Here . . .

Less than a month before his death in September 1865, the Irish mathematician William Rowan Hamilton wrote a letter in four paragraphs to his son. In that letter, Hamilton recalled, among other things, a walk along the Royal Canal in Dublin, Ireland. It was October 16, 1843. Hamilton was on his way to attend a meeting of the Royal Irish Academy. His wife was with him. When the couple came underneath the Brougham Bridge, Hamilton, who had been struggling for more than a decade with some deep mathematical questions, had a flash of inspiration. "An electric circuit seemed to close; and a spark flashed forth . . . I [could not] resist the impulse—unphilosophical as it may have been—to cut with a knife on a stone of Brougham Bridge, as we passed it, the fundamental formula with the symbols, i, j, k; namely, $i^2 = j^2 = k^2 = ijk = -1$."

Hamilton signed off the letter to his son with these words: "With *this quaternion of paragraphs* [emphasis mine] I close this letter . . . Your affectionate father, William Rowan Hamilton." The use of the word "quaternion" was deliberate. A quaternion is a mathematical entity composed of four elements with very strange and special properties, which Hamilton discovered on that fateful day beneath Brougham Bridge. The equation he etched on the stone there, representing the general form of the quaternion, is one of the most famous examples of mathematical graffiti; the original, which has long since been defaced, was replaced by an official plaque reading:

> *Here as he walked by*
> *on the 16th of October 1843*
> *Sir William Rowan Hamilton*
> *in a flash of genius discovered*
> *the fundamental formula for*
> *quaternion multiplication*
> $i^2 = j^2 = k^2 = ijk = -1$
> *& cut it on a stone of this bridge.*

Quaternions are exotic entities, and they don't concern us. But to create the algebra for manipulating quaternions, Hamilton developed some other mathematical ideas that have become central to machine learning. In particular, he introduced the terms "scalar" and "vector." These days, most of us would likely not have heard of Hamilton, but we are intuitively familiar with the notion of scalars and vectors, even if not their formal definitions. Here's a quick primer.

Consider a man who walks five miles. Given that statement, the only thing we can say about what the man did is denoted by a single number: the distance walked. This is a scalar quantity, a stand-alone number. Now, if we were told that the man walked five miles in a northeasterly direction, we would have two pieces of information: the distance and the direction. This can be represented by a vector. A vector, then, has both a length (magnitude) and a direction. In the following graph, the vector is an arrow of magnitude 5.

If you closely examine the vector, you'll see that it has two components: one along the x-axis and another along the y-axis. It's equivalent

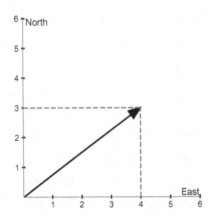

to saying that the man went four miles in the direction due east and three miles in the direction due north. The vector representing the actual walk is an arrow going from $(0, 0)$ to $(4, 3)$, giving both the direction and the distance. The magnitude of the vector is simply the length of the hypotenuse of the right-angled triangle formed by the vector and its components along the x- and y-axes. So, the vector's magnitude, or length, is equal to $\sqrt{4^2 + 3^2} = 5$.

Thinking in terms of vectors, without using formal ways of representing and manipulating them, predates Hamilton. For example, by the late 1600s, Isaac Newton was already using geometric ways of thinking about vector-like entities such as acceleration and force. Newton's Second Law of Motion says that the acceleration experienced by an object is proportional to the force acting upon it and that the object's acceleration and the force have the same direction. The first corollary to Newton's Laws of Motion, in his *Principia*, states, "A body by two forces conjoined will describe the diagonal of a parallelogram, in the same time that it would describe the sides, by those forces apart." This is a statement about using geometry to add two vectors, even though Newton didn't call the quantities vectors.

To understand vector addition, we can go back to our man who walked five miles, represented by a vector going from $(0, 0)$ to $(4, 3)$. After reaching the destination, the man turns more northward such that in the coordinate plane, he reaches $(6, 9)$: He has effectively walked two more miles in the direction due east and six more miles in the direction due north. This is represented by a second vector, an arrow drawn from $(4, 3)$ to $(6, 9)$. This new vector has an x component of 2 and a y component of 6. What is the total distance the man walked? And what is the net distance in the xy coordinate space, from origin to the final destination? This graph shows you the answers to both:

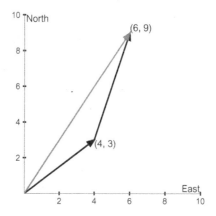

The magnitude of the two individual vectors, or walks, is $\sqrt{4^2 + 3^2} = \sqrt{25} = 5$ and $\sqrt{2^2 + 6^2} = \sqrt{4 + 36} = \sqrt{40} = 6.32$. So, the total distance the man walks is $5 + 6.32 - 11.32$ miles.

The resultant vector is an arrow drawn from the origin to the final destination, which is $(6, 9)$, and its magnitude is $\sqrt{6^2 + 9^2} = \sqrt{36 + 81} = \sqrt{117} = 10.82$. The net distance in the xy coordinate space is 10.82 miles.

This now helps us make sense of what Newton was saying. Let's say the acceleration caused by one force acting upon an object is given by the vector (2, 6) and that the acceleration caused by another force on the same object is given by the vector (4, 3). Both forces are acting on the object at the same time. What is the total acceleration of the object? According to Newton's corollary, the geometric interpretation involves drawing a parallelogram, as shown in the following figure; the net acceleration, then, is given by the diagonal vector (6, 9):

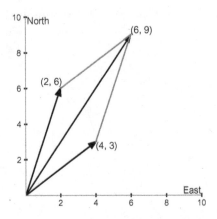

If the acceleration is in units of meters per second per second (m/s^2), then the net acceleration is given by the magnitude of the vector (6, 9), which equals 10.82 m/s^2, in the direction of the arrow.

I have chosen to add the same vectors in this case as in the example of the man walking, but here the two vectors represent acceleration, not distance, and they both have their tails at (0, 0). What this tells you is that the vector (2, 6) is the same vector regardless of whether its tail is at (0, 0) or at (4, 3), as in the previous example. An important property of vectors is that we can move the arrow representing a vector in the coordinate space, and if we don't change the length of the arrow and its orientation, it's the same vector. Why? Well, because we haven't changed its length or its direction, the two properties that define the vector.

None of this was formally understood as the beginnings of vector analysis when Newton published his *Principia* in 1687. His contemporary Gottfried Wilhelm Leibniz (1646–1716), however, had more than an inkling about this new way of thinking. In 1679, in a letter to another luminous contemporary, Christiaan Huygens, Leibniz wrote, "I believe that I have found the way . . . that we can represent figures and even machines and movements by characters, as algebra represents numbers or magnitudes." Leibniz never quite formalized his intuition, but his prescience—as we'll see when we understand the importance of vectors for machine learning—was astounding. Following Leibniz, a host of other mathematicians, including Johann Carl Friedrich Gauss (1777–1855), developed methods for the geometric representation of certain types of numbers in two dimensions, setting the stage for Hamilton's discovery of quaternions and the formalization of vector analysis.

VECTORS BY THE NUMBERS

Vector analysis doesn't have to be geometric. It can come down to manipulating numbers written in a certain format. And in fact, for machine learning, that's how we need to think about vectors. For example, the accelerations caused by the two forces in the previous example are simply arrays of two numbers each, [4, 3] and [2, 6], respectively. Adding them is the same as adding the individual components of each vector (stacked vertically, as a column). You don't have to fuss with arrows:

$$\begin{bmatrix} 4 \\ 3 \end{bmatrix} + \begin{bmatrix} 2 \\ 6 \end{bmatrix} = \begin{bmatrix} 6 \\ 9 \end{bmatrix}$$

Subtracting vectors is similar.

$$\begin{bmatrix} 4 \\ 3 \end{bmatrix} - \begin{bmatrix} 2 \\ 6 \end{bmatrix} = \begin{bmatrix} 2 \\ -3 \end{bmatrix}$$

What just happened? Why is the y component of the resultant vector negative? If these numbers still represent acceleration, then subtraction meant that the second force was acting against the first force; along the x-axis, the acceleration is just a little bit less than when we were adding the two vectors, but it is still positive; along the y-axis, however, the force is now acting against the initial direction of motion, resulting in a deceleration.

One can multiply a vector by a scalar—simply multiply each element of the vector by the scalar.

$$5 \times \begin{bmatrix} 4 \\ 3 \end{bmatrix} = \begin{bmatrix} 20 \\ 15 \end{bmatrix}$$

Geometrically, that's the same as stretching the arrow (or vector) five times in the same direction. The magnitude of the original vector is 5. Scaling it 5 times gives us a new magnitude of 25. If you were to calculate the magnitude of the new vector using its scaled-up coordinates, you'd again get:

$$\sqrt{20^2 + 15^2} = \sqrt{400 + 225} = \sqrt{625} = 25$$

There's yet another way to represent vectors. Restricting ourselves to two dimensions, think of a vector of length one, **i**, along the x-axis and a vector of length one, **j**, along the y-axis. Note that **i** and **j** are in lowercase and boldface; this signifies that they are vectors. So, **i** can be thought of as an arrow that points from (0, 0) to (1, 0) and **j** as an arrow that points from (0, 0) to (0, 1). Each has a magnitude of 1 and is also called a unit vector. Given this, the vectors (4, 3) and (2, 6), in Cartesian coordinates, can be written as $4\mathbf{i} + 3\mathbf{j}$ and $2\mathbf{i} + 6\mathbf{j}$, respectively. That's the same as saying that the vector $(4, 3)$ is 4 units along the x-axis and 3 units along the y-axis and that the vector $(2, 6)$ is 2 units along the x-axis and 6 units along the y-axis. The use of $\mathbf{i}$ and $\mathbf{j}$ is shorthand for representing vectors. It's also important to point out that a unit vector is simply a vector with a magnitude of 1; it doesn't have to lie along the perpendicular axes of some coordinate space.

These ideas apply to higher dimensions, too, and we'll come to that. For now, getting a handle on the mathematical manipulation of 2D vectors and their corresponding geometric meanings will go a long way toward helping us understand the role of their higher-dimensional counterparts in machine learning.

THE DOT PRODUCT

Another important operation with vectors is something called the dot product. Consider vector $(4, 0)$, call it $\mathbf{a}$, and vector $(5, 5)$, call it $\mathbf{b}$. (Again, the boldface and lowercase for letters $\mathbf{a}$ and $\mathbf{b}$ signify that they are vectors.) Conceptually, the dot product $\mathbf{a.b}$—read that as "a dot b"— is defined as the magnitude of $\mathbf{a}$ multiplied by the projection of $\mathbf{b}$ onto $\mathbf{a}$, where the projection can be thought of as the "shadow cast" by one vector onto another.

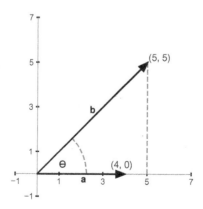

The magnitude of **a** is denoted by $\|\mathbf{a}\|$ or $|\mathbf{a}|$. The projection of **b** onto **a** is given by the magnitude of **b**, or $\|\mathbf{b}\|$, multiplied by the cosine of the angle between the two vectors. For the vectors we have chosen, the angle between them is 45 degrees (or $\dfrac{\pi}{4}$ radians), as shown in the preceding graph. So:

$$\mathbf{a}.\mathbf{b} = \|\mathbf{a}\| \times \|\mathbf{b}\| \times \cos(\pi / 4)$$

$$\cos(\pi / 4) = \frac{1}{\sqrt{2}}$$

$$\|\mathbf{a}\| = \sqrt{4^2 + 0^2} = 4$$

$$\|\mathbf{b}\| = \sqrt{5^2 + 5^2} = \sqrt{50} = 5\sqrt{2}$$

$$\Rightarrow \mathbf{a}.\mathbf{b} = 4 \times 5\sqrt{2} \times \frac{1}{\sqrt{2}} = 20$$

Note: the symbol $\Rightarrow$ means "which implies that."

Now let's make a couple of small tweaks. Let the vector **a** be given by (1, 0), vector **b** by (3, 3). Vector **a** has a magnitude of 1, so it's a "unit vector." Now, if you were to take the dot product **a.b**, you'd get:

$$\mathbf{a}.\mathbf{b} = \|\mathbf{a}\| \times \|\mathbf{b}\| \times \cos(\pi / 4)$$

$$= 1 \times 3\sqrt{2} \times \cos\left(\frac{\pi}{4}\right)$$

$$= 1 \times 3\sqrt{2} \times \frac{1}{\sqrt{2}}$$

$$= 3$$

The dot product turns out to be equal to the x component of vector **b**, or the shadow cast by **b** onto the x-axis, the direction of the

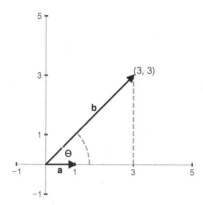

unit vector. This gives us a crucial geometric intuition: If one of the vectors involved in a dot product is of length 1, then the dot product equals the projection of the other vector onto the vector of unit length. In our special case, the unit vector lies along the x-axis, so the projection of vector **b** onto the x-axis is simply its x component, 3.

But here's something amazing about dot products. Even if the unit vector is not along one of the axes, this geometric truth still holds. Let's say **a** is $\left(\frac{1}{\sqrt{2}}, \frac{1}{\sqrt{2}}\right)$. Its magnitude is 1, so it's a unit vector, but it's at a 45-degree angle to the x-axis. Let's say **b** is the vector (1, 3). The dot product **a.b** is $\|\mathbf{a}\| \times \|\mathbf{b}\| \times \cos(\theta)$, which equals $1 \times \|\mathbf{b}\| \times \cos(\theta)$, which in turn is the projection of the vector **b** onto the straight line that extends along vector **a** (see figure on next page).

Another important thing the dot product tells us about two vectors is whether they are at right angles, or orthogonal, to each other. If they are at right angles, then cosine of (90°) equals zero. So, regardless of the length of the vectors, their dot product, or the projection of vector **b** onto vector **a**, is always zero. Conversely, if the dot product of two vectors is zero, they are orthogonal to each other.

How would we calculate the dot product if we were to use the

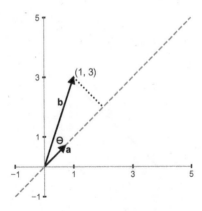

other method for representing vectors, using their components, and we didn't know the angle between the two vectors?

Say, $\mathbf{a} = a1\mathbf{i} + a2\mathbf{j}$ and $\mathbf{b} = b1\mathbf{i} + b2\mathbf{j}$. Then:

$$\mathbf{a.b} = (a1\mathbf{i} + a2\mathbf{j}).(b1\mathbf{i} + b2\mathbf{j}) = a1b1 \times \mathbf{i.i} + a1b2 \times \mathbf{i.j} + a2b1 \times \mathbf{j.i} + a2b2 \times \mathbf{j.j}$$

Note that the second and third terms in the equation turn out to be zero. The vectors $\mathbf{i}$ and $\mathbf{j}$ are orthogonal, so $\mathbf{i.j}$ and $\mathbf{j.i}$ are zero. Also, both $\mathbf{i.i}$ and $\mathbf{j.j}$ equal 1. All we are left with is a scalar quantity:

$$\mathbf{a.b} = a1b1 + a2b2$$

MACHINES AND VECTORS

If all this feels far removed from machine learning, perceptrons, and deep neural networks, rest assured it's not. It's central to the plot. And we are getting there, by leaps and bounds, yet by stepping carefully only on the stones necessary for sure footing.

It's time to revisit the perceptron and think of it in terms of vectors. The intent is to gain geometric insights into how data points and the weights of a perceptron can be represented as vectors and how to visualize what happens when a perceptron tries to find a linearly separating hyperplane that divides the data points into two clusters. Much of it has to do with using dot products of vectors to find the relative distances of the data points from the hyperplane, as we'll see.

Recall the generic equation for a perceptron, which says that the perceptron outputs 1 if the weighted sum of its inputs plus some bias term, b, is greater than 0; otherwise, it outputs -1.

$$g(\mathbf{x}) = w1x1 + w2x2 + \cdots + wnxn + b = \sum_{i=i}^{n} wixi + b$$

$$f(z) = \begin{cases} -1, & z \leq 0 \\ 1, & z > 0 \end{cases}$$

$$y = f(g(\mathbf{x})) = \begin{cases} -1, & g(\mathbf{x}) \leq 0 \\ 1, & g(\mathbf{x}) > 0 \end{cases}$$

We have made a subtle change to the notation we used previously: The argument to the function g is now a vector; in the previous chapter, because we hadn't yet introduced the notion of vectors, we simply had $g(x)$ instead of $g(\mathbf{x})$. Let's stick to the two-dimensional case, with data points given by different values for $(x1, x2)$ and the weights of the perceptron given by $(w1, w2)$. The perceptron first computes the weighted sum of the inputs:

$$w1x1 + w2x2$$

If this weighted sum is greater than some threshold, call it $-b$, then the perceptron's output, y, is 1. Else it is -1. So:

$$y = \begin{cases} -1, & w1x1 + w2x2 \leq -b \\ 1, & w1x1 + w2x2 > -b \end{cases}$$

This can be rewritten as:

$$y = \begin{cases} -1, & w1x1 + w2x2 + b \leq 0 \\ 1, & w1x1 + w2x2 + b > 0 \end{cases}$$

Let's put on our vectors hat. The set of weights (*w1, w2*) is nothing but a vector **w**. But what exactly does **w** represent?

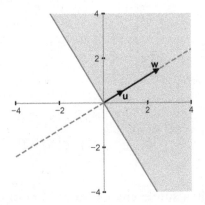

The figure above shows a weight vector, **w** = (2.5, 1.5). It also shows a unit vector in the same direction, **u**. The dashed line gives us the direction along which the two vectors lie. Let's draw a solid black line perpendicular, or orthogonal, to vectors **w** and **u**. This line separates the shaded area from the rest of the coordinate space. So, if we were trying to find a line that clearly delineated the xy plane into two regions, shaded and unshaded, all we would need to specify such a boundary would be the vector **w**, or the corresponding unit vector, **u**. If the solid line, or boundary, in the preceding figure is the separating hyperplane, then the vector **w** is orthogonal to it and characterizes that hyperplane. The boundary is a line when we are dividing 2D space, a plane when partitioning a 3D volume, and a hyperplane in higher dimensions.

Our earlier look at the perceptron learning algorithm showed that it tries to find a hyperplane that divides the coordinate space into two. So, the perceptron finds, or learns, an appropriate set of weights. These weights constitute a vector, **w**, which is orthogonal to the hyperplane. As you change the weights of the perceptron, you change the direction of **w**, and so you change the orientation of the hyperplane, which is always perpendicular to **w**. And what's true of **w** is also true of the unit vector **u** that lies in the same direction. So, one way of rephrasing what the perceptron does is to say that it finds the vector **w**, which is the same as saying that it finds the corresponding perpendicular hyperplane.

Now consider the data points that either lie or don't lie in the shaded area. Each data point is given by ($x1$, $x2$) and can be thought of as a vector, too. Then the weighted sum ($w1x1 + w2x2$) is the same as the dot product of the vector representing the data point with the weight vector. Note that if the data point lies on the hyperplane, which in the 2D case is just a line, then the vector ($x1$, $x2$) will be orthogonal to **w**, making the dot product equal zero. On the next page is a graphical look at the dot product of data points and the weight vector. For convenience, we'll work with a weight vector of unit length. It doesn't change anything conceptually, but it does simplify the math. Let's start with vector **a**, given by data point (3, 1).

Because **w** is a unit vector, its dot product with **a** equals the projection of **a** onto the dashed line. The point at which **a** lands on the line perpendicular to the hyperplane is a measure of the distance of the point (3,1) from the hyperplane.

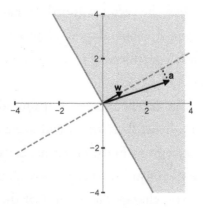

Next, let's look at this somewhat busy but important depiction of the dot product of the weight vector with four different data points, or vectors, **a** $(3, 1)$, **b** $(2, -1)$, **c** $(-2, 1)$, and **d** $(-1, -3)$.

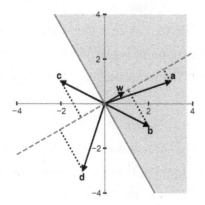

It's clear that the dot product of each vector with **w** is telling you something about that vector: its distance from the hyperplane and whether it's to one side of it (dot product is +ve) or to the other (−ve). In this scenario, points **a** and **b** are linearly separated from points **c** and **d**. (Points lying in the gray shaded area represent $y = 1$; points lying in the unshaded area and points lying on the dividing line itself represent $y = -1$.)

So, let's say the perceptron, at first attempt, finds the weights and the hyperplane as depicted above. But let's also say that according to our labeled training data, points **a**, **b**, and **c** should have been on one side of the hyperplane and only point **d** on the other. For argument's sake, let's say that **a**, **b**, and **c** represent people classified as those who like thriller movies; **d** represents a person who doesn't. This means that the perceptron hasn't yet found the correct hyperplane. One thriller lover has been classified as a thriller hater. That's where the bias term comes in. Adding a bias term to the equation is the same as moving the hyperplane away from the origin, but without changing its orientation. For example, after iterating through the training data, the perceptron could have found this hyperplane:

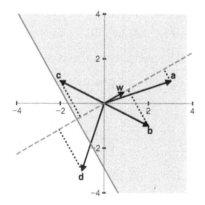

It's clear by looking at the figure above that if the data are linearly separable into two clusters, then there exist many, many separating hyperplanes (for different values of the bias term and different orientations of **w**). Just think of how many straight lines you can draw that go through the space between **c** and **d**: in principle, infinitely many. The perceptron guarantees only that it'll find one, and not necessarily the best one. We'll come to what "best" means in more detail, but it has to do with prediction. After all, the perceptron is learning the weights and the bias term in order to classify some as-yet-unseen data point with respect to the hyperplane. For example, given two characteristics of some person that we are using to classify that person as a thriller lover or a thriller hater, on which side of the hyperplane would the person have to be to be classified as one or the other? A good or best possible hyperplane will minimize future prediction errors. (Defining a "future" prediction error, let alone minimizing it, is a nontrivial, or not an easy, problem.)

These graphs are a way of developing an intuitive sense of what was happening when a perceptron learned. If you were to try to write a computer program to simulate a perceptron, you wouldn't be drawing charts and graphs. You'd be manipulating numbers. Fortunately, the numerical representations we have seen of vectors so far are already enough to showcase the power of these abstractions. In our 2D example, data points $(x1, x2)$ are just arrays of numbers, each array with two elements. The weight vector is similarly another array of two numbers. Finding the dot product is a matter of manipulating these arrays.

More generically, these arrays are called matrices, which contain rows and columns of numbers. For example, if there are m rows and n columns, then we have what's called an $m \times n$ matrix (read as an "m by n matrix"). A vector is a particular form of matrix with either one row or one column: either $m=1$ or $n=1$. We saw these earlier, only the term "matrix" hadn't yet been introduced. But that's what vectors are: matrices with just one column or one row. Here's the example of adding two one-column matrices to get a third one-column matrix.

$$\begin{bmatrix} 4 \\ 3 \end{bmatrix} + \begin{bmatrix} 2 \\ 6 \end{bmatrix} = \begin{bmatrix} 6 \\ 9 \end{bmatrix}$$

Flip one of the one-column matrices on its side, and you get a matrix with a single row:

$$\begin{bmatrix} 4 & 3 \end{bmatrix}$$

So, in formal notation, a one-column matrix with two elements is given by:

$$\begin{bmatrix} a11 \\ a21 \end{bmatrix}$$

The notation says that the column matrix has two rows (indexed by numbers 1 and 2) and that each row has just one element (index 1). When you flip the matrix on its side, the numbering changes. (Note that the row index is 1, while the columns have indices 1 and 2.)

$$\begin{bmatrix} a11 & a12 \end{bmatrix}$$

This is called taking the "transpose" of a matrix. (It looks trivial, or easy, for a column matrix, but it does get more involved for higher-order matrices, which we'll come to in later chapters.) Taking the transpose is a key aspect of calculating the dot product between two column matrices. We'll use boldface capital letters to signify matrices. Let **A** be the column matrix $\begin{bmatrix} a11 \\ a21 \end{bmatrix}$ and **B** the column matrix $\begin{bmatrix} b11 \\ b21 \end{bmatrix}$. You cannot take a dot product of two column matrices. That's because to take the dot product, the number of columns in the first matrix must equal the number of rows in the second one. So, in our case, one of them must be transposed. The transpose of **A** is written as $\mathbf{A}^T$. The dot product **A.B** is written as $\mathbf{A}^T\mathbf{B}$ or $\mathbf{B}^T\mathbf{A}$. (They are one and the same thing in this case.)

$$\mathbf{A}.\mathbf{B} = \mathbf{A}^T\mathbf{B} = \begin{bmatrix} a11 & a12 \end{bmatrix} \times \begin{bmatrix} b11 \\ b21 \end{bmatrix} = a11b11 + a12b21$$

Note that this is exactly the value you'd get if you wrote the vectors in terms of their unit vectors $\mathbf{i}$ and $\mathbf{j}$. If $\mathbf{a} = a11\mathbf{i} + a12\mathbf{j}$ and $\mathbf{b} = b11\mathbf{i} + b21\mathbf{j}$, then:

$$\mathbf{a}.\mathbf{b} = (a11\mathbf{i} + a12\mathbf{j}) . (b11\mathbf{i} + b21\mathbf{j})$$

$$\Rightarrow \mathbf{a}.\mathbf{b} = a11b11 \times \mathbf{i}.\mathbf{i} + a11b21 \times \mathbf{i}.\mathbf{j} + a12b11 \times \mathbf{j}.\mathbf{i} + a12b21 \times \mathbf{j}.\mathbf{j}$$

$$\Rightarrow \mathbf{a}.\mathbf{b} = a11b11 + a12b21$$

Here's another cool thing about using matrices, rather than arrows, to represent vectors: You can just manipulate the numbers and get a scalar value for the dot product without worrying about the cosine of the angle between them. What this means is that if you have a bunch of data points, each represented by a vector, and you want to find their relative distances from a hyperplane characterized by a weight vector $\mathbf{w}$, all you do is take the dot products of each data point with $\mathbf{w}$, and you'll have the necessary information.

And if one of the data points is on the hyperplane, its dot product with the weight vector would be zero, signifying that the data point is orthogonal to the weight vector and that its distance from the hyperplane is zero.

PUTTING IT TOGETHER

All this is leading up to a rather elegant shorthand notation for the perceptron.

Consider inputs $[x1, x2, \ldots, xn]$. You can write this as a column vector **x**. Similarly, the weights, using one weight for each input, $[w1, w2, \ldots, wn]$, are the column vector **w**. Note that we have made another subtle shift in notation: We use square brackets to contain the elements of **w** and **x**, [], instead of parentheses, (), to signal that **w** and **x** are matrices or vectors.

We know that the output of a perceptron involves calculating the weighted sum $w1x1 + w2x2 + \cdots + wnxn$. This is more concisely written as the dot product of **w** and **x**, or $\mathbf{w}^T\mathbf{x}$. Given this, here's what a perceptron does:

$$y = \begin{cases} -1, & \mathbf{w}^T\mathbf{x}+b \leq 0 \\ 1, & \mathbf{w}^T\mathbf{x}+b > 0 \end{cases}$$

Pictorially, let's look again at the perceptron with two inputs and two weights:

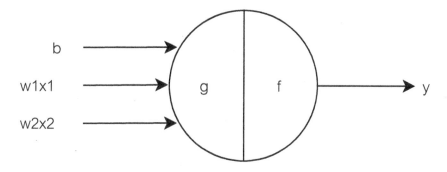

The bias term looks incongruous. There's a neat little trick to subsume it into the weight vector (see first figure on next page).

In this depiction, the bias term b is equal to the weight $w0$ and is multiplied by $x0$. However, $x0$ is always set to 1, ensuring that the bias b is always added to the weighted sum of the other inputs. The weight vector, **w**, is now given by $[w0, w1, w2]$. The input vector, **x**, equals $[x0, x1, x2]$, where $x0=1$.

The generic perceptron, for input vector $\mathbf{x} = [x0, x1, x2, \ldots, xn]$

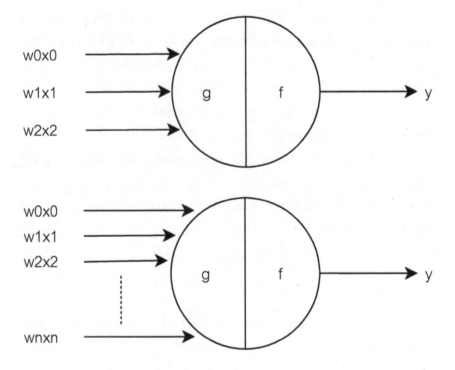

and a weight vector $\mathbf{w} = [w0, w1, w2, \ldots, wn]$ looks like the figure directly above.

The equation of the perceptron looks even simpler:

$$y = \begin{cases} -1, & \mathbf{w}^T\mathbf{x} \leq 0 \\ 1, & \mathbf{w}^T\mathbf{x} > 0 \end{cases}$$

Let's burn this equation into our mind's eye. It's a simple, eloquent statement of these facts: The weight vector $\mathbf{w}$ is perpendicular to the line, or hyperplane, that separates the data points into two clusters. For one cluster of points, $\mathbf{w}^T\mathbf{x}$ is less than or equal to zero, and the output of the perceptron is −1. For the other cluster of points, $\mathbf{w}^T\mathbf{x}$ is greater than zero, and the output of the perceptron is 1. The points that lie on the hyperplane (given by $\mathbf{w}^T\mathbf{x} = 0$) are assigned to the cluster with the label $y = -1$. From a machine learning perspective, the task of a perceptron is to learn the weight vector, given a set of input data vectors, such that the weight vector represents a hyperplane that separates the data into two clusters. Once it has learned the weight vector, and then is given a new data point to classify (say, as "obese" or "not-obese"), the perceptron simply has to calculate $\mathbf{w}^T\mathbf{x}$ for the new instance of data, see if it falls on one side or the other of the hyperplane, and then classify it accordingly.

This has been a somewhat extended journey from Rosenblatt's ideas to a formal notation for a linear transformation of an input to an output, but it's hard to overstate the importance of this formulation. It's one of the cornerstones of our eventual forays into other ML techniques, including modern deep neural networks.

GUARANTEED TO SUCCEED

Soon after Rosenblatt invented the perceptron learning algorithm—we'll come to its exact formulation in a bit—researchers, Rosenblatt included, began analyzing it, developing theorems and proofs to show that it was indeed a computationally viable algorithm. Among these proofs were those that showed that perceptrons would converge upon a solution if one existed, "solution" being defined as a hyperplane that linearly separated the data into two groups. George Nagy remembered the time. "Rosenblatt himself collected these," Nagy told me. "He had a collection of . . . proofs that had been published in the 1960s." One such proof was developed in 1962 by Henry David Block, an applied mathematician at Cornell University who collaborated with Rosenblatt on the mathematical analysis of perceptrons. Block's proof was complicated, but it established upper bounds for the number of mistakes made by the perceptron learning algorithm as it tried to find a linearly separating hyperplane. Block was an accomplished theoretician, at home with reasoning about machines and "the logic of what's possible." When he died in 1978, the Cornell faculty said in their memorial statement, "For all his exceptional intelligence and accomplishments, David Block was a deeply modest, indeed, humble person, tolerant of everything save smugness."

Block's intolerance of smugness comes through in his classic twenty-two-page review of *Perceptrons: An Introduction to Computational Geometry*, a three-hundred-page book by MIT scientists and AI pioneers Marvin Minsky and Seymour Papert. A tour de force of exposition, theorems, and proofs, *Perceptrons* made a huge splash upon its publication in 1969. "We will study in great detail a class of computations that make decisions by weighing evidence," Minsky and Papert write in its introduction. "The machines we will study are abstract versions of a class of devices known under various names; we have agreed to use the name 'perceptron' in recognition of the pioneer work of Frank Rosenblatt." Block praises the book early on in his review: "It is a remarkable book. Not only do the authors formulate a new and fundamental conceptual framework, but they also fill in the details using strikingly ingenious mathematical techniques." One of these ingenious mathematical techniques was Minsky and Papert's version of the convergence proof, but their accompanying notes seemed to irritate Block. The duo had drawn attention to a 1954 paper by Israeli mathematician Shmuel Agmon, who had seemingly anticipated the convergence proof. "In an abstract mathematical sense, both theorem and proof already existed before the perceptron," Minsky and Papert write. "It is quite clear that the theorem would have been instantly obvious had the cyberneticists interested in perceptrons known about Agmon's work."

The dig at cyberneticists rubbed Block the wrong way. "Cybernetics," a term coined by American mathematician Norbert Wiener in his 1948 book of the same name, refers to the study of "control and communication in the animal and the machine." So, those doing research on perceptrons as a means of understanding the human brain and nervous system were cyberneticists. Should they have known of precursors to the convergence proof for perceptrons, which shows that the algorithm will find an answer after a finite number of steps? "Since there is nothing in 'Agmon's work' . . . about the termination of the process after a finite number of steps, this aspect of the theorem at least does not seem to be 'instantly obvious,'" Block quipped in his review. "Furthermore, it is not clear who 'the cyberneticists' are; but presumably the authors do not include themselves in this category. One might wonder why the rebuke does not apply to all those interested in the perceptron." Block followed up with references to 1961 papers by both Minsky and Papert on topics related to perceptrons, implying that Minsky and Papert's castigation should apply equally to them. Block called it as he saw it: "In sum then, Minsky and Papert's formulation of their theory of perceptrons is precise and elegant. Their mathematical analysis is brilliant. Their exposition is lively, often bombastic, and, occasionally, snide."

Putting aside their bombast and snide remarks, we'll focus on the precision and elegance of Minsky and Papert's convergence proof. But first, we need to revisit Rosenblatt's algorithm with more formal notations in hand.

Let's take a potentially real problem. Assuming we have learned from our disastrous experience with the coronavirus pandemic, let's hope we can bring some smarts to how we react during the first months of the next pandemic involving a new infectious respiratory pathogen. (Fingers crossed it doesn't happen anytime soon.) In this more enlightened scenario, hospitals worldwide diligently collect data about the patients they see early on in the pandemic. Each patient is categorized using six variables: $x1 =$ age, $x2 =$ body mass index, $x3 =$ has difficulty breathing (yes $= 1$/no $= 0$), $x4 =$ has fever (yes/no), $x5 =$ has diabetes (yes/no), $x6 =$ chest CT scan ($0 =$ clear,

1 = mild infection, 2 = severe infection). The values for these variables make up a six-dimensional vector. Each patient is an arrow pointing in 6D space, or simply a point in 6D space.

So, for the ith patient, the vector **xi** is given by 6 attributes [*x1, x2, x3, x4, x5, x6*].

Doctors notice that patients are either okay about three days after coming to the hospital and are sent home or they worsen and need ventilator support. So, each patient has an associated outcome $y = -1$ (did not need ventilator support after three days) or $y = 1$ (needed ventilator support after three days).

Hence, the ith patient, **xi**, has a labeled outcome, yi, which can be either -1 or 1.

Doctors in many nations collect data for n patients, creating a set of n data points: $\{(\mathbf{x1}, y1), (\mathbf{x2}, y2), \ldots, (\mathbf{xn}, yn)\}$

Note that **x1, x2 . . . xn** are all vectors. They all have the same dimension, in this case 6. We have to train a perceptron such that given an input, say, **x1** (the information about the first patient), the perceptron should output the corresponding value $y1$. The same goes for **x2, x3, x4**, and so on. In our dataset, each **xi** is classified as belonging to either group -1 or group 1.

We assume that the data, which exist in six dimensions, are linearly separable into two groups. The separating hyperplane would be five-dimensional and impossible to visualize. How would you use this information? Well, first you would train the perceptron with the data that have been collected, so that it would find some separating hyperplane.

Then, if what's true of the patients in this training sample holds for all future patients—this is a major assumption, and we'll examine it more carefully in later chapters—imagine a scenario where a new patient comes to the hospital. You collect the necessary data (the values for *x1, x2, x3, x4, x5*, and *x6*) and plug them into your perceptron. It should tell you whether the patient will need ventilator support in three days, by outputting −1 or 1. This can, for example, be used for triaging decisions. Doctors can, with some confidence, send some people home but keep others for observation.

Training the perceptron means finding the weights [w0, w1, w2, w3, w4, w5, w6] of the weight vector **w**, such that:

$$y = \begin{cases} -1, & \mathbf{w}^\mathrm{T}\mathbf{x} \le 0 \\ 1, & \mathbf{w}^\mathrm{T}\mathbf{x} > 0 \end{cases}$$

Recall that w0 represents the bias term and is included in the weight vector. It's always multiplied by the value 1, or x0.

Given this, the training algorithm requires the following steps:

- **Step 1.** Initialize the weight vector to zero: set $\mathbf{w} = 0$

- **Step 2.** For each data point **x** in the training dataset, do the following:
  o **Step 2a** if $y\mathbf{w}^\mathrm{T}\mathbf{x} \le 0$:
    ◊ the weight vector is wrong, so update it:
    $$\mathbf{w}_{\mathrm{new}} = \mathbf{w}_{\mathrm{old}} + y\mathbf{x}$$

- **Step 3.** If there were no updates to the weight vector in Step 2, **terminate**; otherwise, go to **Step 2** and iterate over all the data points once again.

The perceptron begins by initializing the weight vector to zero and then checks to see if the chosen weight vector correctly classifies each data point one at a time. This is done by first calculating the value of the expression $y\mathbf{w}^\mathrm{T}\mathbf{x}$ for one data point. If the weights are correct for the data point **x** and the expression $\mathbf{w}^\mathrm{T}\mathbf{x}$ evaluates to a negative value, it means that $\mathbf{x}$ lies to the left of the hyperplane; it also means that $\mathbf{x}$ is classified with the label $y = -1$. So, if the expected value of y is -1 and the expression $\mathbf{w}^T\mathbf{x}$ evaluates to a negative number, their product will be positive. Similarly, if the weights are correct and if $\mathbf{w}^T\mathbf{x}$ evaluates to a positive number, it means $\mathbf{x}$ lies on the right side of the hyperplane; and it means that $\mathbf{x}$ is classified with the label $y = 1$. So, if the expected value is 1 and the expression $\mathbf{w}^T\mathbf{x}$ evaluates to a positive number, their product will again be positive. In other words, if the weights are correct, the expression $y\mathbf{w}^T\mathbf{x}$ will always be positive.

But if weights are wrong, then $y\mathbf{w}^T\mathbf{x}$ will always be a negative number. (Expression $\mathbf{w}^T\mathbf{x}$ evaluates to a positive number, but the expected value of y is -1, so $y\mathbf{w}^T\mathbf{x}$ will be negative; or, the expression $\mathbf{w}^T\mathbf{x}$ evaluates to a negative number, but the expected value of y is $+1$, so $y\mathbf{w}^T\mathbf{x}$ will be negative.) So, if $y\mathbf{w}^T\mathbf{x}$ is less than or equal to zero, then something is wrong, and we should update the weights and bias.

As per the algorithm, updating the weights involves adding $y\mathbf{x}$ to $\mathbf{w}$. Why does this work? Intuitively, this update is changing the direction and magnitude of the weight vector (and hence the direction of the hyperplane) in such a way that the data point $\mathbf{x}$, which was on the wrong side of the hyperplane, ends up a little closer to being on the correct side of it. For a given data point $\mathbf{x}$, one might have to make multiple such updates to ensure that $\mathbf{x}$ is correctly classified as being on the correct side of the hyperplane. (For a formal proof, see the mathematical coda on page 57.) Of course, making the correction for one data point means that the hyperplane can go wrong for some of or all the other data points.

So, the perceptron iterates over this process, data point by data point, until it settles on an acceptable set of values for the weights and bias that works for all data points. In doing so, the perceptron finds the linear divide between the two sets of data points.

As computer algorithms go, this is amazingly simple. The question for mathematicians was this: How can we be sure that it will terminate? Why won't it keep going indefinitely, by always getting at least one data point wrong?

That's where the convergence proofs come in—in particular, an especially elegant one by Minsky and Papert in their book, *Perceptrons*. We start by restating the main assumption: There exists a linearly separating hyperplane characterized by the weight vector $\mathbf{w}^*$. The perceptron has to find $\mathbf{w}^*$. There are, of course, many potential such hyperplanes, and the algorithm needs to find only one.

The algorithm starts by using a weight vector $\mathbf{w}$ initialized to zero. Now consider the dot product of $\mathbf{w}$ and $\mathbf{w}^*$. As we update the weight vector $\mathbf{w}$ and it starts pointing more and more in the direction of the desired weight vector $\mathbf{w}^*$, the angle between $\mathbf{w}$ and $\mathbf{w}^*$ approaches zero, regardless of the choice of $\mathbf{w}^*$. The dot product of $\mathbf{w}$ and $\mathbf{w}^*$, given by $\|\mathbf{w}\| \times \|\mathbf{w}^*\| \times \cos(\theta)$, keeps increasing, because $\cos(\theta)$ goes from zero (when the two vectors are perpendicular and most unlike each other) to 1 (when they are parallel and, hence, pointing in the same direction). So, as the algorithm learns, we want $\mathbf{w}.\mathbf{w}^*$ to keep increasing; that's an indication that it is working. However, $\mathbf{w}.\mathbf{w}^*$ can also increase simply because the magnitude of $\mathbf{w}$ keeps increasing while showing no change in direction. In this case, $\mathbf{w}.\mathbf{w}$ (the dot product of $\mathbf{w}$ with itself) will also increase. So, the essence of the proof involves showing that during training, $\mathbf{w}.\mathbf{w}$ increases less rapidly than $\mathbf{w}.\mathbf{w}^*$. If that's the case, the algorithm will converge in a finite number of steps, when $\mathbf{w}$ coincides with $\mathbf{w}^*$. Readers keen to understand the proof can find it in the mathematical coda on page 57.

The proof establishes an inequality. It says that if the algorithm updates the weight vector M times (or makes M mistakes) before finding the solution, then M must be less than or equal to a finite number. It does this by establishing what are called lower and upper bounds for the algorithm, which are measures of *at least* and *at most* how much time and resources the algorithm needs to arrive at the desired solution. Proving such bounds for algorithms is a difficult, intricate, and esoteric task in a field of research called computational complexity theory.

In 2018, Manuel Sabin, a young researcher I met at the University of California, Berkeley, gave an eloquent perspective on such work in a short film that I wrote, hosted, and co-directed (the film was part of a documentary series). "There are deep connections between lower bounds and upper bounds. Oftentimes, you can say they are two sides of the same coin," he said. Lower bounds tell us about whether something is impossible. Say you prove that an algorithm will take exponentially longer to run as you increase the number of data points. You will then encounter problems for which you "won't know the answer until the sun engulfs the earth," Sabin said. "So, lower bounds . . . talks about what is knowable within our lifetimes."

It was no wonder that establishing such bounds for the perceptron learning algorithm was a huge deal in the 1960s. The algorithm will always find a linearly separating hyperplane in finite time if one exists. Minsky and Papert, Block, and others were responsible for a slew of such proofs. Perceptrons were all the rage.

THE FIRST BIG CHILL

But then, Minsky and Papert's 1969 book, which provided such a firm mathematical foundation for research on perceptrons, also poured an enormous amount of cold water on it. Among the many proofs in their book, one addresses a very simple problem that a single layer of perceptrons could never solve: the XOR problem. Look at the four data points shown in the figure on the next page.

No straight line you can draw will separate the circles from the

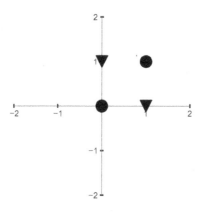

triangles. The points $(x1, x2)$ in this case are: $(0, 0)$, $(1, 0)$, $(1, 1)$ and $(0, 1)$. For the perceptron to separate the circles, represented by the points $(0, 0)$ and $(1, 1)$, from the triangles, represented by $(1, 0)$ and $(0, 1)$, it must be able to generate an output $y = 1$ when both $x1$ and $x2$ are 0 or both $x1$ and $x2$ are 1, and an output $y = -1$ otherwise. No such straight line exists, something that is easy to see visually. Minsky and Papert proved that a single layer of perceptrons cannot solve such problems. The situation illustrated above is the simplest case and calls to mind the XOR gate with two inputs in Boolean logic, where the logic gate outputs a 1 if both the inputs are the same, and 0 otherwise.

It's possible to solve the XOR problem if you stack perceptrons, such that the output of one feeds into the input of another. These would be so-called multi-layer perceptrons. Rosenblatt wasn't oblivious to this problem. "He knew certainly as well or better than Minsky the limitations of a single layer," Nagy told me. However, the problem with multiple layers of perceptrons was that no one knew how to train such networks, including Minsky and Papert. The algorithm we encountered earlier doesn't work if the weights of more than one layer of perceptrons have to be updated.

The hoopla surrounding neural networks subsided. All talk of an electronic computer that would "walk, talk, see, write, reproduce itself and be conscious of its existence" vaporized, as did any notion of sending perceptron devices to other planets as "mechanical space explorers." Funding agencies balked, money disappeared, and a once-promising field of research ground to an almost dead halt. Those in the field refer to the years from 1974 to 1980 as the first AI winter. Sir James Lighthill, the Lucasian professor of applied mathematics at Cambridge University, surveyed the field and, in 1972, published a report about the state of AI. His report even had a section called "Past Disappointments." It begins with these words: "Most workers in AI research and in related fields confess to a pronounced feeling of disappointment in what has been achieved in the past twenty-five years. Workers entered the field around 1950, and even around 1960, with high hopes that are very far from having been realized in 1972. In no part of the field have the discoveries made so far produced the major impact that was then promised."

As far as neural networks are concerned, it'd take a physicist's unique solution to a biological problem to re-energize the field. That was in 1982. Then, in 1986, David E. Rumelhart, Geoffrey E. Hinton, and Ronald J. Williams published a pathbreaking paper on an algorithm called backpropagation. (The idea itself predated their work, but their paper put it firmly on the map.) The algorithm, which showed how to train multi-layer perceptrons, relies on calculus and optimization theory. It'd take fifteen more years before computers became powerful enough to handle the computational demands of artificial neural networks, but the "backprop" paper set a slow-burning revolution in motion.

The precursor to the backpropagation algorithm, with its emphasis on calculus, however, was taking shape at about the same time as Rosenblatt was showing off his perceptron. Toward the very end of the 1950s, over the course of a weekend, a young assistant professor and an immensely talented graduate student invented and implemented an algorithm that would prove to be as important as the perceptron and would contain clues for one day training multi-layer neural networks.

MATHEMATICAL CODA

Feel free to skip the following proof; doing so won't impact your understanding of what comes in subsequent chapters. I should say, however, that it was while listening to recordings of lectures by Kilian Weinberger, professor of computer science at Cornell University, in which he explains this proof to the students of his 2018 course on machine learning, that I realized I wanted to write this book. It's a beautiful proof.

THE ALGORITHM: THE PERCEPTRON UPDATE RULE

(This rule and proof adapted from Weinberger's lecture.)

- **Step 1.** Initialize the weight vector to zero: set $\mathbf{w} = 0$.

- **Step 2.** For each data point $\mathbf{x}$ in the training dataset, do the following:
  o **Step 2a** if $y\mathbf{w}^\mathrm{T}\mathbf{x} \leq 0$:
    ◊ the weight vector is wrong, so update it:
    $$\mathbf{w}_{new} = \mathbf{w}_{old} + y\mathbf{x}$$

- **Step 3.** If there were no updates to the weight vector in step 2, **terminate**, otherwise go to **step 2** and iterate over all the data points once again.

We make an update to the weight vector if $y\mathbf{w}^\mathrm{T}\mathbf{x} \leq 0$ (see the explanation in the "Guaranteed to Succeed" on page 47 for why this is the case):

$$\mathbf{w}_{new} = \mathbf{w}_{old} + y\mathbf{x}$$

For the new weight vector to classify $\mathbf{x}$ correctly, we need to prove that, eventually, $y\,\mathbf{w}^T\mathbf{x} > 0$ (because if it were ≤ 0, it would have required updating). At each step of the update:

$$y\mathbf{w}_{new}^T\mathbf{x} = y\left(\mathbf{w}_{old} + y\mathbf{x}\right)^T\mathbf{x}$$

$$\Rightarrow y\mathbf{w}_{new}^T\mathbf{x} = y\mathbf{w}_{old}^T\mathbf{x} + y^2\mathbf{x}^T\mathbf{x}$$

The second right-hand side term $y^2\,\mathbf{x}^T\mathbf{x}$ is ≥ 0, because $y^2 = 1$, and $\mathbf{x}^T\mathbf{x} \geq 0$. Why is $\mathbf{x}^T\mathbf{x} \geq 0$? Well, it's the dot product of a vector with itself. That's always a positive number or zero. It's akin to squaring a scalar—you'll always get a positive number or zero.

So, $y\mathbf{w}_{new}^T\mathbf{x}$, after one update, is a little less negative than $y\mathbf{w}_{old}^T\mathbf{x}$, which means that the weight vector is moving in the right direction for the one data point $\mathbf{x}$. Eventually, after some unspecified number of updates, the algorithm will classify $\mathbf{x}$ correctly. This process must be repeated for every data point until the weight vector classifies all data correctly.

The proof that follows shows that the number of updates required to find the new, correct weight vector is always finite.

THE PERCEPTRON CONVERGENCE PROOF

Assumptions:

$\mathbf{w}$: the d-dimensional weight vector initialized to zero;

$\mathbf{w}^*$: the d-dimensional weight vector the perceptron has to learn; it's perpendicular to the linearly separating hyperplane. Let $\mathbf{w}^*$ be a unit vector of magnitude 1;

x: the vector representing an input data point, or instance; **x** is a d-dimensional vector, so with elements $[x1, x2, \ldots, xd]$. If there are *n* data points, then each such instance is a row in a larger $n \times d$ matrix **X** (n rows, d columns);

y: the output of the perceptron, for an input vector **x**; the output can be −1 or 1. All the outputs can be collected into a one n-dimensional vector **y**: $[y1, y2, \ldots, yn]$; and

γ (gamma): the distance between the linear separating hyperplane and the closest data point.

The following is the equation for the perceptron (ignoring an explicit bias term; we saw earlier how to incorporate it into this formulation):

$$y = \begin{cases} -1, & \mathbf{w}^T\mathbf{x} \leq 0 \\ 1, & \mathbf{w}^T\mathbf{x} > 0 \end{cases}$$

The goal is to prove that if you keep updating **w**, it will converge to **w*** (meaning, the two vectors will point in the same direction). And because **w***, by definition, is perpendicular to the separating hyperplane, so, too, will be **w**.

First, normalize all the input data points such that the data point farthest from the origin has a magnitude of 1 and all other data points have magnitudes less than or equal to 1. This can be done by dividing each vector **x** by the magnitude of the data point, or vector, that's farthest from the origin. So, the farthest vector will now have a magnitude of 1, and all other vectors will have magnitudes that are less than or equal to 1. This doesn't change the relationship between the data points/vectors because we are simply scaling down their magnitudes by the same amount; their directions remain the same.

Once normalized, $0 < \gamma < = 1$.

Recall that we update the weight vector when an input, $\mathbf{x}$, is classified incorrectly:

$$\text{If } y\mathbf{w}^\mathrm{T}\mathbf{x} \leq 0:$$
$$\mathbf{w}_{\text{new}} \leftarrow \mathbf{w}_{\text{old}} + y\mathbf{x}$$

As $\mathbf{w}$ comes closer to $\mathbf{w}^*$, which is our desired direction, the dot product of the two vectors, or $\mathbf{w}^\mathrm{T}\mathbf{w}^*$, gets bigger.

But $\mathbf{w}^\mathrm{T}\mathbf{w}^*$ can also increase if $\mathbf{w}$ grows in magnitude without changing direction relative to $\mathbf{w}^*$. If $\mathbf{w}$ is growing in magnitude, then $\mathbf{w}^\mathrm{T}\mathbf{w}$, which is the dot product of $\mathbf{w}$ with itself, will also increase. So, the algorithm will converge only if $\mathbf{w}^\mathrm{T}\mathbf{w}^*$ increases faster than $\mathbf{w}^\mathrm{T}\mathbf{w}$, as that would happen only because $\mathbf{w}$ is getting aligned with $\mathbf{w}^*$ and not just increasing in magnitude.

Let's calculate $\mathbf{w}^\mathrm{T}\mathbf{w}^*$ upon each update:

$$\mathbf{w}_{\text{new}}^\mathrm{T}\mathbf{w}^*$$

$$= (\mathbf{w}_{\text{old}} + y\mathbf{x})^\mathrm{T}\mathbf{w}^*$$

$$= \mathbf{w}_{\text{old}}^\mathrm{T}\mathbf{w}^* + y\mathbf{x}^\mathrm{T}\mathbf{w}^*$$

The second term of the right-hand side is $y\mathbf{x}^\mathrm{T}\mathbf{w}^*$. If you have two d-dimensional vectors $\mathbf{a}$ and $\mathbf{b}$, we know that $\mathbf{a}^\mathrm{T}\mathbf{b} = \mathbf{b}^\mathrm{T}\mathbf{a}$. So, $y\mathbf{x}^\mathrm{T}\mathbf{w}^* = y\mathbf{w}^{*\mathrm{T}}\mathbf{x}$. We know that $y\mathbf{w}^{*\mathrm{T}}\mathbf{x} > 0$, because $\mathbf{w}^*$ is the correct presumed weight vector, and it should classify $\mathbf{x}$ correctly.

The dot product of the unit vector $\mathbf{w}^*$ and $\mathbf{x}$ is the distance of $\mathbf{x}$ from the hyperplane characterized by $\mathbf{w}^*$. We defined γ as the distance between the closest data point and the hyperplane. So, $y\mathbf{w}^{*T}\mathbf{x}$ is not only greater than 0, but also always greater than or equal to γ.

Thus,

$$\mathbf{w}_{new}^T\mathbf{w}^* \geq \mathbf{w}_{old}^T\mathbf{w}^* + \gamma$$

Interim result 1: This is telling us something important. The dot product between $\mathbf{w}$ and $\mathbf{w}^*$ grows by *at least* γ with each update.

Now let's examine the rate of growth of $\mathbf{w}^T\mathbf{w}$.

$$\mathbf{w}_{new}^T\mathbf{w}_{new}$$

$$= (\mathbf{w}_{old} + y\mathbf{x})^T (\mathbf{w}_{old} + y\mathbf{x})$$

$$= (\mathbf{w}_{old} + y\mathbf{x})^T\mathbf{w}_{old} + (\mathbf{w}_{old} + y\mathbf{x})^T y\mathbf{x}$$

$$= \mathbf{w}_{old}^T\mathbf{w}_{old} + y\mathbf{x}^T\mathbf{w}_{old} + y\mathbf{w}_{old}^T\mathbf{x} + y^2\mathbf{x}^T\mathbf{x}$$

Since:

$$\mathbf{x}^T\mathbf{w}_{old} = \mathbf{w}_{old}^T\mathbf{x}$$

$$\Rightarrow \mathbf{w}_{new}^T\mathbf{w}_{new} = \mathbf{w}_{old}^T\mathbf{w}_{old} + 2y\mathbf{w}_{old}^T\mathbf{x} + y^2\mathbf{x}^T\mathbf{x}$$

So, the dot product of the new weight vector with itself equals the dot product of the old weight vector with itself plus two new terms. We must figure out the contribution of the new terms.

We know that the first new term $2y\mathbf{w}_{old}^T\mathbf{x} \leq 0$ because $y\mathbf{w}_{old}^T\mathbf{x} \leq 0$. That's the reason we are doing an update to the weight vector.

The second new term is $y^2\mathbf{x}^T\mathbf{x}$. Because y is either $+1$ or -1, $y^2 = 1$. Also, $\mathbf{x}^T\mathbf{x}$ is always less than or equal to 1 (this is because we normalized all the vectors representing data points earlier, so their magnitudes are always less than or equal to 1).

So, the equation becomes:

$$\mathbf{w}_{new}^{T}\mathbf{w}_{new} = \mathbf{w}_{old}^{T}\mathbf{w}_{old} + \left(\textit{negative quantity}\right) + \left(\textit{positive quantity} \leq 1\right)$$

$$\Rightarrow \mathbf{w}_{new}^{T}\mathbf{w}_{new} \leq \mathbf{w}_{old}^{T}\mathbf{w}_{old} + \left(\textit{positive quantity} \leq 1\right)$$

Interim result 2: This is telling us that the dot product of the weight vector with itself grows by *at most* 1 with each update.

Now, on the one hand, we have $\mathbf{w}^{T}\mathbf{w}^{*}$ growing by at least γ with each update and, on the other hand, we have $\mathbf{w}^{T}\mathbf{w}$ growing by at most 1 with each update.

Let's say the algorithm makes M updates to find the linearly separating hyperplane. Our task is to prove that M is a finite number and that the algorithm converges to a solution.

We start with the weight vector initialized to zero, so the initial value of $\mathbf{w}^{T}\mathbf{w}^{*}$ is zero. After the first update, the dot product would have grown at least by γ.

After 1 update: $\mathbf{w}^{T}\mathbf{w}^{*} \geq \gamma$

After 2 updates: $\mathbf{w}^{T}\mathbf{w}^{*} \geq \gamma + \gamma = 2\gamma$

After 3 updates: $\mathbf{w}^{T}\mathbf{w}^{*} \geq 2\gamma + \gamma = 3\gamma$

...

After M updates: $\mathbf{w}^{T}\mathbf{w}^{*} \geq (M - 1)\gamma + \gamma = M\gamma$

So: $M\gamma \leq \mathbf{w}^{T}\mathbf{w}^{*} \ldots (1)$

Similarly, by using interim result 2, which says that $\mathbf{w}^{T}\mathbf{w}$ increases by at most 1 after each update, after M updates, we should have:

$\mathbf{w}^\mathrm{T}\mathbf{w} \leq M \ldots (2)$

Now, because of (1) we have:

$$M\gamma \leq \mathbf{w}^\mathrm{T}\mathbf{w}^*$$

$= ||\mathbf{w}|| \, ||\mathbf{w}^*|| \, cos(\theta)$; this is the definition of the dot product.

$\Rightarrow M\gamma \leq ||\mathbf{w}||$, because $0 \leq cos(\theta) \leq 1$ and $||\mathbf{w}^*|| = 1$, by design.

Therefore:

$\Rightarrow M\gamma \leq \sqrt{\mathbf{w}^\mathrm{T}\mathbf{w}}$, because $||\mathbf{w}|| = \sqrt{\mathbf{w}^\mathrm{T}\mathbf{w}}$, by definition.

The right-hand side can be substituted using the result in (2), giving us:

$$M\gamma \leq \sqrt{M}$$
$$Or,$$
$$M^2\gamma^2 \leq M$$
$$Or,$$
$$M \leq \frac{1}{\gamma^2}$$

After all that analysis, we have arrived at a staggering result: The number of updates that the perceptron makes to find a linearly separating hyperplane is less than or equal to 1 over γ^2. Because gamma is always a positive quantity that's less than or equal to 1, M is always a finite quantity. The perceptron will converge without fail in a finite number of steps.

QED

CHAPTER 3

The Bottom of the Bowl

I t was the autumn of 1959. Bernard Widrow, a young academic on the cusp of turning thirty, was in his office at Stanford University when a graduate student named Marcian "Ted" Hoff came looking for him. The young man arrived highly recommended. The day before, a senior professor at Stanford had reached out to Widrow on Hoff's behalf, saying, "I've got this student named Ted Hoff. I can't seem to get him interested [in my research]; maybe he'd be interested in what you're doing. Would you be willing to talk with him?" Widrow replied, "Sure, happy to."

"So, the next day, knocking on my door was Ted Hoff," Widrow told me.

Widrow welcomed him in and proceeded to discuss his work, which was focused on adaptive filters—electronic devices that *learn* to separate signals from noise—and the use of calculus to optimize such filters. As Widrow chalked up the math on the blackboard, Hoff joined in, and soon the conversation morphed into something more dramatic. During that discussion, the two invented what came to be called the least mean squares (LMS) algorithm, which has turned out to be one of the most influential algorithms in machine learning, having proven foundational for those figuring out how to train artificial neural networks. "When I wrote the LMS algorithm on the blackboard for the first time, somehow I just knew intuitively that this is a profound thing," Widrow told me. "Too bad I didn't have a camera to take a picture."

Widrow grew up in a small town in Connecticut. He could hardly have imagined his luminous academic career. His father ran an ice-manufacturing plant. A curious young Widrow hung around the plant, amid generators, motors, and compressors, always asking questions. He admired the plant's electrician, who taught him the basics of the trade. While Widrow was still in high school, his dad sat him down and asked, "What do you think you want to be when you grow up?"

The teen answered, "I want to be an electrician."

His father said, "You don't want to be an electrician. You want to be an electrical engineer."

That subtle course correction led Widrow to MIT in 1947, where he obtained his bachelor's, master's, and doctorate; he joined MIT as an assistant professor in 1956. One day during the summer of that year, Widrow's colleague Ken Shoulders came into the lab and told him about a workshop on artificial intelligence at Dartmouth College he was attending; did Widrow want to come? "I said, 'What's artificial intelligence?' He said, 'I don't know. But it sounds interesting.' So, I said, 'Sure. I'll go with you.'"

The coining of the term "artificial intelligence" is credited to John McCarthy, a mathematics professor at Dartmouth College. In August 1955, McCarthy; Marvin Minsky, who was then at Harvard University; Nathaniel Rochester of IBM; and Claude Shannon of Bell Telephone Laboratories, put out "A Proposal for the Dartmouth Summer Research Project on Artificial Intelligence." It began with a bold declaration:

We propose that a 2 month, 10 man study of artificial intelligence be carried out during the summer of 1956 at Dartmouth

College in Hanover, New Hampshire. The study is to proceed on the basis of the conjecture that every aspect of learning or any other feature of intelligence can in principle be so precisely described that a machine can be made to simulate it. An attempt will be made to find how to make machines use language, form abstractions and concepts, solve kinds of problems now reserved for humans, and improve themselves. We think that a significant advance can be made in one or more of these problems if a carefully selected group of scientists work on it together for a summer.

Widrow remembered it as an open seminar, no invitation needed. You could go and stay as long as you wanted. You spoke up if you had something to say, or you could simply listen. Widrow listened and then returned to MIT all charged up. He wanted to build a thinking machine. "I spent six months thinking about thinking," he said. "The conclusion was that with the circuitry, the technology that we had at that time, I expected it'd be twenty-five years before we'd be able to build a thinking machine." For a young researcher at the start of his career, it seemed a foolhardy venture. Widrow abandoned his plans and turned to something more concrete: adaptive filters that could learn to remove noise from signals. He was particularly interested in the digital form of adaptive analog filters developed by Norbert Wiener. (We encountered Wiener in the previous chapter as the man who coined the term "cybernetics.")

To understand Wiener's analog filter, consider some continuously varying (hence analog) signal source. Some noise is added to the signal, and the filter's job is to tell signal from noise. Wiener's filter theory showed how this could be done. Others adapted the theory to digital signals. Instead of being continuous, digital signals are discrete, meaning they have values only at certain points in time (say, once every millisecond). Widrow wanted to build a digital filter, but one that could learn and improve over time. In other words, it would learn from its mistakes and become a better version of itself.

At the heart of such an adaptive filter is a nifty bit of calculus. Imagine that the filter, at any given time, makes an error. Let's assume that we are able to keep track of such errors for ten time steps. We must reduce the error the filter makes by looking at its previous ten errors and adjusting its parameters. One measure of the mistakes is simply the average of the previous ten errors. However, errors can be positive or negative, and if you just add them to take the average, they can cancel each other out, giving the wrong impression that the filter's working well. To avoid this, take the square of each error (thus turning it into a positive quantity) and then take the average of the squares of the errors. There are other advantages to squaring the errors and averaging them that have to do with statistics and calculus, but we don't need to focus on those yet. The goal is to minimize this "mean squared error" (MSE) with respect to the parameters of the filter. To restate, we must change the values of the filter's parameters at each time step such that the average, or mean, of the squared errors of the past, say, ten steps is minimized. Understanding how this works requires delving into some simple calculus and learning a method that was first proposed in 1847 by Baron Augustin-Louis Cauchy, a French mathematician, engineer, and physicist. It's called the method of steepest descent.

DOWN FROM ON HIGH

If you have seen pictures of—or, better yet, visited—rice paddies on hillsides, particularly in China, Japan, and Vietnam, you may have marveled at the flat terraces cut into the sides of the hills. If we walk along any one terrace, we remain at the same elevation. The edges of

the terraces trace the contours of the terrain. Imagine standing on some terrace way up a hillside. Down in the valley below is a village. We have to get to the village, but it's getting dark, and we can see only a few feet ahead of us. Let's say the hillside is not too steep and that it's possible to clamber down even the steepest parts. How will we proceed?

We can stand at the edge of the terrace and look for the steepest route to the terrace below. That's also the shortest path down to the next piece of level ground. If we repeat the process from terrace to terrace, we will eventually reach the village. In doing so, we will have taken the path of steepest descent. (This might not be a straight line from our initial position down to the village; we might have had to zigzag down the hillside.)

What we instinctively did was evaluate the slope, or the gradient, of the hillside as we looked in different directions while standing at the edge of a terrace and then took the steepest path down each time. We just did some calculus in our heads, so to speak.

More formally, let's look at going down a slope for a 2D curve, given by the equation $y = x^2$.

First, we plot the curve on the xy plane and then locate ourselves

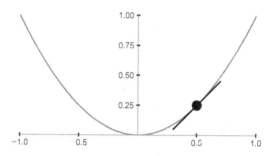

on the curve at some value of x, say, $x = 0.5$. At that point, the curve has a slope.

One way to find the slope of a curve is to draw a tangent to the curve at the point of interest. The tangent is a straight line. Imagine walking a smidgen along the straight line. You would be at a new location, where the x-coordinate has changed by an infinitesimal amount (Δx; read that as "delta x") and the y-coordinate has also changed by a corresponding infinitesimal amount (Δy). The slope is $\frac{\Delta y}{\Delta x}$. (If you think of climbing stairs, then the slope of the stairs is given by the rise divided by the run, where the rise is Δy, or how much you go up vertically with each step, and the run is Δx, the amount you move horizontally with each step.)

Of course, when you do this in our example, you have moved along the tangent to the curve, not along the curve itself. So, the slope really pertains to the tangent and not the curve. However, if the change in the x-direction, Δx, approaches zero, then the slope of the tangent line gets closer and closer to the slope of the curve at the point of interest, until the two become the same when $\Delta x = 0$. But how do you calculate the slope when the denominator in $\frac{\Delta y}{\Delta x}$ is zero? That's where calculus steps in.

Differential calculus is a branch of calculus that lets us calculate the slope of a continuous function (one that has no cusps, breaks, or discontinuities). It lets you analytically derive the slope in the limit $\Delta x \to 0$ (read that as "delta-x tends to zero"), meaning the step you take in the x-direction becomes vanishingly small, approaching zero. This slope is called the derivative of a function.

For our function $y = x^2$, the derivative equals $2x$. (Finding the derivative of a function is at the heart of differential calculus, but we won't get into the details here. For the functions used in this book, I'll simply provide the derivatives. To understand how to find the derivative of a function and for a list of derivatives of common functions, consult Wolfram MathWorld.)

We write our derivative as:

$$\frac{dy}{dx} = 2x$$

This is called the derivative of y with respect to x.

Calculus can cause our eyes to glaze over, if not induce downright dread. But as Silvanus P. Thompson, a professor of physics, electrical engineer, and member of the Royal Society, wrote in his classic *Calculus Made Easy* (first published in 1910), the "preliminary terror" of symbols in calculus "can be abolished once [and] for all by simply stating what is the meaning—in common-sense terms—of the . . . principal symbols." The symbol d, he points out, simply means a "little bit of." So, $\frac{dy}{dx}$ is a little bit of y divided by a little bit of x. The beauty of calculus is that you can calculate this ratio even as that "little bit of x" tends to zero, or $dx \to 0$.

Given the derivative, you now have a way of determining the slope at any point along the curve. So, for the function $y = x^2$, the slope $\frac{dy}{dx} = 2x$, and at $x = 2$ the slope is equal to $2x$, which equals 4.

At $x = 1$, the slope is 2; at $x = 0.5$, the slope is 1; and at $x = 0$, the slope is 0. You can see that when we move along the curve, as the value of x decreases from 2, so does the slope, until the function reaches a minimum (where the slope becomes zero), and then decreases further. The slope in general is zero at the minimum of a function; in this example, the (x, y) coordinates also happen to be (0, 0) at the minimum, but that doesn't have to be so.

We are now equipped to understand the method of steepest descent, also known as the method of gradient descent. Let's say we are at the coordinate (1, 1). We want to reach the bottom of the curve, where the slope is zero and the value of the function is at its minimum. At any point along the curve, there are only two ways you can go. Going one way takes you away from the bottom; going the other way brings you closer to the bottom. The trick to taking a step in the right direction is, first, to calculate the slope, or gradient, at your current location. (The term "gradient" has a more specific meaning, but let's use it here nonetheless.) In this case, for $x = 1$, the gradient is 2. If the function is bowl-shaped, as this one is, then the path toward the minimum involves going in a direction that decreases the gradient. So, we take a step such that the value of the x-coordinate is reduced by some step size (η) multiplied by the gradient at that point:

$$x_{new} = x_{old} - \eta \cdot gradient$$

$$y_{new} = x_{new}^2$$

Let's take a moment to see why taking a step that reduces the value of x reduces the gradient. For our equation, the gradient is given by $2x$. So, if the new value of x is less than the old value of x, the gradient at the new location will be lower than before. The new x-coordinate gives us a new y-coordinate. We end up at a new location. We repeat the process until the gradient becomes zero or close to zero. (We have reached the bottom or near enough to it.) Here's a graph depicting the process:

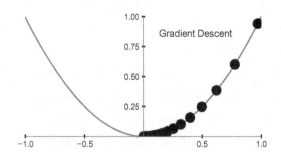

The step size, η, must be some small number, a fraction (say, 0.1). Why? Mainly because as you near the bottom, you want to be very careful you don't overshoot the minimum and end up higher on the other side of the curve. If you do so, depending on the function, the algorithm might begin taking you higher up the curve, away from the minimum. Also, notice that though the step size is the same at each iteration of the algorithm, the size of the jumps along the curve is greater in the beginning and becomes smaller as you near the bottom. Again, why? It's because we are subtracting a multiple of the gradient from the x-coordinate to get a new x-coordinate. The multiple, or step size, doesn't change in our algorithm. But what's changing is the gradient: It's getting smaller. So, the jumps along the curve also get progressively smaller.

Functions like the one depicted above, which have a single, well-defined minimum, are also called convex functions. When we find the bottom of the bowl, technically, we have found the "global" minimum of the function. (If a function has multiple minima, then each of these is called a "local" minimum.)

Now consider the case when the minimization involves a function that takes two inputs. Here's the function:

$$z = x^2 + y^2$$

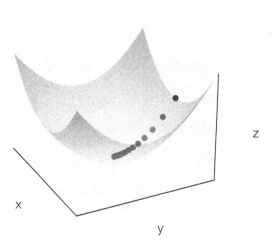

The plot shows the bowl-shaped 3D surface, called an elliptic paraboloid. If you start from any location above the bottom of the bowl, the descent along the surface of this paraboloid can be easily visualized. The difference from the 2D case is that we use the gradient at any location to calculate the new x and y coordinates, instead of just the x-coordinate. (Same operation: Subtract gradient times some step size from each coordinate.) This then gives us a new z-coordinate, and we come down to a new location on the surface. Doing this iteratively gets us to the bottom of the bowl.

Here's a different function to help visualize why it may not be possible to find the minimum for certain functions.

The 3D surface is defined by this equation:

$$z = y^2 - x^2$$

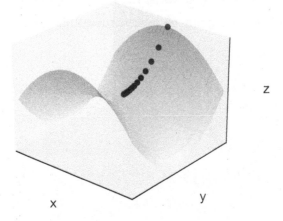

The surface is called a hyperbolic paraboloid. Notice that it looks like a saddle: part convex surface and part concave. In the figure above, we start descending from our location and ostensibly reach a place where the gradient is zero. But this is an unstable place. It's called a saddle point. One false step, and you'll tumble down the surface. This function has no global or local minimum. Also, the initial starting point can dictate whether you even come close to the saddle point while descending. Take this scenario, for instance:

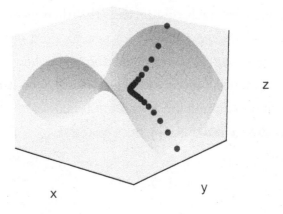

In this case, attempting to descend the gradient by following the same technique (because you start somewhere else) can cause you to veer away from the saddle point.

All this may sound terribly abstract, but gradient descent is crucial not only to Widrow and Hoff's algorithm, but also to modern machine learning. But before we connect gradient descent to Widrow and Hoff's work, there's one important detail we need to address.

Take this function again:

$$z = x^2 + y^2$$

Recall that when we had a function with one variable ($y = x^2$), we could use calculus to determine the derivative ($\frac{dy}{dx} = 2x$) and use this value to perform gradient descent. But what do we do when the function involves multiple variables? Well, there's an entire field of so-called multi-variable, or multi-variate, calculus. And while it can be daunting to confront multi-variate calculus in its entirety, we can appreciate the central role it plays in machine learning by focusing on some simple ideas.

Imagine you are standing at some point on the surface of an elliptic paraboloid, $z = x^2 + y^2$. To figure out the direction of steepest descent, we must be concerned about two directions, given that we have two variables. Following Thompson's exhortation to state things in simple ways, we know that moving along the surface means a small change in the value of the variable z. So, our job is to calculate $\frac{\partial z}{\partial x}$ and $\frac{\partial z}{\partial y}$; or a "tiny change in z divided by a tiny change in x" and a "tiny change in z divided by a tiny change in y," respectively.

In calculus-speak, we are taking the partial derivative of z with respect to x, and the partial derivative of z with respect to y. For our elliptic paraboloid, the partial derivatives are: $\dfrac{\partial z}{\partial x} = 2x$, $\dfrac{\partial z}{\partial y} = 2y$.

Also, note the slight change in the symbol used: ∂x instead of dx and ∂y instead of dy. The curvy "d" signifies a partial derivative of a function w.r.t. ("with respect to") one of many variables. For a conceptual understanding of what comes next, we don't need to worry about how to derive these partial derivatives. It's enough to know that given differentiable functions, calculus shows us how to get at these analytical expressions.

The most important concept here is that the direction of steepest descent, for this example, is given by two partial derivatives. Let's say you are standing at a location where:

$$x = 3, y = 4, \text{ and } z = 3^2 + 4^2 = 25$$

At this location, the two partial derivatives have the values:

$$2x = 2 \times 3 = 6$$

$$2y = 2 \times 4 = 8$$

If you write these numbers in this form, it looks like something very familiar: [6, 8]. It's a vector!

So, if you have to move slightly in the direction of steepest descent, that direction can be inferred from this vector. Recall that a vector has a magnitude (or length) and a direction. In this case, our vector is an arrow going from [0, 0] to [6, 8]. This vector is called the gradient. One technical point: The gradient points away from the minimum. So, to go down toward the minimum, you must take a small step in the opposite direction or follow the negative of the gradient.

If there's one thing to take away from this discussion, it's this: For a multi-dimensional or high-dimensional function (meaning, a function of many variables), the gradient is given by a vector. The components of the vector are partial derivatives of that function with respect to each of the variables.

For our elliptical paraboloid, the gradient is written as:

$$\begin{bmatrix} \partial z / \partial x \\ \partial z / \partial y \end{bmatrix} = \begin{bmatrix} 2x \\ 2y \end{bmatrix} \text{ or } \begin{bmatrix} 2x & 2y \end{bmatrix}$$

The gradient can be written as either a row vector or a column vector.

What we have just seen is extraordinarily powerful. If we know how to take the partial derivative of a function with respect to each of its variables, no matter how many variables or how complex the function, we can always express the gradient as a row vector or column vector. Just to illustrate the power of this approach, consider this slightly more complicated equation:

$$f(x, y, z) = x^2 + 3y^3 + z^5$$

The function f depends on three variables and is plotted in 4D space. There is no way for us to visualize what it looks like. And just by looking at the equation, it's impossible to tell whether the function has a global minimum toward which we can descend. But it's possible to write down the gradient using the partial derivatives. (Again, we are not trying to figure out how exactly to differentiate the function with respect to each variable; let's take it that if the function can be differentiated, calculus will provide an answer. You can use Wolfram MathWorld to find these derivatives.)

$$\begin{bmatrix} \partial f / \partial x \\ \partial f / \partial y \\ \partial f / \partial z \end{bmatrix} = \begin{bmatrix} 2x \\ 9y^2 \\ 5z^4 \end{bmatrix}$$

Now, given some set of values for x, y, and z, we can evaluate the gradient of the function at that point, take a small step in the opposite direction, and update the values of x, y, and z. If the function has a global minimum or local minima, iterating over this process will get us there. Our analysis has also connected the dots between two important concepts: functions on the one hand and vectors on the other. Keep this in mind. These seemingly disparate fields of mathematics—vectors, matrices, linear algebra, calculus, probability and statistics, and optimization theory (we have yet to touch upon the latter two)—will all come together as we make sense of why machines learn.

GLIMMERS OF A NEURON

Bernard Widrow came back from the 1956 AI conference at Dartmouth with, as he put it, a monkey on his back: the desire to build a machine that could think. "It's always there," he told me more than six decades later. "I haven't really ever gotten that out of my system." Yet, in 1956, a young Widrow was savvy enough to realize the futility of building thinking machines, and he turned to more practical things. Building an adaptive filter was one such pursuit.

In the field of signal processing, a filter is something that takes an input signal, processes it, and produces an output signal that has certain desired properties. Let's say you are working on some hobby electronics equipment, and you need to measure a signal. But mixed in with your signal is an annoying hum at a frequency of 60 Hz. That's interference from the AC mains power. A filter can take the noise-laden input, remove only the 60 Hz component, and spit out a clean signal. Such a filter is easy to design, as the noise is well understood; it's always at 60 Hz. But often, a filter needs to learn the characteristics of the noise; it needs to adapt.

Consider an important application for such an adaptive filter: digital communications. Anyone who has ever used a dial-up modem to connect to the internet will remember the distinctive sounds made by the modem. First a dial tone, then the tones of the number being dialed, followed by beeps and bursts of staccato screeches, and then silence after about twenty seconds. That's the sound of a handshake: two digital devices figuring out the best way to talk to each other over a phone line usually used for analog voice signals. The digital devices must transmit and receive streams of zeroes and ones. But analog transmission lines can be noisy—so, you need a filter to remove the noise that could corrupt the data. This includes canceling any echo that a modem may hear of its own transmissions. But it's impossible to build a generic filter for such purposes. The noise can be, and often is, different in each instance of two communicating devices. Part of what happens during a handshake is that an adaptive filter at each end figures out the characteristics of the noise, which it can then remove to create an almost error-free communication channel. (Widrow recalls using a fax machine that made these "handshake" sounds when communicating with some remote fax machine; his grandson, who happened to be around him in those days, started calling the sounds of the handshake "Grandpa music.")

One design of an adaptive filter is shown on the next page.

Here, xn is the input signal; yn represents the corresponding output. The filter turns xn into yn. The output is compared against a desired signal dn, which is the signal the filter ought to have produced. Any discrepancy between yn and dn results in an error en.

$$en = dn - yn$$

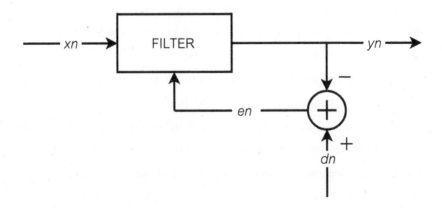

This error *en* is fed back into the filter. An adaptive filter changes itself such that the error is minimized. The black box named FILTER has some characteristics, or parameters, and these parameters can be tweaked to make the filter adaptive.

You might say, if you know the desired signal, what's the point of a filter? Well, you don't know the desired signal for any generic input. But there are ways to know what the filter should produce for known inputs. For example, that's what modems do during the handshake: They transmit a previously agreed-upon signal, so that the other side knows what to expect. That's the desired signal *dn*. But the signal arrives over a noisy transmission line, so the input *xn* is simply *dn* contaminated by noise. But unlike the 60 Hz hum we looked at earlier, this noise is random. The receiver needs a filter that takes *xn* as an input and produces a signal *yn* that is as close to the desired signal *dn* as possible. To do so, the algorithm must learn the statistical properties of the noise, so that it can predict the noise at each time step and subtract it in real time from *xn* to produce the desired signal.

While all this is a far cry from AI and ML, we can see glimmers of machines that learn. This connection—particularly to Rosenblatt's perceptron and artificial neurons—will become even more obvious when we write down the particulars of a filter.

This was slowly becoming obvious to Widrow, too, while he was still at MIT, where he was deeply influenced by the doyen of filter design, Norbert Wiener. At the time, Wiener was MIT's best-known professor. Decades later, Widrow, recalling Wiener's personality in a book, painted a particularly evocative picture of a man whose head was often, literally and metaphorically, "in the clouds" as he walked the corridors of MIT buildings: "We'd see him there every day, and he always had a cigar. He'd be walking down the hallway, puffing on the cigar, and the cigar was at angle theta—45 degrees above the ground. And he never looked where he was walking . . . But he'd be puffing away, his head encompassed in a cloud of smoke, and he was just in oblivion. Of course, he was deriving equations." Even as he approached the steps at the end of some hallway, Wiener would be looking up, not down. "You can see he's going to kill himself—he's going to fall down those steps—but if you disturb him, you might break his train of thought and set science back like ten years! There was always that problem."

Such life-and-death decisions notwithstanding, Widrow embraced Wiener's work. While at MIT, he even came up with different versions of the adaptive filter. Here's an example of one of his designs:

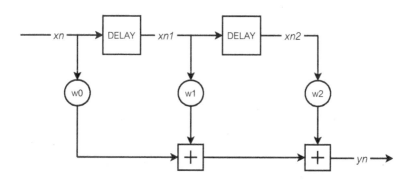

In the filter, the input signal *xn* arrives discretely once every *n*th time step (which can be anything: once per day, per second, per millisecond, per microsecond, and so on), and *yn* is the corresponding output. Each box labeled DELAY takes a signal and delays it by one time step, producing the signal *xn1* from *xn* and *xn2* from *xn1*. After one delay, the signal is multiplied by a weight *w1*, after two delays it is multiplied by *w2*, and so on. The undelayed signal is multiplied by *w0*. All these are summed up. So, for our example on the preceding page, the output signal *yn* can be written as:

$$yn = w0.xn + w1.xn1 + w2.xn2$$

We can treat $[w0, w1, w2]$ as the vector **w**, and $[xn, xn1, xn2]$ as the vector **xn**. Then,

$$\mathbf{w.xn} = w0.xn + w1.xn1 + w2.xn2$$

The diagram shows only two delays, but in principle, there can be any number of them. Now, if *dn* is the desired signal, here's how you would go about optimizing the filter's parameters, to minimize the error between what it generates, which is *yn*, and the desired signal, *dn*.

$$yn = \mathbf{w.xn}, \text{ where:}$$

$$\mathbf{xn} = [xn, xn1, ...]$$

$$\text{and } \mathbf{w} = [w0, w1, ...]$$

$$en = dn - yn$$

$$\Rightarrow en = dn - \mathbf{w.xn}$$

What we have is an expression for the error that the filter makes at the nth time step. It's clear that if the filter predicts a good approximation of the desired signal, then the error will be minimized. To achieve this, the filter must learn the value for **w** at each time step. Of course, such a filter can update its parameters whenever it gets the prediction wrong—hence the name "adaptive filter." It learns. Ideally, over time, the average error made by the filter should tend toward zero. (Maybe now the connections to machine learning are beginning to emerge from this fog of filter theory.)

A small ML digression: How should we calculate the average error? Adding the errors to calculate the mean won't suffice; as we saw earlier, negative and positive errors can negate each other, giving an invalid impression that the average error is low. We could add the absolute value of the errors and take the average: this is called the mean absolute error (MAE). But the math folk prefer to take the average of the square of the error terms and call it a mean squared error (MSE). It turns out that the MSE has some nice statistical properties that the MAE doesn't. Also, the MSE is differentiable everywhere. (A differentiable function is one that has a derivative everywhere in its domain, where a domain could be, say, the xy plane.) The MAE is not. This, too, helps immensely, and we'll see this when we come to training neural networks. One more fact worth mentioning: If you want your error estimate to punish the extreme outliers, then the MSE does that better than the MAE, because the contribution of an error to the average increases as the square of the error in the MSE, while it increases linearly in the MAE.

Back to the filter. We square the error at each time step, add all the squared errors, and then find the expected value. The expected value, or "expectation," of something that is varying randomly has a very specific meaning in probability theory, but let's not worry about that. The key insight here is that we need to minimize the expected value (E) of the squared errors. Let's call that value J:

$$J = E(en^2)$$

$$\Rightarrow J = E((dn - yn)^2)$$

$$\Rightarrow J = E((dn - \mathbf{w.xn})^2)$$

The value of J must be minimized. If you look at the form of the equation that relates J to the filter parameter $\mathbf{w}$, it becomes clear that the function that connects the two will be quadratic (meaning, it'll involve the second power of $\mathbf{w}$). We already saw that such quadratic functions are convex ($y = x^2$, or $z = x^2 + y^2$, for example). So, when J is minimized, we end up at the bottom of some bowl-shaped function. At this point, the slope, or gradient, of J is zero. This gives us another way of finding the optimal value for $\mathbf{w}$. We can simply set the value of the gradient of J with respect to $\mathbf{w}$ to zero and solve the equation:

$$\frac{\partial J}{\partial \mathbf{w}} = \frac{\partial E\left((dn - \mathbf{w.xn})^2\right)}{\partial \mathbf{w}} = 0$$

In 1931, Wiener and German mathematician Eberhard Hopf devised a way to solve such equations, using techniques from linear algebra. But this requires some a priori knowledge about the correlation between the inputs at all the various time steps and the correlation between the inputs and the desired outputs. This is not always known, and even when it is, the calculations can be computationally intensive. Also, Wiener's work applied to analog filters.

We can also minimize J by using the method of steepest descent. Why is that? Well, because it's a bowl-shaped, convex function, we can always find the value for **w** that minimizes the expectation value of the squared errors by iteratively following a path down to the bottom of the bowl. So, regardless of whether the filter is characterized by one coefficient (*w0*), two (*w0, w1*), three (*w0, w1, w2*), or more, the assertion holds. Steepest descent will let you find the minimum. But this method, too, has a limitation: We need to be able to calculate the partial derivatives of *J* with respect to the filter coefficients.

There are other computational concerns.

For instance, given **xn** and the corresponding *yn*, plus the desired output *dn*, one can use the method of steepest descent to calculate the parameters (in our example: *w0, w1, w2*). The trouble is that to find the optimal values for the parameters, you need more and more samples of input, output, and desired output, and these calculations take increasingly longer to finish.

In addition, given that the error calculated for a certain sample of data doesn't fully represent all possible errors, the gradient you calculate at each time step to go toward the minimum is only an approximation. Sometimes it's pointing in the right direction, but most times it's not. In our analogy of walking down a terraced hillside to the village, it's as if in addition to having to navigate in the dark, you were somewhat drunk. Instead of taking the steepest path down to the next terrace, you stagger down willy-nilly. You might even clamber up to the next terrace. The hope is that if you take small enough steps, even this drunkard's walk will get you down to the village. And in practice, algorithms that do this indeed succeed. This method is called stochastic gradient descent (SGD), where the word "stochastic" refers to the fact that the direction of each step in your descent is slightly random.

This is what Widrow was working on while at MIT, before he moved to Stanford. But alongside filters, he was thinking about adaptive neurons, or neural elements, and realizing that training a neuron was no different from training a filter.

A WEEKEND WITH BERNIE

When Ted Hoff walked into Widrow's office at Stanford that fateful day in the fall of 1959, Widrow began discussing such ideas with him. "So, I was up at the blackboard explaining to Ted about the stochastic gradient and quadratic bowl . . . and adaptive filters and adaptive neural elements and . . . talking about how you differentiate to get the components of the gradient," Widrow told me. "I don't know how it happened, but we came up with an idea that we could get a stochastic gradient, a very crude gradient algebraically—without differentiating anything, without averaging anything, and without squaring anything."

The technique they devised could be applied to adaptive filters or artificial neurons. So far, we have learned that the output of our example adaptive filter is given by:

$$yn = w0.xn + w1.xn1 + w2.xn2$$

$$\text{or, } yn = \mathbf{w.xn}$$

Designing a filter that adapts involves learning the values for $w0$, $w1$, and $w2$. If you cast your mind back to Rosenblatt's perceptron, you'll see that it, too, involves learning the weights so that it can correctly classify a new piece of data as falling on one or the other side of a hyperplane. Rosenblatt's algorithm isn't cast in terms of gradient descent. But the Widrow and Hoff algorithm is.

The figure on the next page shows a way to think about the adaptive neuron designed by Widrow and Hoff.

The neuron produces an output y:

$$y = w0x0 + w1x1 + w2x2$$

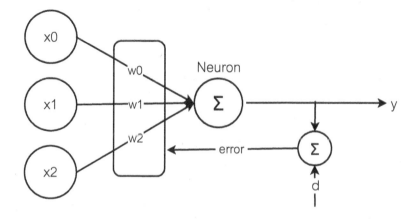

Here, $x0$ is always 1; this makes $w0$ our bias term, b. The actual inputs are $x1$ and $x2$. Together, they make up the vector **x**. The set of coefficients $w0$, $w1$, and $w2$ is the vector **w**. So:

$$y = \mathbf{w}.\mathbf{x}$$

$$\Rightarrow y = \mathbf{w}^{T}\mathbf{x}$$

Assume you have several training samples for which you have the inputs and the corresponding desired outputs (d). Then, the error made by the adaptive neuron for each input is given by:

$$error(e) = d - y = d - \mathbf{w}^{T}\mathbf{x}$$

Consider the problem where the input is a set of 16 values, representing a 4×4 grid of pixels. These pixels can be used to show letters of the alphabet. The letter "T," for example, would light up some of those pixels (meaning, some pixels would have the value "1," and others "0"). The letter "J" would light up a different set of pixels.

Let's say that when the set of pixels representing "T" is the input

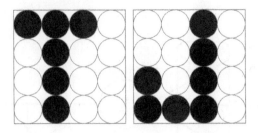

to the neuron, it must output the value 1. And when the input is the set of pixel values representing the letter "J," the neuron must output −1. So, the desired output for "T" is 1, and for "J," it's −1.

Training the neuron involves supplying it one input, representing one letter, at a time. The algorithm uses the input and the desired output to adjust its weights and generate the correct output. But changing the weights so that you get the correct output for the input letter "T" may cause it to make an error for the input letter "J." If that's the case, the algorithm adjusts its weights again. Of course, now the new weights may cause an error for the input letter "T." You repeat the process. And this goes on until the neuron correctly outputs 1 for the letter "T" *and* −1 for the letter "J." The method of steepest descent can be used to train the neuron.

Let's say you had a bunch of training samples: inputs and their corresponding outputs. If you calculate the errors made by the neuron for all input samples and plot the expectation value of squared errors as a function of all the weights, or coefficients, you get a bowl-shaped function (of course, in a higher-dimensional space that we cannot visualize). Then, you could minimize the expectation value using the method of steepest descent. At each step, you calculate the gradient of the function with respect to each weight and then modify the weights by taking a small step in the opposite direction (toward the minimum).

$$\mathbf{w}_{new} = \mathbf{w}_{old} + \mu(-\Delta)$$

where:

$$\mu = \text{step size}$$

$$\Delta = \text{gradient}$$

Recall from our previous discussion that the gradient is simply a vector in which each element is the partial derivative of the mean squared error, *J*, with respect to each weight.

So, for our three weights, the gradient is:

$$\left[\begin{array}{ccc} \dfrac{\partial J}{\partial w0} & \dfrac{\partial J}{\partial w1} & \dfrac{\partial J}{\partial w2} \end{array} \right]$$

Each element of this vector will be an analytic expression that can be calculated using the rules of calculus. Once you have the expressions, you just plug in the current values for the weights, and you get the gradient, which you can then use to calculate the new weights. The problem: You need calculus, and while our gradient has only three elements, in practice, it can have elements that number in the tens, hundreds, thousands, or even more. Widrow and Hoff were after something simpler. This is what they came up with:

$$\mathbf{w}_{new} = \mathbf{w}_{old} + \mu(-\Delta_{est})$$

Instead of calculating the entire gradient, they decided to calculate only an estimate of it. The estimate would be based on just one data point. It didn't involve calculating the expectation value of the error squared. Rather, they were simply estimating it. But estimating a statistical parameter based on just one sample is usually anathema. Even so, Widrow and Hoff went with it. With a little bit of analysis, they came up with their update rule for the weights:

$$\mathbf{w}_{new} = \mathbf{w}_{old} + 2\mu\varepsilon\mathbf{x}$$

where:

μ = step size

ε = error based on one data point

$\mathbf{x}$ = the vector representing a single data point

The error itself is given by:

$$\varepsilon = d - \mathbf{w}^{T}\mathbf{x}$$

This is simple algebra. Basically, for each input, you calculate the error and use that to update the weights.

Widrow and Hoff were aware that their method was extremely approximate. "What you do is you take the single value of the error, square it, swallow hard, because you are going to tell a lie, [and] you say that's the mean squared error," Widrow told me. "It's a pretty noisy version of the average of the square of the error. And then, when you take the derivatives, you can do it analytically, without differentiating. You don't have to square anything. You don't have to average anything. You got an extremely noisy gradient. You take a small step, another small step, another small step."

And yet, the algorithm gets you close to the minimum of the

function. It came to be called the least mean squares (LMS) algorithm. In a video Widrow uploaded in 2012, to explain the algorithm, he credited one of his graduate students for naming the algorithm, but he doesn't remember the student's name. He also said, "I hope that all this algebra didn't create too much mystery. It's all quite simple once you get used to it. But unless you see the algebra, you would never believe that these algorithms could actually work. Funny thing is they do. The LMS algorithm is used in adaptive filters. These are digital filters that are trainable . . . Every modem in the world uses some form of the LMS algorithm. So, this is the most widely used adaptive algorithm on the planet."

Not only would the LMS algorithm find uses in signal processing, but it would also become the first algorithm for training an artificial neuron that used an approximation of the method of steepest descent. To put this into context: Every deep neural network today—with millions, billions, possibly trillions of weights—uses some form of gradient descent for training. It would be a long road from the LMS algorithm to the modern algorithms that power AI, but Widrow and Hoff had laid one of the first paving stones.

On that Friday afternoon in the autumn of 1959, however, all they had were mathematically motivated scribbles on a blackboard. Widrow and Hoff didn't know that the algorithm would work. They needed to simulate it on a computer; they were excited that they had uncovered something extremely important. "Foolishly I was thinking: 'We've discovered the secret of life,'" Widrow told me.

Across the hall from his office was an analog computer, a gift to Stanford from Lockheed. The door was open, and anyone could use the computer. Programming it was akin to operating an old-fashioned telephone switchboard: Take a wire out from a patch panel here, plug it in there, and so on. In a half hour, Hoff had the algorithm running on the analog machine. "He made it work," Widrow said. "I don't know how he knew how to do it. He knew how to program that thing."

Having verified that the algorithm worked, the two had as their next step the building of a single adaptive neuron—an actual hardware neuron. But it was late afternoon. The Stanford supply room was closed for the weekend. "Well, we weren't going to wait," Widrow told me. The next morning, the two of them walked over to Zack Electronics, in downtown Palo Alto, and bought all the parts they needed. They then went over to Hoff's apartment and worked all of Saturday and most of Sunday morning. By Sunday afternoon, they had it working. "Monday morning, I had it sitting on my desk," Widrow recalled. "I could invite people in and show them a machine that learns. We called it ADALINE—'adaptive linear neuron.' It was . . . not an adaptive filter, but an adaptive neuron that learned to be a good neuron."

What ADALINE does, using the LMS algorithm, is to separate an input space (say, the 16-dimensional space defined by 4×4, or 16, pixels) into two regions. In one region are 16-dimensional vectors, or points that represent, say, the letter "T." In another region are vectors that represent the letter "J." Widrow and Hoff chose 4×4 pixels to represent letters, as this was big enough to clearly show different letters, but small enough to work with, given that they had to adjust the weights by hand (using knobs). Anything larger, and they'd have spent most of their time twiddling those knobs. Again, here are the letters "T" and "J" in 4×4-pixel space:

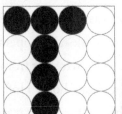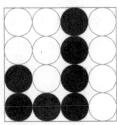

So, each letter is represented by 16 binary digits, each of which can be either 0 or 1. If you were to imagine plotting these letters as points in a 16D space, then "J" would be a point (vector) in one part of the coordinate space, and "T" in another. The LMS algorithm helps ADALINE find the weights that represent the linearly separating hyperplane—in this case, a plane in fifteen dimensions—that divides the input space into two. It's exactly what Rosenblatt's perceptron does, using a different algorithm.

While the perceptron convergence proof we saw in chapter 2 showed clearly why the perceptron finds the linearly separating hyperplane, if one exists, it wasn't exactly clear why the rough-and-ready LMS algorithm worked. Years later, Widrow was waiting for a flight in Newark, New Jersey. He had a United Airlines ticket. "Those days, your ticket was in a jacket. And there was some blank space on it. So, I sat down and started doing some algebra and said, 'Goddamn, this thing is an unbiased estimate.'"

He was able to show that the LMS algorithm, if you took extremely small steps, got you to the answer: the optimal value for the weights of either the neuron or the adaptive filter. "By making the steps small, having a lot of them, we are getting an averaging effect that takes you down to the bottom of the bowl," Widrow said.

Hoff finished his Ph.D. with Widrow and was doing his postdoctoral studies when a small Silicon Valley start-up came calling. Widrow told him to take the job. It was sound advice: The start-up was Intel. Hoff went on to become one of the key people behind the development of the company's first general-purpose microprocessor, the Intel 4004.

Widrow continued using the LMS algorithm to build adaptive filters—for noise cancelation and for antennas that adapt to remove noise and interference. He worked on ADALINE (a single layer of adaptive neurons) and MADALINE (for "Many ADALINE"), which had three layers: input, hidden, and output. But it was hard to train MADALINE. Still, Widrow's work began making waves.

In a 1963 episode of *Science in Action* titled "Computers that Learn," produced by the California Academy of Sciences, the host and presenter, Earl S. Herald, introduces a robotic assembly that seems to be balancing a broom. "This may not seem very startling, because anyone can balance a broom. But this is a machine that can learn to do this . . . This is the story of MADALINE, the machine that in some respects *thinks like a man* [italics mine]." The sexism of the time rears its head again when Herald, barely two minutes into the episode, queries Widrow: "Let me ask you about the name 'ADA-LINE.' Why 'ADALINE'? Why not a masculine name?" Widrow replies, "Well, this happens to spell 'Adaptive Linear Neuron.' And that's it."

The line connecting ADALINE to modern neural networks (which have multiple layers and are trained using an algorithm called backpropagation) is clear. "The LMS algorithm is the foundation of backprop. And backprop is the foundation of AI," Widrow told me. "In other words, if you trace it back, this whole field of AI right now, [it] all starts with ADALINE."

In terms of the backpropagation algorithm, this is a fair assessment. Of course, Rosenblatt's perceptron algorithm can make similar claims. Together, Rosenblatt and Widrow laid some of the foundation stones for modern-day deep neural networks. But these weren't the only such efforts. Other algorithms, also foundational, were being invented, and they'd rule the roost in the decades during which neural network research floundered, primarily because of Minsky and Papert's unduly harsh assessment of its limitations. And these non-neural network approaches were establishing the governing principles for machines that learn based on, for example, probability and statistics, our next waystation.

CHAPTER 4

In All Probability

Probability deals with reasoning in the presence of uncertainty. And it's a fraught business for the best of us. There's no better illustration of how uncertainty messes with our minds than the Monty Hall dilemma. The problem, named after the host of the American television show *Let's Make a Deal,* became a public obsession in 1990 when a reader of the *Parade* magazine column "Ask Marilyn" posed the following question to columnist Marilyn vos Savant:

"Suppose you are on a game show, and you're given the choice of three doors. Behind one is a car; behind the others, goats. You pick a door, say, No. 1, and the host, who knows what's behind the doors, opens another door, say, No. 3, which has a goat. He then says to you, 'Do you want to pick No. 2?' Is it to your advantage to switch your choice?" The person playing the game has a quandary. Do they switch their choice from door No. 1 to door No. 2? Is there any benefit to doing so, in that they will increase their odds of choosing the door hiding the car? Before we look at vos Savant's answer, let's try to tackle the problem ourselves. Here's my intuitive answer:

Before the host opens one of the doors, the probability that a car is behind the door I've picked (Door No. 1) is one-third. But then the host opens Door No. 3 and reveals that there's a goat behind it. Now there are two closed doors, and behind one of them is the car.

I figure that the car is equally likely to be behind one or the other door. There's no reason to switch my choice.

You may or may not have reasoned similarly. Kudos if you *didn't*.

Here's what vos Savant advised regarding whether you should switch your choice: "Yes; you should switch. The first door has a one-third chance of winning, but the second door has a *two*-thirds chance." And she's correct.

Americans were outraged—and not just folks untrained in the nuances of probability theory. As mathematician Anthony Lo Bello writes in an essay about this fracas, "Shortly thereafter, Savant received an avalanche of harsh rebukes from PhD's [*sic*] on the faculties of several American universities, reproving her for giving, as they claimed, the wrong answer; the instructors, three of whose names were published in the issue of 2 December 1990 [of *Parade* magazine], argued that once the host had opened the losing third door, both the first and second doors then each had a probability of 1/2 of winning."

Vos Savant stood her ground and provided the critics with different ways of arriving at her answer. One of her best intuitive arguments, paraphrasing her, asks you to consider a different situation. Say there are a million doors, and behind one of them is a car; all the others hide goats. You choose Door No. 1. There's a one-in-a-million chance you are correct. The host then opens all the other doors you did not choose, except one. Now there are two unopened doors, your choice and the one the host left closed. Sure, the latter door could hide a goat. But of all the doors the host chose not to open, why did he choose that one? "You'd switch to that door pretty fast, wouldn't you?" wrote vos Savant.

Mathematician Keith Devlin gave another take on it. Put a mental box around your choice, Door No. 1, and another box around Doors No. 2 and 3 combined. The box around Door No. 1 has a one-third probability associated with it, and the box around Doors No. 2 and 3 has a two-thirds probability associated with it, in terms of containing the car. Now the host opens one of the doors inside the bigger box to reveal a goat. The two-thirds probability of the bigger box shifts to the unopened door. To switch is the correct answer.

But here's the thing. It's impossible to rely on intuition to solve this problem, because it's just as easy to conceive of it slightly differently and be convinced that you shouldn't switch (as I was in my earlier analysis). And if you didn't switch, you'd be in august company, and I don't mean mine.

In his book *Which Door Has the Cadillac?*, the Hungarian mathematician Andrew Vázsonyi writes about the inability of another Hungarian mathematician, Paul Erdős—"arguably the most prolific mathematician of the 20th century, in terms of both the number of problems he solved and the number of problems he convinced others to tackle"—to agree that switching doors is the better option. While Erdős was visiting Vázsonyi in 1995, the two discussed the Monty Hall dilemma. When Vázsonyi told Erdős that switching increased one's odds of winning, Erdős refused to accept the answer: "He reacted as if he had just been stung by a bee. 'No, that is impossible,' he said. 'It should make no difference if you switch.'" Vázsonyi tried to convince him that probabilities are not static, that they change as contexts change. Erdős wasn't swayed. Eventually, Vázsonyi used a computer program he had written to run one hundred thousand simulations of the game and showed that the host won and you lost two-thirds of the time if you didn't switch, but the host lost and you won two-thirds of the time if you did switch. "Erdős objected that he still did not understand the reason why, but was reluctantly convinced that I was right," Vázsonyi wrote.

Encapsulated in this story about the Monty Hall dilemma is the tale of an eternal dispute between two ways of thinking about probability: frequentist and Bayesian. The former approach, which makes use of the simulation, is what seemingly convinced Erdős. The frequentist notion of the probability of occurrence of an event (say, a coin coming up heads) is simply to divide the number of times the event occurs by the total number of trials (the total number of coin flips). When the number of trials is small, the probability of the event can be wildly off from its true value, but as the number of trials becomes very large, we get the correct measure of the probability. The following figure shows the results of ten thousand trials of the Monty Hall dilemma. (Data scientist Paul van der Laken shows how to plot the probabilities of winning if you switch and if you don't switch. This is one version.)

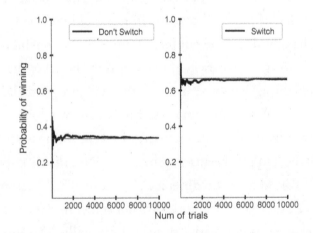

You can see clearly that when the number of trials is small, the probabilities fluctuate. But they settle into the correct values as the trials go beyond about four thousand: 0.67, or two-thirds, for switching, and 0.33, or one-third, for not switching.

But simulations are not the only way of answering such questions. Another approach is to rely on Bayes's theorem, one of the cornerstones of probability theory and, indeed, of machine learning.

TO BAYES OR NOT TO BAYES

There's delicious irony in the uncertainty over Thomas Bayes's year of birth. It's been said that he was "born in 1701 with probability 0.8." The date of his death, however, is firmly established: April 17, 1761, at Royal Tunbridge Wells in England. Two years after his death, a close friend, Richard Price, who was twenty-two years younger, presented a paper to the Royal Society on Bayes's behalf. Bayes and Price were kindred spirits: intellectuals, dissenting ministers, and, of course, mathematicians. Price wrote a letter, with an accompanying essay, dated November 10, 1763, to his friend John Canton, and Canton read the correspondence to the Royal Society on December 23: *An Essay Towards Solving a Problem in the Doctrine of Chances.* Even though Price attributed the essay to Bayes, scholars have estimated that Price made a substantial contribution to its contents. Price submitted another paper on the topic to the Royal Society in 1764, this time as the sole author. Taken together, these submissions cemented the status of Bayes as the man who gave us his eponymous theorem, which birthed an entire way of thinking about probability and statistics and has now become, almost 250 years later, a formidable force in machine learning.

Bayes's theorem gives us a way to draw conclusions, with mathematical rigor, amid uncertainty.

It's best to understand the theorem using a concrete example. Consider a test for some disease that occurs in only about 1 in 1,000 people. Let's say that the test is 90 percent accurate, meaning that it comes back positive nine out of ten times when the person has the disease and that it is negative nine out of ten times when the person doesn't have the disease. So, it gives false negatives 10 percent of the time and false positives 10 percent of the time. For the sake of simplicity, the rate of true positives (the sensitivity of the test) and the rate of true negatives (the specificity) are taken to be the same in this example; in reality, they can be different. Now you take the test, and it's positive. What's the chance you have the disease? We assume that the subject being tested—"you" in this case—has been picked at random from the population.

Most of us would say 90 percent, because the test is accurate 9 out of 10 times. We'd be wrong. To calculate the actual probability that one has the disease given a positive test, we need to take other factors into account. For this, we can use Bayes's theorem.

The theorem allows us to calculate the probability of a hypothesis H (you have the disease) being true, given evidence E (the test is positive).

This is written as $P(H \mid E)$: the probability of H given E.

Bayes's theorem says:

$$P(H \mid E) = \frac{P(H) \times P(E \mid H)}{P(E)}$$

Let's unpack the various terms on the right-hand side of the equation.

P(H): The probability that someone picked at random from the population has the disease. This is also called the prior probability (before taking any evidence into account). In our case, we can assume it is $1/1000$, or 0.001, based on what's been observed in the general population thus far.

P(E | H): The probability of the evidence given the hypothesis or, to put it simply, the probability of testing positive if you have the disease. We know this. It's the sensitivity of the test: 0.9.

P(E): The probability of testing positive. This is the sum of the probabilities of two different ways someone can test positive given the background rate of the disease in the population. The first is the prior probability that one has the disease (0.001) multiplied by the probability that one tests positive (0.9), which equals 0.0009. The second is the prior probability that one doesn't have the disease (0.999) times the probability that one tests positive (0.1), which equals 0.0999.

So, $P(E) = 0.0009 + 0.0999 = 0.1008$

So, $P(H \mid E) = 0.001 \times 0.9 \,/\, 0.1008 = 0.0089$, or a 0.89 percent chance.

That's way lower than the 90 percent chance we intuited earlier. This final number is called the posterior probability: It's the prior probability updated given the evidence. To get a sense of how the posterior probability changes with alterations to the accuracy of the test, or with changes in the background rate of the disease in the population, let's look at some numbers:

For a test accuracy rate of 99 percent—only 1 in 100 tests gives a false positive or false negative—and a background rate of disease in the population of 1 in 1,000, the probability that you have the disease given a positive test rises to 0.09. That's almost a 1-in-10 chance.

For a test accuracy rate of 99 percent (1 in 100 tests gives a false positive or false negative), and a background rate of disease in the population of 1 in 100 (the disease has become more common now), the probability that you have the disease given a positive test rises to 0.5. That's a 50 percent chance.

Improve the test accuracy to 99.9 percent and keep the background rate at 1 in 100, and we get a posterior probability of 0.91. There's a very high chance you have the disease if you tested positive.

With this whirlwind introduction to Bayes's theorem, we are ready to tackle the Monty Hall problem. (This is a bit involved. Feel free to skip to the end of this section if you think it's too much, though it's quite revealing to see how Bayes's theorem gets us to Marilyn vos Savant's answer.)

We start by assuming that the car is hidden at random behind one of the three doors.

Let's start by stating our hypothesis and our priors. We pick Door No. 1. The host opens Door No. 3, behind which is a goat. We must figure out whether it's worth switching our guess from Door No. 1 to Door No. 2, to maximize our chances of choosing the door that hides the car. To do this, we must figure out the probabilities for two hypotheses and pick the higher of the two.

The first hypothesis is: Car is behind Door No. 1, given that host has opened Door No. 3 and revealed a goat. The second hypothesis is: Car is behind Door No. 2, given that host has opened Door No. 3 and revealed a goat. Consider the probability of the first hypothesis:

P (H=car is behind Door No. 1 | E=host has opened Door No. 3, revealing a goat).

From Bayes's theorem:

$$P(H \mid E) = \frac{P(E \mid H) \times P(H)}{P(E)}$$

Where:

P (E|H): the probability that the host opens Door No. 3, given that the car is behind Door No. 1. At the start of the game, you picked Door No. 1. If the car is behind it, the host can see that and, hence, has a choice of two doors to open, either No. 2 or No. 3, both of which hide goats. The probability they'll open one of them is simply 1/2.

P (H): the prior probability that the car is behind Door No. 1, before any door is opened. It's 1/3.

P (E): the probability that the host opens Door No. 3. This must be carefully evaluated, given that the host knows that you have picked Door No. 1 and they can see what's behind each door. So,

P (host picks Door No. 3) = P1 + P2 + P3

P1 = P (car is behind Door No. 1) × P (host picks Door No. 3, given car is behind Door No. 1) = P (C1) × P (H3|C1)

P2 = P (car is behind Door No. 2) × P (host picks Door No. 3, given car is behind Door No. 2) = P (C2) × P(H3|C2)

P3 = P (car is behind Door No. 3) × P (host picks Door No. 3, given car is behind Door No. 3) = P (C3) × P(H3|C3)

Take each part of the right-hand side of the equation:

- P1: P (C1) × P (H3|C1).
  o P (C1) = P (car is behind Door No. 1) = 1/3.
  o P (H3|C1)—if the car is behind Door No. 1, then the probability that the host opens Door No. 3 is 1/2. They could have picked either Door No. 2 or Door No. 3.
  o So, P1 = 1/3 × 1/2 = 1/6.

- P2: P (C2) x P (H3|C2).
  o P (C2) = P (car is behind Door No. 2) = 1/3.
  o P (H3|C2)—if the car is behind Door No. 2, then the probability that the host opens Door No. 3 is 1, because they cannot pick Door No. 2, otherwise it'll reveal the car.
  o So, P2 = 1/3 × 1 = 1/3

- P3: P (C3) × P (H3|C3).
  o P (C3) = P (car is behind Door No. 3) = 1/3.
  o P (H3|C3)—if the car is behind Door No. 3, then the probability that the host opens Door No. 3 is 0, otherwise it'll reveal the car.
  o So, P3 = 1/3 × 0 = 0

So, P (E) = P1 + P2 + P3 = 1/6 + 1/3 + 0 = 3/6 = 1/2

We can now calculate the probability that hypothesis 1 is true, given the evidence:

$$P(H|E) = \frac{\frac{1}{2} \times \frac{1}{3}}{\frac{1}{2}} = \frac{1}{3}$$

The probability that the car is behind the door you have picked is 1/3.

Now let's calculate the probability for the second hypothesis: The car is behind Door No. 2 given that the host has opened Door No. 3, revealing a goat. We can do a similar analysis.

P (E|H): Probability that the host opens Door No. 3, given that the car is behind Door No. 2. The host cannot open Door No. 2. They have to open Door No. 3, so the probability of this event is 1.

P (H): The prior probability that the car is behind Door No. 2, before any door is opened. It's 1/3.

P (E): As computed before, it's ½.

$$P(H|E) = \frac{1 \times \frac{1}{3}}{\frac{1}{2}} = \frac{2}{3}$$

Very clearly, the second hypothesis—that the car is behind Door No. 2, given that the host has opened Door No. 3—has a higher probability compared to the probability that the car is behind Door No. 1 (your original choice). You should switch doors!

If all this feels counterintuitive and you still refuse to change your choice of doors, it's understandable. Probabilities aren't necessarily intuitive. But when machines incorporate such reasoning into the decisions they make, our intuition doesn't get in the way.

WHO GIVES A TOSS?

Most machine learning is inherently probabilistic, even if the algorithm is not explicitly designed to be so. But that notion gets lost in the myriad claims about the capabilities of modern artificial intelligence. Let's take the perceptron algorithm we encountered earlier. Given two sets of data that are linearly separable, the algorithm will find a hyperplane that can divide the data that exists in some coordinate space into two. As we'll see in more detail soon, the algorithm finds *a* hyperplane, not necessarily the best one (for some definition of "best"). Then, given a new instance of data, the algorithm checks to see whether the data point lands on one side of the hyperplane or the other and classifies that data point accordingly. Sounds pretty deterministic, doesn't it? What's probabilistic about the perceptron?

The prediction is probabilistic in the sense that there's a finite chance that the algorithm will make an error when classifying a new data point. The classification depends entirely upon the hyperplane found by the perceptron. An infinite number of hyperplanes can separate the original data into two. So, one hyperplane might classify a new data point as belonging to class A, while another might classify the same data point as belonging to class B. It's possible, mathematically, to derive the risk of error inherent in a perceptron's predictions. That's what makes the prediction probabilistic, even though the algorithm's output is rather black and white (or -1 and 1).

This brings us to a valuable way of thinking about machine learning: in terms of probabilities, distributions, and statistics. To get there, we need a crash course in the basics behind these ideas.

We start with the notion of an experiment. An experiment can be anything: the toss of one coin, or two consecutive tosses of a coin, or the measurement of the temperature outside. All experiments have outcomes, and depending on how you define an experiment, you get a different set of outcomes. In each of these experiments, we can assign a number to that outcome, and this number is known as a random variable. Let's call it X (you can call it anything). Here are examples of how X can take on numerical values:

For one toss of a coin:

$$X = \begin{cases} 0 \;\; \textit{the coin toss came up heads} \\ 1 \;\; \textit{the coin toss came up tails} \end{cases}$$

For two consecutive tosses of a coin:

$$X = \begin{cases} 0 \;\; \textit{the coin tosses came up HH} \\ 1 \;\; \textit{the coin tosses came up HT} \\ 2 \;\; \textit{the coin tosses came up TH} \\ 3 \;\; \textit{the coin tosses came up TT} \end{cases}$$

For the measurement of temperature:

$$X = \{\text{a real-valued number between abs zero } (-273 \text{ C}) \text{ and } \infty$$

Let's toss our single coin, say, ten times. For each toss, the random variable X can be either 0 or 1. We plot the value of X on the x-axis, against the number of trials on the y-axis, to get a bar chart. For example, something like this (6 heads and 4 tails):

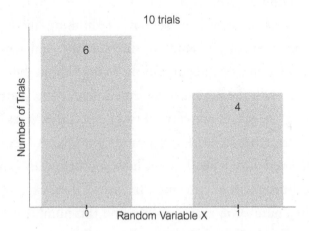

Given the relatively small number of trials, the number of heads versus the number of tails can vary a lot. We can plot the same data in terms of the experimental probability of X being 0 or X being 1. The use of the adjective "experimental" before the word "probability" signifies that it's an empirical result. Experimental, or empirical, probability is somewhat different from theoretical probability.

$$\text{Theoretical probability of an event} = \frac{\text{No. of favorable outcomes}}{\text{Total no. of possible outcomes}}$$

The theoretical probability of getting heads on a single coin toss is simply one-half, but the empirical probability depends upon the outcomes of our actual experiments. I'm going to avoid the adjective "empirical" or "theoretical" in the discussions that follow unless the type of probability isn't clear from the context.

For our experiment with 10 coin tosses, the probability of $X = 0$ is 0.6, and the probability of $X = 1$ is 0.4. The total probability should add up to 1.

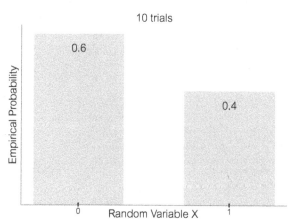

What we have just seen is the simplest example of a probability distribution. It's called a Bernoulli distribution, and it dictates the way the values of a "discrete" random variable X are distributed. In this case, X can take on only discrete values, 0 or 1. Formally, the Bernoulli probability distribution is specified by the function P(X):

$$P(X=x)=\begin{cases} 1-p, & x=0 \\ p, & x=1 \end{cases}$$

P(X) is also called the probability mass function, and it states that the probability of the random variable X taking on the value 1 is p, and the probability of X being 0 is $(1-p)$. For a fair coin, one that is equally likely to come up heads or tails, p equals 0.5.

This prepares us for the idea of sampling from an underlying distribution. An underlying distribution is the ground truth for some random variable—in this case, the outcome of the toss of a fair coin. Every toss of the coin is a sample from the underlying distribution. Here's an example of what happens when we sample a 100,000 times. (Thanks to something called the square root law, the counts of heads and tails will differ by a value that's on the order of the square root of the total number of trials; in this case, it will be on the order of the square root of 100,000, or about 316.)

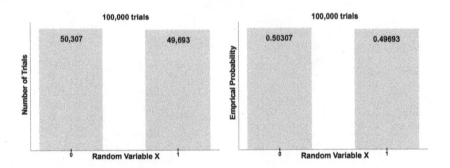

In machine learning, we start with data. The distribution of the data we have in hand is representative of some underlying distribution of the data. So, if all we had were the results of 100,000 coin tosses, then that distribution of heads and tails would be our best insight into the underlying distribution describing the toss of a fair coin. Just hold that thought in mind while we take one more example of a discrete distribution.

Consider a weird digital display that, when you press a button, shows a number between 0 and 6. Here, the random variable X is the number that is displayed. So, X can be one of $[0, 1, 2, 3, 4, 5, 6]$. But the display is rigged. The probabilities for the different values of X are not equal. Let's say the underlying distribution is given by:

$$P(X = x) = \begin{cases} 1/32, & x = 0 \\ 1/16, & x = 1 \\ 1/8, & x = 2 \\ 9/16, & x = 3 \\ 1/8, & x = 4 \\ 1/16, & x = 5 \\ 1/32, & x = 6 \end{cases}$$

These are the theoretical probabilities.

If we pushed the button 1,000 times, we would be sampling the underlying distribution 1,000 times, and we might get this distribution of the observed values of X and the corresponding empirical probabilities:

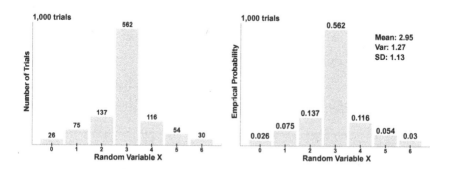

Given this distribution, there are some statistical parameters of interest. One is something called the expected value. We encountered it while discussing Bernard Widrow's LMS algorithm and put off an explanation. Well, you get the expected value of X by taking each value of X and multiplying it by its probability and summing them all up. So, for our experiment:

$$E(X) = \sum_{k=1}^{N} x_k P(X = x_k)$$

$\Rightarrow E(X) =$

$0 \times P(0) + 1 \times P(1) + 2 \times P(2) + 3 \times P(3) + 4 \times P(4) + 5 \times P(5) + 6 \times P(6)$

$\Rightarrow E(X) =$

$0 \times 0.032 + 1 \times 0.056 + 2 \times 0.116 + 3 \times 0.584 + 4 \times 0.127 + 5 \times 0.056 + 6 \times 0.029$

$\Rightarrow E(X) = 3$

This is the value you'd expect to get for the random variable X over some large-number trials. We know this by another name: the mean of the distribution. If the probabilities of all the values of X were identical, then the expected value, or mean of the distribution, would be the same as the arithmetic average. (Sum up all the values and divide by the total number of values.)

Now come two other extremely important statistical parameters: the variance and the standard deviation. First, the variance:

$$var(X) = \sum_{k=1}^{N} (x_k - E(X))^2 P(X = x_k)$$

Basically, take each value of X, subtract from it the expected value of X, square it, multiply the result with the probability of that value of X, and sum over all values of X. That's the variance.

The standard deviation is defined as the square root of the variance. In standard terminology:

$$var(X) = \sigma^2$$
$$sd = \sqrt{\sigma^2} = \sigma$$

Both the variance and the standard deviation are indicative of the dispersion, or spread, of X about the mean.

We will change tack now. What if the random variable took on continuous values, instead of discrete ones? There's folklore that one of the most common distributions in nature for continuous random variables is the so-called normal distribution, with the familiar bell-shaped curve. I thought so, too, until Philip Stark, a professor at the University of California, Berkeley, and an expert on probability and statistics, disabused me of the notion. "The joke is that theoreticians think it's an empirical fact, and experimentalists think it's a theoretical fact," he told me, while acknowledging he couldn't recall who first came up with the quip. "The normal approximation works when it works. The problem is knowing when it works." Oh, well. It was a nice delusion while it lasted. Still, it's well worth taking a closer look at the normal distribution, given the outsize role it plays in machine learning.

Consider a random variable that's equal to a person's average resting body temperature, in Fahrenheit. We know that our body temperature varies from day to day, from hour to hour; not by much, unless you are ill, but it varies nonetheless. Yet, we all have an average resting body temperature, which, it turns out, is slightly different for each one of us. Let's plot the average resting body temperature of a very large sample of individuals (see figure, top of next page).

The x-axis is the value of the random variable X, which equals the average resting body temperature in degrees Fahrenheit (F). For now, let's take the y-axis as a measure of the empirical probability

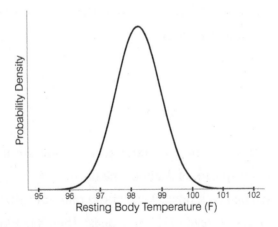

Resting Body Temperature (F)

that X takes on some value between 95 and 102. (There's a more precise meaning for what the y-axis stands for, but we'll come to that.)

This idealized curve peaks at 98.25°F and is symmetric about it. This value is the mean of the distribution, and the curve is called a "normal," or Gaussian, distribution.

Our curve has a standard deviation of 0.73, a parameter that has a very specific meaning in the context of a normal distribution. If you draw two vertical lines one standard deviation to the left of the mean $(98.25 - 0.73)$ and one standard deviation to the right of the mean $(98.25 + 0.73)$, you get a region under the curve that contains 68 percent of the observed values of X. The region is shown in gray in the following image (see figure, next page). And almost all the observed values of X will lie within 3 standard deviations of the mean.

Again, the variance is simply the square of the standard deviation. So, the variance and standard deviation are telling you something about the spread of values away from the mean. A larger standard deviation would give you a broader, squatter plot. (If the mean is zero and the standard deviation equals 1, we have what's called a "standard" normal distribution.

Let's revisit the y-axis in our plot of the continuous random variable. While a discrete random variable is characterized by its

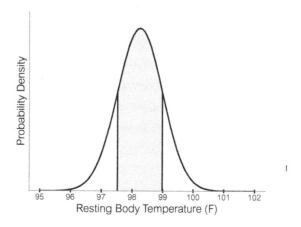

probability mass function (PMF), a continuous random variable is characterized by what's called the probability density function (PDF).

In the case of a discrete random variable, one can use a PMF to determine the probability that X has a certain value. (In one of our experiments above, the probability that $X = 0$, for heads, is 0.50279.) But one cannot do something similar for a continuous random variable. When the variable's value is continuous, it means that you can keep getting more and more precise about its exact value. Let's say the thermometer recording body temperature is arbitrarily precise. That implies the thermometer reading can be one of an infinite number of possible values between 95 and 102. So, even though a normal distribution can be used to characterize the random variable, the probability that it has some specific, infinitely precise value is actually zero.

That's why when dealing with probability density functions and continuous random variables, one can speak in terms only of the probability that the random variable will take on a value between two numbers (say, between 98.25 and 98.5). Then, the probability that the random variable has a value in that range is given by the area under the probability density function, bounded by the end points of that range. Also, because the total probability must add up to 1, the area under the entire PDF equals 1.

The key message so far, for our purposes, is this: Whether it's a probability mass function for a discrete random variable or a probability density function for a continuous random variable, some well-known and analytically well-understood functions, with characteristic parameters, can be used to describe the probability distributions. For example, we just need the probability p for the Bernoulli distribution. For the normal distribution, we need the mean and variance; those two numbers give you the exact shape of the bell curve. These parameters are a way to model some underlying distribution.

With these barest of bare-minimum basics of probability and statistics in hand, we can get back to thinking about machine learning as probabilistic reasoning and statistical learning.

SIX OF ONE, HALF A DOZEN OF THE OTHER

Let's start with the most common form of machine learning, one we have already encountered, called supervised learning. We are given some labeled data, $\mathbf{X}$. Each instance of $\mathbf{X}$ is a d-dimensional vector, meaning it has d components. So, $\mathbf{X}$ is a matrix, where each row of the matrix is one instance of the data.

$$[x1, x2, x3, x4, \ldots, xd]$$

Each instance of $\mathbf{X}$ could represent, say, a person. And the components $[x1, x2, x3, \ldots, xd]$ could be values for the person's height, weight, body mass, cholesterol levels, blood pressure, and so on. Associated with each instance of $\mathbf{X}$ is a label, y. Let's say y is -1 if the person did not have a heart attack in the five years following the date their physiological parameters were measured, and 1 if they did. In supervised learning, some algorithm—the perceptron, for example—is given the training data: a set of data points representing n people (so $\mathbf{X}$ is an n x d matrix, n rows, d columns); each row of $\mathbf{X}$ has a corresponding label y, equal to -1 or 1. All values of y taken together form the vector $\mathbf{y}$. The algorithm uses these data to learn something about the underlying distribution of $\mathbf{X}$ and $\mathbf{y}$.

Let's say that P $(\mathbf{X}, \mathbf{y})$ is the underlying probability distribution, which captures our knowledge about all humans as to their risk of having a heart attack in the next five years, given a person's current physiological state. When we create a dataset of several individuals, assuming that these individuals are randomly chosen, the dataset is akin to drawing from, or sampling, this underlying distribution. The ML algorithm, given data about a new unlabeled individual, must predict whether that person is at risk of a heart attack in the next five years. Now, if you knew the underlying distribution, you could very simply figure out the probability that the person was at risk given $\mathbf{x}$ and the probability that the person was not at risk given $\mathbf{x}$ (where $\mathbf{x}$ refers to the vector for a single person or an instance of $\mathbf{X}$).

$$P \ (y = \text{at-risk} \mid \mathbf{x}) \text{ and } P \ (y = \text{not-at-risk} \mid \mathbf{x})$$

Then, one way to make a prediction would be to choose the category that had the higher probability. Later in the chapter, we'll come to just how you can do this (it involves using Bayes's theorem), but for now, all we need to appreciate is that this is the best an ML algorithm can do, because it has access to the underlying distribution. Such a classifier is called a Bayes optimal classifier.

But in just about every case, it's impossible to know the underlying distribution. So, the task of probabilistic ML algorithms, one can say, comes down to estimating the distribution from data. Some algorithms do it better than others, and all make mistakes. So, when you hear claims that an AI is making accurate predictions, remember that it's well-nigh impossible to be 100 percent accurate. Whether an algorithm is implicitly (as in the case of the perceptron) or explicitly probabilistic (we'll see examples of these in a bit), it can be wrong. And yet, this is not a knock against machine learning. As humans, while we seem to think we make rational, error-free decisions, we also make probabilistic decisions. It's just that these probabilistic goings-on happen under the hood, so to speak, and we are mostly unaware of them.

Estimating underlying distributions is not trivial. For starters, it's often easier to make some simplifying assumptions about the shape of the distribution. Is it a Bernoulli distribution? Is it a normal distribution? Keep in mind that these idealized descriptions of distributions are just that: idealized; they make the math easier, but there's no guarantee that the underlying distribution hews exactly to these mathematical forms. Also, when we have data, we have access to rates. For example, how many times a biased coin came up heads. We must turn rates into probabilities: The two are not the same, and equating them can be problematic; as Stark told me, "That's a huge epistemic jump." Nonetheless, it's one we make with caution.

Let's say you do assume the type of underlying distribution. In each case, the distribution is characterized by some parameters. We saw that a Bernoulli distribution, for example, is characterized by the value p, which then allows you to write down this probability mass function:

$$P(X = x) = \begin{cases} 1 - p, & x = 0 \\ p, & x = 1 \end{cases}$$

A normal distribution is characterized by the mean and standard deviation. There are other types of distributions. Some have their own set of parameters, denoted by the Greek letter θ (theta). (Let's ignore for now so-called nonparametric distributions, which are not specified with some set of parameters.) The underlying distribution is then written as:

$$P_\theta(\mathbf{X}, \mathbf{y})$$

Or we can refer to both $\mathbf{X}$ and $\mathbf{y}$ with a single letter "D" (for "data"), and write the distribution in this way:

$$P_\theta(D) \ or, \ P(D; \theta)$$

All this is leading up to a broad statement about ML algorithms. We can focus on two important approaches. (There are others, but these two get us to the heart of some interesting issues.)

- In the first method, given data, the ML algorithm figures out the best θ, for some choice of distribution type (Bernoulli or Gaussian or something else), which maximizes the likelihood of seeing the data, D. In other words, you are estimating the best underlying distribution, with parameter θ, such that if you were to sample from that distribution, you would maximize the likelihood of observing the labeled data you already had in hand. Not surprisingly, this method is called maximum likelihood estimation (MLE). It maximizes P $(D \mid \theta)$, the probability of observing D given θ, and is loosely associated with frequentist methodology.

As a concrete example, let's take two populations of people, one tall and the other short. We have a few hundred samples of the heights of people from each group. Our job is to estimate the underlying distribution P (D) by maximizing P $(D \mid \theta)$. Let's say that each set of heights (short and tall) is modeled as a Gaussian distribution, with its own mean and variance, and the overall distribution will be a combination of these two Gaussians. MLE makes no assumptions about which Gaussians are more likely than others, meaning that all values for the parameters are equally likely. Given this assumption, or lack of one, MLE maximizes P $(D \mid \theta)$, where θ here refers to the mean and variance. Again, by treating all values of θ as equally likely, MLE gives us the θ that maximizes the likelihood of observing the data we collected.

- In the second method, given the sampled data, the ML algorithm maximizes P $(\theta \mid D)$, i.e., it finds the most likely θ, given the data. Hidden in that statement is something that causes frequentists to tear their hair out, as Kilian Weinberger, professor of computer science at Cornell University, eloquently told his students in one of his ML lectures. The idea that you are going to find the most likely θ implies that θ itself follows a distribution, meaning it is being treated as a random variable. This second method now makes assumptions about which θ is most likely, without having seen the data. This is the prior probability distribution. Bayesian statisticians argue that it's entirely reasonable to have a prior belief for the value of θ.

The argument will become clearer if we revisit our tall-short dataset. Surely, not all Gaussian distributions are equally likely. We can, based on our knowledge about the world, make a fair assumption that the Gaussian for short people has a mean of, say, five feet, while the Gaussian for tall people has a mean of six feet or something along those lines. (You get the picture.) And we can make similar assumptions about their variances.

With this prior distribution in hand and the sampled data, one can estimate the posterior distribution, which is the most likely θ, given the data. This second method is called MAP, for "maximum a posteriori" estimation. It's a Bayesian approach, though not the only one.

In both MLE and MAP, the actual math can get sophisticated, but conceptually, it involves these basic steps:

- Write down the function that needs to be maximized, while incorporating any necessary assumptions.

- Take the derivative of the function. In the case of MLE, the derivative is taken with respect to x, the data; in the case of MAP, the derivative is taken with respect to θ. Now set the derivative to zero. (This is the place where the function has no slope; it's at a maximum. Of course, the derivative can be zero at a minimum, too, and there are ways to check.) Now solve the equation(s) you get by setting the derivative to zero.

- Sometimes—in fact, most times—there's no closed-form solution to the problem. In this case, instead of trying to find the maximum, you take the negative of the function and try to find the minimum. We already know how to find the minimum, at least for convex functions: You do gradient descent. That'll give you the relevant results.

MLE is powerful when you have a lot of sampled data, while MAP works best with fewer data. And as the amount of sampled data grows, MAP and MLE begin converging in their estimate of the underlying distribution.

Most of us are intuitively frequentists. But the Bayesian approach to statistics is extremely powerful. (Note: Bayesian statistics is not the same as Bayes's theorem. Even frequentists value Bayes's theorem. They just object to this whole idea of having prior beliefs about the parameters of a distribution when trying to discern the properties of that very distribution from data.)

One of the first large-scale demonstrations of using Bayesian reasoning for machine learning was due to two statisticians, Frederick Mosteller and David Wallace, who used the technique to figure out something that had been bothering historians for centuries: the authorship of the disputed *Federalist Papers*.

WHO WROTE THEM PAPERS?

Months after the U.S. Constitution was drafted in Philadelphia in the summer of 1787, a series of essays, published anonymously under the pen name "Publius," began appearing in newspapers in New York State. Seventy-seven such essays were published, written to convince New Yorkers to ratify the Constitution. These essays, plus eight more, for a total of eighty-five, were then published in a two-volume set titled *The Federalist: A Collection of Essays, Written in Favour of the New Constitution, as Agreed upon by the Federal Convention, September 17, 1787.* Eventually, it became known that the essays had been written by Alexander Hamilton, John Jay, and James Madison, three of the "founding fathers" of the United States. About two decades later, and after Hamilton had died (following a fatal duel between him and Aaron Burr, the then-U.S. vice president), the essays began to be assigned to individual authors. For seventy of the papers, the writers were known. But of the remaining papers, twelve were thought to have been written by either Hamilton or Madison, and three were thought to have been co-authored.

You'd think that Madison, who was still alive, would have clearly identified the authors of each paper. But as Frederick Mosteller writes in *The Pleasures of Statistics*, "the primary reason the dispute existed is that Madison and Hamilton did not hurry to enter their claims.

Within a few years after writing the essays, they had become bitter political enemies and each occasionally took positions opposing some of his own Federalist writings." They behaved like lawyers writing briefs for clients, Mosteller writes: "They did not need to believe or endorse every argument they put forward favoring the new Constitution." Consequently, the authorship of these fifteen documents remained unresolved.

In 1941, Mosteller and a political scientist named Frederick Williams decided to tackle the problem. They looked at the lengths of sentences used by Madison and Hamilton in the papers whose authorship was *not* in dispute. The idea was to identify each author's unique "signatures"—maybe one author used longer sentences than the other—and then use those signatures to check the sentence lengths of the disputed papers and, hence, their authorship. But the effort led nowhere. "When we assembled the results for the known papers the average lengths for Hamilton and Madison were 34.55 and 34.59, respectively—a complete disaster because these averages are practically identical and so could not distinguish authors."

Mosteller and Williams also calculated the standard deviation (SD), which provided a measure of the spread of the sentence lengths. Again, the numbers were very close. The SD for Hamilton was 19, and 20 for Madison. If you were to draw the normal distribution of sentence lengths for each author, the two curves would overlap substantially, providing little discriminatory power. This work became a teaching moment. Mosteller, while lecturing at Harvard, used this analysis of *The Federalist Papers* to educate his students on the difficulties of applying statistical methods.

By the mid-1950s, Mosteller and statistician David Wallace, who was at the University of Chicago, began wondering about using Bayesian methods for making inferences. At the time, there were no examples of applying Bayesian analysis to large, practical problems.

It was about then that Mosteller received a letter from the historian Douglass Adair, who had become aware of the courses being taught by Mosteller at Harvard. Adair wanted Mosteller to revisit the issue of the authorship of *The Federalist Papers*. "[Adair] . . . was stimulated to write suggesting that I (or more generally, statisticians) should get back to this problem. He pointed out that words might be the key, because he had noticed that Hamilton nearly always used the form 'while' and Madison the form 'whilst.' The only trouble was that many papers contained neither of them," Mosteller writes. "We were spurred to action." There was no deadline. "True, Adair was in a hurry to know, but history is good at waiting."

One of their ideas that bore fruit was to look at so-called function words, words that have a function rather than a meaning—prepositions, conjunctions, and articles. First, they had to count the occurrence of such words in documents written by Hamilton and Madison. It was a laborious process. With the help of others, the duo began typing each word from each article, one word per line, on a long paper tape. Then they began the even more laborious task of cutting the paper tape into slips, such that each slip had just one word on it, and then arranging the slips in alphabetical order. "That was in 1959–60; it all seems primitive, even laughable now," Mosteller writes. "When the counting was going on, if someone opened a door, slips of paper would fly about the room."

Eventually they figured out how to use a computer to count and alphabetize the words. But the computer came with its own idiosyncrasies. "The program did this beautifully up to some indeterminate point around 3000 words, and then it would go crazy, destroying everything it had done so far," Mosteller writes, adding that "1500 words of *The Federalist* was as much as anyone (even a computer) could stand, however important these political writings may be." And so it went, a few thousand words at a time, until they had the counts for certain function words that appeared in a large number of articles written by Hamilton and Madison.

Now it was time to figure out the authorship of one of the disputed papers. They used Bayesian analysis to calculate the probability of two hypotheses: (1) the author is Madison, and (2) the author is Hamilton. If hypothesis 1 has a greater probability, the author is more likely to be Madison. Otherwise, it's Hamilton. Take one function word, say, "upon," and calculate the probability of hypothesis 1 given the word and hypothesis 2 given the word, and ascribe authorship appropriately. Of course, using multiple words at once makes the analysis sharper.

The key insight here is that given a bunch of known documents by Madison, the usage of some word, such as "upon," follows a distribution. Madison used the word more in some documents, less so in others. The same can be said of Hamilton. As we saw in the issue with sentence length, if these distributions are alike, they cannot be used to tell the authors apart. But if they are different, they possess the power to discriminate. Mosteller makes this point eloquently: "The more widely the distributions of rates [of words] of the two authors are separated, the stronger the discriminating power of the word. Here, [the word] *by* discriminates better than [the word] *to*, which in turn is better than [the word] *from*."

Mosteller and Wallace then turned such evidence from word rates into an appropriate model to do statistical inference. They tried various models; each model implied certain assumptions about the underlying probability distribution that made the math tractable. The results were unanimous. "By whatever methods are used, the results are the same: overwhelming evidence for Madison's authorship of the disputed papers. Our data independently supplement the evidence of the historians. Madison is extremely likely, in the sense of degree of belief, to have written the disputed Federalist papers, with the possible exception of paper number 55, and there our evidence yields odds of 80 to 1 for Madison—strong, but not overwhelming."

Patrick Juola, professor of computer science at Duquesne University in Pittsburgh, Pennsylvania, and a modern-day expert in stylometry (the use of the statistics of variations in writing style to determine authorship), said that Mosteller and Wallace's work was a seminal moment for statisticians. "It was very influential in statistical theory. And they were justifiably lauded," Juola told me. "Historians had been looking at the problem for a hundred years. And the historians had mostly come to the same decisions that Mosteller and Wallace did. And what made [their] study so groundbreaking was [that] for the first time, this was done in a completely objective, algorithmic fashion, which is to say it was *machine learning* [italics mine]."

A WADDLE OF PENGUINS

To get further insights into the probabilistic nature of machine learning, let's head to the Palmer Archipelago, Antarctica. There, a team led by marine biologist Kristen Gorman painstakingly collected data on 334 penguins from three islands. Yes, penguins. Three species of penguins: Adélie, Gentoo, and Chinstrap. Each penguin is characterized by its species name, the island where it lives, its bill length (in millimeters), its bill depth (mm), its flipper length (mm), its body mass (grams), its sex (male or female), and the year it was studied, data that were made freely available by Gorman and her colleagues Allison Horst and Alison Hill.

For our purposes, let's disregard the information about the island of origin and the year the penguin was studied. Sans those data, each penguin has these five attributes: bill length, bill depth, flipper length, body mass, and sex. These attributes can be thought of as the components of a vector $[x1, x2, x3, x4, x5]$, where $x1 =$ bill length, $x2 =$ bill depth, and so on.

So, each penguin is characterized by a vector $\mathbf{x} = [x1, x2, x3, x4, x5]$. And each penguin has a label $y =$ Adélie (0), Gentoo (1), or Chinstrap (2). A penguin, then, is a point in 5D space, and that point can be classified as belonging to one of three species.

The task for an ML algorithm is to learn the correlation among the attributes of a penguin and the species to which those attributes belong. Basically, the algorithm needs to learn a function that maps $\mathbf{x}$ to y.

$$f(\mathbf{x}) = y$$

Then, given a new $\mathbf{x}$, it can spit out the predicted value for y (0, 1, or 2). Or, we can say that the ML algorithm must estimate the underlying distribution $P(\mathbf{X}, \mathbf{y})$. And then, given some new data $\mathbf{x}$, it can calculate $P(y =$ Adélie $| \mathbf{x})$ and $P(y =$ Gentoo $| \mathbf{x})$ and $P(y =$ Chinstrap $| \mathbf{x})$. The largest of the three conditional probabilities gives us the most likely species, given the new, unknown penguin's attributes.

For a moment, let's take just two species. If the 5D data are linearly separable—meaning one can draw a 4D hyperplane that cleanly separates, say, the data representing Adélie penguins from those of the Chinstrap penguins in 5D coordinate space—then we can use a perceptron algorithm to find that hyperplane. Then, given data about a new, as-yet-unclassified penguin, the perceptron can tell us whether the penguin falls on one side of the hyperplane or the other and classify it accordingly. But we know by now that the perceptron algorithm finds one of the infinitely many possible hyperplanes. The perceptron's ability to classify new data can be error-prone. An Adélie could get classified as a Chinstrap, and vice versa.

But there's a bigger problem staring at us: the assumption of linearly separable data. For starters, even if the data representing a few hundred penguins were linearly separable, there's no guarantee the distinction would hold if you kept collecting more and more data. But even with a small sampling of penguins, as is the case here, it's clear that the assumption is suspect. We can see it for ourselves.

It's hard to visualize data in anything more than two dimensions, so let's look at the data in different ways using only two features—say, bill length and depth—to get a sense of the problem. First, here's a plot of two species of penguins, Adélie and Gentoo, characterized by those two attributes. In these two dimensions, the two species show a separation, but only just about. One Gentoo penguin has attribute values that are very much like those of the Adélie penguins; if it weren't for the one outlier, the separation would be cleaner.

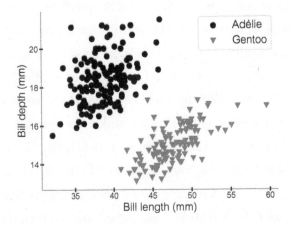

To mix things up, let's plot all three species on the same graph, for the same two attributes (see figure opposite).

The picture is much more muddled now. If we had to build an ML model that could cleanly separate the three species of penguins from one another, it's not going to be clear-cut. Even with this limited sampling of the penguins, the data overlap, particularly when we compare the Adélie and Chinstrap penguins or the Chinstrap and Gentoo penguins.

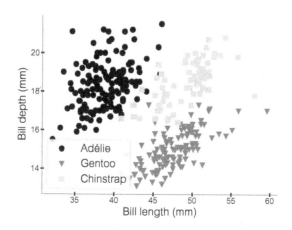

So, any classifier we build that learns the function $f(\mathbf{x})$ to map the features of a penguin to its species will always make some mistakes. Or, looking at it another way, if the classifier is given new data about a penguin, and the classifier predicts that the penguin is, say, an Adélie, then that prediction will have a certain probability of being wrong. Our task is to build a classifier that minimizes the likelihood of a mistake.

This is where an entire field of machine learning, called Bayesian decision theory, comes in. It establishes the bounds for the best we can do given the data at hand. But first, to make things even easier to visualize and grasp, let's whittle the data down to just one attribute.

Consider the following histogram showing the numbers of Adélie penguins plotted against their bill depth (see top, next page).

There are ten bins for the value of bill depth, and in each bin, there are some Adélie penguins whose bill depths belong in that bin. The plot gives you a rough sense of the distribution of bill depths of Adélie penguins.

In nature, the distribution would likely be continuous. The chart that follows shows a normal bell-shaped distribution with a mean and standard deviation fitted to the data we have. (Notice that the y-axis now reads "probability density," rather than "number of

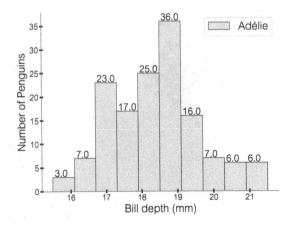

penguins"—it's giving us a way to get at the probability that the bill depth has some value in Adélie penguins.)

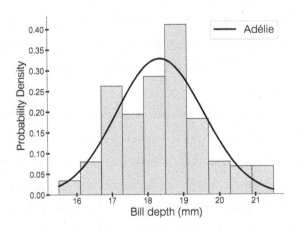

Let's imagine for a moment that the smooth curve above is the actual, underlying distribution of bill depths of Adélie penguins. If we had access to that curve, it would allow us to calculate the probability that the bill depth has some value, given the penguin is an Adélie. (I'm being a bit imprecise here, in talking about the probability of an Adélie penguin having a specific bill depth; we know from our earlier analysis that when the distribution is continuous, we can talk of the probability only for some range of bill depths.) So, we calculate something called a class-conditional probability, meaning, a probability conditioned on the fact that the penguin belongs to a particular class, in this case Adélie.

So, the distribution gives us P ($\mathbf{x} \mid y =$ Adélie). Ideally, the P needs a subscript, indicating that it's the probability for bill depth, but it's clear from the context, so I'm going to eschew the subscript.

We could do the same for Gentoo penguins. Here's a plot of the sampled data:

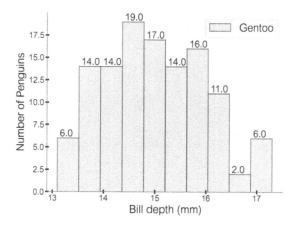

We can fit a normal distribution to the data:

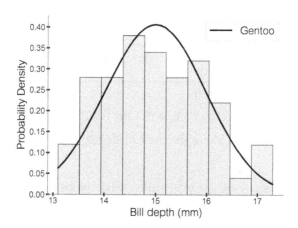

Again, assuming the curve is nature's real, underlying distribution of bill depths of Gentoo penguins, and assuming we have access to that distribution, then we can calculate, for some **x**:

$$P\ (\mathbf{x}\ |\ y = \text{Gentoo})$$

Here are the two curves in the same plot, side by side:

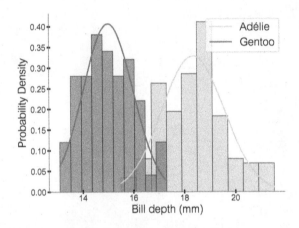

It's clear that Gentoo penguins have a smaller mean bill depth and that the bill depths are somewhat more tightly clustered around the mean than they are for Adélie penguins, which have a larger mean bill depth. From the perspective of making predictions, if we had access to these supposed underlying natural distributions, and we were then given the bill depth for an unidentified penguin—all we were told is that it's either a Gentoo or an Adélie—then we could calculate two probabilities:

$P\ (y = \text{Gentoo}\ |\ \mathbf{x})$, which is the probability that the penguin is a Gentoo, given a value for the bill depth; and

$P\ (y = \text{Adélie}\ |\ \mathbf{x})$, the probability that the penguin is an Adélie, given the bill depth.

If the former is greater, then we predict that the penguin is a Gentoo; if the latter value is larger, then we predict that it's an Adélie. But how do we calculate the two probabilities? This is where Bayes's theorem comes in.

Recall that, in terms of a hypothesis (H) and evidence (E):

$$P(H \mid E) = \frac{P(H) \times P(E \mid H)}{P(E)}$$

We have two hypotheses: (1) The penguin is a Gentoo, and (2) the penguin is an Adélie. The evidence we have is some bill depth.

So, we must calculate the probabilities of each of our two hypotheses:

$$P\,(y = \text{Gentoo} \mid \mathbf{x}) = \frac{P(\mathbf{x} \mid y = \text{Gentoo}) \times P(y = \text{Gentoo})}{P(\mathbf{x})}$$

$$P(y = \text{Adélie} \mid \mathbf{x}) = \frac{P(\mathbf{x} \mid y = \text{Adélie}) \times P(y = \text{Adélie})}{P(\mathbf{x})}$$

Let's tackle the first hypothesis and see how we can arrive at the probability for it. It involves calculating the values for each term on the right-hand side of the equation.

P ($y =$ Gentoo): This is simply the "prior" probability that the penguin is a Gentoo. We can estimate this from the data at hand. In our sample of penguins, there were 119 Gentoo penguins and 146 Adélie penguins. So, an estimate of the prior probability that a penguin is a Gentoo is simply 119 / (119+146) = 0.45.

P ($\mathbf{x} \mid y =$ Gentoo): We can read off this value from the distribution depicted above. Find the bill depth on the x-axis and figure out the probability on the y-axis on the "Gentoo" part of the plot.

P($\mathbf{x}$): This is the probability that the bill has some particular depth. In much the same way that we calculated the probability that someone could test positive when administered a test for a disease (where we had to account for both true positives and false negatives), we can also take into account that we are dealing with two types of penguins. So:

$$P(\mathbf{x}) = P\left(\mathbf{x} \mid Ad\acute{e}lie\right) \times P\left(Ad\acute{e}lie\right) + P\left(\mathbf{x} \mid Gentoo\right) \times P\left(Gentoo\right)$$

We can read off P ($\mathbf{x}$ | Adélie) from our distribution. P (Adélie) is the prior probability that a penguin is an Adélie. We know how to calculate this. The same goes for Gentoo penguins. Also, note that P($\mathbf{x}$) is the same for both hypotheses and is therefore often ignored in the calculations, especially in situations where it can be tricky or even impossible to determine.

Using these data, we can calculate P ($y =$ Gentoo | $\mathbf{x}$): the "posterior" probability that the penguin is a Gentoo, given some bill depth $\mathbf{x}$.

We can do the same analysis for Adélie penguins and get the posterior probability that the penguin is an Adélie, given the same bill depth $\mathbf{x}$. Then, we predict that the penguin is an Adélie or a Gentoo based on whichever posterior probability is higher.

This simple classifier that we just analyzed, with only one feature of penguins (bill depth) and two types of penguins, is called the Bayes optimal classifier. It's the best any ML algorithm can ever do. And in our analysis, the result was contingent upon knowing or estimating the underlying distribution of data.

But even the Bayes optimal classifier makes errors. Let's say you are handed data about an unclassified penguin, and it has a bill depth of about 16 mm. Our calculations might come up with, for example, a probability of 0.8 that the penguin is a Gentoo and 0.2 that it's an Adélie. So, using our algorithm, we predict that the penguin is a Gentoo, but there's a 20 percent chance we are wrong. It can be shown mathematically that this error cannot be improved upon by any other technique, so it sets a lower bound for the prediction risk.

If all this seems too easy, or trivial, let's start pouring cold water. For starters, we assumed that we had access to or could estimate the underlying natural distributions. Of course, we almost *never* have access to the true underlying distribution—which is why we do machine learning in the first place. As we saw earlier, ML algorithms are basically trying to get at the best possible approximation of the underlying distribution from a sampling of data. There are any number of ways of doing this, including two we saw earlier: maximum likelihood estimation (MLE) and maximum a posteriori (MAP) estimation.

Also, it just so happens that in the case we analyzed, bill depth can help distinguish Adélie penguins from Gentoo penguins without huge errors being made. But that's not the case if one compares Adélie and Chinstrap penguins. Here's a plot of the two penguin species, overlaid. They are indistinguishable when evaluated using only bill depth. Even the Bayes optimal classifier will get things wrong a lot of the time.

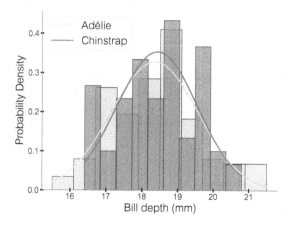

This is where extra features come in. If we were to add bill length to the mix, and plot the two types of penguins on the xy plane, here's what we'd get:

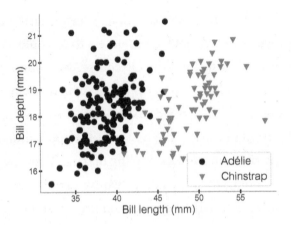

There's some overlap between the circles (Adélie) and triangles (Chinstrap), but the two are mostly distinct groups. We can again build a Bayes optimal classifier if we can estimate the underlying distributions. Getting to these distributions is going to take some mental calisthenics. Just as we fit a bell-shaped curve to represent the probability density function for bill depth, we can fit a bell-shaped surface to represent the PDF for bill length and depth taken together.

For example, above is such a 3D plot. The 2D surface at the bottom shows the "heat map" of the distribution of points: The whiter regions closer to the center will have more points, and the points will get scarcer as you move outward, toward darker regions. The 3D surface is the probability density function.

Now imagine such surfaces for our plot of bill length and depth for the two types of penguins. There would be two, one centered over the circles and another over the triangles. The precise shapes of these surfaces would be slightly different. Even by simply eyeballing the 2D scatter plot, you can imagine that the surface over the Adélie penguins would be more rounded and spread out, whereas the one over the Chinstrap penguins would be narrower and more ellipsoidal. Those two surfaces would overlap, just like the two curves did when we were interested only in bill depth.

If we could estimate those underlying distributions, we'd be able to classify a new penguin (given its bill length and depth) as either an Adélie or a Chinstrap. And in much the same way, the classification would be error-prone, but it's the best we can do.

All this must still seem straightforward (and some of the ease might have to do with the disarming penguins and their tractable characteristics). But let's start thinking about why this method, the Bayes optimal classifier, gets computationally impossible very quickly.

At the heart of this approach is the ability to estimate probability distributions given a set of features. For one feature, bill depth, we had to estimate the shape of a 2D function. Maybe a set of one hundred or so penguins of a certain class would be enough to get a good sense of the underlying function. We then bumped up the set of features to two (bill length and depth) and had to estimate the shape of a 3D surface. The same sample size, one hundred penguins per class, may still be adequate to get at that 3D surface. But the sample size becomes an issue as we add more features.

In real-life ML problems, the features can number in the tens, hundreds, thousands, or even more. This is where the scope of the problem becomes terrifying. Estimating the shape of the probability distribution with reasonable accuracy in higher and higher dimensions is going to require more and more data. A few hundred samples are not going to cut it. And the more data you add, the more compute-intensive estimating the distribution gets, if it's possible at all.

So, some simplifications are in order.

IT PAYS TO BE NAÏVE

Let's restate our problem. If we have, say, five features that are being used to describe a penguin (bill depth, bill length, flipper length, body mass, and sex), then we see that each penguin is essentially a vector (a point) in 5D space. The feature vector **x** is:

$$[x1, x2, x3, x4, x5]$$

If we are given these attributes for some as-yet-unidentified penguin, then our job is to figure out:

- P ($y =$ Adélie | **x**): the probability the penguin is an Adélie, given the evidence, or feature vector, **x**;

- P ($y =$ Gentoo | **x**): the probability the penguin is a Gentoo, given **x**; and

- P ($y =$ Chinstrap | **x**): the probability the penguin is a Chinstrap, given **x**.

Take any one of these computations:

$$P(y = \text{Adélie} \mid \mathbf{x}) = P(y = \text{Adélie} \mid x1, x2, x3, x4, x5)$$

Computing this will require first estimating the class condition probability density function P $(\mathbf{x} \mid y = \text{Adélie})$:

$$P(\mathbf{x} \mid y = \text{Adélie}) = P(x1, x2, x3, x4, x5 \mid y = \text{Adélie})$$

This is a complicated surface in six dimensions, which depends on all five features. We have already established that reconstructing or estimating this is near impossible with limited samples of data and constrained computational resources.

Here's a trick that statisticians and probability theorists use to make the problem more tractable. They assume that all features are sampled from their own distributions independently of one another. So, the values for bill depth in Adéline penguins are values sampled independently from an underlying distribution for bill depth alone, and the values for bill length are values sampled independently from an underlying distribution for bill length alone. This implies that the variation in, say, bill depth has nothing to do with variation in bill length. This is, of course, never really going to be true in nature. But it's an assumption that works wonders when it comes to making the mathematics easier. Given this assumption of mutually independent features, we can use Bayes's theorem to get at what we desire:

$$P(y = \text{Adélie} \mid \mathbf{x}) = \frac{P(\mathbf{x} \mid y = \text{Adélie}) \times P(y = \text{Adélie})}{P(\mathbf{x})}$$

The function that we need to estimate or know a priori and one that causes problems in higher dimensions is:

$$P(\mathbf{x} \mid y = \text{Adélie}) = P(x1, x2, x3, x4, x5 \mid y = \text{Adélie})$$

The mutual independence assumption makes the task simpler. Given that assumption (and using A for Adélie):

$P(x1, x2, x3, x4, x5 \mid y = A)$

$$= P(x1 \mid y = A) \times P(x2 \mid y = A) \times P(x3 \mid y = A) \times P(x4 \mid y = A)$$
$$\times P(x5 \mid y = A)$$

The problem has been broken down into many sub-problems, each involving the estimation of a probability distribution for just one feature, or random variable. This can be done with fewer samples and is computationally far less intensive. Using more compact mathematical symbols, we have:

$$P(\mathbf{x} \mid y = A)$$

$$= \prod_{i=1}^{5} P(x_i \mid y = A)$$

The "pi" symbol signifies multiplication; it's multiplication's equivalent of the "sigma" symbol for addition. With this simplification in hand, we can compute the various class-conditional probabilities (the penguin is an Adélie given the 5D evidence, $\mathbf{x}$; the penguin is a Gentoo given $\mathbf{x}$; and a Chinstrap given $\mathbf{x}$), and then basically predict the type of penguin based on the highest conditional probability. Such a classifier, with the assumption of mutually independent features, is called a naïve Bayes or, somewhat pejoratively, an idiot Bayes classifier. But it's a powerful technique that works well in many situations. For example, such a classifier does well in predicting whether an email is spam.

By now, you may be wondering, even worried about, how exactly we estimate the probability distributions, even if the features are taken to be mutually independent. Well, we have already seen an example of this, when we fit a curve over the histogram of bill depths for a given penguin type. Let's revisit it:

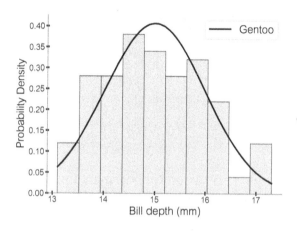

We assume that the underlying distribution is a Gaussian, or normal, distribution, and we basically use the sampled Gentoo penguin data (of their bill depths) to find a curve with a mean and standard deviation—these constitute the parameter θ of the distribution—that best fits the data. Once we have θ, we have an estimate of the underlying distribution, and we don't need any more data. In this case, we have modeled our random variable as continuous. We do this for each feature and use each probability density function for the calculations.

Or we can also simply model each feature as a discrete random variable. In the figure on the next page, there are ten bins. Each bin has penguins with bill depths that fall within a certain range.

For example, there are 19 Gentoo penguins in the fourth bin, out of a total of 119. So, the probability that the bill depth falls in the fourth bin is 19/119 = 0.16. Similarly, the probability that the bill depth falls in the eighth bin is 11/119 = 0.09. And so on . . .

Calculating such probabilities for the discrete random variable,

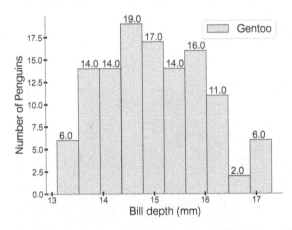

we saw earlier, gives us the probability mass function. We can use these probabilities to make our predictions. It's obvious that the more samples we have, the better the histogram will be in representing the true underlying distribution and, thus, will make the predictions more accurate.

WRAP-UP

It's understandable if this foray into probability and statistics felt a bit overwhelming, especially if you came to it—as I once did—with little prior knowledge of the subject. We have tried to grapple with two massive fields of mathematics, all in the space of a chapter, and connect them to machine learning. I'd be surprised if it didn't feel a touch too much. Even if everything else becomes a blur, we can take away from this chapter a few succinct conceptual messages.

In supervised machine learning, all data is drawn (or sampled) from an underlying distribution. D is our data. One part of D is a matrix of feature vectors, $\mathbf{X}$. Each row represents one instance of the data (say, features for one penguin, $\mathbf{x}$). The data D also has a corresponding label for each row of $\mathbf{X}$ (say, the species of penguin). These labels form a column vector **y**. The data D is said to be sampled from the underlying distribution P (**X, y**). So:

$$D \sim P(\mathbf{X}, \mathbf{y})$$

The true nature of the overall underlying distribution is almost always hidden from us. The task of many ML algorithms is to estimate this distribution, *implicitly or explicitly,* as well as possible and then use that to make predictions about new data.

Let's say the estimated distribution is given by:

$$P_\theta(\mathbf{X}, \mathbf{y})$$

The symbol θ represents the parameters of the distribution. The parameters mean different things for different types of distributions. For example: A Bernoulli distribution requires figuring out one parameter "*p*"; a normal distribution requires figuring out the mean and standard deviation. (I'm ignoring a whole class of distributions that don't have parameters and, hence, are called nonparametric.) The process starts with making an assumption about the type of underlying distribution—is it, for example, a Bernoulli or a normal distribution or something else?—and then figuring the best θ.

Estimating θ can be done, broadly speaking, in one of two ways. (There are other methods, but these two give us a great sense of how things are done in machine learning.) The first is called maximum likelihood estimation (MLE), which, given the data, tries to find the θ that maximizes the likelihood of the data. What that means is that $P_\theta(\mathbf{X}, \mathbf{y})$ will give us different probability distributions for different θ, and the algorithm finds the θ that maximizes the probability of observing the data we have in hand.

The second method of estimating the probability distribution is called maximum a posteriori (MAP) estimation. This assumes that θ is itself a random variable, which means that you can specify a probability distribution for it. (As we saw earlier, it's a Bayesian claim that makes frequentists livid.) So, MAP starts with an initial assumption about how θ is distributed. This is also called the prior. For example, if you are modeling a coin toss, you can assume a priori that the coin is fair; or you can assume that it's biased. Then, given the data and the prior, MAP finds the posterior probability distribution $P_\theta(\mathbf{X}, \mathbf{y})$, such that if you were to sample several instances of data from this distribution, the probability that the sampled data matched the original data would be maximized.

If we can somehow learn or estimate the entire joint probability distribution $P_\theta(\mathbf{X}, \mathbf{y})$, which is some complex surface in a hyperdimensional space, we will have a model of all the data, the feature vectors, and the labels. This enables us to do something very powerful: generate new data that resemble the training data by sampling from the distribution, giving us what has come to be called generative AI.

ML algorithms can also use the model to make predictions about new, unlabeled data. The naïve Bayes (or idiot Bayes) classifier is an example: It first learns the joint probability distribution, albeit with some simplifying assumptions, and then uses Bayes's theorem to discriminate between different classes of data.

There are algorithms that eschew learning the complex joint probability distribution; instead, they focus on the conditional probabilities of the data belonging to one class or the other. This approach allows one to do something called discriminative learning. An algorithm can do discriminative learning by calculating the probability distribution $P_\theta(y|\mathbf{x})$. This means that given a new feature vector $\mathbf{x}$ and some optimal θ, we now can calculate the probability of the most likely class for **x**: The class that has the higher conditional probability gets the nod, as the prediction of our ML algorithm.

Any algorithm that figures out how to separate one cluster of data points from another by identifying a boundary between them is doing discriminative learning. It doesn't have to deal specifically in probability distributions. For example, maybe it finds a linear hyperplane à la the perceptron, or finds a curved nonlinear surface or boundary, an example of which we'll see in the next chapter. An example of this latter algorithm—whose roots probably lie in intuitions harbored by the first humans—got its start at Stanford in the 1960s (a few years after Bernard Widrow developed ADALINE). It came to be called the nearest neighbor (NN) algorithm, and it showed a very different way to do pattern recognition. And in much the way the perceptron's convergence proof made people sit up and take notice, the NN algorithm achieved the same, doing almost as well, in ideal scenarios, as the Bayes optimal classifier, which we now know is the best ML game in town. But the NN algorithm does so without making any assumptions about the underlying distribution of the data.

CHAPTER 5

Birds of a Feather

N o street in the Cholera area was without death." This is just one of the many stark, sobering sentences found in a report submitted by the Cholera Inquiry Committee in July 1855, about a particularly severe outbreak of the disease that had struck a London parish the previous year. The outbreak was concentrated in what came to be called the "Cholera area" of Soho, in the city's West End. "In Broad Street, the very heart of the area, the deaths were rather more than 10 per cent, or 1,000 to every 10,000 persons living. In Cambridge Street, Pulteney Court, and Kemp's Court, the population was also decimated," the members of the committee wrote.

One of the committee members was a physician named John Snow, who had been making major contributions to two fields of medical science, anesthesiology and epidemiology. Today, anesthesiologists revere Snow for his scientific study of ether and chloroform. His methods allowed him to administer "chloroform to Queen Victoria for the births of Prince Leopold and Princess Beatrice," bringing "obstetric anesthesia into acceptance against religious, ethical, and medical beliefs." And epidemiologists celebrate Snow for his extraordinary analysis of the 1854 cholera outbreak. He was able to show that the outbreak was clustered around a water pump on Broad Street, which lent credence to his hypothesis that cholera was a waterborne disease. Snow's epidemiological legwork forced authorities to inspect the pump and its surroundings, and they eventually established that a cesspool with decaying brickwork, located within a few feet of the Broad Street well, was leaking wastewater into the soil around the well. The pump was drawing water from that well.

The Cholera Inquiry Committee report contains a section written by Snow, including an annotated map of Soho's "Cholera area" that's considered a classic by epidemiologists. But more recently, the map caught the attention of computer scientists, because the technique Snow used is a striking illustration of something that forms the conceptual heart of a popular and powerful ML algorithm.

Snow's map had a few key elements. First was a dotted line that circumscribed a region in Soho; all deaths due to cholera during six weeks in August and September 1854 occurred in this region. Each death was denoted as a small black rectangle, marking the address of the house in which the person had died or contracted the disease. (Some houses had multiple such markers.) Water pumps were drawn as small black dots. Most important, Snow drew an inner black dotted line that showed "the various points which have been found by careful measurement to be at an equal distance by the nearest road from the pump in Broad Street and the surrounding pumps." In other words, if you stood anywhere on this inner dotted line, you'd be equidistant from the location of the disease-ridden Broad Street pump and some other pump in Soho, as long as you walked along streets and roads to get to the pumps (so, not as the crow flies). When inside the perimeter of this latter dotted line, people were closer to the Broad Street pump; outside, they were closer to some other pump.

After making allowances for one confounding pump, Snow concluded, "It will be observed that the deaths very much diminish, or cease altogether, at every point where it becomes decidedly nearer to send to another pump than to the one in Broad Street." People who were nearer to some other pump and who went there for water, rather than to the Broad Street pump, were better off. The Broad Street pump was the problem.

Snow's inner dotted line represents the contours of what in modern parlance is called a Voronoi cell, after the Ukrainian mathematician Georgy Voronoi (or Voronoy, as the name is also spelled), who developed the formal mathematics for the eponymous diagrams decades after Snow's analysis. Think of the 2D map of Soho, with a sprinkling of water pumps, each pump represented by a small black dot. You can draw a Voronoi cell around each dot, or "seed," such that any point inside the cell is closer to its seed than to any other seed. So, for a Voronoi diagram drawn for a mid-nineteenth-century map of Soho, each cell has a water pump as its seed, and every location within each cell is closer to its "seed" water pump than to any other pump. There are different ways to measure closeness from someplace inside the cell to the pumps. Normally, you'd use straight lines, an "as the crow flies" measure of distance. But in this case, Snow had to be smarter. The closest pump had to be discerned based on the distance covered to the pumps when one walked along the streets.

Here's an example of a simple Voronoi diagram:

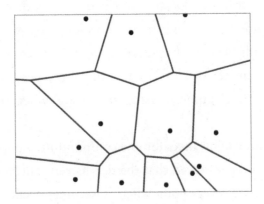

The diagram is a tessellation of irregular polygons, or cells. Think of each dot as a water pump. For now, let's stick to the "as the crow flies" metric to measure the distance to a pump. In the Voronoi diagram above, if we are within a cell, the closest pump is the one inside the cell. If we are walking along a polygon edge, and because that edge is shared by two cells, we are equidistant from the two pumps that lie within those cells. And if we are standing at the vertex formed by the intersection of edges, we are equidistant from three (or more) pumps.

What does this have to do with machines that learn? Quite a lot. Let's start with a hypothetical problem. Imagine Midtown Manhattan, with its mostly neat grid of streets and avenues.

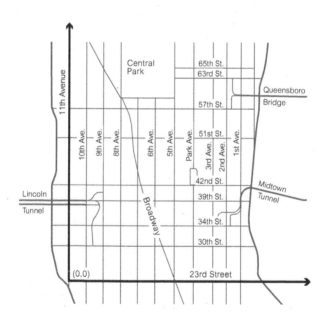

Let's say the U.S. Postal Service installs six brand-spanking-new branches in this neighborhood. We are given the task of assigning each building in Midtown to the nearest new post office branch. (Ignore the fact that buildings have postcodes; using such codes makes the task trivial.) How would we do it? We could come up with a Voronoi diagram for all of Midtown on the xy plane (substituting post office branches for water pumps). In the map shown on the previous page, the point (0, 0) is the bottom-left corner, at the intersection of Twenty-Third Street and Eleventh Avenue. Each post office branch gets an (x, y) coordinate relative to (0, 0), based on which we can construct a Voronoi diagram. Once we have the Voronoi diagram, the assignment of buildings to post office branches becomes straightforward. If a given building lies within a Voronoi cell, it's served by the post office branch that is the seed for that cell. If the building is on the edge of two cells or on a vertex, it's equidistant from multiple post office branches, so we assign it to the branch that's handling the least number of buildings.

But what's the correct notion of distance from a building to a post office? Let's assume we use the "as the crow flies" measure of distance, also called the Euclidean distance (after the Greek mathematician Euclid). If the post office branch is at coordinate $(x1, y1)$ and the apartment building is at $(x2, y2)$, then the Euclidean distance is given by:

$$\sqrt{(x2 - x1)^2 + (y2 - y1)^2}$$

This is simply the length of the hypotenuse formed by a right-angled triangle, with the coordinates $(x1, y1)$ and $(x2, y2)$ forming two vertices of the triangle. The triangle has two sides that are perpendicular to each other. One side, along the x-direction, has the length $(x2-x1)$ and the other, in the y-direction, has the length $(y2-y1)$. It's trivial to calculate the length of the hypotenuse (see figure opposite).

But it turns out that this is not a good measure of distance in a place like Midtown Manhattan. People aren't crows, and they want

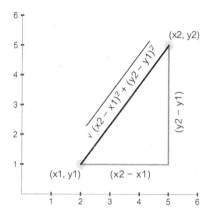

the distance to the nearest post office branch measured in terms of the distance traveled by sidewalk/street. Well, there's a simple measure of such a distance:

$$(x2 - x1) + (y2 - y1)$$

Because of Midtown Manhattan's grid (ignoring Broadway, which cuts across the grid), this is the same as walking $(x2 - x1)$ units of length along streets and $(y2 - y1)$ units of length along avenues, even if you have to zigzag your way down different streets and avenues. No wonder this measure of distance is formally called the Manhattan distance between two points. Now, if someone constructs a new building on vacant land, that's a new data point. It's simple to figure out that building's post office branch: Find the building's Voronoi cell and assign that building to the cell's seed, or post office branch.

The problem we've just analyzed is more generally cast as the search for nearest neighbors. Software implementations of such searches rank among the most influential algorithms in machine learning. We'll soon see why. But first, we must go back in time to the Islamic Golden Age and the work of Abu Ali al-Hasan Ibn al-Haytham, or Alhazen, a Muslim Arab mathematician, astronomer, and physicist. It was Alhazen who, in his attempt to explain visual perception, came up with a technique that closely mirrors modern nearest neighbor search algorithms. Marcello Pelillo, a computer scientist at the University of Venice, Italy, has been doing his best to draw attention to Alhazen's ideas.

THE MAKINGS OF AN ALGORITHM

One day, when he wandered into a bookstore in New Haven, Connecticut, Pelillo stumbled upon a slim book called *Theories of Vision from Al-Kindi to Kepler*. It was the late 1990s, and Pelillo was then a visiting professor at Yale. Besides doing research in computer vision, pattern recognition, and machine learning, he had a penchant for the history and philosophy of science and a love of math. The slim book, at just over two hundred pages, was alluring. It argued that Alhazen was "the most significant figure in the history of optics between antiquity and the seventeenth century." Before Alhazen, humanity's attempts at understanding vision—our ability to see and perceive the world around us—were, in hindsight, very strange. One idea was known as the "intromission" theory, which essentially posited that we see an object because bits of matter of some form emanate from that object and enter our eyes: "Material replicas issue in all directions from visible bodies and enter the eye of an observer to produce visual sensation." Some believed that those bits of matter were atoms. "The essential feature of this theory is that the atoms streaming in various directions from a particular object form coherent units—films or *simulacra*—which communicate the shape and color of the object to the soul of an observer; encountering the *simulacrum* of an object is, as far as the soul is concerned, equivalent to encountering the object itself."

Less influential by this time was an alternative idea, under the rubric of "extramission" theories, which argued that our eyes emanate rays that intercept objects, allowing us to see those objects. Euclid, back in about 300 B.C., gave the first entirely geometrical account, using seven theorems of how such rays could explain aspects of our vision. Then there were those who tried, unsuccessfully, to combine the intromission and extramission theories into a cohesive explanation of vision.

All this was patently wrong, but, again, only in hindsight. Alhazen came up with an alternative theory that put paid to these ideas. He proposed a new type of intromission, one that relied not on bits of matter leaving an object and entering our eyes but, rather, one that required light radiating out in straight lines from every point of a colored object. Some of that light would enter our eyes and lead to perception. We don't have to concern ourselves with Alhazen's amazing analysis of the eye's anatomy or the optics of it all. Suffice it to say his work was instrumental in "transforming the intromission theory into a mathematical theory of vision."

Marcello Pelillo was most interested in Alhazen's account of what happens once the light and color are registered in the eye: the act of recognizing what the eye is seeing. Alhazen wrote, "When sight perceives some visible object, the faculty of discrimination immediately seeks its counterpart among the forms persisting in the imagination, and when it finds some form in the imagination that is like the form of that visible object, it will recognize that visible object and will perceive what kind of thing it is."

Basically, Alhazen argued that once a visible object registered in the eye, some cognitive process—the "faculty of discrimination"—compared what was being seen to what had already been seen and categorized in one's imagination, or memory. So, if what's being seen is a dog, that image is recognized as such when cognition connects it to some stored memory of a dog.

Alhazen even had a solution for when no such comparison was possible because the object had never been seen before. "If it does not find a form similar to the form of that visible object among the forms persisting in the imagination, it will not recognize that visible object or perceive what kind of thing it is," he wrote.

Note that Alhazen talked of one form being "similar" to another, but he didn't say what "similarity" meant. In computer science, similarity has to do, for example, with the distance of one data point from another in some hyperdimensional space, be it Euclidean, Manhattan, or some other measure of distance. (The closer that two data points are to each other according to some given measure, the more similar they are.) We'll get back to these issues soon enough.

When Pelillo looked at Alhazen's writing, it became clear to him that Alhazen's method was "a surprisingly clear, almost algorithmic, exposition" of an idea that was formally invented in the 1950s and analyzed mathematically in the '60s, thanks mainly to Thomas Cover, a young, whip-smart information theorist and electrical engineer at Stanford, and Cover's precocious graduate student Peter Hart. Their algorithm came to be called the nearest neighbor (NN) rule; it became an extremely important algorithm for pattern recognition, which classifies data as belonging to one category or another. (Is what's being seen a dog or a cat?)

"I don't know whether [Alhazen's work] was the very first time that that idea was put forward, namely, that in order for me to recognize an object, I have to compare that object with something that I have in my memory, and then I just look for the closest one according to a certain notion of similarity," Pelillo told me. "[That] is exactly the nearest neighbor rule. My conjecture is that probably it was the first time."

PATTERNS, VECTORS, AND NEIGHBORS

Alhazen had clearly envisioned aspects of Cover and Hart's NN algorithm almost a thousand years before them, but Peter Hart thinks the intuition goes back farther, probably to our cave-dwelling forebears. To make his point, he starts with some simple mathematics, of the kind we have already encountered. Think of 2D vectors and the xy plane. Each point in the xy plane, given by some point (x, y) is a vector, an arrow drawn from the origin (0, 0) to (x, y). The same is true of the 3D xyz coordinate system: Each vector is an arrow drawn from (0, 0, 0) to (x, y, z). Similarly, a 3D vector is simply a point in 3D space. This can be extended to any number of dimensions. We run out of letters of the alphabet soon, so it's customary to refer to vectors using $[x1, x2, x3, \ldots, xd]$, for a d-dimensional vector. The key now is to connect vectors to patterns.

Let's say we are looking at a 7×9 image, a total of 63 pixels, where each pixel can be either white (0) or black (1). You can easily depict the digits 0 to 9 using such an image by making some pixels black and others white. And each image, or pattern, can be written as a vector, $[x1, x2, \ldots x63]$: a set of 63 numbers, where each number is either a 0 or a 1. We have simply transformed each 7×9 image into a 63-dimensional vector.

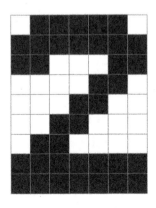 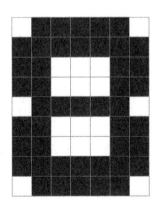

Now, what if you were shown a blank 7×9 grid on the touch screen of your tablet and were asked to draw the numeral 2 or the numeral 8 using your finger? Each time you draw the numeral, some squares in the grid turn black, while others remain white. The pattern then gets stored as a number that is 63 bits long. You do that a few times and then pass the tablet to someone else, and they do the same. Many people take turns at generating the data, and soon, you have hundreds of samples of vectors representing two hand-drawn digits, 2 and 8. Each pattern, mathematically, is a point in the 63-dimensional vector space. Ask yourself this: Given that each vector is a point (which is how machine learning thinks of vectors), how would these vectors be clustered in that hyperdimensional space?

Well, most of us will draw the numeral 2 in much the same way, but each effort might be slightly different from another, even if the drawings were made by the same person. (Because we are using black and white pixels, the difference may not be significant between drawings, but it would be a lot more if, say, finger pressure converted each pixel into something on the grayscale and gave it a number from 0 to 255. But let's go with 0 and 1 for white and black.) So, each time the pattern 2 is stored as a set of 63 numbers, it represents a vector, a point that's more or less in the same location as the vectors representing other hand-drawn 2s. Now, the points representing all the hand-drawn 2s will be clustered near one another in the 63-dimensional space. The same goes for the numeral 8. But the two numerals are different enough that the vectors constituting the cluster for the numeral 2 will be in one region of the 63D space, and the cluster of vectors for the numeral 8 will be somewhere else.

Assume that the touch screen also generates a label for each pattern, tagging it as either 2 or 8. What we have done now is generate a sample dataset where each vector has an associated label. The question now for us—or, rather, for any ML algorithm—is this: Given a new unlabeled, or untagged, pattern, can the algorithm tell whether it's a 2 or an 8?

Algorithmically, there's something very simple one can do. Just plot the new, unlabeled vector as a point. Find the point that's nearest to it in the 63D space. If the nearest point has the label 2, then the new point is most likely a 2, too. If the nearest neighbor is an 8, the new entrant is most likely an 8. "That's the nearest neighbor rule. That's the caveman intuition: If they look alike, they probably are alike," Hart told me.

Cave dwellers and Alhazen's seminal work notwithstanding, the first mathematical mention of the nearest neighbor rule appeared in a 1951 technical report of the U.S. Air Force School of Aviation Medicine, Randolph Field, Texas. The authors were Evelyn Fix and Joseph L. Hodges, Jr. In 1940, Fix came to work at the University of California, Berkeley, as a research assistant in the Statistical Laboratory, assigned to a project for the National Defense Research Committee. U.S. researchers were getting drawn into the war raging in Europe. "The war years were hard," Hodges and others wrote in a memorial tribute to Fix.

They brought difficult, but occasionally interesting problems. Every demand on the Laboratory emphasized urgency; the practical solutions of the problems meant the determination of optimal plans, the probability of success of this plan, of that plan, numbers and more numbers. High speed computers did not exist; all the numerical work had to be done on desk calculators consuming much time and effort. Endowed with unusual energy and with a special spirit of getting the job done and done right, Evelyn [Fix] spent days and nights at her machine, aided by a group of students and some faculty wives, so that the needed results could be transmitted on time, usually to New York but

occasionally directly to England. During these years Evelyn also
continued her own studies and lectured to students.

Fix's efforts gave her valuable expertise in the practical use of statistics and probability theory. She got her Ph.D. in 1948 and stayed on at UC Berkeley, enjoying many productive collaborations. One of them was with Joseph Hodges, which resulted in the technical report of 1951. The very last equation of this extremely short but important paper refers to the rule we elucidated earlier: Given a set of labeled, or tagged, data points, a new, unlabeled data point can be assigned the same label, or tag, as that of its nearest neighbor in the hyperdimensional vector space.

As a graduate student looking for a doctoral thesis topic related to pattern recognition, Peter Hart stumbled upon the Fix and Hodges paper and the nearest neighbor rule. He was intrigued and wanted to figure out its theoretical properties. "The most practical thing in the world is a good theory," Hart told me. "If you know the theoretical properties of a procedure, you can have confidence employing that without having the bother of conducting endless experiments to figure out what it does or when it works and when it doesn't work."

Hart approached Thomas Cover, who had just joined Stanford as an acting assistant professor, and the two discussed working on the theoretical properties of the nearest neighbor rule. Their two-hour conversation left Hart convinced he wanted Cover as his thesis advisor; but there was an administrative hitch. Because he was only an "acting" assistant professor, Cover couldn't formally be the first reader on a dissertation. Hart was prescient, though. "Even back then I was a pretty good judge of talent," he told me. "I thought, you know, by the time I need a signature, I bet he'll get promoted all the way up to assistant professor." Hart signed on with Cover as the young academic's very first graduate student and began working on understanding the theory behind the nearest neighbor rule. His work established the lower and upper bounds for the algorithm: the good and the bad. The good was almost as good as the best possible solution, if you assumed that the number of data samples went to infinity. The bad wasn't that bad at all. Crucially, the strength of the nearest neighbor rule was that it didn't make any assumptions about the underlying data distribution.

IT DOESN'T GET SIMPLER

ML algorithms don't get much simpler than the nearest neighbor rule for classifying data. Especially considering the algorithm's powerful abilities. Let's start with a mock dataset of gray circles and black triangles.

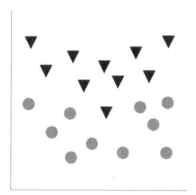

Recall the perceptron algorithm. It will fail to tell apart the circles from the triangles, because this dataset is not linearly separable: There's no single straight line you can draw to delineate the two classes of data. A naïve Bayes classifier can find a windy line that separates the circles from the triangles, though. We'll come back to that in a bit, but for now, let's tackle the nearest neighbor algorithm. The problem we must solve is this: When given a new data point, we have to classify it as either a circle or a triangle.

The nearest neighbor algorithm, in its simplest form, essentially plots that new data point and calculates its distance to each data point in the initial dataset, which can be thought of as the training data. (We'll use the Euclidean distance measure for our purposes.) If the data point nearest to the new data is a black triangle, the new data is classified as a black triangle; if it's a gray circle, the new data is classified as a gray circle. It's as simple as that. The following two panels show how a new data point is labeled based on its nearest neighbor. (The new data point is shown as a star, but is colored either gray or black, depending on whether it's classified as a gray circle or a black triangle.) The original dataset is the same as the one shown in the previous panel.

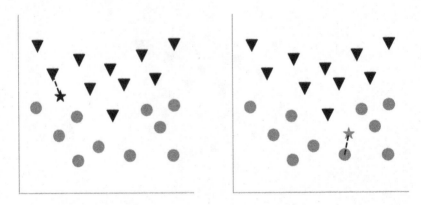

Going back to the perceptron algorithm, recall that the linearly separating hyperplane divides the coordinate space into two regions. The nearest neighbor algorithm does the same, except in this case, the boundary between the two regions is not a straight line (or a hyperplane in higher dimensions). Rather, it's squiggly, nonlinear. Look at the two plots above, and you can imagine a boundary such that if the new data point fell on one side of the boundary, it'd be closer to a gray circle, or else to a black triangle. Here's what the boundary looks like for the same dataset when the NN algorithm examines just one nearest neighbor. You can see that a new data point (a gray star) that's closest to a gray circle lies in the region that contains all the gray circles, and one that's closest to a black triangle lies in the region containing all the black triangles.

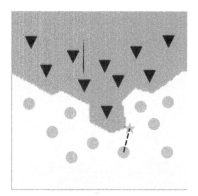 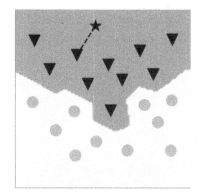

This simple algorithm—we'll come to the details in a moment— achieves something quite remarkable: It finds a nonlinear boundary to separate one class of data from another. But the simplicity of the algorithm that uses just one nearest neighbor belies a serious problem. Can you figure it out before reading further?

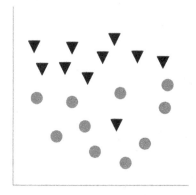

To help understand the potential problem, consider another dataset (shown at the bottom of the previous page), one that includes a data point that's misclassified by humans as a black triangle and that lies amid the gray circles. What do you think might happen, in terms of finding the boundary separating the circles from the triangles? The machine, it must be said, would have no way of knowing that the errant black triangle had been misclassified as such.

Given the data, the algorithm will find a nonlinear boundary that's quite intricate. Here's the solution:

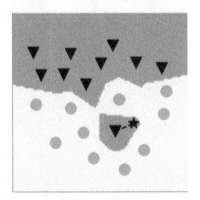 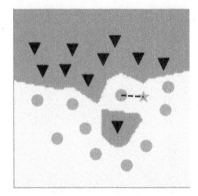

Notice how the nonlinear boundaries split up the coordinate space into more than two gray-and-white regions. There's a small "island" surrounding the misclassified black triangle. If your new data point is within that small island, it'll get classified as a black triangle even though it's surrounded by gray circles.

What we have seen is an example of what ML researchers call overfitting. Our algorithm has overfit the data. It finds a boundary that doesn't ignore even a single erroneous outlier. This happens because the algorithm is paying attention to just one nearest neighbor. There's a simple fix, however, that addresses this problem. We can simply increase the number of nearest neighbors against which to compare the new data point. The number of neighbors must be odd (say, three or five or more). Why an odd number? Well, because if it were even, we could end up with a tie, and that's of no use. An odd number ensures we'll get an answer, right or wrong. This is assuming that we are working only with data that can be clustered into two classes (in this case, the gray circles and the black triangles).

Here's the same dataset, but now the algorithm looks for three nearest neighbors and classifies the new data point based on the majority vote:

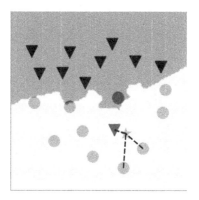

The nonlinear boundary no longer gives undue attention to the one lone triangle amid the circles. If a new data point were to fall near this lone triangle, it'd still be classified as a circle, because the triangle would be outvoted by the nearby circles. The boundary has become somewhat smoother; it's not contorting to account for the noise in the data, which in our case is the misclassified triangle. Such smoother boundaries, using a larger number of nearest neighbors, are more likely to correctly classify a new data point when compared with the boundary we got using just one nearest neighbor. The algorithm is said to be generalizing better to unseen data. (Though, there's a gray circle that's ended up on the wrong side of the boundary. We'll come to such transgressors in a moment.)

Here's another example (see panel on next page), with the number of nearest neighbors being considered bumped up to seven. The shape

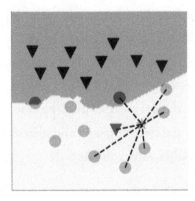

of the nonlinear separating boundary looks slightly different for the same initial dataset.

Note something crucial, though. If you examine the nonlinear boundary that the algorithm achieves using seven nearest neighbors, you can see that while the errant triangle falls within the region meant for circles, its influence is largely diminished. That's good, because the errant triangle is "noise," a circle that was accidently misclassified in the training data as a triangle. But there's a circle that, unfortunately, falls inside the region meant for triangles. This circle, however, was correctly classified in the training data and yet has ended up on the wrong side of the boundary. This is the price you pay if you don't want to overfit. The classifier—which is characterized by the boundary—can misclassify some data points in the training dataset. The reason this is desirable, despite some errors made in the training data, is because when you test this classifier using data it hasn't yet seen, it'll likely make fewer errors than if you used a classifier that had overfit the training data. Just keep this in mind for now; we will come to a more serious analysis of overfitting versus generalization later.

As simple as this algorithm is, the mathematics needed to determine its efficacy—in terms of the probability that the algorithm makes errors while classifying new data—was anything but simple.

Peter Hart recalled struggling initially to develop the intuition needed to prove that the algorithm could converge to a result and perform satisfactorily when compared with the Bayes optimal classifier (which, as we saw, is the best a machine algorithm can do). Of course, the Bayes optimal classifier is an idealization, in that one assumes access to the underlying probability distributions of the data, or our best estimates of such distributions. The NN algorithm functions at the other extreme. All one has is data, and the algorithm makes barely any assumptions about, and indeed has little knowledge of, the underlying distributions. There's no assumption, for example, that the data follows a Gaussian (bell-shaped) distribution with some mean and variance.

Needing to make sense of the math, Hart sought out Kai-lai Chung, a brilliant Chinese American mathematician at Stanford. Hart explained to Chung the problem he was trying to solve. Chung asked Hart if he knew of two mathematical results called Jensen's inequality and the dominated convergence theorem. Hart said that he did. "And, with a straight face, he said, 'Well, you know enough. Now you just have to be smarter.' And then he waved me out of his office," Hart told me.

And so, Hart did just that: He got smarter.

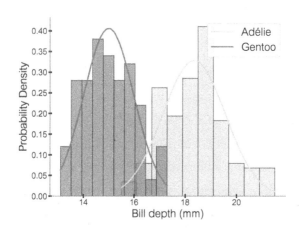

We can get a taste of the intuitions that Hart wanted to turn into rigorous results. (The actual theorems and proofs are a touch too abstruse for us.) Let's go back to the two penguin species, Adélie and Gentoo, and one feature, bill depth (see figure, previous page).

If you had access to the two underlying distributions, then given a new, unclassified penguin and its bill depth, you could use the Bayes theorem to simply calculate the probability that the penguin is an Adélie given the bill depth and the probability that the penguin is a Gentoo given the bill depth. Let's say that, for some given bill depth, the probability of the penguin being an Adélie turns out to be 0.75 and of it being a Gentoo, 0.25. For the Bayes optimal classifier, the higher probability wins each time. The algorithm will always classify the new penguin as an Adélie, even though there is a 25 percent chance it could be wrong.

What about the nearest neighbor algorithm? Here's a mental picture of what the 1–nearest neighbor, or 1-NN, rule accomplishes. It looks for points representing Adélie penguins and Gentoo penguins in the immediate neighborhood of the new data point. If the algorithm had access to all possible points representing the two types of penguins, then 75 percent of those nearby data points would be those of Adélie penguins and 25 percent would represent Gentoo penguins. But we have only a small sample of penguins. And the 1-NN algorithm must make its decision based on that limited dataset. It's as if it had a biased coin that came up heads 75 percent of the time and tails 25 percent of the time. The coin, of course, is specific to a new, unclassified penguin's bill depth: heads, it's an Adélie; tails, it's a Gentoo. So, unlike the Bayes optimal classifier, which will always claim it's an Adélie, the 1-NN rule will say that the new penguin is an Adélie three-quarters of the time and a Gentoo one-quarter of the time. This intuition in hand, Hart eventually figured out the math needed to establish the lower and upper bounds of the errors

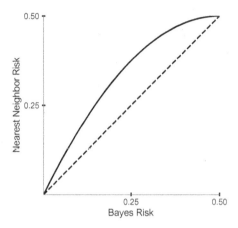

made by the 1-NN rule and then extended it to k nearest neighbors, the k-NN rule. It was a seminal, memorable result. The above plot shows a comparison between probability of error (or risk) of the Bayes optimal classifier versus the NN classifier.

The k-NN algorithm can do no better than the Bayes optimal classifier (the dashed line, the lower bound). For 1-NN and large samples of data (n), the algorithm's upper bound of the risk of being wrong is shown as the solid parabolic line: It can do no worse. But as k increases, and k/n remains small, the classifier's performance starts approaching that of the Bayes optimal classifier: The parabola flattens and gets even closer to the dashed line.

Again, the intuition for it goes something like this: As you collect more and more samples, the immediate neighborhood of the new data point gets dense with data points representing Adélie and Gentoo penguins. For our example, the local region around the new data point will have 75 percent Adélie penguins and 25 percent Gentoo penguins. If the total number of samples gets very large, then the probability that a majority of the k nearest neighbors are Adélie penguins will approach one. In this idealized scenario, the k-NN algorithm (for large values of k) will always classify the new data point as an Adélie—as would the Bayes optimal classifier.

All this work, from start to finish, took about three months. Hart had started talking with his advisor, Tom Cover, in the spring of 1964. By late spring, Cover was heading to Cambridge for a summer stint at MIT. "We already had these results," Hart said. "Tom, even as a brand-new advisor, was very well aware of the fact that you're not supposed to give a Stanford Ph.D. on the basis of three months' worth of dissertation work, no matter how fabulous the results. So, he looks at me and he says, 'Can you extend these results?'"

Hart had already proven the results for almost all types of probability distributions: continuous ones, distributions that had discontinuities (or breaks), and those with infinitely many discontinuities. Cover asked Hart to extend the math to all measurable functions (where the functions represented probability distributions). "Now we get into the realm of measure theory. Nobody who's not a mathematician has ever heard of it. You don't want to go there. This is like a pure mathematician's generalization. [There's this] famous quote, 'Here's to pure mathematics—may it never be of any use to anybody,'" Hart said. "I kept a straight face and nodded. Tom took off for Cambridge."

Hart came home to the "love of his life," who had started off as a math major but then switched to history and would become a well-published author. He told her about Cover's suggestion and added, "I have no idea how to even begin." The couple took the summer off and learned how to sail at the Stanford sailing club, at times running their fifteen-foot sloop into some trees in the middle of a lake. The summer ended, and Cover came back and asked Hart about his progress. "I very truthfully replied, 'I didn't make any progress at all.' Tom just nodded and said, 'Yeah, I didn't think you would,'" Hart said.

Hart did some more work to optimize the algorithm. It was more than enough for a dissertation: all of sixty-five pages, triple-spaced, typed up on an IBM Selectric typewriter. He got his Ph.D. in 1966. "I was barely twenty-five, and I was launched," he said.

The k-NN algorithm has been extraordinarily successful, both because of and despite its simplicity. From the perspective of someone writing a piece of code, here's some pseudo-code to illustrate how little it takes. (Let's stick with Adélie and Gentoo penguins for now, so two classes of penguins, and two features, bill depth and bill length; the algorithm can be easily generalized to include more than two classes and any number of features.)

- **Step 1.** Store all instances of sample data.
  - o Each penguin is a vector $[x1, x2]$, where $x1$=bill depth and $x2$=bill length. The entire dataset is stored in a matrix $\mathbf{X}$, where $\mathbf{X}$ has m rows (number of penguins) and n columns (number of features).
  - o Each penguin is also associated with a label y, which is equal to -1 (Adélie) or 1 (Gentoo). So, $\mathbf{y}$, which stores all the corresponding labels, is an m-dimensional vector.

- **Step 2.** Given a new data point, representing an unclassified penguin, in the form of a vector $\mathbf{x}$ with elements for bill depth and bill length $[x1, x2]$, do the following:
  - o Calculate the distance of the new data point to each of the data points in the original dataset, $\mathbf{X}$. This gives us a list of m distances, $\mathbf{d}$.
  - o Sort the list $\mathbf{d}$ in the order of increasing distance (the first element has the minimum distance to the new point, and the last element has the maximum).
  - o As you sort $\mathbf{d}$, simultaneously rearrange the elements of $\mathbf{y}$, so that the appropriate labels (-1 or 1) remain associated with each penguin in the sorted list.

- **Step 3.** Take the first k elements of the sorted list **d**. These represent the k nearest neighbors. Collect the labels (-1 or 1) associated with each of these nearest neighbors. Count the number of 1s and the number of -1s.

- **Step 4.** If the 1s outnumber -1s, the new data point has the label 1 (Gentoo); else it's an Adélie.

What can such a simple algorithm achieve? How about all the stuff that you get asked to buy on the internet? If companies, which shall not be named, want to recommend that you buy certain books or watch certain movies, they can do this by representing you as a vector in some high-dimensional space (in terms of your taste in books or movies), find your nearest neighbors, see what they like, and recommend those books or movies to you. Even fruit flies are thought to use some form of a k-NN algorithm to react to odors: When a fly senses some odor, it makes the connection between the new odor and another odor most like it for which it already has the neural mechanisms to respond behaviorally.

Perhaps the most important feature of the k-NN algorithm is that it's a so-called nonparametric model. Cast your mind back to the perceptron. Once you have a trained model, using some initial training dataset, the perceptron is simply characterized by its weight vector, **w**. The number of elements of this vector equals the number of parameters that define the perceptron. This number is not dependent on the amount of training data. You could train the perceptron with one hundred instances of data or a million, but at the end of the training session, the hyperplane would still be defined by **w**.

A nonparametric model, by contrast, has no fixed number of parameters. The k-NN model is an example. You basically store all the instances of the training data (whether one hundred or one million) and use all the instances when doing the inference about a new piece of data. And therein, unfortunately, lies one of the biggest concerns with the k-NN algorithm. As the size of datasets has exploded, making inferences using k-NN requires increasing amounts of computational power and memory, to the point where it can become mind-numbingly slow and resource-intensive.

There's one more glaring disadvantage, brought about by the strange behavior of data in very high dimensions. Our 3D minds are incredibly ill-equipped to appreciate all that can go wrong.

THE CURSE OF DIMENSIONALITY

In the preface to his 1957 book, *Dynamic Programming,* the American applied mathematician Richard Bellman wrote about the problems of dealing with extremely high-dimensional data and coined the phrase "the curse of dimensionality."

There are many ways to appreciate this curse. Let's start with something rather simple. Take a sample of data that can be described using one feature: something that takes a value between 0 and 2. Let's assume that the random variable representing the value of the data sample is uniformly distributed, meaning that the random variable can take any value between 0 and 2 with equal probability.

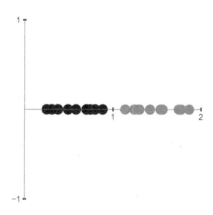

If we were to sample twenty times from this distribution, we might get a sampling that looked something like the plot shown on the previous page, with an almost equal number of data points between 0 and 1 as there are between 1 and 2. (Note that the y-axis is irrelevant in this plot; all the points lie on the x-axis.)

Now imagine that the object you are describing requires two features, each with a value that can be between 0 and 2. Again, you sample 20 points from a uniform distribution, but now this distribution is over the 2D xy plane: The probability of drawing a sample from anywhere in this 2x2 square is the same. This is what you might get:

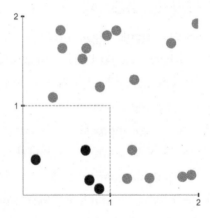

Note that the region of space for which the feature values lie between 0 and 1 forms only a quarter of the total space. (In the 1D space, it formed half the length of the total line segment.) So, now you are likely to find far fewer data samples in this region of space, which is the unit square. (In the example plot above, only 4 out of 20 end up in our prescribed region.)

Let's move on to three dimensions. Now there are three features, and each can have a value anywhere between 0 and 2. Again, we are interested in the volume of space for which the features lie between 0 and 1; the volume is the unit cube. In the 3D case, the volume of interest is now an eighth of the total volume. So, if you drew 20 samples of data that were uniformly distributed over the total volume, which is a cube with sides 2 units long, then the number you'd find in the unit cube would be drastically reduced. (In the example shown below, only 2 are black dots; the gray dots lie outside.)

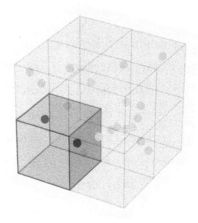

ML algorithms can be thought of as methods that are often examining such volumes of space in order to see, for example, whether one data point is like another. And these data are usually randomly sampled from some underlying distribution. In our toy example with features that have values between 0 and 2, when the number of dimensions (or the number of features that are needed to describe a data point) rises, say, to 1,000 or 10,000 or more, the chance of finding a data point within a unit hypercube rapidly diminishes. (The length of each side of a unit hypercube is equal to 1.) That's assuming, of course, that we are sticking to 20 randomly drawn samples scattered over this extremely high-dimensional space; in this case, a unit hypercube in the hyperdimensional space may be devoid of any data. As Julie Delon of the Université Paris–Descartes says in her talks on the subject, "In high dimensional spaces, nobody can hear you scream."

One way to mitigate the problem would be to increase the number of data samples (so that somebody can hear you scream in your immediate neighborhood). Unfortunately, for the solution to work, this number must grow exponentially with the number of dimensions, and so, the method runs out of steam very quickly. The curse takes over.

In his lectures, Thomas Strohmer, professor of mathematics at the University of California, Davis, describes another way to appreciate the curse of dimensionality. Let's take the k-NN algorithm: It works by calculating distances between a new data point and each sample in the training dataset. The assumption is that similar points have smaller distances between them than those that are dissimilar. But something very curious happens to distances between data points in high-dimensional space. It has to do with the behavior of the volumes of objects such as hyperspheres and hypercubes.

Let's start with a 2D circle of radius one, also called a unit circle. Take a smattering of 20 data samples distributed uniformly over the area circumscribed by the circle. Intuition tells us that the samples are spread evenly over the entire area, and our intuition is correct. The same intuition holds true for a unit sphere with a radius of one. We can visualize the volume of the sphere and the data points distributed uniformly inside that volume. However, our imagination and intuition falter when we move to higher dimensions. To see why, consider the volume of a unit sphere in some higher dimension, d. The volume is given by this formula:

$$V(d) = \frac{\pi^{\frac{d}{2}}}{\frac{d}{2}\Gamma\left(\frac{d}{2}\right)}, \text{ where } \Gamma \text{ is the Gamma function}$$

For whole numbers:

$$\Gamma(n) = (n-1)! = (n-1) \times (n-2) \times \ldots \times 2 \times 1$$

The Gamma function is also defined for real and complex numbers.

We don't need to worry about the specifics of the rest of this formula. As Strohmer points out, all we need to know is that the term $\Gamma\left(\dfrac{d}{2}\right)$ in the denominator increases much, much faster than the term $\pi^{\frac{d}{2}}$ in the numerator, for increasing values of the dimension, d. This has extraordinary consequences. As the number of dimensions tends to infinity, the volume of the unit sphere tends to zero! However, the volume of a unit hypercube is always 1 regardless of the dimensionality of the hypercube.

This allows us to compare what happens to the volume of a sphere that's embedded, or inscribed, within a cube, such that the sphere touches each of the cube's surfaces. (This problem is elegantly analyzed by Alon Amit, in a detailed post on Quora.) Again, let's start with dimensions that are familiar. Here are the two volumes in 3D space:

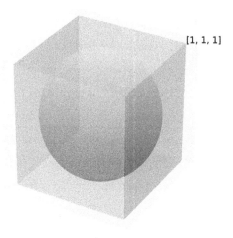

[1, 1, 1]

Let the cube and the sphere be centered at the origin, and the surfaces of the cube, at the point where they touch the sphere, be a unit length away from the origin. But the vertices of the cube are farther away.

For example, the vertex at $(1, 1, 1)$ is at a Euclidean distance of:
$\sqrt{(1-0)^2 + (1-0)^2 + (1-0)^2} = \sqrt{3} = 1.732$, from the origin, which is defined by $(0, 0, 0)$.

So are the 7 other vertices.

Similarly, in 4D space, the cube has 16 vertices. The vertex at $(1, 1, 1, 1)$ is at a distance of:

$$\sqrt{(1-0)^2 + (1-0)^2 + (1-0)^2 + (1-0)^2} = \sqrt{4} = 2$$

So are the 15 other vertices.

Similarly, for a 5D hypercube, the 2^5 $(= 32)$ vertices are 2.23 units away; and for a 10D hypercube, the 2^{10} $(= 1,024)$ vertices are each 3.16 units away. This gets out of hand very quickly. A 1,000-dimensional hypercube has 2^{1000} $(= 10.72^{300})$ vertices, which is way, way more than the number of atoms in the observable universe, and each of these vertices is 31.6 units away from the origin.

Despite the enormous number of vertices and their increasing distance from the origin, the surfaces of the hypercube, at the point where they touch the unit hypersphere, are still only 1 unit away from the origin. What does this say about how much of the volume of the hypercube is occupied by the enclosed hypersphere and how much of it by the volume that extends to the vertices?

We know that in 3D space a large fraction of the volume of the cube is taken up by the enclosed sphere. This fraction starts decreasing as we move up in dimensions. We saw that as the number of dimensions tends to infinity, the volume of the unit hypersphere tends to zero. This means that the internal volume of the hypercube taken up by the unit hypersphere vanishes, most of the volume of the hypercube ends up near the vertices, and all the vertices are equally far away from each other.

What's all this got to do with the k-NN algorithm and machine learning? Well, let's say that data points that we are interested in are embedded in the volume of a hyperdimensional cube. They are vectors, or points, in this space. As the dimensionality grows, these points don't occupy the internal volume of the unit sphere, because that's going to zero; there's no volume there to be occupied. The data points end up populating the corners of the hypercube. But given the extraordinarily large number of corners, most corners are devoid of data points, and the data points that do lie in some corners end up being almost equidistant from all other points, whether they belong to the same class or not. The whole idea of measuring distances to determine similarity falls apart. The k-NN algorithm's central premise, that nearby points are similar, doesn't hold water anymore. The algorithm works best for low-dimensional data.

Given this curse, machine learning sometimes turns to a powerful technique that has long been the staple of statisticians: principal component analysis (PCA). Often, it turns out that though the data may be very high-dimensional, much of the variation in the data that is needed to distinguish clusters lies in some lower-dimensional space. PCA is a powerful technique to reduce the data to some tractable number of lower dimensions, allowing an ML algorithm to do its magic.

After having introduced the curse of dimensionality, Bellman writes in *Dynamic Programming,* "Since this is a curse which has hung over the head of the physicist and astronomer for many a year, there is no need to feel discouraged about the possibility of obtaining significant results despite it." Far from being discouraged, PCA reveals the awesome power of dimensionality reduction. That's our next stop.

CHAPTER 6

There's Magic in Them Matrices

W hen Emery Brown was doing his medical residency to become an anesthesiologist, one of his attending doctors said to him, "Now, watch this." All of a sudden, the patient in whom they were inducing anesthesia fell unconscious. It was a profound moment. Now, after decades of practice, Brown—a professor of anesthesia at Harvard Medical School's Massachusetts General Hospital, a computational neuroscientist at MIT, and a trained statistician and applied mathematician—still finds the transition from consciousness to unconsciousness in his patients "amazing." Except, these days, he's the attending telling his residents to watch not just the patients' physiological patterns (such as changes in breathing), but also the EEG signals being recorded from their brains.

Most anesthesiologists don't pay much attention to EEG signals as a means of monitoring a patient's state of consciousness. Brown and his colleagues want to change that. They want ML algorithms to help anesthesiologists determine the dosage of anesthetics, either to induce unconsciousness or to bring patients out of it. And that means listening to the brain. Part of being able to do that involves collecting high-dimensional EEG data. (The dimensionality is determined by how much data there is and the number of features in each instance of the data, which, in this case, depends on the number of electrodes being used, the different frequencies at which the signals are being analyzed, and the duration of the recordings.) But working with high-dimensional data can drain computational resources. In one study done by Brown's team, each person's data, from just one electrode, yielded 100 different frequency components per time interval and 5,400 two-second time intervals (for a total of three hours of data). That's a 100 x 5400 matrix, or 540,000 data points, for one electrode per person. The question the researchers were asking of this data was this: If one looks at the power in the EEG signal in each of the 100 frequency bands in any given time interval, can one tell whether a person is conscious or unconscious?

One way to make the problem tractable is to borrow a tool from the statistician's toolbox: a simple, elegant, and long-standing method called principal component analysis (PCA), which involves projecting high-dimensional data onto a much smaller number of axes to find the dimensions along which the data vary the most. The trick lies in finding the correct set of low-dimensional axes. First, we need to get an intuition for PCA, one of the most important methods in all of data science and machine learning.

BABY PCA

Here's a very simple example of some made-up data to illustrate the basic idea behind principal component analysis.

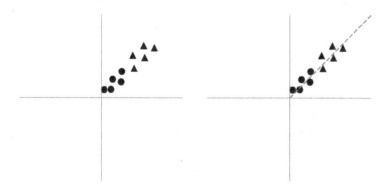

Consider the first plot. Each data point, shown as a circle or a triangle, is characterized by two values, or features, *x1* (plotted along the x-axis) and *x2* (plotted along the y-axis). As depicted, there is as much variation in the data along the x-axis as there is along the y-axis. Our job now is to reduce the dimensionality of this data, from two to one, such that most of the variation in the data is captured along one dimension. Can we draw a line representing one axis, or dimension, and project the data onto that axis?

This example was chosen because it is particularly easy and intuitive. There's a relatively obvious answer. We can draw a dashed line that runs at an angle of 45 degrees and make that the x-axis.

Now imagine the dashed line as being the new x-axis. Draw another line at 90 degrees to it, making that the y-axis. Here's what the data look like in the transformed coordinate space:

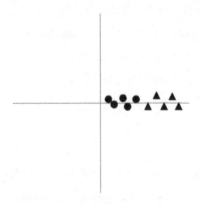

Now you can clearly see that there's more variation in the data along the x-axis than along the y-axis. It's also clear that if we now project the data onto the new x-axis, we'll see a clear separation between the circles and the triangles, but if you were to project the data onto the y-axis, the points representing the two shapes would be bunched together. So, if we had to pick one axis, or dimension, to analyze the data, we'd pick the new x-axis. If we project the data onto that axis, we'd get this plot:

We've just performed a principal component analysis. We took a two-dimensional dataset; found a one-dimensional component, or axis, that captured most of the variation in the data; and projected the data onto that one-dimensional axis. You might wonder about the rationale for doing so. Well, for one, what we did makes it easy to find (and, in this case, visualize) the separation in the data—the circles lie to the left, and the triangles to the right. It's easy for a classification algorithm, such as the perceptron algorithm, to find that boundary. (In this 1D case, the boundary is any point that separates the circles from the triangles.) The algorithm need work only in 1D space. Once it has found that boundary, then given a new data point of unknown type—we don't know if it's a circle or a triangle—we can just project it onto the single "principal component" axis and see if it falls to the right or the left of the boundary and classify it accordingly. This, of course, assumes that the new data point is drawn from the same distribution of data on which we performed PCA.

Granted, this was a trivial example. We didn't gain much, computationally speaking, by reducing dimensions from two to one to separate the circles from the triangles. But if the original dataset had been high-dimensional (as it was in Brown's anesthesia study), then reducing the number of dimensions to some smaller number, such that those lower dimensions, or principal components, capture most of the variation in the data, would be a huge computational advantage. There's always a risk that the dimensions along which there isn't much variation, which we are throwing away, are important. Also, we are assuming that the dimensions along which there's a lot of variation have a high predictive value. Such risks notwithstanding, we'd be projecting data from tens or hundreds of thousands of dimensions (or even more) down to a handful and then using computationally tractable algorithms to find patterns in the data.

To make more formal sense of all this, we begin with an introduction to the German word *Eigen,* the first mention of which (in the context that interests us) appears in a 1912 work by the German mathematician extraordinaire David Hilbert (1862–1943), titled *Grundzüge einer allgemeinen Theorie der linearen Integralgleichungen* (*Fundamentals of a General Theory of Linear Integral Equations*). *Eigen* means "characteristic, peculiar, intrinsic, or inherent." Hilbert used *Eigenfunktionen,* for "eigenfunctions," and *Eigenwerte,* for "eigenvalues." Our focus will be on two uses of "eigen": eigenvalues and eigenvectors. They will lay the groundwork for our understanding of principal component analysis.

EIGENVALUES AND EIGENVECTORS

Much of machine learning, as you well know by now, comes down to manipulating vectors and matrices. A vector is simply a set of numbers arranged as a row or a column. The number of elements in the vector is its dimensionality.

$$[3 \quad 4 \quad 5 \quad 9 \quad 0 \quad 1] \text{ is a row vector}$$

$$\text{Whereas} \begin{bmatrix} 3 \\ 4 \\ 5 \\ 9 \\ 0 \\ 1 \end{bmatrix} \text{ is a column vector}$$

These are two ways of representing the same vector. Its dimensionality, in this case, is 6. If you were to think of a 6-dimensional coordinate space (say, with axes x, y, z, p, q, r), then this vector would be a point in that 6D space. It's, of course, challenging for us to visualize anything in higher than three spatial dimensions. But conceptually, this is not a difficult idea: Just like the vector [3 4 5] is a point in 3D space (3 units along the x-axis, 4 units along the y-axis, and 5 units along the z-axis), [3 4 5 9 0 1] is a point in 6D space, with the requisite number of units along each axis.

We also know from our earlier discussion about vectors that sometimes it's worth thinking of a vector as having a direction: it's the orientation of the line drawn from the origin to the point in n-dimensional space. But for the purposes of machine learning, it's best to get used to vectors simply as a sequence of numbers, or as a matrix with one row or one column.

To recap, a matrix is a rectangular array of numbers. Generically, an $m \times n$ matrix has m rows and n columns. Here's an example of a 3×3 matrix. The rows run horizontally, the columns vertically.

$$\begin{bmatrix} a_{11} & a_{12} & a_{13} \\ a_{21} & a_{22} & a_{23} \\ a_{31} & a_{32} & a_{33} \end{bmatrix}$$

So, a_{12} is an element of the matrix that belongs to the first row, second column, and a_{32} is an element that belongs to the third row, second column. More generically, an $m \times n$ matrix is given by:

$$\begin{bmatrix} a_{11} & \cdots & a_{1n} \\ \vdots & \ddots & \vdots \\ a_{m1} & \cdots & a_{mn} \end{bmatrix}$$, and a_{ij} is an element of row i and column j.

Earlier, we saw some of the basic operations you can do with vectors. The one operation that's of concern to us now is the multiplication of a vector by a matrix. Consider:

$\mathbf{Ax} = \mathbf{y}$, where $\mathbf{A}$ is a matrix and $\mathbf{x}$ and $\mathbf{y}$ are vectors

Taking an example, and expanding the elements, we get:

$$\begin{bmatrix} a_{11} & a_{12} & a_{13} \\ a_{21} & a_{22} & a_{23} \end{bmatrix} \begin{bmatrix} x_1 \\ x_2 \\ x_3 \end{bmatrix} = \begin{bmatrix} a_{11}x_1 + a_{12}x_2 + a_{13}x_3 \\ a_{21}x_1 + a_{22}x_2 + a_{23}x_3 \end{bmatrix} = \begin{bmatrix} y_1 \\ y_2 \end{bmatrix}$$

If the matrix $\mathbf{A}$ has m rows ($m{=}2$, in the above example) and n columns ($={}3$, in our example), then the vector $\mathbf{x}$ has to be a column vector with n elements (or rows), or dimensionality of n ($={}3$, above). If you look carefully, a matrix-vector multiplication involves taking the dot product of each row of the matrix with the column vector. You are treating each row of the matrix as a row vector. That's why the number of columns of the matrix $\mathbf{A}$ must equal the number of rows, or dimensionality, of the column vector $\mathbf{x}$.

In the above example, the output vector $\mathbf{y}$ has a dimensionality of 2. This output dimensionality depends entirely on the number of rows in the matrix $\mathbf{A}$. If matrix $\mathbf{A}$ has 4 rows, the output vector $\mathbf{y}$ would have a dimensionality of 4.

$$\begin{bmatrix} a_{11} & a_{12} & a_{13} \\ a_{21} & a_{22} & a_{23} \\ a_{31} & a_{32} & a_{33} \\ a_{41} & a_{42} & a_{43} \end{bmatrix} \begin{bmatrix} x_1 \\ x_2 \\ x_3 \end{bmatrix} = \begin{bmatrix} a_{11}x_1 + a_{12}x_2 + a_{13}x_3 \\ a_{21}x_1 + a_{22}x_2 + a_{23}x_3 \\ a_{31}x_1 + a_{32}x_2 + a_{33}x_3 \\ a_{41}x_1 + a_{42}x_2 + a_{43}x_3 \end{bmatrix} = \begin{bmatrix} y_1 \\ y_2 \\ y_3 \\ y_4 \end{bmatrix}$$

Now, each vector is a point in some n-dimensional space. In our example above, the input vector **x** is a point in 3D space. But the output vector is a point in 4D space. Multiplying a vector by a matrix can transform the vector, by changing not just its magnitude and orientation, but the very dimensionality of the space it inhabits.

If you want to preserve the dimensionality of the vector during a vector-matrix multiplication, what should be the shape of the matrix? A moment's thought, and it's clear that the matrix must be square. For the dot products to work, the number of the matrix's columns should be the same as the dimensionality of the vector **x**. The number of its rows should also be the same as the dimensionality of the vector **x**, to get an output vector **y** with the same number of elements. It's this operation—the multiplication of a vector with a square matrix—that gets us to the concept of eigenvectors and eigenvalues.

Such a multiplication simply moves a vector from one location in its coordinate space to another point in the same space or moves a point from one location to another. In general, moving a point—say, in 2D space—from one location to another will change both the magnitude and the orientation of the vector.

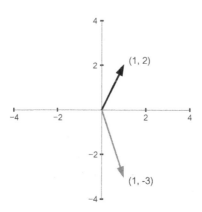

For example: the vector $\begin{bmatrix} 1 \\ 2 \end{bmatrix}$ multiplied by the matrix $\begin{bmatrix} 1 & 0 \\ 1 & -2 \end{bmatrix}$

results in the vector $\begin{bmatrix} 1 \\ -3 \end{bmatrix}$. The graph on the previous page shows the transformation.

In the figure, the old vector is the arrow pointing to (1, 2), and the new vector is pointing to (1, -3). Note that the new vector has changed in magnitude *and* orientation. For almost all the vectors that are in this 2D plane, multiplying by a 2x2 matrix (let's restrict ourselves to a square matrix with real numbers as its elements) will result in a similar transformation: a change in magnitude and orientation.

But there are some orientations associated with each square matrix that are special, or characteristic (hence, the notion of "eigen"). There are algebraic ways of figuring out what these directions are for a given matrix. For our purposes, let's take it as given that there are such methods. In fact, if you are programming in Python, there's code that will do this for you, or you could just type the matrix values into a Web interface provided by Wolfram Alpha, and it'd spit out the values for you. For our example matrix $\begin{bmatrix} 1 & 0 \\ 1 & -2 \end{bmatrix}$, here are those orientations:

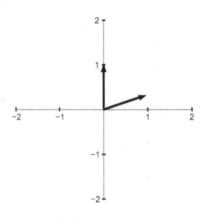

Depicted in the figure are two vectors of length 1, or so-called unit vectors. These represent special orientations for our example matrix. If you take a vector that lies along one of these orientations and multiply it by the example matrix, you'll get a new vector that has the same orientation but may have a different length. In other words, the new vector is simply rescaled, or multiplied by some scalar value. Note that you can multiply the old vector by a negative scalar value and get a vector that is flipped over, relative to the origin, but is still considered to have the same orientation, because it lies on the same line.

These special orientations, or vectors, associated with a square matrix are called eigenvectors. Corresponding to each eigenvector is an eigenvalue. So, if you take a vector with the same orientation as one of the eigenvectors and multiply it by the matrix, you'll get a new vector that is scaled by the corresponding eigenvalue. Continuing with our example, the two eigenvalues for our example matrix are −2 and 1, and the corresponding eigenvectors are [0, 1] and [3, 1]. Again, you can find these eigenvectors and eigenvalues using either algebraic methods or code, or simply by asking Wolfram Alpha.

So, let's take a vector that lies along the y-axis, say, [0, 2], and multiply it by our matrix. We get:

$$\begin{bmatrix} 1 & 0 \\ 1 & -2 \end{bmatrix} \begin{bmatrix} 0 \\ 2 \end{bmatrix} = \begin{bmatrix} 0 \\ -4 \end{bmatrix} = -2 \times \begin{bmatrix} 0 \\ 2 \end{bmatrix}$$

The new vector is a scaled version of the original vector (by −2, the eigenvalue), but it lies along the same line as before (see figure, next page). So, −2 is an eigenvalue, and the corresponding eigenvector is [0, 1].

More generally, eigenvectors and eigenvalues are written in this way:

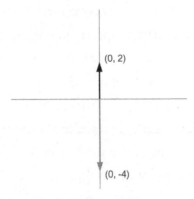

(0, 2)

(0, -4)

$\mathbf{Ax} = \lambda\mathbf{x}$, where $\mathbf{A}$ is a matrix and $\mathbf{x}$ is an eigenvector and λ is an eigenvalue. That's saying that multiplying the vector $\mathbf{x}$ by the matrix $\mathbf{A}$ results in a vector that equals $\mathbf{x}$ multiplied by a scalar value λ.

For a 2×2 matrix, there are at most two eigenvectors and two eigenvalues. The eigenvalues may or may not be distinct.

In his Stanford lectures, Anand Avati shows a neat way to visualize what a matrix does to vectors and the connection of that transformation to eigenvectors and eigenvalues. Let's start with a set of unit vectors, arranged such that their tips (the points) form the circumference of a circle of unit radius. Multiply each of those vectors with a square matrix. When you plot the transformed vectors, you get an ellipse. The matrix has squished and stretched the circle into an ellipse.

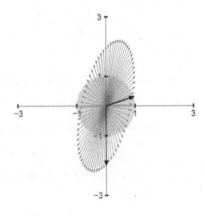

Again, for our example matrix $\begin{bmatrix} 1 & 0 \\ 1 & -2 \end{bmatrix}$, you get the plot shown on the previous page. Notice the two black vectors. Those are the directions of the eigenvectors, one of which scales a unit vector by -2 and the other by 1, as dictated by the corresponding eigenvalues.

Now we come to a very special type of matrix: a square symmetric matrix (with real values, for our purposes; no imaginary numbers, please).

One such matrix would be: $\begin{bmatrix} 3 & 1 \\ 1 & 2 \end{bmatrix}$

Note that the matrix is symmetric about the diagonal that goes from the top left (number 3) to the bottom right (number 2). (We'll use such square symmetric matrices when we come to principal component analysis.) Here's what this matrix would do to a set of unit vectors that formed a circle:

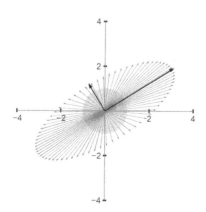

There's something quite elegant about the transformation. Each original input unit vector is transformed into an "output" vector, and the output vectors taken together form an ellipse. It turns out that the eigenvectors lie along the major and minor axes of the ellipse.

These eigenvectors are perpendicular to each other; they are called orthogonal eigenvectors. Note that the eigenvectors won't be orthogonal when the matrix is not square symmetric (as in the previous example).

We have been looking at 2x2 matrices operating on 2D vectors. But everything we have discussed holds true for a space of any dimension. Say you were working in 10,000 dimensions. Then a set of unit vectors in 10,000-dimensional space (the equivalent of a circle in 2D space) would be transformed by a square, symmetric matrix (which has 10,000 rows and 10,000 columns) into the equivalent of an ellipsoid in 10,000-dimensional space.

In the 2D case, the square symmetric matrix with real-valued elements has two eigenvectors and two corresponding eigenvalues. In the 10,000-dimensional case, the matrix has 10,000 eigenvectors and 10,000 eigenvalues, and those 10,000 eigenvectors would be orthogonal to each other. It's pointless attempting to visualize it.

COVARIANCE MATRIX

We have one more crucial concept to get through before we can tackle a real dataset with principal component analysis. Let's start with a simple 3×2 matrix.

$$
X = \begin{bmatrix} h1 & w1 \\ h2 & w2 \\ h3 & w3 \end{bmatrix}
$$

It's a tiny dataset that represents three data points: ($h1$, $w1$), ($h2$, $w2$), and ($h3$, $w3$). Let's say that each row of the matrix represents a person, with the first column of the row being the person's height and the second column their weight. If we plot the height on the x-axis and the weight on the y-axis, we'll have three points, each representing one person.

For argument's sake, consider a plot of 500 such persons. The data would be represented by a 500×2 matrix (500 rows, 2 columns). If all the people in the dataset were men of similar phenotype and genotype, from the same geographical region and ethnicity, who ate the same kind of food and had much the same behaviors regarding exercise, you'd expect their heights and weights to be related. As the height increases, so does the weight. But what if the data included people who were heavier or skinnier? Now you'd see many people with the same height but with wildly different weights. What if you added women to the mix? The relationship between the height and weight would again likely change somewhat.

There's a way in which this information can be captured in a matrix. Let's go back to our small 3×2 matrix $\begin{bmatrix} h1 & w1 \\ h2 & w2 \\ h3 & w3 \end{bmatrix}$.

First, from each element of the matrix, we subtract the expected value, or the mean, of that feature. So, for the first column, the heights have a mean of $E(h)$; and similarly, the mean for the weights is $E(w)$. When we subtract these mean values from their respective elements in the matrix, this is what we get:

$$X = \begin{bmatrix} h1 = h1 - E(h) & w1 = w1 - E(w) \\ h2 = h2 - E(h) & w2 = w2 - E(w) \\ h3 = h3 - E(h) & w3 = w3 - E(w) \end{bmatrix}$$

This procedure of setting each element to its mean-corrected value is also called centering. The reasons for doing this are a bit involved, so let's take it as something that is done implicitly. For the calculations that follow, assume that the matrix $\mathbf{X}$ is mean-corrected.

Now we take the dot product of the transpose of $\mathbf{X}$ with itself. We saw earlier that the transpose of a column vector turns it into a row vector, and vice versa. The transpose of a matrix, $\mathbf{X}^T$, similarly flips the rows and columns. So,

$$\mathbf{X}^T = \begin{bmatrix} h1 & h2 & h3 \\ w1 & w2 & w3 \end{bmatrix} \quad \text{(Note: this is a mean-corrected matrix)}$$

$$\mathbf{X}^T.\mathbf{X} = \begin{bmatrix} h1 & h2 & h3 \\ w1 & w2 & w3 \end{bmatrix} \begin{bmatrix} h1 & w1 \\ h2 & w2 \\ h3 & w3 \end{bmatrix}$$

$$= \begin{bmatrix} \left(h1^2 + h2^2 + h3^2\right) & \left(h1w1 + h2w2 + h3w3\right) \\ \left(h1w1 + h2w2 + h3w3\right) & \left(w1^2 + w2^2 + w3^2\right) \end{bmatrix}$$

This matrix, the result of taking the dot product of a 2×3 matrix with a 3×2 matrix, has two rows and two columns, and hence, is a square matrix.

Take a close look at the values of each element of the matrix. The first element (row 1, column 1) is simply the sum of the squares of the heights of the three people in our original dataset. Or, rather, it's the sum of the squares of mean-corrected heights.

$$h1^2 + h2^2 + h3^2 = (h1 - E(h))^2 + (h2 - E(h))^2 + (h3 - E(h))^2$$

As we saw in chapter 4, if height were a random variable, then this sum is also the variance of h. Similarly, the diagonal element (row 2, column 2) is the sum of the squares of the three mean-corrected weights and, hence, is the variance of w.

$$w1^2 + w2^2 + w3^2 = (w1 - E(w))^2 + (w2 - E(w))^2 \\ + (w3 - E(w))^2$$

So, the diagonal terms of the $\mathbf{X}^T.\mathbf{X}$ matrix are the variances of the individual features: The larger these values are, the more variance, or spread, there is in the dataset for that aspect of people.

The off-diagonal elements tell us something even more interesting. First, both off-diagonal elements are the same. This is a square symmetric matrix. (Keep this in mind, for we'll come back to why it is important.) The off-diagonal element is the sum of the products of the mean-corrected height and weight of each person and gives us what's called the covariance between pairs of random variables.

Let's take a small example. Here are the heights (in feet) and weights (in pounds) of three people, in matrix form:

$$\mathbf{X} = \begin{bmatrix} 5 & 120 \\ 6 & 160 \\ 7 & 220 \end{bmatrix}$$

Mean of heights is: $(5 + 6 + 7)/3 = 6$
Mean of weights is: $(120 + 160 + 220)/3 = 166.67$
The mean-corrected matrix is:

$$\mathbf{X} = \begin{bmatrix} 5-6 & 120-166.67 \\ 6-6 & 160-166.67 \\ 7-6 & 220-166.67 \end{bmatrix} = \begin{bmatrix} -1 & -46.67 \\ 0 & -6.67 \\ 1 & 53.33 \end{bmatrix}$$

$$\mathbf{X}^T.\mathbf{X} = \begin{bmatrix} -1 & 0 & 1 \\ -46.67 & -6.67 & 53.33 \end{bmatrix} \begin{bmatrix} -1 & -46.67 \\ 0 & -6.67 \\ 1 & 53.33 \end{bmatrix} = \begin{bmatrix} 2 & 100 \\ 100 & 5066.67 \end{bmatrix}$$

Now let's suppose that the three people had somewhat different weights, for the same heights. The first two persons, who are 5 feet and 6 feet tall, respectively, are heavier, and the 7-foot-tall person is severely underweight.

$$X = \begin{bmatrix} 5 & 160 \\ 6 & 220 \\ 7 & 120 \end{bmatrix}$$

After mean correction:

$$X = \begin{bmatrix} -1 & -6.67 \\ 0 & 53.33 \\ 1 & -46.67 \end{bmatrix}$$

$$X^T.X = \begin{bmatrix} -1 & 0 & 1 \\ -6.67 & 53.33 & -46.67 \end{bmatrix} \begin{bmatrix} -1 & -6.67 \\ 0 & 53.33 \\ 1 & -46.67 \end{bmatrix} = \begin{bmatrix} 2 & -40 \\ -40 & 5066.67 \end{bmatrix}$$

Note that the off-diagonal values are lower (-40) than in the previous case (100). These off-diagonal values are telling us that the heights and weights in the first case are more related to each other (an increase in height is associated with an increase in weight) than the heights and weights in the second case (where one person's weight drops dramatically despite the increase in height).

The upshot of all this is that the diagonal elements capture the variance, or spread, in the values of individual features of a dataset, whereas the off-diagonal elements capture the *covariance* between the features. In our example, it's the covariance of the height and weight. In theory, you can have any number of features in the dataset (height, weight, cholesterol level, diabetes status, etc.). If so, the matrix we've just calculated—also called the covariance matrix—will get bigger and bigger, and each off-diagonal element will capture the covariance of a different pair of features. But it'll always remain square and symmetric.

All this analysis has been leading up to this statement: *The eigenvectors of a covariance matrix are the principal components of the original matrix* $\mathbf{X}$. Explaining exactly why requires far more analysis, but here's an intuition that might help: The covariance matrix describes how the dimensions relate to one another, and the eigenvectors of the covariance matrix yield the primary dimensions along which the original data vary. It's challenging, however, to arrive at the intuition, so we'll leave that aside; rather, let's focus on how to make use of the statement.

You start with, say, an $m \times 2$ matrix $\mathbf{X}$, with m rows and 2 columns, where m is the number of individuals and 2 is the number of features. Calculate the mean-corrected covariance matrix $\mathbf{X}^{\mathrm{T}}.\mathbf{X}$. This will be a 2x2 square, symmetric covariance matrix. Find its eigenvectors and eigenvalues. Then, for each eigenvector of the covariance matrix, the associated eigenvalue tells you how much variance there is in the data along the direction of the eigenvector. For example, you might discover—once you calculate the two eigenvectors and their eigenvalues—that almost all the variation in the original data lies in the direction of one of the eigenvectors (the major axis of the ellipse). You can ignore the other direction, for it tells you little. A 2D problem has been reduced to a 1D problem. All you must do now is project the original data onto the axis represented by that one eigenvector.

Again, reducing 2D to 1D is trivial and usually unnecessary. But if the data has hundreds of features (with each feature describing, say, some aspect of an individual), then finding the handful of eigenvectors of the covariance matrix or the principal components of the original dataset makes our task immensely easier, in terms of understanding the patterns hiding in the data.

It's worthwhile examining another example problem, which John Abel, a postdoc on Brown's team, often uses to highlight ways in which PCA may be useful. Let's say we have a dataset of vehicles that are categorized based on six features, such as the height, length, number of wheels, number of passengers, size, and shape. Each feature corresponds to a dimension along which the vehicle is being analyzed. Most of the variation in this dataset will likely lie along the dimensions that map onto the size and shape of vehicles. If you did principal component analysis on this dataset, the first principal component would capture most of this variation. And if your intent was to use the variation in size and shape to classify the vehicles, then the first principal component would be extremely useful. But what if the vehicles had one other feature: say, number of ladders? The only type of vehicle that would have ladders would be a fire truck. All other vehicle types would have zero ladders. So, in the original dataset, there would be very little variation along this dimension. If you did PCA, and looked only at the first principal component, it would not be informative about the number of ladders. If your task were to classify vehicles as fire trucks, then finding the first principal component and discarding the rest (particularly, information about the number of ladders) would likely make it impossible to tell which vehicle was a fire truck and which one wasn't. As Kenny Rogers sang, "You've got to know when to hold 'em and know when to fold 'em."

THE IRIS DATASET

Many books and lectures on machine learning invariably mention the Iris dataset. It is data about, as the name suggests, irises. The data were first formally published in a 1936 paper titled "The Use of Multiple Measurements in Taxonomic Problems," by Ronald Aylmer Fisher, a British biologist, mathematician, statistician, and geneticist, among other things. Fisher was also a staunch eugenicist. It is little wonder that the paper, published originally in the *Annals of Eugenics* and now made available online by the journal *Annals of Human Genetics,* comes with this disclaimer: "The work of eugenicists was often pervaded by prejudice against racial, ethnic and disabled groups. Publication of this material online is for scholarly research purposes [and] is not an endorsement or promotion of the views expressed in any of these articles or eugenics in general."

The Iris dataset is a bit of a marvel as a didactic tool for modern machine learning. Fisher used it to illustrate some statistical techniques. But he wasn't the creator of the data. They were collected, painstakingly, by an American botanist named Edgar Anderson, who, in his paper titled "The Irises of the Gaspe Peninsula," poetically recalled how he went about gathering them. Anderson wrote about the abundance of these flowers on a stretch from L'Isle-Verte to Trois-Pistoles on the peninsular coast in Quebec, Canada: "There for mile after mile one could gather irises at will and assemble for comparison one hundred full-blown flowers of *Iris versicolor* and of *Iris setosa canadensis,* each from a different plant, but all from the same pasture, and picked on the same day and measured at the same time by the same person with the same apparatus. The result is, to ordinary eyes, a few pages of singularly dry statistics, but to the biomathematician a juicy morsel quite worth looking ten years to find."

Anderson's data, as collated in Fisher's paper, were of three types of irises: *Iris setosa, Iris versicolor,* and *Iris virginica.* For each flower, Anderson measured four characteristics, or features: the sepal length, the sepal width, the petal length, and the petal width. The sepal is the green, leaflike protection around a flower bud that opens out underneath a blossoming flower. There are 50 entries per type of flower. All those data are captured in a 150x4 matrix (150 rows, one row for each flower, 4 columns, one column per feature of the flower). There's also a 150-column vector (or the fifth column of the matrix) that tells you the type of the flower. We'll leave this information aside for now.

Here's our problem: Can we visually discern any structure or pattern in this dataset? We cannot plot the data, because there are four features, and hence, each flower exists as a vector in 4D space. So, we cannot visually tell anything about the axis or axes along which you find the most variance among the flowers. What if we find the two main principal components and project the data down to 2D space? Then we can plot the data and see if any pattern emerges.

We start with the data matrix $\mathbf{X}$, which contains the information about 150 flowers. Assume $\mathbf{X}$ is mean-corrected.

The covariance matrix is: $\mathbf{X}^{T}.\mathbf{X}$

Because $\mathbf{X}$ is a 150x4 matrix and $\mathbf{X}^{T}$ is a 4×150 matrix, the covariance matrix is the dot product of a (4×150) matrix with a (150×4) matrix. So, it's a (4×4) matrix. Given that the covariance matrix is square symmetric with real values, it has 4 orthogonal eigenvectors. So, each eigenvector is a 4D row or column vector. Put the four of them together, and you get another (4×4) matrix. Call it $\mathbf{W}$.

We must ensure that $\mathbf{W}$ is ordered: The first column is the eigenvector with the largest eigenvalue, the second column with the next biggest, and so on. The first eigenvector is the direction in which the data have the most variance; the variance associated with the next eigenvector is a little less, and so on.

We'll take the first two eigenvectors. These are our two main principal components. We are taking two so that we can plot and easily visualize the data; within the confines of an ML algorithm, you can work with any number of lower dimensions. Arrange the two eigenvectors side by side, and we get a 4×2 matrix; call it $\mathbf{W}_r$ (for $\mathbf{W}$-reduced).

We now must project the original dataset $\mathbf{X}$ onto these two axes. The original dataset had 4 columns, or features. The transformed dataset, call it $\mathbf{T}$, will have two columns, or features. Taking the dot product of $\mathbf{W}_r$ and $\mathbf{X}$ gives us $\mathbf{T}$.

$\mathbf{T} = \mathbf{X} . \mathbf{W}_r$

$\mathbf{X}$ is a (150×4) matrix.

$\mathbf{W}_r$ is a (4×2) matrix.

So, $\mathbf{T}$ is a (150×2) matrix.

Our 150 flowers have now been reduced from 4D vectors to 2D vectors. In the original dataset, each feature, or dimension, had a meaning: sepal length or petal width, for example. But in the 2D space, the two features don't have a physical meaning. But each feature in two dimensions encapsulates something about how much each of the original dimensions contributes to it.

Now let's see what happens when all the 150 flowers are plotted on a 2D plane, where the x-axis is the first principal component and the y-axis is the second principal component. You get the figure shown on top of the next page. It's kind of hard to tell anything except that one group of points is well separated from another, larger group.

It's somewhat informative, but we can do more. It's time to look at the fifth column of data that we have kept aside. The fifth column had associated each row in the original 150x4 matrix with a flower type. What if we plot the same figure that we just did but give a different shape and color (gray circle, gray square, or black triangle) to

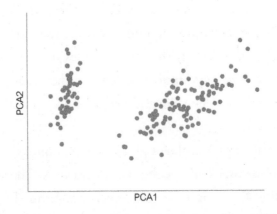

the data point, depending on whether it's *Iris setosa, Iris versicolor,* or *Iris virginica.* Something magical happens. The flowers clearly cluster in the 2D plot:

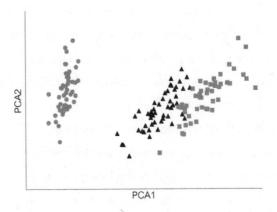

We have just seen the power of principal component analysis. By reducing the dimensionality of the data from four to two, we can visualize the data. And it so happened that the two main principal components captured almost all the variance in the data—there are ways to figure out exactly how much—and the variance was such that it allowed us to clearly see the pattern in 2D. We got lucky.

However, there can be high-dimensional data that shows considerable variance along most of, if not all, its principal components. For example, in the 2D case, when the unit circle was transformed into an ellipse, what if the major and minor axes of the ellipse were almost equally long? In that case, both axes would contain equal amounts of variation. In such a situation, there's little benefit to doing this analysis. You may as well stick to your original data, as there's no way to effectively reduce the dimensionality and not lose valuable information.

There's another way of thinking about what we've just done. We projected our data into a lower-dimensional, more computationally tractable space and then labeled the various flowers as being of one type or another. Here's where machine learning comes in. If we are now given a new data point, but it's missing the label for the type of flower, what can we do? Well, first we project that data point onto the same two principal components and plot it. We can see where it lands and tell, just by eyeballing it, the type of flower it is. Or we could use some of the algorithms we saw earlier, such as the nearest neighbor algorithm, to classify the new data point.

But what if we didn't have the original labels? Let's say Anderson, despite his finicky data collection habits, forgot to write down the type of flower alongside each row describing the four features of the flower. What's an ML engineer to do?

Well, there's a whole field called unsupervised learning that tries to find patterns or structure in unlabeled data. One analysis method that might be considered a precursor to unsupervised learning is clustering, an intuitive example of which is called the K-means clustering algorithm. It needs to be told how many clusters there are in the data. Given that information, the algorithm iteratively tries to find the geometric center of each cluster. Once it finds those "centroids,"

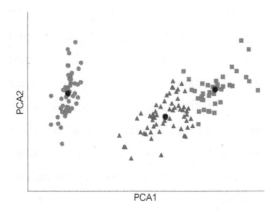

it assigns the appropriate label (in this case, 0, 1, or 2) to each data point, depending on its closest centroid. We can run this algorithm on the low-dimensional Iris dataset, sans the labels. The algorithm finds three centroids, shown as black dots.

You can see that despite our not knowing the flower types, the combination of principal component analysis and K-means brings us close to identifying distinct clusters in the dataset. Though, if you look closely, the clusters identified in this manner don't exactly match up with the original clusters, but they are close. Also, of course, in this case we wouldn't know what each cluster meant—is it *Iris setosa, Iris versicolor,* or *Iris virginica*? Nonetheless, the ability to find clusters in data, particularly high-dimensional data, is invaluable.

We now have the tools to tackle the problem we opened the chapter with—Emery Brown and his team's work with people under anesthesia.

CONSCIOUSNESS AND ANESTHESIA

Principal component analysis could one day help deliver the correct dose of an anesthetic while we lie on a surgeon's table. At least, Brown and his colleagues would like to add PCA-enabled machine learning to an anesthesiologist's tool kit. And their study demonstrated in no small measure some of the steps needed to get there.

First, the data. The team collected what has to be one of the cleanest datasets of EEG signals of people being put under an anesthetic. Ten subjects were each administered the anesthetic propofol over a period of about 2.5 hours. The propofol was gradually increased until the estimated concentration of the anesthetic in the blood at a given location in the body went from 0 to 5 micrograms per milliliter and then back down to zero. Every two seconds, the subject was asked to respond to an auditory command by pressing an appropriate button. The response was used to assess their state of consciousness. Meanwhile, the researchers recorded EEG signals using sixty-four scalp electrodes. "It's a very rich dataset in the sense that it [was collected] in such a tightly controlled environment," team member John Abel told me. Such data would have been near impossible to gather from patients undergoing surgery in an OR. "It's challenging to collect EEG in the OR. Recording EEG is low on the list of priorities when you're actually doing surgery."

For the PCA part of their analysis, the team looked at the EEG signals recorded at just one location on the prefrontal cortex. Using the data collected from that one electrode, they calculated the power spectral density: the power in the signal as a function of frequency. So, for every two-second time interval, this resulted in a vector of a hundred dimensions, where each element of the vector contained the power in the signal in some frequency band. The overall frequency ranged from 0 to 50 Hz, with each band corresponding to a hundredth of that range.

If the subject is monitored for three hours, say, then the monitoring generates a 100-dimensional vector every two seconds, for a total of 5,400 such vectors. Once the data acquisition and processing are complete, a subject's EEG is encapsulated in a (5400×100) matrix,

S. Each row of the matrix represents the power spectral density for a two-second interval; each column represents the power spectral density in each frequency bin.

$$\begin{bmatrix} s_{11} & \cdots & s_{1n} \\ \vdots & \ddots & \vdots \\ s_{m1} & \cdots & s_{mn} \end{bmatrix}, \text{ where } m = 5{,}400 \text{ (rows)}, n = 100 \text{ (columns)}$$

The other data that's generated apart from the time series of the power spectral density is the inferred state of the subject: conscious or not. Every two seconds, you get a 1 if the subject is inferred to be conscious, 0 if not. That's another 5,400-dimensional vector **c**, one entry for each 2-second time slot.

$$\begin{bmatrix} c_1 \\ \vdots \\ c_m \end{bmatrix}, m = 5400$$

The team collected such data for ten patients. We are now ready to do PCA. Here's one way to go about it.

Let's take matrices for only seven of the ten subjects. (We'll leave three aside for testing, which we'll come to in a bit.) First, stack the matrices of all seven, one below the other, so that we get a $(37{,}800 \times 100)$ matrix. The reason for doing this? It increases the amount of information you have in each of the 100 columns. Each column now contains the power spectral density for not just one subject, but seven.

This giant $(37{,}800 \times 100)$ matrix is our matrix **X**. Perform mean correction.

The covariance matrix is $\mathbf{X}^T\mathbf{X}$, which is a $(100 \times 37{,}800)$ matrix dotted with a $(37{,}800 \times 100)$ matrix, giving us a (100×100) matrix **W**. This has 100 eigenvectors and 100 eigenvalues. We'll take the first three eigenvectors (associated with the three biggest eigenvalues), and we get a (100×3) matrix $\mathbf{W}_r$.

These three eigenvectors are our first three principal components. It turns out, said Abel, that the first eigenvector is not very informative with respect to the state of consciousness. While it does capture the maximum amount of variation in the data along that axis, that variation doesn't reveal much about whether a patient is conscious or unconscious. (This is the kind of poking around that a data scientist must do to extract information from the data.) So, we drop the first principal component and just use the next two. So, $\mathbf{W}_r$ now is a (100×2) matrix.

Now we can project any subject's high-dimensional data onto these two principal components, or axes. This involves taking the dot product of the matrix for one subject, a (5400×100) matrix, with $\mathbf{W}_r$, a (100×2) matrix. The result: a (5400×2) matrix. Each row of the matrix represents the state of consciousness of the patient projected down from a hundred dimensions (of power spectral density data) to two. There are 5,400 such states, for every two-second time slot. If you plot these states on the xy plane, using gray circles for "conscious" and black triangles for "unconscious" (recall that we have this data in the form of a 5,400-dimensional vector for each subject), here's what you get, as an example:

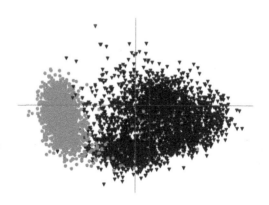

This is pretty amazing. The conscious and unconscious states needn't have separated. But they do, albeit not very cleanly—you can see some black triangles among the gray circles, and vice versa—and this is where machine learning enters the picture. Given such data in two dimensions, one can build an efficient classifier that finds the boundary that best separates the gray circles from the black triangles. A linear classifier that finds a good-enough straight line to separate the two clusters will do—"good" here implies the best possible. It's clear that there's no line that can be drawn that will classify all the gray circles as lying on one side and all the black triangles as lying on the other: There's some overlap in the data, and so, there will be some mistakes. The task is to minimize the mistakes. The perceptron algorithm, for instance, will never find a solution, because a linearly separating hyperplane doesn't exist in this case. But a naïve Bayes classifier will find a solution, and of course, so will a k-nearest neighbor algorithm. (In the final chapter, we'll address this rather profound issue of choosing a simple model versus a more complex model—a topic that is typically referred to as the bias–variance problem, and the perils and promises of preferring one over the other.)

Once you have trained a classifier, you can test it. This is where those three subjects we kept aside come in. We can pretend we don't know the state of consciousness of the subject in any given two-second time slot. All we have to do is project the 100-dimensional vector that captures that state down to two dimensions (the two principal axes used above), and see what the classifier says it should be: gray (conscious) or black (unconscious). But we also have actual data about the state of the subject for that two-second time slot, the so-called ground truth. We can compare the prediction against the ground truth and see how well the classifier generalizes data it hasn't seen. The aim of this entire effort is to ensure that one builds a classifier that minimizes prediction error. However, as was mentioned in chapter 2, minimizing prediction error is no simple matter. The overall objective matters, and the nuances depend on the exact problem being tackled. But let's say that the prediction error was minimized keeping the right objective in mind. Only then can something like this be introduced into a real-world setting, involving a patient undergoing surgery and a machine that's recommending the dosage of the anesthetic to an anesthesiologist, who factors it into their decision-making process. While there's considerably more research and engineering required to build such a machine, predicting the state of consciousness of a patient by using EEG data would be central to such an effort. And principal component analysis might play a role.

So far, we have encountered situations where high-dimensional data posed problems. PCA showed us one way to find a lower-dimensional space in which to make sense of data. But sometimes, data in low dimensions can be problematic. For example, what if all you had was the lower-dimensional data that could not be linearly separated, but you wanted to use a linear classifier, because it works so well? It'd be impossible to do so in the lower-dimensional space. Well, you could do the opposite of what PCA does and project the data into higher dimensions, sometimes even into an infinite-dimensional space, where there always exists some linearly separating hyperplane. An algorithm that used this trick and, the subject of the next chapter, rocked the machine learning community in the 1990s.

CHAPTER 7

The Great Kernel Rope Trick

B ernhard Boser was biding his time at AT&T Bell Labs in Holmdel, New Jersey. It was the fall of 1991. He had been offered a position at the University of California, Berkeley, but there were still three months to his start date. At Bell Labs, he had been a member of the technical staff, working on hardware implementations of artificial neural networks. But in those intervening three months, he didn't want to start a new hardware project. Looking to keep busy, he started talking to one of his colleagues at Bell Labs, Vladimir Vapnik, an eminent Russian mathematician, a formidable expert in statistics and machine learning, and a recent immigrant to the United States. Vapnik asked Boser to work on an algorithm that Vapnik had designed back in the 1960s and that now appeared in an addendum to the English-language translation of his seminal book, *Estimation of Dependencies Based on Empirical Data*. The addendum was called "Remarks about Algorithms." Vapnik wanted Boser to implement the algorithm detailed in Remark No. 4, "Methods for Constructing an Optimal Separating Hyperplane."

A separating hyperplane, as we saw earlier, is the linear boundary between two regions of coordinate space: a line separating two regions of 2D space, or a plane separating two regions of 3D space, or a hyperplane dividing some higher-dimensional space into two. Such a separating hyperplane delineates data points into two clusters. Points that lie to one side of the hyperplane belong to one category, and those that lie on the other side belong to another. Given labeled data, the perceptron algorithm devised by Frank Rosenblatt can find such a hyperplane, if one exists. However, for a linearly separable dataset, there exists an infinity of separating hyperplanes. And some are better than others.

Below is an example of the perceptron algorithm finding a hyperplane that separates the circles from the triangles. It's a perfectly valid hyperplane, given the initial set of data on which the perceptron is trained.

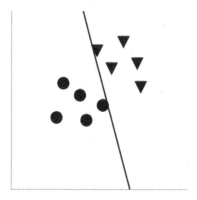

Now imagine you are given a new data point, a triangle that lies close to the original cluster of triangles. The perceptron must classify it based on the hyperplane it previously found. Here's what it'll do: It'll classify the point as a circle (shown in gray). And it will be wrong.

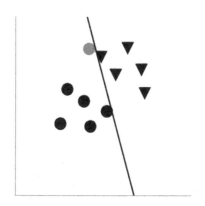

It's easy to imagine another hyperplane—shown as a dashed gray line, say, one that's rotated a few degrees—that would correctly classify the new point as a triangle.

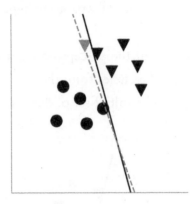

Of course, even with the new hyperplane, it's possible that a new data point gets misclassified. And while one can eyeball a 2D plot of points to imagine yet another hyperplane that might do better, this is not a sustainable method. Also, let's not forget that this process of finding a hyperplane often involves operating in dimensions that are far greater than two, making visualization impossible. What's needed is a systematic method for finding the best possible separating hyperplane that would minimize errors when classifying new data points. Vapnik's method did just that: It found an optimal hyperplane from an infinity of choices.

The first figure on the opposite page visualizes Vapnik's algorithm.

Given some linearly separable sets of data points, the algorithm finds a hyperplane (the black line) that maximizes the margins on either side of it. Note that some data points are black, while the others are gray. The black ones are nearest to the separating hyperplane. In the example, there's one black circle and two black triangles. The separating hyperplane is equidistant from the black circle and the two black triangles. It's as if we cleared a path through the thicket of data points, a "no-one's-land," if you will. By definition, no data points

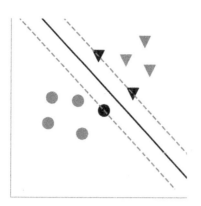

lie inside the path. The closest ones from either cluster come at most to the edges, or margins, of the path, and those are the ones in black. The hyperplane is the line that goes through the middle of the path.

Once you find such a hyperplane, it's more likely to correctly classify a new data point as being a circle or a triangle than the hyperplane found by the perceptron. Boser implemented and tested the algorithm in no time at all. It worked.

The math behind Vapnik's algorithm is elegant and puts to use much of the terminology we have encountered so far. But it's an involved analysis. (See a pointer to an excellent exposition of the math.) We'll aim for an intuitive understanding.

The goal of the analysis is to find the hyperplane depicted below. Note that the figure now has a vector **w**. This is the weight vector

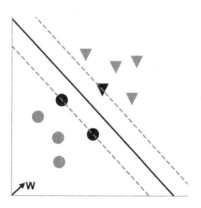

characterizing the hyperplane and is perpendicular to it. The hyperplane is also characterized by a bias b, which is its offset from the origin. Also note this time that there are two black circles and one black triangle and that each serves as an instance of data closest to the hyperplane. This is deliberate, to make the point that the number of data points of each class that lie on the edges of the maximally wide path can be anything; it depends on your training dataset. The only guarantee is that there is bound to be, by definition, at least one of each category.

Let's say that circles are labeled -1 and triangles $+1$. There are n data points (both circles and triangles). After some nifty vector algebra, Vapnik proved that the weight vector that maximizes the separation between points on either side of the hyperplane can be found by minimizing the function $\dfrac{\|\mathbf{w}\|^2}{2}$, where $\|\mathbf{w}\|$ is the magnitude of the weight vector, while simultaneously satisfying this equation for every data point $\mathbf{x}_i$ (a vector) and its associated label, y_i (a scalar, equal to -1 or $+1$):

$$y_i(\mathbf{w}.\mathbf{x}_i + b) \geq 1$$

$\mathbf{w}.\mathbf{x}_i$ is the dot product of the weight vector with the ith data point. The above equation is also called the margin rule; it ensures that points on either side of the hyperplane can get only so close and no closer, thereby creating the no-one's-land.

So, we have some function, given by $\dfrac{\|\mathbf{w}\|^2}{2}$, which must be minimized. If it were simply a question of finding the minimum of a quadratic function (a polynomial of degree 2, which is what we have), that would be straightforward. The function is bowl-shaped, and we can use gradient descent to find the minimum. But minimizing while accounting for the second set of equations $y_i(\mathbf{w}.\mathbf{x}_i + b) \geq 1$, complicates things somewhat.

We now have a constrained optimization problem. We must descend the bowl to a location that simultaneously satisfies the constraint and is a minimum. One solution for such a problem was devised by Joseph-Louis Lagrange (1736–1813), an Italian mathematician and astronomer whose work had such elegance that William Rowan Hamilton—we met Hamilton in chapter 2; he was the one who etched an equation onto the stones of an Irish bridge—was moved to praise some of Lagrange's work as "a kind of scientific poem."

NOT JUST THE BOTTOM OF THE BOWL

Before we come to Lagrange's work, here's a fun, but entirely unreasonable, mental exercise to motivate the mathematical discussion to follow. Imagine you are clambering up the slope of a hill over a valley. You are a prospector and have been told that there is a vein of some rather exotic mineral beneath the hills that forms a circle centered on the valley floor and about a mile in radius. It's rather far away to dig horizontally toward the vein from the bottom of the valley. But there's another option. The surrounding hillsides go up very gently. You could walk up the slopes such that you were over the vein and, yet, be at a height that's far less than a mile—say, a few hundred feet at most—and dig down from there. So, you walk up and reach a location that's directly over the supposed vein of mineral underground. But there's a problem. As you walk the hillside along a circular path around the valley, making sure you are always above the mineral vein, you are tracing a circle, but your altitude might go up and down, because the hillside is not necessarily level. Your job is to find the place on that circular path that has the least altitude, so that when you do drill down, it'll require the minimum amount of digging.

What we have just done is pose a constrained optimization problem. If you had simply been told to find the place with the least altitude in the valley (the minimum), well, that would have been easy. You just walk down to the valley floor, doing your own version of gradient descent. But now you must find a minimum altitude (a value along the z, or vertical, direction) given a constraint, which is that you must be a certain horizontal distance away from the valley's bottom. The x and y coordinates (measured along the plane of the valley floor) must lie on a circle with a radius of one mile, with the circle centered on the middle of the valley.

Here's a depiction of the problem:

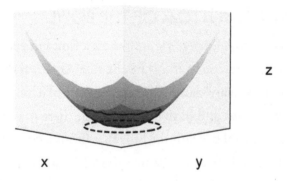

The dashed circle is the mineral vein. The solid wavy line is the path you walk along on the slopes, such that you are directly above the vein. Note that the altitude varies as you walk along the solid line, and you must find the spot where the altitude is at a minimum (there may be multiple such locations). Of course, if you were an actual prospector, you could just walk around with an altimeter and find the lowest point on that path and start drilling down. How would you do it mathematically?

The mathematical equation depicting the surface shown above is a bit gnarly:

$$f(x, y) = x^2 + \sin^4(xy) + xy$$

Given the x and y coordinates, the function calculates the height of the surface in the z direction. Let's take a much simpler function to work with:

$$f(x, y) = xy + 30$$

Here's how the function looks. You can see that it rises along two sides and drops off along two other sides. Such a surface has a saddle point, the flat bit in the middle, but it has no maximum or minimum.

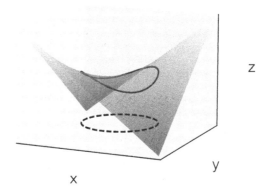

Now think of our constrained optimization problem. Let's add the constraint that the (x, y) coordinates must lie on a circle of radius 2. So, the (x, y) coordinates are constrained by the equation of a circle:

$$x^2 + y^2 = r^2 = 2^2 = 4$$

In the figure, the dashed circle lies on the xy plane. The solid circle is what you get when you satisfy the constraint as you move along the 3D surface. Even though the original 3D surface sans the constraints had no minimum or maximum, the constrained path along the surface does have a minimum and maximum.

Lagrange came up with an elegant solution to find the extrema (the minima and the maxima) of such a constrained path. To understand his solution, we need a few different ways of looking at the problem. For starters, here's a depiction of the surface using contour lines (or the terraces of rice paddies on hillsides that we encountered earlier, which are paths along the hillsides that are at the same altitude, or height).

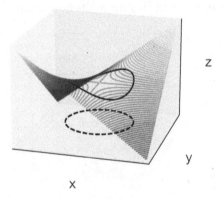

Because we must find the minimum and maximum along the solid circle, we are really interested in the smallest and the largest values of the contour lines, respectively, that touch the solid line. It's clear that we can ignore contour lines that don't intersect the constraining curve. They are of no interest, for they clearly don't satisfy the constraint. The contour lines that either touch or intersect the curve do satisfy the constraint at certain points. Let's think about them, while focusing on finding the minimum, first. To find a minimum, we need to go down a slope. As we do, we encounter different contour lines, including ones that intersect the constraining curve, one that just touches the constraining curve at a single point, and then contour lines that don't intersect the curve. As we move from higher ground to lower ground, the values of these contour lines, or the heights they represent, keep decreasing. The contour line that grazes the constraining curve is the one of interest to us. It represents the minimum height while simultaneously satisfying the constraint. The same analysis holds for finding the maximum. In both cases, we are interested in contour lines that tangentially touch the constraining curve.

It's easier to see this in 2D. Here are the contour lines projected down to the 2D xy plane (fewer lines are shown for clarity). Note that the constraining curve is a circle, as it should be.

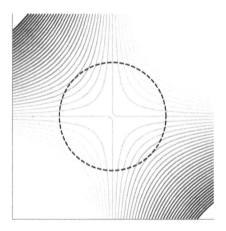

The contour lines get darker as they decrease in value (the surface is falling) and fade away with increasing value (the surface is rising). In this figure, you can see four contour lines touching the constraining curve. We must find the values of those contour lines. They represent the extrema of our surface, given the constraint.

Lagrange noticed that the tangent to the constraining curve and the tangent to the contour line, at each extremum, are essentially the same line at the point of contact. If we draw an arrow that is perpendicular to each of those tangent lines, those two arrows will point in the same direction. But what does an arrow that's perpendicular to the tangent to the contour line represent? We have seen it before. It's the gradient of the surface, the direction of steepest ascent. So, what we are saying is that at the point where the tangents to the constraining curve and the contour line are parallel, or are in essence the same line, their gradients point in the same direction.

Recall that the gradient is a vector. The fact that two gradients point in the same direction doesn't mean they have identical lengths, or values. They may differ in their magnitude: One could be a scalar multiple of the other.

For our example function, the gradient of the 3D surface is given by:

$\nabla f(x,y)$; Read that as "delta f of x y"

Let's call the constraining function $g(x,y)$. So:

$$g(x,y) = x^2 + y^2 = 4$$

The gradient of the constraining function is:

$$\nabla g(x,y)$$

Lagrange's insight was:

$$\nabla f(x,y) = \lambda \nabla g(x,y)$$

The gradient of one function is a scalar multiple, λ, of the gradient of the other function.

We saw in chapter 3 that the gradient of a function that represents a surface in 3D space is a two-dimensional vector. The first element of the vector is the partial derivative of the function with respect to x, and the second element of the vector is the partial derivative with respect to y.

$$\nabla f(x,y) = \begin{bmatrix} \partial f / \partial x \\ \partial f / \partial y \end{bmatrix}$$

$$f(x,y) = xy + 30$$

$$\rightarrow \partial f / \partial x - y \text{ and } \partial f / \partial y = x$$

$$\Rightarrow \nabla f(x,y) = \begin{bmatrix} y \\ x \end{bmatrix}$$

Similarly,

$$g(x,y) = x^2 + y^2$$

$$\Rightarrow \nabla g(x,y) = \begin{bmatrix} \partial(x^2 + y^2) / \partial x \\ \partial(x^2 + y^2) / \partial y \end{bmatrix} = \begin{bmatrix} 2x \\ 2y \end{bmatrix}$$

Now, according to Lagrange's method:

$$\nabla f(x,y) = \lambda \nabla g(x,y)$$

Or,

$$\begin{bmatrix} y \\ x \end{bmatrix} = \lambda \begin{bmatrix} 2x \\ 2y \end{bmatrix}$$

This gives us two equations:

$$y = \lambda 2x \text{ and } x = \lambda 2y$$

But we have three unknowns, (x, y, λ), and only two equations. We need at least one more equation to solve for all the unknowns. That's, of course, the constraining equation:

$$x^2 + y^2 = 4$$

Solving these three equations, we get values for the three unknowns:

$$\lambda = +1/2, -1/2$$
$$x = +\sqrt{2}, -\sqrt{2}$$
$$y = +\sqrt{2}, -\sqrt{2}$$

We don't really care about the value for lambda. That was just a placeholder, a trick to let us calculate the values for the (x, y) coordinates of the extrema.

Those coordinates are:

$$\left(\sqrt{2},\sqrt{2}\right), \ \left(\sqrt{2},-\sqrt{2}\right), \ \left(-\sqrt{2},\sqrt{2}\right), \text{ and } \left(-\sqrt{2},-\sqrt{2}\right)$$

Plug these values into the equation representing the surface, and you get the values for the corresponding z coordinates:

$$f\left(\sqrt{2},\sqrt{2)}\right) = \sqrt{2}.\sqrt{2} + 30 = 32$$

$$f\left(\sqrt{2},-\sqrt{2)}\right) = \sqrt{2}. - \sqrt{2} + 30 = 28$$

$$f\left(-\sqrt{2},\sqrt{2)}\right) = -\sqrt{2}.\sqrt{2} + 30 = 28$$

$$f\left(-\sqrt{2},-\sqrt{2)}\right) = -\sqrt{2}. - \sqrt{2} + 30 = 32$$

There are two points that represent the constrained minima and two that represent the constrained maxima. This makes sense, because the surface is symmetric about the center, and the constraining curve is a circle. Here's what the points look like in the 2D and 3D contour plots:

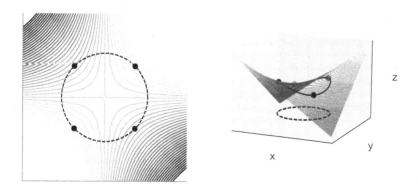

More generally, the problem of constrained optimization can be thought of as finding the extrema of the so-called Lagrange function, given by:

$$L(x,\lambda) = f(x) - \lambda g(x)$$

The logic here is straightforward. First, let's take the gradient of both sides of this equation.

$$\nabla L(x,\lambda) = \nabla f(x) - \nabla \lambda g(x)$$

At the extrema, the gradient of L must be zero. If we set the left-hand side to zero, then we get back the equality that we analyzed above:

$$\nabla f(x) = \nabla \lambda g(x)$$

What this means is that the optimization problem boils down to finding the extrema of the Lagrange function. The example we looked at was rather easy, and we could find the extrema analytically. But in most real-world cases, the process is far more complicated. Also, we looked only at a constraint that was an equality. Constraints can also be inequalities (say, something must be greater than or equal to some number). Regardless, it's this method, often called the method of Lagrange multipliers (λ being the Lagrange multiplier) that will help us move farther along in our discussion of finding the optimal separating hyperplane.

THE OPTIMAL MARGIN

Our purpose, before we segued into talking about Lagrange multipliers, was to find the weight vector $\mathbf{w}$ such that $\frac{\|\mathbf{w}\|^2}{2}$ was minimized. There was an additional constraint, which was that the following equation (the margin rule) had to be satisfied for data points that either lie on or beyond the margins of no-one's-land:

$$y_i(\mathbf{w}.\mathbf{x}_i + b) \geq 1$$

Well, we are in Lagrange territory.

You'd write down the Lagrange function by treating $\frac{\|\mathbf{w}\|^2}{2}$ as $f(x)$ and $(y_i(\mathbf{w}.\mathbf{x}_i + b) - 1)$ as $g(x)$ and then follow the process described above. However, the equations that you get are not always solvable analytically, and you need specialized mathematical techniques to find the Lagrange multipliers. (There are as many of these multipliers as there are constraining equations, and we have one such equation for each data point.)

We'll focus on the results of the constrained optimization. The first result is that the weight vector turns out to be given by this formula:

$$\mathbf{w} = \sum_i \alpha_i y_i \mathbf{x_i}$$

Each α_i (alpha sub-i) is a scalar and is specific to a given data point and its associated label, $(\mathbf{x_i}, y_i)$. These alphas are the Lagrange multipliers. (We are calling them alphas now instead of lambdas, to be consistent with much of the literature.) Given some training data, specialized optimization techniques can give us the alphas, and thus help us calculate the weight vector and the bias term. A further key insight that arises from the mathematical analysis is that the alphas depend *only on the mutual dot product of the vectors representing the data samples*. Keep this in mind.

The weight vector, as you can see from the equation above, turns out to be a linear combination of vectors that represent the data samples, with the coefficients of the combination being the alphas. This is an amazing result.

So, once we have the alphas, we can calculate the weight vector, which along with the bias, b, determines the hyperplane. Then it's easy to figure out whether a new data point—let's call it $\mathbf{u}$—lies to one side of the hyperplane or the other.

$$\text{The label for a new data point } \mathbf{u} = \begin{cases} -1, & \mathbf{w}.\mathbf{u} + b < 0 \\ +1, & \mathbf{w}.\mathbf{u} + b \geq 0 \end{cases}$$

We can substitute the value for $\mathbf{w}$ from the above equation, to get the second result, the decision rule:

$$\text{The label for a new data point } \mathbf{u} = \begin{cases} -1, & \left(\sum_i \alpha_i y_i \mathbf{x_i}.\mathbf{u}\right) + b < 0 \\ +1, & \left(\sum_i \alpha_i y_i \mathbf{x_i}.\mathbf{u}\right) + b \geq 0 \end{cases}$$

Note that the decision rule similarly depends only on the dot product of the new sample, with each of the vectors representing the training data. It turns out that α_i will be zero for samples that don't lie on the margins; so, effectively, we are dealing with only those data points that lie on the margins.

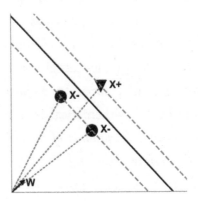

The plot above shows only the data that lie on the margins. These data points are, of course, vectors, and because they help define, or anchor, the margins, they are called support vectors. Also, all this analysis holds for vectors of any dimension, not just the 2D vectors we used for easy visualization.

If this rather involved discussion got us to appreciate one thing, it is this: The optimal separating hyperplane depends only on the dot products of the support vectors with each other; and the decision rule, which tells us whether a new data point $\mathbf{u}$ is classified as +1 or −1, depends only on the dot product of $\mathbf{u}$ with each support vector. So, if your dataset had 10,000 data points, but only ten of them were support vectors, you would need to worry about calculating only the mutual dot products of these ten vectors and the dot product of the new data point with each support vector. (This recap glosses over the elaborate optimization that's required to find the α_i for each support vector.)

Regardless, it's a rather extraordinary finding, and it falls out of the algorithm that Vapnik designed in 1964. It's the algorithm that Boser worked on at Bell Labs in the fall of 1991. He finished implementing and testing it for linearly separable datasets, but he still had time to kill before moving to Berkeley. Vapnik suggested that Boser try classifying linearly inseparable datasets by projecting the data into higher dimensions. Boser began thinking about it. The idea is that even though the data is linearly inseparable in its original, low-dimensional space, one can project it into some higher dimension, where it could potentially be linearly separable, and one could use the optimal margin classifier to find the higher-dimensional hyperplane. If you projected the hyperplane back into the low-dimensional space, it'd look like some nonlinear curve separating the data into clusters.

There are many ways to project data into higher-dimensional spaces. For our purposes, such projections come with two major concerns. One has to do with Vapnik's original algorithm, which requires taking mutual dot products of data samples. Let's say the original dataset was in ten dimensions. That would require taking dot products of ten-dimensional vectors. If this data is linearly inseparable in 10D space, and if it were to be projected into 1,000 dimensions, where the data cleanly clumped into two separable categories, then each data point would be represented by a 1,000-dimensional vector. The algorithm requires dot products of these extremely large vectors. As you go into higher and higher dimensions, searching for that optimal space where you can find a linearly separating hyperplane, the computational costs of calculating dot products can get prohibitively high.

The other concern has to do with the fact that sometimes one wants to project data into a space that has infinite dimensions. (We'll soon see how that's possible.) This has enormous advantages, because in an infinite-dimensional space, you can always find a separating hyperplane. But it isn't obvious how to compute dot products of vectors of infinite dimensions, let alone store such vectors in computer memory. How, then, do you find the hyperplane?

One morning, on their way to work together, Boser began

discussing his project with his wife, Isabelle Guyon, an ML expert whose mind had a much more mathematical bent. She also worked at Bell Labs. Guyon had thought a lot about such problems, especially for her Ph.D. thesis. She immediately suggested a solution that would bypass the need to compute dot products in the higher-dimensional space. It involved a neat trick, one whose history goes back to work by other Russian mathematicians in the 1960s. Guyon's insight, and her subsequent involvement in the project with Vapnik and Boser, led to one of the most successful ML algorithms ever invented.

THE KERNEL TRICK

In the early 1980s, Isabelle Guyon was a young engineering student in Paris, interested in cybernetics and looking for an internship. One of her professors, Gérard Dreyfus, who later became her dissertation advisor, told her to read a paper by a physicist named John Hopfield. The paper described a novel way of constructing neural networks that could be trained to store memories. These networks, which came to be called Hopfield networks (the subject of the next chapter) and were designed for storing memories, caused a flutter among neural network researchers. As an intern, Guyon began working on them and continued the research while doing her master's degree. She developed a more efficient method for training Hopfield networks and tried to use those networks to classify images of handwritten digits. But the peculiar nature of the networks made them rather ineffective at such classification tasks. Guyon moved on to other algorithms for pattern recognition. She picked up the "bible" of the field at the time, a book on pattern classification by Richard Duda and Peter Hart— we met Hart in chapter 5, as the co-inventor of the Cover-Hart k-nearest neighbor algorithm—and began implementing and benchmarking various pattern recognition algorithms.

Two ideas that Guyon encountered while obtaining her doctorate directly connect to her later work at Bell Labs. One was the idea
of optimal margin classifiers. Even as she built linear classifiers using Hopfield networks and other algorithms, Guyon became aware
of work by two physicists, Werner Krauth and Marc Mézard, who
were working nearby in Paris, at the École Normale Supérieure.
Krauth and Mézard had published a paper in 1987 showing how
to train a Hopfield network such that the network stored memories with minimum overlap. Their idea was, in a manner of speaking,
an algorithm for finding an optimal margin to separate two regions
of coordinate space. Their paper was published a year before Guyon
defended her Ph.D. thesis, for which she had tested numerous algorithms for linear classification—but none of these was an optimal
margin classifier, meaning the algorithms found some linear boundary, not necessarily the best one. Guyon could have used Krauth
and Mézard's algorithm to implement an optimal margin classifier; she didn't. "One of the examiners of my Ph.D. asked me why I
did not implement the algorithm of Mézard and Krauth and bench-
mark it against the other things I was trying. I said, 'Well, I didn't
think it would make that much of a difference,'" Guyon told me.
"But the reality is that I just wanted to graduate, and I didn't have
time."

So, when Bernhard Boser told Guyon about Vapnik's optimal
margin classifier, which he, Boser, had implemented in the fall of 1991,
it rang a bell. Vapnik's request that Boser push data that was linearly inseparable in lower dimensions into some higher dimensions
rang even louder bells. Guyon had come across such ideas while doing her Ph.D. One of the key papers she had studied on the subject
was written in 1964, by three Russian researchers, M. A. Aizerman,
E. M. Braverman, and L. I. Rozonoer, who had worked in the same
institute as Vapnik, but independently of him.

In their paper, the Russian trio, inspired by ideas in physics, had developed an algorithm that allowed Rosenblatt's perceptron to find nonlinear boundaries. We can cut to the chase and examine the essence of what they did, eschewing much of the contortions that imbue early works. Recall that Rosenblatt's perceptron algorithm works only when the data is linearly separable. Here's a simple dataset for which it wouldn't work:

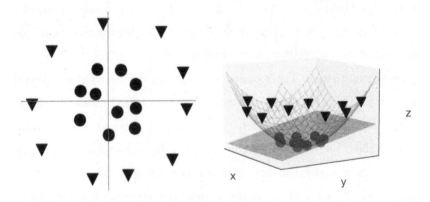

In the figure on the left, there's no way to draw a straight line, or a linearly separating hyperplane, to demarcate the circles from the triangles. But if we project these data into three dimensions in such a way that the triangles rise above the circles (the figure on the right), we can find such a separating hyperplane.

Here's one way to do it. Each original data point is two-dimensional, characterized by features $x1$ and $x2$ (the values along each of the two axes, in this case) and a label y, which can be either 1 (circles) or −1 (triangles). We can project these data into three dimensions by creating a third feature, $(x1^2 + x2^2)$, which can be plotted on the z-axis. So, now each data point in three dimensions is represented by $(x1, x2, x1^2 + x2^2)$, for the values along the x, y, and z axes. When plotted in 3D, the triangles rise above the circles; a perceptron can find the depicted hyperplane to separate the two.

For the problem we've just tackled, it wasn't very difficult to come up with a third feature to help separate the data into two clusters. But what if the 2D data look like this?

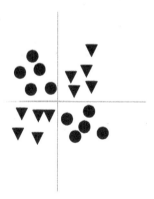

Now it's not immediately obvious what to choose for the third feature; $(x1^2 + x2^2)$ won't work. We need a more disciplined way to project data into higher dimensions. The method would have to work even if the lower-dimensional space were itself much higher than 2D (thus making it impossible for us to visualize). Also, once we project the data into higher dimensions, finding a linearly separating hyperplane in the augmented space involves taking the dot product of the higher-dimensional vectors, which can be computationally intractable. So, somehow, the algorithm needs to simultaneously do two things: (1) create new features such that the data can be mapped into some higher-dimensional space, and (2) avoid having to perform dot products in that new space and still be able to find the separating hyperplane.

Aizerman, Braverman, and Rozonoer showed just how to do that for the perceptron algorithm in their 1964 paper. In their reformulation of the algorithm, the weight vector characterizing the hyperplane is cast in terms of a linear combination of the vectors that make up the training dataset, and the decision rule to classify a data point depends only on the dot product of that data point with every other data point in the training dataset.

We'll explore the ideas put forth by Aizerman, Braverman, and Rozonoer but avoid using the exact mappings the trio used; instead, we'll use a mapping that was developed about a decade later, as it's simpler to understand. Let's start with data in two dimensions and map it into data in three dimensions, using three features. Given a vector $\mathbf{x}_j$ in the low-dimensional space (2D in our case), it gets mapped to the vector $\phi(\mathbf{x}_j)$ in the high-dimensional space (3D in our case).

$$\mathbf{x}_j \longrightarrow \phi(\mathbf{x}_j)$$

Our map goes like this: $[x1 \ x2] \rightarrow [x1^2 \ x2^2 \ \sqrt{2}x1x2]$

So, if a point $\mathbf{a}$ in 2D is given by $[a1 \ a2]$ and a point $\mathbf{b}$ is given by $[b1 \ b2]$, then the same points, when projected into 3D space, become $[a1^2 \ a2^2 \ \sqrt{2}a1a2]$ and $[b1^2 \ b2^2 \ \sqrt{2}b1b2]$.

To find a linearly separating hyperplane, we'd have to take dot products of vectors in the higher-dimensional space. In this toy example, it's no skin off our backs to perform dot products of all the vectors in the 3D space. But in the real world, the dimensionality of the augmented space can be humungous, making the computation far too resource-intensive (in terms of time and memory requirements). But Aizerman, Braverman, and Rozonoer showed us a cool trick that avoids this complication altogether.

To restate, to find the linearly separating hyperplane in the higher-dimensional space, we have to calculate dot products of $\phi(\mathbf{x}_j)$ with $\phi(\mathbf{x}_i)$, for all combinations of i and j.

What if we could do calculations with the two lower-dimensional vectors, $\mathbf{x}_i$ and $\mathbf{x}_j$, that gave us the same answer as the dot product of the corresponding vectors in the higher-dimensional space? What if we could find a function K, such that:

$$K(\mathbf{x}_i, \mathbf{x}_j) \rightarrow \phi(\mathbf{x}_i) \cdot \phi(\mathbf{x}_j)$$

In other words, if we were to pass the two low-dimensional vectors to the function K, then the function should output a value that equals the dot product of the augmented vectors in the higher-dimensional space. Let's look at a concrete example of the vectors **a** and **b**:

$$\mathbf{a} = [a1 \ a2]$$

$$\mathbf{b} = [b1 \ b2]$$

$$\phi(\mathbf{a}) = \left[a1^2 \ a2^2 \ \sqrt{2}a1a2\right]$$

$$\phi(\mathbf{b}) = \left[b1^2 \ b2^2 \ \sqrt{2}b1b2\right]$$

$$\phi(\mathbf{a}).\phi(\mathbf{b}) = \left[a1^2 \ a2^2 \ \sqrt{2}a1a2\right] \cdot \left[b1^2 \ b2^2 \ \sqrt{2}b1b2\right]$$

$$= (a1^2 b1^2 + a2^2 b2^2 + 2a1a2b1b2)$$

We need a function K, which produces the same output. Here's one such function:

$$K(\mathbf{x}, \mathbf{y}) = (\mathbf{x}.\mathbf{y})^2$$

Feed this function the two lower-dimensional vectors, **a** and **b**, and see what happens:

$$K(\mathbf{a}, \mathbf{b}) = (\mathbf{a}.\mathbf{b})^2$$

$$= ([a1 \ a2].[b1 \ b2])^2$$

$$= (a1b1 + a2b2)^2$$

$$= (a1^2 b1^2 + a2^2 b2^2 + 2a1a2b1b2)$$

So, $K(\mathbf{a}, \mathbf{b}) = \phi(\mathbf{a}).\phi(\mathbf{b})$

This is stupendous. Because we have been toying with 2D and 3D spaces, the import of this may not be obvious. Let's, for a moment, imagine that $\mathbf{a}$ and $\mathbf{b}$ are 100-dimensional vectors and that $\phi(\mathbf{a})$ and $\phi(\mathbf{b})$ are million-dimensional. If we can find the appropriate mapping of $\mathbf{x}_j \rightarrow \phi(\mathbf{x}_j)$, such that $K(\mathbf{x}_i, \mathbf{x}_j) \rightarrow \phi(\mathbf{x}_i).\phi(\mathbf{x}_j)$, then we will be in a position to calculate the dot products of the high-dimensional vectors without ever stepping into that million-dimensional space; we can compute in one hundred dimensions.

The function K is called a kernel function. The method of using a kernel function to compute dot products in some higher-dimensional space, without ever morphing each lower-dimensional vector into its monstrously large counterpart, is called the kernel trick. It's one neat trick.

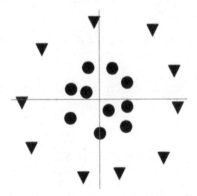

We can visualize the "kernelized" perceptron algorithm, using the mapping we've just analyzed. Let's start with circles and triangles that are linearly inseparable in two dimensions (see above). Each data point is projected into three dimensions, and then the perceptron algorithm is used to find a linearly separating hyperplane. The figure opposite shows what happens in three dimensions.

You can see that two types of data points are clearly separated in

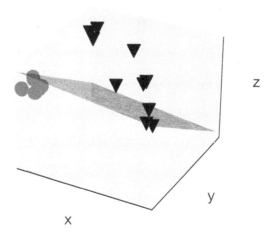

3D, allowing the algorithm to find a plane (in this case, any plane) that separates the circles from the triangles. Now, given any new data point in 2D, we can project it into 3D space and classify it as a circle or a triangle, depending on its position relative to the hyperplane. When this delineated 3D space is projected back into the original 2D space, we get a nonlinear boundary that separates the circles from the triangles (see figure, next page).

Guyon had played around with kernels during her Ph.D. thesis, and she did so even after she started working. In particular, she had been using something called a polynomial kernel, introduced by MIT computational neuroscientist Tomaso Poggio in 1975. Here's the general form of the polynomial kernel:

$$K(\mathbf{x}, \mathbf{y}) = (c + \mathbf{x}.\mathbf{y})^d, \text{ where } c \text{ and } d \text{ are constants}$$

If you choose the constants to be 0 and 2 for c and d, respectively, you'll get back the kernel we just used for the perceptron algorithm:

$$K(\mathbf{x}, \mathbf{y}) = (\mathbf{x}.\mathbf{y})^2$$

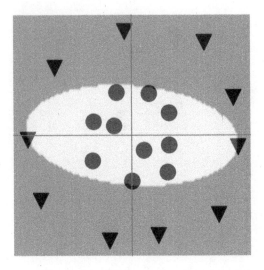

Let's play around with one more variation, where the constants are 1 and 2, to get a better sense of why this works.

$$K(\mathbf{x}, \mathbf{y}) = (1 + \mathbf{x}.\mathbf{y})^2$$

For 2D data points:

$$\mathbf{a} = [a1 \ a2]$$

$$\mathbf{b} = [b1 \ b2]$$

We have:

$$K(\mathbf{a}, \mathbf{b}) = (1 + [a1 \ a2].[b1 \ b2])^2$$

$$= (1 + a1b1 + a2b2)^2$$

$$= 1 + (a1b1 + a2b2)^2 + 2(a1b1 + a2b2)$$

$$= 1 + a1^2 \ b1^2 + a2^2 \ b2^2 + 2a1a2b1b2 + 2a1b1 + 2a2b2$$

The question now is this: What should the mapping $\mathbf{x}_j \rightarrow \phi(\mathbf{x}_j)$ be, such that:

$$K(\mathbf{x}_i, \mathbf{x}_j) \rightarrow \phi(\mathbf{x}_i) \cdot \phi(\mathbf{x}_j)$$

With a little bit of fiddling around, we can discover the mapping. (Don't worry if it's not immediately obvious. This is not trivial; in fact, finding such mappings is quite the art.)

$$\mathbf{x}_j \rightarrow \phi(\mathbf{x}_j)$$

$$\Rightarrow \left[x1 \; x2\right] = \left[1, x1^2, x2^2, \sqrt{2}x1x2, \sqrt{2}x1, \sqrt{2}x2\right]$$

(I have added commas to separate the elements of the larger vector, just for clarity; normally, one wouldn't use commas.)

So:

$$\mathbf{a} = \left[a1, a2\right] \rightarrow \left[1, a1^2, a2^2, \sqrt{2}a1a2, \sqrt{2}a1, \sqrt{2}a2\right]$$

$$\mathbf{b} = \left[b1, b2\right] \rightarrow \left[1, b1^2, b2^2, \sqrt{2}b1b2, \sqrt{2}b1, \sqrt{2}b2\right]$$

We have the 2D coordinates, or vectors, $\mathbf{a}$ and $\mathbf{b}$ transformed into their 6D counterparts, $\phi(\mathbf{a})$ and $\phi(\mathbf{b})$. The question is: Does $\phi(\mathbf{a}) \cdot \phi(\mathbf{b})$, evaluated in the 6D space, give the same result as the kernel function operating on $\mathbf{a}$ and $\mathbf{b}$ in 2D space? Let's check:

$$\phi(\mathbf{a}) \cdot \phi(\mathbf{b}) = \left[1, a1^2, a2^2, \sqrt{2}a1a2, \sqrt{2}a1, \sqrt{2}a2\right]$$

$$\cdot \left[1, b1^2, b2^2, \sqrt{2}b1b2, \sqrt{2}b1, \sqrt{2}b2\right]$$

$$= 1 + a1^2 b1^2 + a2^2 b2^2 + 2a1a2b1b2 + 2a1b1 + 2a2b2$$

$$= K(\mathbf{a}, \mathbf{b})$$

Voilà! They are the same. So, the kernel function lets us calculate the dot product of 6D vectors, but we never have to formulate those vectors, or compute, in 6D space. For our polynomial kernel, we used the constant values of 1 and 2. You can verify that the kernel function works for any value of the constants, and so we can project the data into ever-higher dimensions, where we are more and more likely to find a linearly separating hyperplane.

(An aside: The size of the higher-dimensional space is given by $\binom{n+d}{d} = \frac{(n+d)!}{d!\,n!}$; n is the size of the original, low-dimensional space, and d is the value of the constant used in the polynomial kernel. Another aside: Why is it so important to work with linear classifiers or to do linear regression?)

Guyon knew of these kernels, but she hadn't connected the dots between optimal margin classifiers that worked with linearly separable data and linear classifiers, like the perceptron algorithm, that could use the kernel trick to do their magic in higher dimensions. That would have to wait until 1991, when her husband told her about Vapnik's idea of pushing data into higher dimensions by creating new features and building an optimal margin classifier in the high-D space. These features could be generated by multiplying individual features, for example:

$$\mathbf{x}_j \longrightarrow \phi(\mathbf{x}_j)$$

From 2D to 3D: $[x1\ x2] = [x1\ x2\ x1x2]$
Or, from 3D to 7D:

$$[x1\ x2\ x3] = [x1\ x2\ x3\ x1x2\ x1x3\ x2x3\ x1x2x3]$$

Vapnik wanted Bernhard Boser to implement the algorithm by creating new features in this manner and then explicitly do the dot products in the higher-dimensional space. When Boser mentioned this to Guyon that morning on their way to work, she immediately saw the futility of such an algorithm. "I told Bernhard, there's no point in making these [dot] products of features," she said. "Let's use the kernel trick." She explained the trick to her husband and then quickly rewrote Vapnik's optimal margin algorithm to use a kernel. "I rewrote it in a way that made it apparent how to kernelize it. Everywhere there was a dot product [in higher dimensions], I replaced it by a kernel. Once you see that, it's trivial," she said.

We saw earlier that the hyperplane found using a kernel and then projected back into two dimensions might look like this:

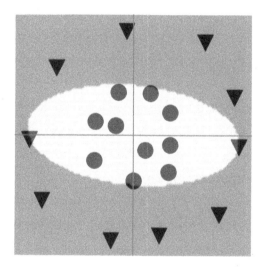

Even a cursory visual inspection suggests that the boundary is too close to the circles, and it'd be easy to misclassify a new point as a triangle when in fact it is a circle. The solution would be to use an optimal margin classifier in the higher dimensions, rather than a perceptron. The algorithm would find support vectors in the higher dimensions and the appropriate hyperplane running through the middle of no-one's-land. Projected back to 2D, you'd get this new boundary:

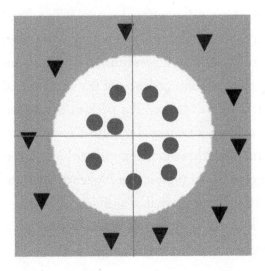

Now the chances of correctly classifying new data points are higher compared with those for the perceptron's sub-optimal decision boundary.

Initially, Guyon and Vapnik argued over whether the kernel trick was important. Boser, meanwhile, was more practical. "This was a very simple change to the code. So, I just implemented it, while [they] were still arguing," Boser told me.

Guyon then showed Vapnik a footnote from the Duda and Hart book on pattern classification. It referred to the kernel trick and to the work of mathematicians Richard Courant and David Hilbert, giants in their fields. According to Guyon, this convinced Vapnik. "He said, 'Oh, wow, this is something big,'" Guyon said.

The reference to Hilbert is particularly enticing. So-called Hilbert spaces allow for infinite-dimensional vectors. There's a kernel, called the radial basis function (RBF) kernel, that equates $K(\mathbf{a}, \mathbf{b})$ with the dot product of two corresponding high-dimensional vectors $\phi(\mathbf{a})$ and $\phi(\mathbf{b})$, even though it's impossible to do the mapping from the low-dimensional vector to the high-dimensional space ($\mathbf{a} \longrightarrow \phi(\mathbf{a})$, for example). That's because the higher-dimensional space is infinite.

And yet, one can calculate $K(\mathbf{a}, \mathbf{b})$. The import of this is rather stunning: Given some simple assumptions about the dataset, it's possible to turn the problem, regardless of the complexity of the decision boundary in lower dimensions, into a linearly separable problem in infinite dimensions. For the curious, here's the kernel function:

$$K(\mathbf{a}, \mathbf{b}) = \exp\left(-\gamma \|\mathbf{a} \quad \mathbf{b}\|^2\right), \text{ where } \gamma > 0$$

The RBF kernel is the "Brad Pitt of kernels," Weinberger joked in his lectures on machine learning. It's so perfect, "people sometimes faint when they see it."

Understanding Weinberger's paean to the RBF kernel demands a segue into decision boundaries. A decision boundary through some coordinate space (such as 2D or 3D) can be thought of as a function. For example, the nonlinear decision boundary we found earlier, using the kernelized perceptron algorithm, is equivalent to finding a function that takes in two values, $x1$ and $x2$, and helps us draw a curve that resembles the decision boundary. These boundaries can be extremely complex, especially when the input space itself is considerably higher dimensional than the two or three we have been visualizing and when the two classes of data are way more mixed than we have seen thus far. An RBF kernel, because it can help an algorithm *always* find a linearly separable hyperplane in some infinite-dimensional space, can find *any* decision boundary, or function, when mapped to the lower-dimensional space, no matter how complex. It's said to be a "universal function approximator." Keep this phrase in mind, for we'll devote an entire chapter to it when we discuss how certain types of artificial neural networks are also universal function approximators; given enough neurons, they can solve any problem.

The combination of Vapnik's 1964 optimal margin classifier and the kernel trick proved incredibly powerful. No dataset was off-limits now. It didn't matter how intermingled the different classes of data were in the original low-dimensional space. One could project the data into extremely high dimensions and then use the optimal margin classifier to find the best linearly separating hyperplane, but do so using the kernel function, and thus avoid ever having to compute in the high-dimensional space.

Boser did most of the work implementing and testing the algorithm, particularly on the favorite dataset of the time: the Modified National Institute of Standards and Technology (MNIST) database of handwritten digits. Meanwhile, Guyon took it upon herself to write a paper to be submitted to the annual Computational Learning Theory (COLT) conference. Her colleagues and friends at Bell Labs, particularly Esther Levin and Sara Solla, had written papers for this prestigious conference. "It was kind of thought [that] if you have a paper in COLT, you are a real machine learning person, because it's a hard-core theory conference," Guyon said.

Guyon and Boser went to meet the COLT conference organizers, Manfred Warmuth and David Haussler. "We asked them whether they thought it was a paper that would fit into that conference. We gave a talk, and then they told us, 'Oh, yeah, we like application papers.' For us, it was the most theoretical work that we ever did, and for them, it was an application paper," Guyon told me, laughing at the memory.

Warmuth recalled being approached by Guyon and Boser. He and Haussler were fascinated by the simplicity of the technique and "of course by the KERNEL TRICK!!!" Warmuth wrote me in an email. They accepted the paper, titled "A Training Algorithm for Optimal Margin Classifiers," and it appeared in July 1992 in the *Proceedings of the Fifth Annual Workshop on Computational Learning Theory*.

It took a decade, but the paper eventually became a classic. Meanwhile, others at Bell Labs furthered the work. Kristin Bennett's

Ph.D. work on mathematical programming, which refers to the use of mathematical models to solve problems, in this case ML problems, inspired Vapnik and Corinna Cortes, a Danish data scientist who was then at Bell Labs and is now a VP at Google Research, to develop what they called a "soft-margin" classifier. This approach, published in 1995, made allowances for problematic data points that would otherwise have made it impossible to find a linearly separating hyperplane, even in the higher-dimensional space.

Vapnik and Cortes called their algorithm the support vector network. Bernhard Schölkopf, a German computer scientist, who is now the director of the Max Planck Institute for Intelligent Systems, in Tübingen, Germany, renamed it by coining the term "support vector machine," helping distinguish the algorithm from neural networks. Thus did "support vector machine" (SVM) enter the lexicon of machine learning.

With the math behind us, it's rather simple to recap what SVMs do: They take datasets that are linearly inseparable in their original, relatively low-dimensional space and project these data into high enough dimensions to find an optimal linearly separating hyperplane, but the calculations for finding the hyperplane rely on kernel functions that keep the algorithm firmly anchored in the more computationally tractable lower-dimensional space. Support vectors, we saw, refer to those data points that lie on the margins of no-one's-land. The technique doesn't find any old hyperplane in the higher dimensions; it finds an optimal one. When projected back to lower dimensions, this hyperplane can resemble a very convoluted but nonetheless optimal decision boundary.

SVMs took off, becoming the darlings of the ML community through much of the 1990s and 2000s. While Guyon had been instrumental in redesigning Vapnik's optimum margin classifier to incorporate the kernel trick, she credits Vapnik for recognizing the power of kernelized SVMs and for making sure the wider community understood it. "I didn't really recognize that this was an important invention," she said. "For me it was just a trick, a computational trick, and it was giving very nice results."

Given Vapnik's evangelism, it's only relatively recently that the broader ML community acknowledged Guyon and Boser, whose contributions had been somewhat overshadowed, as it were, by Vapnik's stature. Even without SVMs, Vapnik had contributed heavily to the theory of machine learning. "Manfred [Warmuth] and I gave Vapnik a kind of superstar status from the beginning," David Haussler wrote me in an email. Haussler and Warmuth had coined the term "Vapnik-Chervonenkis (VC) dimension," which uses math developed by Vapnik and fellow mathematician Alexey Chervonenkis to provide a measure of an ML model's capacity to classify data correctly. "After that, with the help of AT&T Bell Labs, where he was treated as the ultimate guru, there emerged a narrative that Vapnik was the true genius behind the emerging revolution in machine learning. I know he personally felt a bit overwhelmed by it," Haussler wrote in his email.

As far as SVMs go, this storyline is changing. In 2020, the BBVA Foundation gave its Frontiers of Knowledge Award to Isabelle Guyon, Bernhard Schölkopf, and Vladimir Vapnik; to Guyon and Vapnik for inventing support vector machines and to Schölkopf for furthering their power with the use of kernel methods. "The human tendency [is] to adopt a simple narrative with a single hero when in fact the reality is quite a bit more complex," Haussler wrote to me.

The BBVA Foundation's citation goes on to say, "Thanks to SVM and kernel methods, intelligent machines can now be trained to classify datasets with human precision, or at times even better, enabling them to recognize everything from voices, handwriting or faces to cancer cells or the fraudulent use of credit cards. SVMs are now being used in genomics, cancer research, neurology, diagnostic imaging, and even in HIV drug cocktail optimization, as well as finding diverse applications in climate research, geophysics and astrophysics."

As we'll see in upcoming chapters, with the thawing of the first AI winter, research in artificial neural networks began burgeoning in the 1980s. But the abrupt arrival of SVMs and kernel methods in 1992 derailed the advance of neural networks for a while. "It's like Vapnik took a big beam of light and showed it to everybody: 'Look, there is this opportunity of applying this kernel trick,'" Guyon said. And then Schölkopf and his colleague Alex Smola wrote a comprehensive book on kernel methods, illustrating much of what one could do with the kernel trick. "And that was it," Guyon said. "It was incredible. Neural networks dominated machine learning in the eighties. And in the nineties, all of a sudden, everybody switched to kernel methods."

Now neural networks are dominating modern machine learning again. Intriguingly, theoretical advances are beginning to show tantalizing links between neural networks and kernel machines. To appreciate this connection, we need to step back a decade or so, to the early 1980s, when the ML community started paying serious attention to neural networks—thanks to the work of John Hopfield, whose eponymous networks inspired Guyon's foray into machine learning. Hopfield, a physicist, was at a crossroads in his career and was looking to work on something big. He could not have imagined the changes he would inspire.

CHAPTER 8

With a Little Help from Physics

In the late 1970s, Princeton University physicist John Hopfield faced a familiar career question: "Now what?" He was looking for a new research direction. The dilemma wasn't new for him. Hopfield had spent the 1960s making seminal contributions to solid-state and condensed matter physics. But by the end of that decade, he had run out of steam. He couldn't find interesting problems to which to apply his "particular talents." So, he turned to biology, focusing on cellular biochemical reactions, such as those involved in the synthesis of proteins. Hopfield looked at transfer RNA, or tRNA, molecules that "recognize" the correct amino acids and bring them to the site of protein synthesis in cells. Every aspect of life depends upon this process proceeding without errors. But given how error-prone biological processes can be, how does biology get it right? Biochemists, at the time, tended to think of a process as simply going from step A to B to C. Hopfield realized that there were multiple pathways from A to C and that the ability to take one of many pathways was necessary for reducing errors, allowing the system to proofread, as it were. "You can't make things error-free enough to work if you don't proofread, because the [biological] hardware isn't nearly perfect enough," Hopfield told me.

Hopfield published his "biology" paper in 1974. "This was the first paper I had ever written containing words like 'nucleoside' or 'synthetase' or 'isoleucine' or even 'GTP,'" he would later write. In 1976, Hopfield gave a talk at Harvard about his ideas on proofreading and predicted what biochemists should see for certain reactions in terms of the quantities and ratios of molecules. As far as he was concerned, these were theoretical predictions and yet to be corroborated by experiments. After the talk, a scientist in the audience told Hopfield that he had seen such "stoichiometry" ratios in his studies of bacteria. Researchers had found that the antibiotic streptomycin interferes with the bacteria's ability to proofread; as a result, the bacteria synthesize numerous erroneous and functionally lethal proteins, causing them to die. Hopfield was elated at the empirical validation of his theoretical work. "It was one of the biggest—and most delightful—surprises of my scientific career," he wrote.

That momentous occasion aside, this foray into biology set the stage for another of Hopfield's fundamental contributions, this time in computational neuroscience—or, to take a broader view of it, in machine learning and AI. The 1974 paper was a clear elucidation of the idea that networks of reactions (in this case, consisting of multiple molecular pathways from the same starting point to the same end point) had functions that went beyond what could be understood by looking at individual molecules. "A network could 'solve a problem' or have a function that was beyond the capability of a single molecule and a linear pathway," Hopfield wrote. "Six years later I was generalizing this view in thinking about networks of neurons rather than the properties of a single neuron."

But before he could embark on this work, Hopfield had to identify a "PROBLEM" to work on (the all caps being his way of emphasizing that the problem had to be substantial). This took a while. A chance invitation to attend semi-annual meetings of the Neuroscience Research Program at MIT, about five hours northeast from Princeton, gave Hopfield the necessary stimulus. "How mind emerges from brain is to me the deepest question posed by our humanity. Definitely A PROBLEM," he wrote. It became clear to him, while he was attending those meetings, that the work the neuroscientists were doing—"primate neuroanatomy, insect flight behavior, electrophysiology in aplasia, learning in rat hippocampus, Alzheimer's disease, potassium channels, human language processing"—was exploring their own special corners of the field. Hopfield was after something more integrative, something that required the tools of his trade: theoretical physics. Specifically, he was searching for a basic and potentially far-reaching insight into how the brain computes.

A machine computes by changing configurations from one "state" to another (according to some prescribed rules specified, say, by a programmer), until eventually the machine reaches an end state. The end state represents a solution that can be read off. A computer, then, is a dynamical system, one whose behavior can be seen as evolving, or transitioning from state to state, with each tick of the clock, with rules that specify the state transitions and the set of allowable states, the so-called state space. "I'd seen enough [at the NRP meetings] to understand that if you could describe the equations of how neural activity propagated from one neuron to another, you had a dynamical system," Hopfield told me. "All computers are dynamical systems. There had to be this link between neurobiology and digital or analog computers."

Also, Hopfield's work on proofreading in biochemical processes was evidence that dynamical systems that could take multiple pathways through the state space to "converge" to the same final state could reduce the errors that accumulate during computation. Hopfield kept looking for a neurobiological problem that was amenable to such a solution. He finally hit upon one: associative memory. The term may be cryptic to most of us, but it's something with which we are intuitively familiar. Think about how the strains of a song or the hint of an aroma can bring to mind an entire episode from our lives. Our brains are somehow able to use a fragment of the original experience to bring into conscious awareness an entire stored memory. Well, that's associative memory. Hopfield was after a computational model of the same. Could a network of artificial neurons that had stored within them some memories be capable of retrieving a particular memory given only some sliver of it? Could he solve the problem in terms of the dynamics of the network converging to a solution? "It took me quite a while to find any problem in neuroscience which looked like that computation, and I finally realized associative memory did," Hopfield said.

Understanding the essence of such a computation requires delving into physics, this time the physics of ferromagnetism and a simplified mathematical model of it. The parallels to computing with neurons are striking.

FLIP-FLOP

Some simple math connects phenomena as seemingly diverse as the process that gives us window glass, the magnetization of materials, and the workings of some types of neural networks, at least the artificial kind.

Let's start with window glass. One method for making such glass is to start with the raw materials—usually silica (sand), soda ash, and limestone, with silica being the primary component. The mixture is melted to form molten glass and then poured into a "float bath." The bath gives plate glass its flatness and helps cool the molten material from temperatures of over 1,000°C down to about 600°C. This flat material is further "annealed," a process that releases any accumulated stresses in the glass. The key, for our purposes, is that the resulting glass is neither a solid with an ordered crystalline structure nor a liquid. Instead, it's an amorphous solid where the material's atoms and molecules don't conform to the regularity of a crystal lattice.

There's an interesting analog in magnetism. Certain materials, for example, are ferromagnetic, a state in which the magnetic moments of the material's atoms (or ions) are all aligned, generating a net magnetism. A ferromagnet is analogous to a solid with a definite crystalline structure. However, if the magnetic moments of the atoms, or ions, are randomly oriented, the material has no permanent magnetism—analogous to the structure of glass. Each individual magnetic moment is the outcome of the spin of an elementary particle in the material. Hence, materials with disordered magnetic moments are called spin glasses.

In the early 1920s, the German physicist Wilhelm Lenz and his graduate student Ernst Ising developed a simple model of such materials. It came to be called the Ising model. For his doctoral thesis, Ising analyzed a one-dimensional case of magnetic moments. The engendering spins can be either up ($+1$) or down (-1). In the model, any given spin state is influenced only by its immediate neighbors. For example, if one spin state is -1, but both its neighbors are $+1$, then the spin will flip directions. It's clear that such a system will have some dynamics, because as each spin state reacts to its nearest neighbors, the effects of spin flips will ripple back and forth through the system. If all the spins taken together constitute the system's state, then the system traverses a state space, going from one state to another, possibly settling into some stable state or continually oscillating. Ising showed that a 1D system cannot be ferromagnetic (meaning, the spins will never all align in one direction). He even argued—erroneously, it turned out—that state transitions from disorderly to orderly would not happen even in the three-dimensional case.

In 1936, Rudolf Ernst Peierls, a German physicist who left Germany during the Nazi era and became a British citizen, rigorously studied the model for the 2D case. (It was Peierls who attributed the model to Ising, giving it its name.) "For sufficiently low temperatures the Ising model in two dimensions shows ferromagnetism and the same holds *a fortiori* also for the three-dimensional model," Peierls wrote. (I had to look up "a fortiori." As per the Oxford English Dictionary, it means "used to express a conclusion for which there is stronger evidence than for one previously accepted.")

Here's how a 2D model of spins, or magnetic moments, might look:

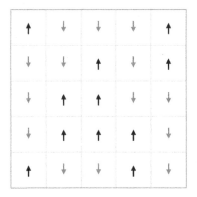

The black "UP" arrows are assigned a value of +1, and the gray "DOWN" arrows are assigned −1. What's shown could be the state of a 2D system at some instant in time. Except for the arrows along the edges of the square, each arrow has four nearest neighbors (left and right and up and down; the diagonals are ignored):

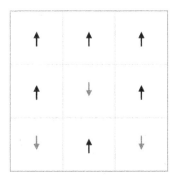

Given a certain state of the system, each spin is going to be influenced by one of two things: some external magnetic field and the magnetic fields induced by its nearest neighbors. The latter, in turn, depend on the strength of the interaction between two spins—for example, the closer they are in the material's lattice, the stronger the interaction—and on whether the material is ferromagnetic or anti-ferromagnetic. (In ferromagnetic material, the spins align with their nearest neighbors; in anti-ferromagnetic material, the spins prefer to be in opposition.)

Let's stick to ferromagnetic materials. From the perspective of a physicist, the question that comes to mind is this: Why should a ferromagnetic material that has disordered spins in its lattice end up in a state where all the spins are aligned in one direction, creating macroscopic magnetism? To answer this question, we have to look to something called the Hamiltonian, an equation that allows one to calculate the total energy of a system. (Yes, the equation is named after the mathematical graffiti artist we met in chapter 2, William Rowan Hamilton.)

Let's say that σ_i gives us the value for the spin of the ith element in a 2D system: It's either $+1$ or -1. There are many ways to write down the Hamiltonian of a system (depending on the assumptions one makes). Here's one:

$$H = -\sum_i \sum_{j, i \neq j} J\sigma_i\sigma_j - \sum_j h\sigma_j$$

The first term in the equation involves taking each pair of nearest neighbors in the lattice, multiplying their spins, multiplying the result with some constant J that denotes the strength of the interaction between two adjacent spins, and then adding up the result for all such pairs. The double-sigma notation $\sum_i \sum_{j, i \neq j}$ means sum over all adjacent pairs of spins, except for when $i=j$. (As an aside, if the no-tation simply says $\sum_i \sum_j$, then we sum over all adjacent pairs, even when $i=j$.)

The second term of the Hamiltonian takes each spin and multi-plies it by some external magnetic field, h, and sums the result for all spins. If there's no external field, then this term is zero.

Note that each term is preceded by a minus sign. This has the following physical significance: If two adjacent spins have the same direction $(+1, +1)$ or $(-1, -1)$, their product will be positive. So, prefixing a minus sign makes the whole term negative. This causes the Hamiltonian, and hence the system's energy, to decrease in value. However, if two adjacent spins have opposing values, their product will be negative, and taking the negative of that term results in a positive value, raising the energy. So, if two spins are aligned, they lower the energy of the system; if they are in opposition, they raise it. Even this cursory analysis tells us that if all the spins were to be aligned, the energy of the system would reach a minimum.

This should ring a bell. (Think back to gradient descent and reaching the bottom of a bowl.) Physical systems prefer configura-tions of lower, rather than higher, energy. In the Hamiltonian de-scribed above, if the constant $J > 0$, the material is a ferromagnet; if $J < 0$, it's anti-ferromagnetic, and if J_{ij} is random, thus signifying a different J for each pair of spins, then the material is a spin glass.

Given his work in condensed matter and solid-state physics, Hop-field knew something about spin glasses. Also, he had identified the neurobiological "PROBLEM" he wanted to address: How does a neu-ral network recover a stored memory based on partial information? The Ising model was almost tailor-made to describe the simple neu-ral network he had in mind. By making one more important as-sumption about how the artificial neurons were connected to each other (and we'll come to the details), Hopfield could design a network whose dynamics ensured that storing or retrieving the memory was akin to putting the ensemble of neurons, and hence the network, into some stable low-energy state. This state was characterized by the strengths of the connections, or the weights, between the neurons. If you were to read off the outputs of the neurons in this stable state, they would be representative of some memory. Then, if you were to perturb the system by changing some inputs to the neurons, and hence their outputs, this would constitute a partial disruption of memory. If you read off the outputs of neurons now, they would represent distorted memory. But this perturbation would put the system into some high-energy state, and the network would dynamically find its way to the stable state. Because that low-energy, stable state represents the memory, then that memory could be retrieved. The dynamical process restores the memory.

The math of how this happens is our first foray into modern neural networks. To get there, we have to harken back to the first artificial neuron, designed in the 1940s, which we encountered in chapter 1, the McCulloch-Pitts (MCP) neuron.

NEURAL NETWORKS: THE REVIVAL BEGINS

John Hopfield was among the few researchers who did not give up on neural networks, despite the blow dealt to the field by Marvin Minsky and Seymour Papert in their 1969 book, *Perceptrons*. (We'll meet other researchers in subsequent chapters, in particular Geoff Hinton and Yann LeCun, who also kept the faith.) Recall that Frank Rosenblatt and others had shown, using the perceptron convergence theorem, that the perceptron will always find a linearly separating hyperplane if the dataset can be cleanly divided into two categories. Teaching the perceptron using training data involves finding the correct set of weights for the perceptron's inputs. However, this algorithm works only for a single-layer perceptron (meaning, you have to provide inputs to a perceptron and read off its output; you cannot feed the output of one perceptron as input to another). Minsky and Papert proved mathematically—and elegantly so—that single-layer perceptrons are ineffective when the data are not linearly separable in some given set of dimensions. They then conjectured that while multi-layer perceptrons, where the output of one layer becomes an input to the next, could solve such problems, there was likely no way to train such networks.

"Minsky didn't see how to do learning in multi-layer networks and surmised that perhaps multi-layer networks couldn't actually do anything that single-layer networks couldn't. Once the convergence theorem on single-layer networks was done and one understood what [such] networks could or couldn't do, that was sort of the end of the subject," Hopfield told me. "Minsky had missed the point."

Many others hadn't. In the 1970s, researchers were beginning to probe how to train multi-layer perceptrons (or multi-layer neural networks). The outline of an algorithm that would soon be called backpropagation, or backprop, was taking shape. But the computing power in those days wasn't up to the task. "Nobody could do backprop on any interesting problem in [the 1970s]. You couldn't possibly develop backprop empirically," Hopfield said.

This was the state of affairs when Hopfield entered the field, as he tried to answer his own question: "What next?" He started with an artificial neuron that was part Rosenblatt's perceptron and part the McCulloch-Pitts neuron.

Consider a neuron that has two inputs, $x1$ and $x2$. In Hopfield's version, the inputs are restricted to bipolar values of 1 or −1 (an unfortunate nomenclature, given the import of the word "bipolar" in psychiatry and psychology). Each input is multiplied by its

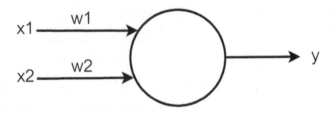

corresponding weight, *x1* by *w1*, and *x2* by *w2*. The weighted inputs are then summed, to give us: *w1x1 + w2x2*.

If the weighted sum is greater than 0, then the neuron outputs a 1 (so, $y = 1$). Otherwise, it outputs a −1 ($y = -1$).

Normally, there's an extra bias term; we saw this in chapter 1. So, the output of the neuron will be +1 if *w1x1 + w2x2 + b* > 0; and −1 otherwise. But for the analysis that follows in this chapter, we will ignore the bias term without losing any generality.

Here's the formal equation for the neuron's output:

$$y = \begin{cases} +1 \text{ if } w1x1 + w2x2 > 0 \\ -1 \text{ if } w1x1 + w2x2 \leq 0 \end{cases}$$

That's it; that's our neuron. Hopfield's next intuition was to create networks of neurons bi-directionally connected to each other. In other words, if the output of neuron A goes as input to neuron B, then the output of neuron B forms an input to neuron A. Let's analyze a simple two-neuron network (see figure, next page).

The output of neuron 1, *y1*, becomes the input to neuron 2. And the output of neuron 2, *y2*, becomes the input to neuron 1. And each input is multiplied by its corresponding weight: *w12y2* for the output of neuron 2 serving as input to neuron 1; and *w21y1* for the output of neuron 1 serving as input to neuron 2.

The weights have a numbering that tells us the direction of the

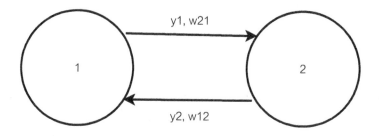

input: $w21$ means the signal is going from neuron 1 to neuron 2; $w12$ signifies the signal is going from neuron 2 to neuron 1. Let's take a moment to grasp what's happening here. The neurons have no other input except what's coming from other neurons in the network. Also, note that a neuron doesn't talk to itself, meaning the output of neuron 1 doesn't become an input to itself.

This means that the outputs of neurons 1 and 2 are:

$$y1 = \begin{cases} +1 \text{ if } w12\,y2 > 0 \\ -1 \text{ if } w12\,y2 \leq 0 \end{cases}$$

$$y2 = \begin{cases} +1 \text{ if } w21\,y1 > 0 \\ -1 \text{ if } w21\,y1 \leq 0 \end{cases}$$

Two neurons don't really make much of a network, and also, they're not enough to get a sense of the succinct mathematical formalism that can be used to describe such networks. Consider a network with three neurons (see figure, next page).

Now we can write these equations for each neuron:

$w12y2 + w13y3$: the weighted sum, or the output, of neuron 1
$w21y1 + w23y3$: the weighted sum, or the output, of neuron 2
$w31y1 + w32y2$: the weighted sum, or the output, of neuron 3

This weighted sum of the inputs to each neuron, i, can be compactly described as follows. (Note the "." between the terms wij

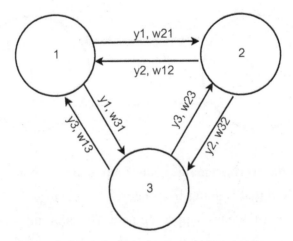

and yj returns, for clarity's sake; it's not the dot product; rather it's just two scalars being multiplied.)

$$\sum_{j,i\neq j} wij.yj$$

This is a summation over all j, except for when $i{=}j$ (to prevent each neuron from influencing itself). For each neuron, if its weighted sum is greater than 0, the output of the neuron is 1; or else it's −1. Succinctly, the output of the ith neuron is:

$$yi = \begin{cases} +1 \text{ if } \sum_{j,i\neq j} wij.yj > 0 \\ -1 \text{ if } \sum_{j,i\neq j} wij.yj \leq 0 \end{cases}$$

This compact formula describes a network with any number of neurons, in which the neurons are connected to one another. Can you see the similarities with the Ising model of magnetism? Let's say that you have 100 neurons, and each neuron's output is randomly set to either +1 or −1. What happens next? Think about a spin glass, in which the magnetic moments in a material are randomly ordered.

Each magnetic moment is going to react to its nearest neighbors and flip or not flip. In our network, something similar happens. Each neuron is listening to every other neuron. Take neuron 1. It's getting inputs from 99 other neurons. Then, neuron 1 will calculate the weighted sum of the inputs from 99 neurons and will set its output to +1 if the weighted sum is greater than zero; otherwise to −1. If the new output is the negative of the neuron's previous output (−1 versus 1, or vice versa), then that counts as a flip.

We haven't yet talked about how the weights (*w12*, *w13*, *w21*, *w23*, *w31*, *w32*, in the case of 3 neurons) are set or calculated. We'll come to that. For now, let's assume that the weights are *not* symmetric, meaning *w12* is not necessarily equal to *w21*, and so on. This is the sort of network, with asymmetric weights, that John Hopfield began studying at first.

He devised a method of calculating the energy of such networks. He defined it as:

$$E = -\frac{1}{2} \sum_{i} \sum_{j,\, i \neq j} wij.yi.yj$$

Of course, these networks are simulations inside a computer, so they don't really have a physical energy. But one can use this formula to calculate a number that's analogous to physical energy. In the next section, "Take Me Home," we'll analyze why this behaves like energy, but for now, let's take Hopfield's word for it.

In the 3D Ising model of materials, it can be shown that ferromagnetic materials will dynamically settle into the lowest energy state, and this state is one in which all the magnetic moments are aligned. Hopfield was after similar dynamics in a network of bidirectionally connected neurons. But given the energy function I've just described, a network with asymmetric weights will not settle into the lowest energy configuration; the network is said to be unstable.

Then Hopfield had an insight. What if the weights were symmetric? So, *w12* is equal to *w21*, and *w13* is equal to *w31*, and so on.

"As soon as I got to symmetric connections, oh, I knew it'd work," Hopfield told me. "Stable points were guaranteed."

What's all this got to do with associative memory? Recall that that's how this story began—with Hopfield looking for a neurobiological problem to solve with neural networks. Well, let's give the game away a bit in advance, before coming to how it actually works. Imagine a way of setting the weights of the network such that a given pattern of outputs of the neurons represents a stable state, an energy minimum. (The outputs are equivalent to the spin states of the spin glass.) If the network is in this state, it is not going to change any further. This pattern of outputs can be thought of as the memory you want to store in the network. Now you are given a pattern that's a corrupted version of that memory. A few bits are +1 instead of −1, and vice versa (where each bit is the output of one neuron). Let's leave the weights of the neurons untouched, but let's force their outputs to represent this corrupted pattern. What Hopfield found is that when you do this, the network is no longer stable, and its dynamics take over: Each neuron flips (or not) until the network reaches a stable state. And if the corrupted state you forced the network into wasn't very different from the stored memory, the network will reach the stable state that represents the memory. The outputs of the neurons, once the network reaches this stable state, will not flip anymore. You can simply read off the outputs: You have recalled the memory.

"Once I understood that I needed symmetric connections—and the Ising model for magnetism had a lot to offer—I put things together, and then it was just clear," Hopfield said. "It was just sitting down and grinding things out."

TAKE ME HOME

There are many moving parts to understanding a Hopfield network, and they involve coming to grips with different conceptual ideas. One, what does it mean to store a memory? (We got a glimpse of the answer in the previous section.) Two, what does it mean for a network to be stable? Three, how does one select the weights of the network in order to store a memory? Four, what do storing memories and stable states have to do with each other? Five, what does energy have to do with all this?

Let's start with a simple 3-neuron network. The weights of the network can be written in matrix form:

$$\begin{bmatrix} w11 & w12 & w13 \\ w21 & w22 & w23 \\ w31 & w32 & w33 \end{bmatrix}$$

Generically, *wij* represents the weight of the connection going from neuron j to neuron i. There are some obvious aspects to this matrix. First, because a neuron doesn't talk to itself, the diagonal elements of the matrix will be zero. Also, the matrix, as per Hopfield's requirement, is symmetric about its diagonal: *wij = wji*

$$\begin{bmatrix} 0 & w12 & w13 \\ w21 & 0 & w23 \\ w31 & w32 & 0 \end{bmatrix}$$

The network has 3 neurons and, hence, 3 outputs, so we can store any pattern that's 3 bits long. Let's say we want to store the pattern "−1, 1, −1." This means that when the output of neuron 1 is

"−1," neuron 2 is "1," and neuron 3 is "−1," the network should be in a stable state. We have to select the weights appropriately. Choosing or finding the appropriate weights (whatever the procedure for doing so) is akin to teaching the network; the process is called learning. For this, Hopfield turned to a decades-old idea, one we encountered in chapter 1: "Neurons that fire together wire together." Here, "wiring together" means changing the weights between two neurons such that the activity of the neurons is reinforced. Choosing the weights to accomplish this is called Hebbian learning.

So, if neuron 1 has an output of $y1$, and neuron 2 has an output of $y2$, then Hebbian learning says that the weights between those two neurons are given by:

$$w12 = w21 = y1.y2$$

Given that we are sticking to symmetric connections, that's all there is to it, really. Multiply the two outputs, and you get the value for the weights of the symmetric connections between two neurons. If two neurons are each outputting the same value, either +1 and +1 or −1 and −1, then the mutual weights are set to 1. If the two neurons are producing different values (−1 and +1 or +1 and −1), then the mutual weights are set to −1.

Because we want the network, in its stable state, to output "−1, 1, −1" ($y1 = -1$, $y2 = 1$, $y3 = -1$), this gives us the following weights:

$$w12 = w21 = y1.y2 = -1 \times 1 = -1$$
$$w13 = w31 = y1.y3 = -1 \times -1 = 1$$
$$w23 = w32 = y2.y3 = 1 \times -1 = -1$$

More generally:

$$wij = yi.yj$$

Consequently, our weight matrix looks like this:

$$\begin{bmatrix} 0 & -1 & 1 \\ -1 & 0 & -1 \\ 1 & -1 & 0 \end{bmatrix}$$

Notice that it's symmetrical about the diagonal, whose elements are all zero.

Here's a very simple method that uses matrices and vectors to generate the weight matrix:

$$\begin{bmatrix} 0 & w12 & w13 \\ w21 & 0 & w23 \\ w31 & w32 & 0 \end{bmatrix} = \begin{bmatrix} 0 & y1.y2 & y1.y3 \\ y2.y1 & 0 & y2.y3 \\ y3.y1 & y3.y2 & 0 \end{bmatrix}$$

The vector representing the memory we want to store is given by:

$$\mathbf{y} = \begin{bmatrix} y1 & y2 & y3 \end{bmatrix}$$

We can get a matrix from our memory vector by multiplying the transpose of the memory vector with itself. This is also called the outer product of vectors. (Note that this is not the dot product, which yields a scalar value.)

$$\begin{bmatrix} y1 \\ y2 \\ y3 \end{bmatrix} \times \begin{bmatrix} y1 & y2 & y3 \end{bmatrix}$$

$$= \begin{bmatrix} y1 \times \begin{bmatrix} y1 & y2 & y3 \end{bmatrix} \\ y2 \times \begin{bmatrix} y1 & y2 & y3 \end{bmatrix} \\ y3 \times \begin{bmatrix} y1 & y2 & y3 \end{bmatrix} \end{bmatrix}$$

$$= \begin{bmatrix} y1.y1 & y1.y2 & y1.y3 \\ y2.y1 & y2.y2 & y2.y3 \\ y3.y1 & y3.y2 & y3.y3 \end{bmatrix}$$

$$= \begin{bmatrix} 1 & y1.y2 & y1.y3 \\ y2.y1 & 1 & y2.y3 \\ y3.y1 & y3.y2 & 1 \end{bmatrix}$$

The final matrix is almost what we want, except for the diagonal elements, which turn out to be 1, because 1×1 or -1×-1 is each equal to 1. To get to our desired weight matrix, we simply subtract a 3×3 identity matrix from our result.

$$\begin{bmatrix} 1 & y1.y2 & y1.y3 \\ y2.y1 & 1 & y2.y3 \\ y3.y1 & y3.y2 & 1 \end{bmatrix} - \begin{bmatrix} 1 & 0 & 0 \\ 0 & 1 & 0 \\ 0 & 0 & 1 \end{bmatrix} = \begin{bmatrix} 0 & y1.y2 & y1.y3 \\ y2.y1 & 0 & y2.y3 \\ y3.y1 & y3.y2 & 0 \end{bmatrix}$$

So, finding the Hebbian weights for any stored pattern, or vector, **y** simply becomes:

$$\mathbf{W} = \mathbf{y}^\mathsf{T}\mathbf{y} - \mathbf{I}$$

Where, **I** is the identity matrix of the appropriate size. For example, if the stored pattern has 10 bits, then we require 10 neurons, and both the weight matrix and the identity matrix will be 10×10.

Once the network's weights are initialized using this method, the question to answer is this: Why is the pattern stable, or why does the network not change states? By "stable," we mean a state in which no neuron's output should ever flip.

Consider the ith neuron, with the output yi.

We know that:

$$yi = \begin{cases} +1 \text{ if } \sum_{j,i \neq j} wij.yj > 0 \\ -1 \text{ if } \sum_{j,i \neq j} wij.yj \leq 0 \end{cases}$$

But we have also set, as per the Hebbian rule:

$$wij = yi.yj$$

Therefore:

$$\sum_{j,i \neq j} wij.yj = \sum_{j,i \neq j} yi.yj.yj = \sum_{j,i \neq j} yi.yj^2 = yi \sum_{j,i \neq j} yj^2$$

yj^2 is always 1 (regardless of whether yj is +1 or −1)

So, $\sum_{j,i \neq j} yj^2$ is always positive

So, $yi \sum_{j,i \neq j} yj^2$ always has the same sign as yi

So, $\sum_{j,i \neq j} wij.yj$ always has the same sign as yi

This means the neuron will never flip. None of the neurons in the network will flip. We have proven that if the weights are set according to the Hebbian learning rule (for a given pattern of desired outputs), then that pattern is a stable state for the network.

We have addressed the first three questions asked at the beginning of this section. Now it's time to tackle the concept of energy in a Hopfield network. We want the stable, stored pattern to represent an energy minimum. This means that any perturbation to the pattern (say, if the output of neuron 1 is forcibly flipped from −1 to 1) should increase the energy of the network, thus causing it to slide back, metaphorically speaking, to its minimum-energy state. The descent back to an energy minimum, if it happens as desired, is the equivalent of recalling a stored memory.

For a more detailed account of why this works, see the mathematical coda on page 272. What follows here is an intuitive take. Recall that Hopfield defined the energy of his network as:

$$E = -\frac{1}{2}\sum_i \sum_{j,\,j\neq i} wij.yi.yj$$

It turns out that when the weights of the network have been set using the Hebbian learning rule, then the following are true:

- In the stable state, which represents a stored memory, the network's energy (as defined by the equation above) is at a local minimum. The network can have multiple local minima (each potentially representing a different stored memory). In a stable state, neurons don't flip their outputs any further, and the network remains at that energy minimum.

- However, if you were to perturb the network, say, by making it store a pattern that's a slightly corrupted form of a stored memory, this would cause the energy of the network to increase. This perturbed state is unstable, and the neurons will start flipping. It can be shown that when a neuron flips, the overall energy of the network decreases. These dynamics continue until the network reaches a stable state, or a local energy minimum—at which point, the dynamics cease.

- Once the network reaches an energy minimum, the neurons stop flipping. At this stage, the outputs of the neurons potentially represent some stored memory. Whether or not the stored memory is the one you intended to retrieve depends on the initial perturbation—if the perturbation is too large, it's possible that the network's dynamics take it to a different energy minimum than the one corresponding to the stored memory you wanted to retrieve.

Here's a demonstration of what's possible with Hopfield networks. Say you want to store a black-and-white 28×28 image of a handwritten digit. That's 784 pixels to depict a digit. Each pixel can be 0 or 1. For our purposes, because we are using bipolar neurons, we can think of "0" as being equivalent to "−1." Basically, any image is a vector with 784 elements in it, with each element being either −1 or +1. To store such a vector, we need 784 neurons. Using the Hebbian rule, we can calculate the weights of the 784-neuron network for any image we want to store.

Let's say **y1** represents image 1 (the numeral 5), and **y2** represents image 2 (the numeral 8). These digits are modified versions of images from the MNIST database of handwritten digits.

To store the first digit, the weight matrix is calculated as follows:

$$\mathbf{W1} = \mathbf{y1}^T\mathbf{y1} - \mathbf{I}$$

Where, **W1** is a 784×784 matrix, and **I** is a 784×784 identity matrix. This single operation updates the weights of the network such that image 1 becomes a stored memory. If you were to read out the outputs of the neurons at this stage, you could reconstruct the image, as each neuron outputs the corresponding pixel value.

But what if we wanted to store another image in the same network? If we wanted to store only the second image, we'd set the weights to **W2**, where:

$$\mathbf{W2} = \mathbf{y2}^{\mathrm{T}}\mathbf{y2} - \mathbf{I}$$

But if you wanted to store both images in the same network, then the composite weight matrix would be:

$$\mathbf{W} = \frac{1}{2}(\mathbf{W1} + \mathbf{W2})$$

This is the same as:

$$\mathbf{W} = \frac{1}{2}\left(\mathbf{y1}^{\mathrm{T}}\mathbf{y1} + \mathbf{y2}^{\mathrm{T}}\mathbf{y2}\right) - \mathbf{I}$$

More generally, if you wanted to store n memories, then:

$$W = \frac{1}{n}\sum_{i=1}^{n} yi^T yi - I$$

(An aside: Hopfield showed that if you have *n* neurons, the network can store at most *0.14×n* memories. So, a network with 784 neurons can store about 109 memories. If you think of each memory as a vector in n-dimensional space, then these 109 vectors will need to be almost mutually orthogonal, otherwise they'll interfere with one another. There have been considerable advances in the past few years to increase the storage capacity, leading to networks called modern Hopfield networks.)

Let's say we stored the two images as memories in our 784-neuron Hopfield network. Now we want to retrieve a memory given some fragment of it. Let's take the digit 8 and randomly change some pixels.

We feed this image to our network. "Feeding the image" means setting each neuron's output to either +1 or −1, depending on the values of the corresponding pixels in the perturbed image. Our algorithm for retrieving an image goes like this:

- **Step 1.** Calculate the energy of the perturbed network.

- **Step 2.** Pick a neuron at random from 1 to 784.

- **Step 3.** Calculate its output based on the outputs of all other neurons and the weight matrix.

- **Step 4.** Figure out whether the neuron should flip or not. Flip it if necessary.

- **Step 5.** Calculate the new energy.
  - **Step 5a.** If (old energy – new energy) $<= e$, where e is some really small value, then terminate the process. This basically means that the change in energy after the neuron has flipped is extremely small, so we are likely near some local minimum.
  - **Step 5b.** If (old energy – new energy) $> e$, then go to step 1 (essentially, iterate over all the neurons at random, over and over, until you reach an energy minimum).

Using this algorithm, the network, when fed a noisy input image, retrieves the stored image:

We can also create perturbed images by randomly initializing a 28×28 image with $+1$ and -1 for its pixel values (below, left), feeding it to the network, and seeing what it retrieves (below, right). In this case, the network retrieves the digit 8, but it could also have come back with the digit 5.

Note that if you are given a Hopfield network with some stored memories, all you have access to are the weights of the network. You really don't know what stored memories are represented by the weight matrix. So, it's pretty amazing that when given the perturbed image shown above, our Hopfield network dynamically descends to some energy minimum. If you were to read off the outputs at this stage and convert that into an image, you would retrieve some stored memory.

Occasionally, something strange happens. In the figures on the next page, for example, given a different perturbed image (left), the network retrieves a slightly different image (right).

What happened? It's clear that the retrieved number is the digit 8, but the image has been inverted: Black pixels have turned white, and vice versa. The values of the pixels are the outputs of the neurons. As it turns out, the energy landscape (or energy as a function

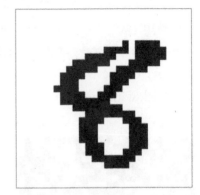

of the weights and outputs of the neurons) has two minima for each stored memory. If one set of outputs (hence, pixel values) gives you one minimum, outputs that are flipped (1 becomes −1, or white becomes black and vice versa) give you the other minimum in the energy landscape, but an identical one in terms of the energy. So, depending on your initial starting point, as dictated by the perturbed image, you can land in one or the other minimum. So, in some cases, we end up with a bit-flipped image.

We, however, stored two images in the network, representing the numerals 5 and 8. Sometimes, the randomly perturbed image descends to an energy minimum that represents the digit 5 or its bit-flipped sibling (see panels, bottom of previous page).

It's also possible that if you took the image of the digit 8, per-turbed it, and set the network to represent the perturbed image, it might descend to an energy minimum that resulted in the retrieval of an image of the digit 5. That's because the perturbation landed the network on a part of the energy landscape that was somehow closer to the minimum representing 5 than to the minimum representing 8.

If you ever do build your own Hopfield network, it's not at all vain to store your own photograph and see if it can be retrieved (per-fectly normal behavior). Here's one such outcome.

The image on the top left is what was stored, the image on the top right is the same image with a lot of noise added, and the bottom image is what the network retrieved, given the noisy image.

When interviewing John Hopfield, I found it awkward to refer to his eponymous network by name. "It feels weird to be calling them Hopfield networks while I'm talking to you, but you must have experienced this all along," I said.

"I've given up on that," said Hopfield, smiling.

It might be passé now, but in 1981, when Hopfield finished his work, no one was particularly interested in publishing it. No neurobiologist would have looked at what Hopfield had written and claimed it had anything to do with neurobiology. "There would have been no hope of getting it [into] a refereed publication," Hopfield told me. As it happened, Hopfield was a member of the National Academy of Sciences, for his earlier work in physics. "If you were an academy member, you could essentially, on your own say-so, publish a few papers a year," he said. "Nobody would criticize them at all, unless they were immoral."

But back in 1981–82, the *Proceedings of the National Academy of Sciences* (*PNAS*) published almost nothing in mathematics or computer science. And those disciplines were at the heart of Hopfield's paper. Plus, he had one more problem: *PNAS* had a five-page limit. Hopfield had to distill his work down to five pages while simultaneously hoping to attract the attention of mathematically minded computer scientists and neurobiologists. The paper was published. Reminiscing about the process in his essay "Now What?," Hopfield quotes Hemingway:

Concerning the writing of non-fiction, Ernest Hemingway remarked, "If a writer of prose knows enough about what he is writing about he may omit things that he knows and the reader, if the writer is writing truly enough, will have a feeling of those things as strongly as though the writer had stated them." The PNAS *length limitation forced me to be highly selective in what was said—and what was omitted. Had Hemingway been a physicist, he would have recognized the style. In hindsight, the omission of the almost obvious probably increased the impact of the paper. The unstated became an invitation for others to add to the subject, and thus encouraged a community of contributors to work on such network models. Successful science is always a community enterprise.*

Hopfield's 1982 *PNAS* paper has become a classic in the field. It fostered the understanding that neurobiological systems—our brains included, of course—are dynamical and can be mathematically modeled as such. This was a huge advance. Then there was the question of learning. (After all, this is a book on machine learning.) Hopfield networks are what are called one-shot learners. Given one instance of data, the network can memorize it. But an awful lot of the learning our brains do is incremental: Given enough data, we slowly learn about patterns in them.

Incremental training was a key goal for neural network researchers. We saw in chapter 1 how to incrementally train a single-layer perceptron, or neural network. But such networks had enormous limitations. The goal was to move to multi-layer neural networks, but no one knew yet how to efficiently train them. By 1986, that, too, had changed, irrevocably, with the publication of the first detailed exposition of the backpropagation algorithm. And within a few years of that, another paper, by a mathematician named George Cybenko, further inflamed passions about neural networks: Cybenko showed that a certain kind of multi-layer network, given enough neurons, could approximate any function in terms of transforming an input into a desired output. Before we tackle backpropagation, we'll jump ahead to one of the classic findings about neural networks, the universal approximation theorem.

MATHEMATICAL CODA
CONVERGENCE PROOF / HOPFIELD NETWORK

Theorem: If a Hopfield network in a stable state is perturbed, then it will dynamically transition through a series of states until it reaches and settles into a stable state that represents an energy minimum.

The proof that follows is inspired by a brilliant exposition of it in Raúl Rojas's book *Neural Networks: A Systematic Introduction*. Let's begin with a network of what are called bipolar neurons, which produce an output of $+1$ or -1. The neurons are connected to each other with symmetric weights. A neuron's output does not feed back to itself. The network's weight matrix is given by an $n \times n$ matrix for a network of n neurons:

$$\begin{bmatrix} 0 & w12 & \cdots & w1n \\ w21 & 0 & \cdots & w2n \\ \vdots & \vdots & \vdots & \vdots \\ wn1 & wn2 & \cdots & 0 \end{bmatrix}$$

For a pattern to be stored in the network, we use the Hebbian learning rule.

$$wij = yi.yj$$

More generally, if there are n neurons, the stored memory is n bits long and is given by the vector $\mathbf{y} = [y1 \quad y2 \cdots yn]$. The weight matrix can be calculated as follows:

$$\mathbf{W} = \mathbf{y}^T\mathbf{y} - \mathbf{I} = \begin{bmatrix} 0 & y1y2 & \cdots & y1yn \\ y2y1 & 0 & \cdots & y2yn \\ \vdots & \vdots & \vdots & \vdots \\ yny1 & yny2 & \cdots & 0 \end{bmatrix}$$

Whether or not a neuron flips depends on the weights and the outputs of all the other neurons to which it's connected. For neuron i, it depends on:

$$yi_{new} = yi_{old} \times \sum_{j, i \neq j} wij.yj$$

yi_{old}: the current state of neuron i before it responds to other neurons

yi_{new}: the new state of neuron i after it responds to other neurons

The quantity $\sum_{j, i \neq j} wij.yj$ is often called the "field" of neuron i (analogous to the magnetic field experienced by a single magnetic moment inside some material). If the field of a neuron has the opposite sign to its current state, the neuron flips; otherwise, it doesn't.

Hopfield defined the energy of the network in these terms:

$$E = -\frac{1}{2} \sum_{i} \sum_{j, j \neq i} wij.yi.yj$$

Let's take a network with 3 neurons. So, the weights are $w11$, $w12$, $w13$, $w21$, $w22$, $w23$, $w31$, $w32$, and $w33$. We know that $w11$, $w22$, and $w33$ are zero. Here's the energy, with all the terms expanded:

$$E = -\frac{1}{2} \begin{bmatrix} w12\,y1\,y2 + w21\,y2\,y1 + w13\,y1\,y3 + \\ w31\,y3\,y1 + w23\,y2\,y3 + w32\,y3\,y2 \end{bmatrix}$$

This can be reorganized, with a focus on neuron 1:

$$E = -\frac{1}{2}\left[y1(w12\,y2 + w21\,y2 + w13\,y3 + w31\,y3) + w23\,y2\,y3 + w32\,y3\,y2\right]$$

We know that *w12* = *w21*, *w13* = *w31*, and so on . . . So, rewriting again:

$$E = -\frac{1}{2}\left[2y1(w12\,y2 + w13\,y3) + w23\,y2\,y3 + w32\,y3\,y2\right]$$

This can be generalized:

$$E = -\frac{1}{2}\left[2y1\sum_{j\neq 1}w1j.yj + \sum_{i,i\neq 1}\sum_{j,j\neq 1, j\neq i} wij.yi.yj\right]$$

The equation has two terms, one that is specific to *y1* and another that is about all the other neurons except *y1*. Let's say that it's neuron 1 that flips. So, we are concerned with two outputs of the first neuron:

$y1_{old}$: the current state of neuron 1, before it responds to other neurons

$y1_{new}$: the new state of neuron 1, after it responds to other neurons

Using the equation specific to neuron 1, we have two energies, one before the neuron flips and one after:

$$E_{old} = -\frac{1}{2}\left[2y1_{old}\sum_{j\neq 1}w1j.yj + \sum_{i,i\neq 1}\sum_{j,j\neq 1, j\neq i} wij.yi.yj\right]$$

$$E_{new} = -\frac{1}{2}\left[2y1_{new}\sum_{j\neq 1}w1j.yj + \sum_{i,i\neq 1}\sum_{j,j\neq 1, j\neq i} wij.yi.yj\right]$$

The difference in energy after neuron 1 flips is:

$$\nabla E = E_{new} - E_{old}$$

$$= -\frac{1}{2}\left[2y1_{new}\sum_{j\neq1}w1j.yj + \sum_{i,i\neq1}\sum_{j,j\neq1,j\neq i}wij.yi.yj\right]$$

$$-\left(-\frac{1}{2}\left[2y1_{old}\sum_{j\neq1}w1j.yj + \sum_{i,i\neq1}\sum_{j,j\neq1,j\neq i}wij.yi.yj\right]\right)$$

$$\nabla E = E_{new} - E_{old} = -\frac{1}{2}\left[2y1_{new}\sum_{j\neq1}w1j.yj\right] + \frac{1}{2}\left[2y1_{old}\sum_{j\neq1}w1j.yj\right]$$

$$\nabla E = -\frac{1}{2}(2y1_{new} - 2y1_{old})\sum_{j\neq1}w1j.yj$$

$$\nabla E = -(y1_{new} - y1_{old})\sum_{j\neq1}w1j.yj$$

If you were wondering about ½ before the energy function, this is where it comes in handy. The ½ cancels out the 2 before the summation. (Such are the tricks of mathematicians.)

So, this is the change in energy, when some ith neuron (in our case, neuron 1) flips states from +1 to −1 or vice versa. For the sake of generality, we'll abandon being specific about neuron 1 and just refer to the ith neuron as the one that flips. Recall that $\sum_{i,j\neq i}wij.yj$ is the field of the ith neuron. It'll always have the opposite sign to that of yi_{old}. That's why the neuron flips.

So, if yi_{old} is +1, then yi_{new} is −1, because $\sum_{i,j\neq i}wij.yj$ has a negative sign.

$$\Delta E = -(yi_{new} - yi_{old})\sum_{j\neq i}wij.yj = -(-1-1))\times NegNumber$$

$$= + 2 \times NegNumber$$

$$= NegNumber$$

If yi_{old} is -1, then yi_{new} is $+1$, because $\sum\limits_{i, j \neq i} wij.yj$ has a positive sign.

$$\Delta E = -\left(yi_{new} - yi_{old}\right)\sum\limits_{j \neq i}wij.yj = -\left(+1-(-1)\right) \times PosNumber$$

$$= - 2 \times PosNumber$$

$$= NegNumber$$

Regardless of whether the ith neuron flips from $+1$ to -1 or from -1 to $+1$, the change in energy is a negative number, meaning the total energy of the system goes down. "Since there is only a finite set of possible states, the network must *eventually* reach a state for which the energy cannot be reduced further," Rojas writes.

So, if a series of neuron flips keeps reducing the energy of the network until it reaches a state where no neuron flips, then that state represents a local energy minimum. It's a stable state. Once the network settles into that state, it cannot change states any further.

QED

CHAPTER 9

The Man Who Set Back
Deep Learning (Not Really)

George Cybenko was surprised by the reception he got. He was only one among the many luminaries teaching summer school on deep learning in 2017, in Bilbao, Spain. By then, deep learning—or the process of training neural networks that have three or more layers (one input layer, one output layer, and one or more so-called hidden layers tucked in between the input and output)—had taken over the world of machine learning. Nearly thirteen hundred people attended the school, and Cybenko taught an hours-long mini-course to about four hundred of them. During breaks, students came up and requested selfies with him. "I felt like a rock star," Cybenko, a professor of engineering at Dartmouth College, Hanover, New Hampshire, told me.

That feeling was somewhat spoiled by a blog post Cybenko later read about the summer program. The blogger mentioned that another highly regarded AI researcher, Li Deng, one of the pioneers of the deep learning revolution, had reportedly quipped that the very theorem that made Cybenko feel like a rock star at the summer school may have substantially set back the field of deep learning. "So, in some circles, I'm the guy that delayed deep learning by twenty years," a somewhat amused Cybenko told me. To be held up, even in jest, as the person whose work hampered an entire field for two decades is quite an allegation. "It misunderstood what I did," Cybenko said.

So, what did Cybenko do that brought him celebrity status among deep learning aficionados on the one hand and, yet, caused some to joke about its deleterious effect on the other? To answer these questions, we must jump ahead somewhat in the time line of research into neural networks.

To recap what we know so far, in the late 1950s and early '60s, Frank Rosenblatt and Bernard Widrow devised single-layer neural networks and the algorithms to train them, making these networks the focus of machine learning for almost a decade. Then, in 1969, Minsky and Papert published their book, *Perceptrons,* in which they elegantly proved that single-layer neural networks had limitations, while insinuating (without proof) that multi-layer neural networks would likely be similarly useless, effectively killing that field of research and bringing about the first AI winter.

Yet, not everyone gave up. In 1981–82, John Hopfield figured out Hopfield networks. These networks, however, were one-shot learners. They didn't need the kind of training that multi-layer neural networks required to learn incrementally from data. By the mid-1970s and early '80s, a handful of researchers had begun elucidating the fundamental elements of an algorithm that could be used to train multi-layer networks. Then, in 1986, David Rumelhart, Geoffrey Hinton, and Ronald Williams published a seminal paper in the journal *Nature,* showing off the strengths of a training algorithm called backpropagation, thus greasing the wheels of deep learning and setting it in motion. (Though, as we'll see in the next chapter, they weren't the first to think of backpropagation; its history goes back to Rosenblatt.)

It's these wheels on which Cybenko's work allegedly put the brakes. His landmark paper was published in 1989. Given the chronology of the developments, it'd make sense to understand backpropagation first and then deal with Cybenko's theorem. But we'll reverse the order. Coming to grips with Cybenko's work first will set us up for a better understanding of deep neural networks and backpropagation and will give us a great excuse to delve into some delicious details about functions and why they can be regarded as vectors and how all that gets pulled together in Cybenko's "proof by contradiction." His proof showed that a neural network with just one hidden layer, given enough neurons, can approximate any function, meaning it can turn an input into any desired output. Think about it: One hidden layer, with an arbitrarily large number of neurons, can represent any function, no matter how complicated. For example, the function could be one that takes an input and produces a simple tone or a complex speech waveform; or recognizes images; or even generates new images. The theorem is called the universal approximation theorem.

The implication of the backpropagation algorithm, detailed in the 1986 Rumelhart, Hinton, and Williams paper, was that multilayer neural networks could now be trained, while one kept in mind practical concerns such as lack of both computing power and training data. At the time, Cybenko, who had done his Ph.D. in the mathematics of signal processing, was intrigued by the promise of these networks. "We had these negative results by Minsky and Papert, and yet people were doing stuff and getting things done. That motivated me to get to the bottom of it," he told me. "What *can* a single-hidden-layer network do?"

Before we get to multi-layer networks, here's a depiction of a single-layer perceptron, or a single-layer neural network, with no hidden layer:

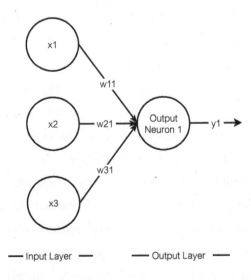

— Input Layer —　　　　— Output Layer —

The input layer simply refers to the inputs to the neural network. They are not artificial neurons in themselves. For example, in the figure above, the input to the neural network is a three-dimensional vector $[x1, x2, x3]$. This vector, stacked vertically, represents the input layer. There is only one layer of actual artificial neurons in the network, hence the name "single-layer neural network." And that's the output layer. The figure shows only one neuron as part of the output layer, but there can be any number of them, stacked vertically. Each neuron in the output layer receives the entire vector as input. Each element of the vector is multiplied by its own weight. Each output neuron computes the weighted sum of its inputs, adds a bias, and then uses a thresholding function to generate its output.

So, for a bipolar neuron, which produces either +1 or −1:

$$y = \begin{cases} -1 \text{ if weighted sum} + \text{bias} \leq 0 \\ +1 \text{ if weighted sum} + \text{bias} > 0 \end{cases}$$

Recall from chapter 1 that we can write the equations for a single neuron as follows:

$$g(\mathbf{x}) = w1x1 + w2x2 + \cdots + wnxn + b = \sum_{i=i}^{n} wixi + b$$

$$f(z) = \begin{cases} -1, & z \leq 0 \\ 1, & z > 0 \end{cases}$$

$$y = f(g(\mathbf{x})) = \begin{cases} -1, & g(\mathbf{x}) \leq 0 \\ 1, & g(\mathbf{x}) > 0 \end{cases}$$

The perceptron training algorithm we encountered in chapter 1 can be used to train this network. To further recap, training via supervised learning means taking several instances of labeled training data (where each labeled instance is some value for $\mathbf{x}$ on the input side and a value for the corresponding output, y) and iterating over these instances to arrive at some near-optimal set of weights and bias, so that the network finds some linearly separating hyperplane. Once we have the weights and bias, then given some new $\mathbf{x}$, it's easy to estimate the output y.

For the example network above, the algorithm must learn the values for this weight matrix and the bias term:

$$\begin{bmatrix} w11 \\ w21 \\ w31 \end{bmatrix} \text{ and } b$$

However, the perceptron training algorithm works only for a single-layer network. If you have something like the network shown on the next page, it will fail. (Note that the weights now have subscripts to indicate the pertinent layer.)

The network shown has one hidden layer of neurons—hidden because the layer is not directly exposed on the output side. The outputs of the hidden neurons feed into the neurons of the output layer.

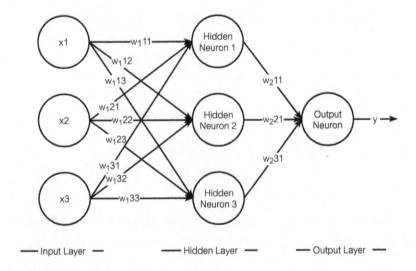

In this example, again, we have only one neuron in the output layer, but there can be as many as we want, and if you have more than one output neuron, each output becomes an element of the output vector, **y**. The important thing to notice here is that there are now two weight matrices, one for the connections between the inputs and the hidden layer and another for the connections between the hidden and output layers. (If there were more hidden layers, the number of matrices would correspondingly increase.) Leaving aside the bias terms—they are always present and must be learned, too—the two weight matrices for the network shown above are:

$$\mathbf{W}_1 = \begin{bmatrix} w_1 11 & w_1 12 & w_1 13 \\ w_1 21 & w_1 22 & w_1 23 \\ w_1 31 & w_1 32 & w_1 33 \end{bmatrix}$$

$$\mathbf{W}_2 = \begin{bmatrix} w_2 11 \\ w_2 21 \\ w_2 31 \end{bmatrix}$$

(A note on notation: The weights have subscripts, where each subscript refers to the layer, and two numbers: The number on the left refers to the neuron in the previous layer, whose output serves as input to the neuron in the current layer; and the number on the right denotes the neuron receiving the input in the current layer (later in this book, the two numbers will appear as superscripts). Also note that this indexing is reversed compared to the notation used for Hopfield networks. We could have chosen the same notation, but you'll often encounter these differing ways of indexing the weights, biases, and outputs, so this just serves to keep us on our toes. Henceforth, we'll stick to this notation.)

If a network requires more than one weight matrix (one for the output layer and one for each hidden layer), then it's called a deep neural network: the greater the number of hidden layers, the deeper the network.

The perceptron training algorithm doesn't work when the network is characterized by more than one weight matrix. By the mid- to late 1980s, researchers were successfully training some deep neural networks thanks to the backpropagation algorithm (which we'll come to in the next chapter); the algorithm could deal with hidden layers. "But, at the time, there was no understanding. You could train it to do *what*? What, if any, were the limitations? There was an effective algorithm, but sometimes it worked, sometimes it didn't," Cybenko said.

Essentially, a deep neural network, with its multiple weight matrices, transforms an input **x** into an output **y**, where both the input and output are vectors. This can be written as:

$$\mathbf{y} = f(\mathbf{x})$$

A neural network—we'll drop the word "deep" where it's clear from the context—then approximates some desired function. So, while training a network means finding the optimal values for the weight matrices, it's also akin to finding the function that best approximates the correlation between the inputs and the outputs. But what does approximating a function achieve? Well, for one, a function can represent a decision boundary. If a new data point falls to one side or the other of the boundary, it can be classified accordingly. Or take another example: The function can also be used for regression, meaning the function is the curve that best fits the training data; then, given a new data point, the function can be used to predict the output. Or, in the context of ChatGPT and other instances of generative AI, the function could represent an AI's ability, first, to learn an extremely complicated probability distribution that models the training data and, then, to sample from it, thus enabling the AI to generate new data that are in accordance with the statistics of the training data.

Cybenko wanted to understand the strengths and limitations of neural networks. Can they approximate any function? What if the network doesn't have the capacity, in terms of number of neurons, to approximate the desired function? What can an idealized neural network, with as many neurons as needed, do or not do?

STACK 'EM UP

There's an intuitive way to understand how a sufficiently large number of neurons in one hidden layer can approximate any given function. Let's take a complicated enough function (so that the ghosts of Minsky and Papert can't accuse us of going easy on neural networks):

$$y = f(x) = \sin\left(\pi x / 3\right) + \cos\left(\pi x / 5\right) + e^{-2\pi x} + \sqrt{|x|}$$

As complicated as this looks, it's still just a one-dimensional function, in that the scalar output *y* depends only on the scalar input *x*. A plot of this function looks like this:

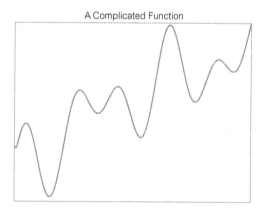

A Complicated Function

There's an intuition from calculus that can help us understand how a neural network might transform inputs to outputs in a manner that closely matches this function. Let's say we want to find the area under the portion of the curve that's shown above. We can do so approximately. It involves drawing a bunch of rectangles of equal width, which we try to fit under the curve. The area under the curve can be estimated by summing up the area of all the rectangles we managed to fit under the curve. The thinner the rectangles, the more of them we can fit and the closer we get to the correct answer. Integral calculus takes this to the limit, letting us calculate the area by allowing the width of the rectangles to tend to zero. The figures on the next page show some examples.

We are not interested in integral calculus or the area under the curve. But the method tells us something about how a single-hidden-layer neural network might get at the problem of approximating any function.

What if we designed individual neural units, where each neural unit is made of two or more neurons that each produced an output

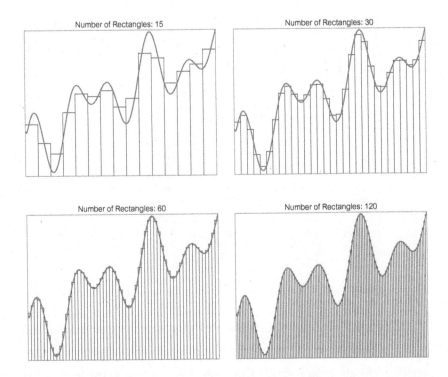

that equaled the height of a rectangle of a required size and had the necessary width? Examine the first of the four figures above, which approximates the area under the curve for fifteen rectangles. What if each of those rectangles were the output of a neural unit? Each unit would represent a function that had a certain value, equal to the height of the rectangle (the value along the y-axis), for a small range of input values equaling the width of the rectangle (the values along the x-axis). For all other values along the x-axis, the unit outputs a zero. We could just stack these rectangles next to each other and sum them up, and we'd have an approximation of some function.

Let's build a network that can help us approximate a function in this manner. For a detailed visual analysis of this approach, including some nifty interactive graphics, see the notes for a link to Michael

Nielsen's highly original explanation: "A visual proof that neural nets can compute any function." Nielsen develops the necessary intuition using neurons that have a step activation function (defined further down). We'll directly use a type of "nonlinear" neuron, based on the one Cybenko used in his proof.

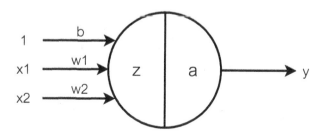

In the example above, the neuron takes in two inputs, *x1* and *x2*, and produces an output *y*, which depends on two processing stages (the bias *b* will always be multiplied by the input 1):

$$z = w1x1 + w2x2 + b$$

$$y = a(z)$$

If $a(z) = z$, we have a simple linear neuron

$$a(z) = z$$

$$\Rightarrow y = w1x1 + w2x2 + b$$

In formal lingo, the function $a(z)$ is called an activation function. In the neurons we encountered in chapters 1 and 2, $a(z)$ was a threshold function, or a step activation function. An example of such a function would be:

$$\text{If } z > 0: a(z) = 1$$
$$\textit{Else}: a(z) = 0$$

Cybenko's neurons used the sigmoid activation function, $a(z) = \sigma(z)$, where:

$$\sigma(z) = \frac{1}{1 + e^{-z}}$$

Here's what the function looks like, for a 1D input x, such that $z = wx + b$:

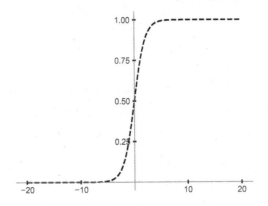

Note that the function $\sigma(z)$, plotted on the y-axis, goes smoothly from almost 0 to almost 1. (This smoothness, rather than the abrupt transition we see in the functions that have a step, is important for training networks with hidden layers; it's something we'll look at in detail in the next chapter.) In this depiction, the midpoint of the rise occurs exactly at $x = 0$. But that midpoint, as well as the steepness of the rise from near 0 to near 1, can be controlled by changing the values of w and b.

In the context of our neuron, z is the weighted sum of the inputs plus the bias term. So, the neuron's output, y, can be written this way:

$$z = \mathbf{w}^\mathsf{T}\mathbf{x} + b$$
$$y = \sigma(z)$$

By varying $\mathbf{w}$ and b, one can vary the value of z, and thus the shape and position of the sigmoid. Here are two different outputs for a one-dimensional input and output, for example:

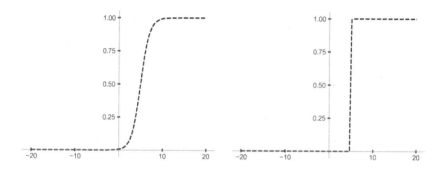

The first shows a sigmoid shifted to the right of the origin (because of a change in the bias), and the second shows a sigmoid that rises almost vertically (because of an increase in the weight) and is also shifted to the right (because of an accompanying change in the bias). In the second plot, you could just as well have changed the bias such that the steeply rising curve moves to the left.

Using a sigmoidal neuron as the element of the hidden layer, the figure on the next page shows a one-dimensional version of the network Cybenko analyzed (with 1D here meaning that both the input and output vectors have only one element each; there is an arbitrary number of neurons in the hidden layer).

The basic idea is that each hidden neuron is generating some sigmoidal curve, where the steepness of the curve is controlled by the neuron's weight and where the location at which the curve rises along the x-axis is controlled by the neuron's bias. The output neuron is simply doing a linear combination of the outputs of the hidden neu-

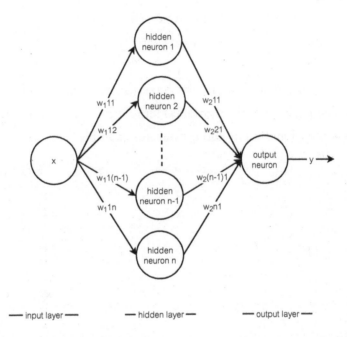

— input layer —   — hidden layer —   — output layer —

rons: It multiplies each hidden neuron's output by some weight (which can be negative, causing the curve to fall rather than rise) and then sums up the weighted outputs of the hidden neurons to produce the final output.

Before we analyze simple examples of such summations, let's examine the mathematical formalism of the one-hidden-layer network that Cybenko studied. The network has the following characteristics:

An input vector of d dimensions: $\mathbf{x}$

Number of neurons in the hidden layer: n

Weight matrix for the hidden layer: $\mathbf{W}$; this is a $d \times n$ matrix

Output: y

Given these parameters, the equation Cybenko was examining was this:

$$y = f(\mathbf{x}) = \sum_{i=1}^{n} \alpha_i \sigma\left(\mathbf{W}_i^T \mathbf{x} + b_i\right)$$

The expression inside the parentheses evaluates to the output of the ith hidden neuron before it encounters the activation function. The output is then passed through the sigmoid activation function and then multiplied by the weight α_i. All the alphas, $i = 1$ to n, taken together form the weights of the output layer. So, the final output is a linear summation of the outputs of the n hidden layer neurons. Cybenko wanted to prove that this summation, given enough hidden neurons, could approximate any desired function $f(\mathbf{x})$.

To understand what happens in such a network, we can switch back to the simplest case of 1D input and output. Let's look at what happens if we take any two hidden neurons. Here are two possible outputs:

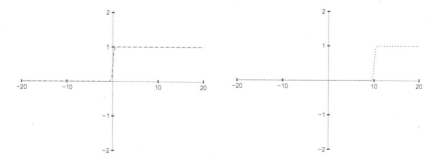

You can see that the second hidden neuron's output is shifted to the right along the x-axis. Let's say that the output neuron does a linear combination of the outputs of the two hidden neurons, multiplying the first output by 1 and the second output by −1 (equivalent to flipping it about the x-axis) and then adding them up. The bold line shows the final output:

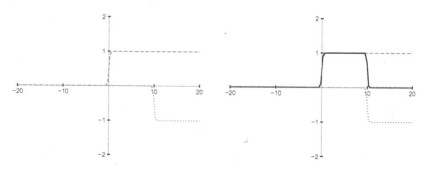

We have produced an approximately rectangular output. A similar thing can be done with two other hidden neurons to produce a rectangle that's shifted farther to the right and is taller and skinnier. The dashed and dotted lines are the outputs of two hidden neurons

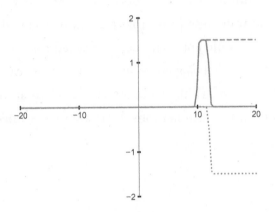

multiplied by 1.5 and −1.5, respectively; these are the coefficients of the linear summation. The solid gray line is the sum of those outputs.

Here are the two rectangles next to each other:

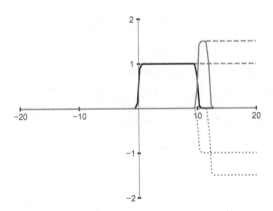

The output neuron can of course do a linear summation of the outputs of all four neurons at once. We'd get the bold line shown in the top figure on the page opposite, as the final output.

Essentially, we have generated two rectangles of different heights

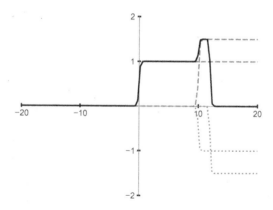

and widths (using bespoke weights and biases for the hidden neurons) and added them using similarly bespoke linear coefficients to produce the final output, which looks like some nonlinear function. (What we just did hews closely to Nielsen's exposition of how to use neurons with a step activation function to generate and sum such rectangles; we used the sigmoid activation function.)

Here's an attempt at approximating the function $y = x^2$, using 10 sigmoidal neurons:

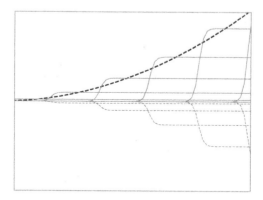

The black dashed line shows the function to be approximated. The light gray lines, solid and dashed, show the outputs of individual hidden neurons. The output of each hidden neuron is multiplied by an appropriate value (the linear coefficient), either positive or negative. These outputs rise from zero to some positive value (and stay there) for some neurons, shown as gray solid lines, and drop from zero to some negative value (and stay there) for others, shown as gray dashed lines. Also, the rise or fall happens at different points along the x-axis, thanks to the biases of the individual hidden neurons. The result of summing up all those biased and weighted outputs is a linear combination. Here's what it looks like for our example:

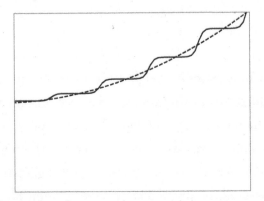

This linear combination of the outputs of 10 sigmoidal neurons, shown as the black solid line, almost approximates the function, but it's clearly not good enough. Increase the number of neurons from 10 to 20 or 100 (the next two figures, respectively), and the power of this approach becomes obvious. With 100 neurons, it's visually impossible to tell apart the actual function from its approximation.

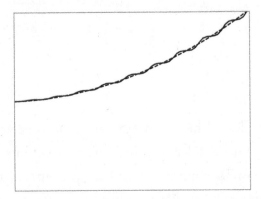

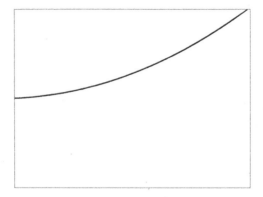

The function approximated above is simple. Below is a more complex function and its approximation with 300 neurons.

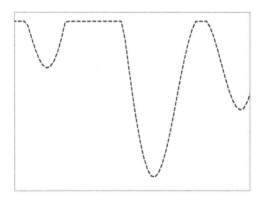

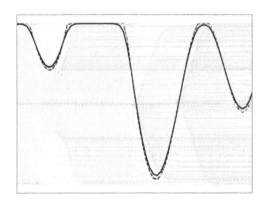

The dashed black line is the function we want to approximate. The individual outputs of the sigmoidal neurons, appropriately weighted and biased, are shown in gray. The final output, the linear combination of those outputs, is shown in solid black. It's astonishing to see how a few hundred neurons are sufficient to get very close to the original function.

A note of caution here: I hand-designed the weights and biases used in these examples to show how these networks work. In practice, a network would have to learn the correct values for these parameters. A training algorithm, such as backpropagation, will find the weights and biases using training data. If there is some unknown complicated function that maps the inputs to the outputs or represents the probability distribution over the data, then training the network is akin to finding the best possible set of weights and biases to approximate that function.

Also, we have dealt with the simple case of a scalar input and a scalar output. Real-world problems require input vectors that can have dimensions of tens of thousands or even millions. But the same ideas hold, regardless of the dimensionality of the input and output vectors.

Despite all this analysis, we have only developed an intuition for why a single-hidden-layer neural network, with enough neurons, can approximate any function. It's not proof. That requires some nifty mathematics.

Cybenko had the necessary mathematical chops. In particular, he was an expert in functional analysis, or the analysis of operations of vectors and operations of functions. (Functions, as we'll see in some detail, are vectors in an infinite-dimensional space.) In 1988, Cybenko worked on the problem for the better part of the year and wrote a small technical report showing that a network with two hidden layers can approximate any function. The proof was mathematically rigorous. Cybenko wanted to go further. "I had this feeling it should be able to do it with one hidden layer," he said. He was right.

Cybenko's proof itself is too complex for us, and it relies on other complex theorems. We'll have to settle for a bird's-eye view of his work. But first, a small segue to talk about functions as vectors.

FUNCTIONS AS VECTORS

Of all the concepts in this book, the idea of a function as a vector may cause the most head-scratching, but it's also among the most beautiful and powerful ideas we'll encounter. Take the function $y = sin(x)$, for example. What follows is a plot of the function, for x ranging from 0 to 10 radians. How does one think of this function as a vector?

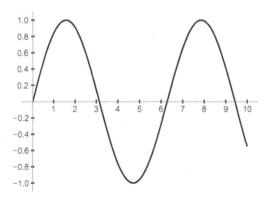

Well, let's just consider the x values $[0, 1, 2, 3, 4, 5, 6, 7, 8, 9, 10]$. At each of these locations on the x-axis, the function has a corresponding value on the y-axis. These values can be written down as: $[0.0, 0.84, 0.91, 0.14, -0.76, -0.96, -0.28, 0.66, 0.99, 0.41, -0.54]$.

We've just approximated the function using a sequence of 11 numbers. This sequence is a vector in 11-dimensional space.

Let's do the same for $y = cos(x)$; the figure is shown on the next page.

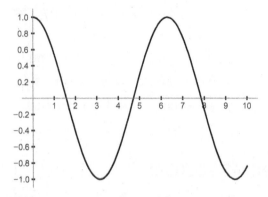

This function, for the same set of coordinates on the x-axis, can be written down as: [1.0, 0.54, -0.42, -0.99, -0.65, 0.28, 0.96, 0.75, -0.15, -0.91, -0.84]. This is a different vector in the same 11-dimensional space. Just imagine 11 axes that are orthogonal to each other in 11D space. (Well, we cannot actually visualize it, but these mathematical spaces exist.) The functions *sin*(*x*) and *cos*(*x*), evaluated for 11 values of *x* between 0 and 10 (inclusive), turn into vectors in this 11D space.

We can do this for any function. First map the function on the xy plane, for a certain range of values on the x-axis, and then determine the value of the function for a preselected array of x-axis values. This output array can be thought of as a vector whose dimensionality is determined by the number of points at which you chose to evaluate the function. In our example, it's 11 locations along the x-axis, ranging from 0 to 10, inclusive.

Now comes another conceptual leap, toward infinity. We've considered only 11 points on the x-axis, between the end points 0 and 10, inclusive. But the line segment between 0 and 10 is infinitely divisible: There is an infinite number of points in that interval. So, technically, we can have an infinite sequence of real numbers that represent each function between 0 and 10. We mere mortals have problems visualizing anything beyond three dimensions, let alone

11D space. Mathematicians, however, revel in going beyond. There are spaces with infinite dimensions, or with an infinite number of axes. Any function, then, can be thought of as a point in this infinite-dimensional space.

The march toward infinity doesn't stop here. What if, instead of evaluating the function between 0 and 10, as we did in our example, we let the x-axis extend to minus infinity on one side and plus infinity on the other? The function, evaluated at an infinite number of points, along an axis that is itself infinite in length, results in a point in yet another infinite-dimensional space.

Let's add one more complication. The functions we have looked at so far have been one-dimensional: They take in a scalar input and spit out a scalar output. But functions can take in vectors as inputs and produce vectors as outputs. We don't have to fret about this, but know that that's the most general way to think about what a neural network is doing: transforming one vector to another vector. Take a neural network with one hidden layer. The input column vector, $\mathbf{x}$, is multiplied by a matrix of weights of the hidden layer, producing another column vector, each element of which is passed through the sigmoid function, which results in another column vector. This column vector—the output of the hidden layer—is then multiplied by the weights of the output layer, producing yet another vector: the output vector, $\mathbf{y}$.

Cybenko thought more generally about his one-hidden-layer network. Each hidden neuron implements some sigmoidal function. We've just learned that each such function is itself a vector in some infinite-dimensional space. An output neuron implements a linear combination of the vectors of functions implemented by neurons of the hidden layer. The question Cybenko asked was this: If you performed every possible linear combination of this arbitrarily large number of sigmoid functions (or, rather, their associated vectors), could you get to every possible function (or vector) in the vector space of functions?

"Vector space" is a technical term, referring to objects such as vectors, matrices, and functions that live in that space. For example, 2D vectors live in the xy plane; 3D vectors live in the xyz coordinate space. These objects must satisfy certain properties in order for the space to be called a vector space. But we don't need to know those details to get a sense of Cybenko's approach.

Cybenko's proof by contradiction starts with the assumption that a neural network with one arbitrarily large hidden layer *cannot* reach all points in the vector space of functions, meaning it cannot approximate all functions. He then shows that the assumption leads to a contradiction and, hence, is wrong. It wasn't a proof by construction, in that Cybenko did not prove some assertion. Rather, it was classic reductio ad absurdum. He started by assuming that some proposition was true and ended up showing that the proposition was false. "I ended up with a contradiction," Cybenko said. "The proof was not constructive. It was an existence [proof]."

Because his proof that neural networks could indeed approximate any function given enough hidden neurons focused on networks with just one hidden layer, it apparently caused some researchers to spend their time building networks with just one hidden layer, rather than go deep by increasing the number of hidden layers. "I didn't say you should use one layer," Cybenko said. "People concluded [that you] only need one layer."

The revolution in deep learning that began around 2010 happened because researchers began to take seriously the "deep" in "deep learning"—and started to increase the number of hidden layers to well beyond one. But it took almost two decades after Cybenko's proof for this revolution to take off—and to be fair to

Cybenko, the revolution needed other ingredients that weren't available in the 1990s: massive amounts of training data and computing power.

Still, the proof was a big deal. In the concluding paragraph of his 1989 paper, Cybenko speculated that while the approximating properties of neural networks were extremely powerful, it was unclear just how many neurons would be required to approximate any function with enough accuracy. "We suspect quite strongly that the overwhelming majority of approximation problems will require astronomical numbers of terms," Cybenko wrote. "This feeling is based on the curse of dimensionality that plagues multidimensional approximation theory and statistics."

But the deep neural networks that are dominating today's efforts in AI—with billions, even hundreds of billions of neurons and tens, even hundreds of hidden layers—are challenging the theoretical foundations of machine learning. For one, these networks aren't as susceptible to the curse of dimensionality as was expected, for reasons that aren't entirely clear. Also, the massive numbers of neurons and, hence, parameters should overfit the data, but these networks flout such rules, too. However, before we can appreciate such mysteries, we need to examine the algorithm that allowed researchers to start training deep neural networks in the first place: backpropagation.

CHAPTER 10

The Algorithm that Put Paid
to a Persistent Myth

I t's AI folklore that Minsky and Papert killed research on neural networks, starting in the late 1960s, by proving that single-layer perceptrons could not solve something as simple as the XOR problem. I brought up the Minsky-Papert proof early on in my conversation with Geoffrey Hinton, one of the key figures behind the modern deep learning revolution. Hinton got interested in neural networks in the mid-1960s, when he was still in high school in the United Kingdom.

"This was before the Minsky and Papert proof about [neural networks] not working for XOR," I said.

"Yes," Hinton said, but then immediately lodged a protest. "I can't let it go [about] it not working for XOR. I reserve the right to complain about that." And he did. (More of that later.)

In high school, Hinton was influenced by a mathematician friend who was wondering how memories are stored in the brain. It was about then that scientists figured out how to make 3D holograms. "He got interested in the idea that the brain might be like a hologram in that memory is not localized," Hinton said. While his friend was exploring how memories are stored, Hinton became interested in how brains learn; he wanted to understand the mind. This pursuit led him to study physics and physiology at university, but all they taught about the brain was how action potentials, or electrical signals, travel along axons of neurons. Not exactly an elucidation of how the brain works. A disappointed Hinton turned to philosophy. "I thought philosophers had something to say about it. And then I realized they didn't," he told me. "They didn't have the Feynman concept of understanding the mind—that you need to figure out how to build one to understand it."

A frustrated Hinton even tried studying experimental psychology—again, to no avail. "What they did was design experiments to distinguish between two hypotheses, both of which were obviously hopeless," he said. "That didn't satisfy me."

Disenchanted, he dabbled in some carpentry and took some time off to read. He was deeply influenced by Donald Hebb's book *The Organization of Behavior*. In 1972, Hinton joined the school of artificial intelligence at the University of Edinburgh, to work for his doctorate with Christopher Longuet-Higgins, a theoretical chemist who had moved from Cambridge to Edinburgh and would later co-found the Department of Machine Intelligence and Perception (an outcome of the United Kingdom Science Research Council's decision to fund a center to further the emerging field of AI).

Hinton recalled Longuet-Higgins as having been interested in holograms and memories and making holographic memories using neural networks. But by the time Hinton got to Edinburgh, Longuet-Higgins had switched sides, going from believing in neural networks and connectionism to thinking that symbolic AI was the answer. He had also taken on one other student and had gotten him to work on symbolic AI. "He spent the whole time trying to get me to switch," Hinton said of Longuet-Higgins.

But Hinton wasn't convinced about using symbolic AI and logic to achieve artificial intelligence. "I never really liked logic," he told me. "I never believed people were logical." But people are intelligent, so intelligence must not be simply the outcome of applying rules of logic, which is what symbolic AI does—use rules of logic to manipulate symbols to arrive at answers. Hinton wanted to work on neural networks. He negotiated an arrangement with Longuet-Higgins to let him do so for six months, determining that if he hadn't produced anything good by then, he would switch. "And after six months, I said, 'Yeah, well, I haven't produced anything good. But I think I'm going to be able to, so I need another six months,'" Hinton said. "It kept going like that."

Hinton did finish his Ph.D. His work involved solving constrained optimization problems using neural networks. "But they weren't learning," he said of his neural networks. He was convinced, however, that multi-layer neural networks could one day be made to learn. This was the mid-1970s. By then, Minsky and Papert had proven that single-layer perceptrons could not solve the XOR problem. Hinton acknowledges that their proof was substantial, in that it was general, and that the XOR problem was a specific instance of a class of problems that single-layer perceptrons couldn't solve. Still, Hinton wasn't impressed. "It basically was a con job in that they proved that a simple kind of net couldn't do things. And they had no proof that a more complicated net couldn't do them. It was just kind of by analogy: 'Since we proved the simple nets can't do it, forget it,'" he told me. "And people fell for it."

Hinton didn't. Neither had Rosenblatt. Recall our encounter with Rosenblatt's student George Nagy in chapter 1: Nagy told us that Rosenblatt was well aware of the problem of training multi-layer perceptrons; Rosenblatt addressed it in his 1961 tome, *Principles of Neurodynamics*, which Hinton had devoured.

In chapter 13 of that book, a section heading reads, "Back-Propagating Error Correction Procedures." In that section, Rosenblatt clearly lays out the problem for a three-layer perceptron, which has a sensory layer (S), which receives inputs; a response layer (R), which produces outputs; and a layer (A) in between the two, creating a network that goes from S to A to R (S → A → R). Rosenblatt writes, "The procedure to be described here is called the 'back-propagating error correction procedure' since it takes its cue from the error of the R-units, propagating corrections back towards the sensory end of the network if it fails to make a satisfactory correction quickly at the response end."

The basic idea is rather straightforward (in hindsight, of course): Determine the error made by the network by comparing the produced output with the expected output and then figure out how to change the weights of the network based on the error such that the network produces the correct output. The perceptron training algorithm we encountered in chapters 1 and 2 can adjust the weights only of the final A → R layer. Rosenblatt's three-layer network had a pre-determined set of weights for the S → A layer. But he understood that those weights, too, should be amenable to training. "It would seem that considerable improvement in performance might be obtained if the values of the S to A connections could somehow be optimized by a learning process, rather than accepting the arbitrary or pre-designed network with which the perceptron starts out," he writes.

His book lays out one such procedure, to backpropagate errors, if modifying the weights of the A → R layer isn't enough. But it didn't work well. Even so, Rosenblatt had introduced the idea of backprop-agation as a means for training multi-layer networks, but hadn't figured out exactly how to do it. (He built the Mark I Perceptron we saw in chapter 1 using such layers, sans backpropagation.)

He had also identified another problem with training neural networks. Consider this three-layer neural network:

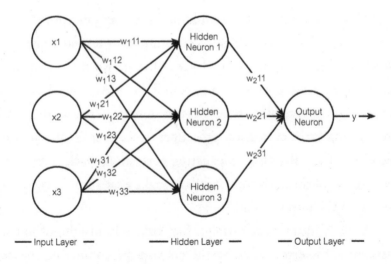

For now, let's set aside the problem of training such a network. Let's assume that before training begins, all the weights are initialized to zero. (We are ignoring the bias term associated with each neuron here, for simplicity.) That means that for any given input $\mathbf{x} = [x1, x2, x3]$, each hidden neuron is going to produce the same output. The neuron in the final layer produces some output. We calculate the error and update each weight such that the error is reduced a little. Because the initial weights were all the same, the change to each weight will be identical, making them equal to each other even after the update. This continues until the network converges on a set of weights that work well for the training dataset. Unfortunately, the weights for each hidden neuron will have the same set of values, so each hidden neuron will process the input data in exactly the same manner as every other hidden neuron; in essence, all neurons have learned the same thing. To put it differently, they have all picked up on the same feature in the data. We could just as well have used only one hidden neuron because of the symmetry in the weights of the neurons in the hidden layer.

Rosenblatt recognized this problem of symmetry in neural networks. He proved, using an illustrative example, that a three-layer neural network could not solve a simple problem if it started off with symmetric weights and used a deterministic procedure to update the weights. "While this theorem shows that a deterministic procedure cannot be guaranteed to work, it remains to be shown that a non-deterministic procedure will work. In the most extreme case, we could employ a procedure which randomly varies the value of every connection, independently of the others, as long as errors continue to occur," he writes.

Rosenblatt was suggesting a stochastic process for updating the weights. Hinton read this to mean that the output of the neurons should be stochastic, which meant introducing an element of randomness to a neuron's output. This would ensure that the weights were updated differently during each pass of the training data and that the final trained network would have the requisite asymmetry, enabling the neurons to detect different features in the data.

"I was convinced by his argument. The neurons had to be stochastic," Hinton said. So, he continued thinking about training multi-layer neural networks with stochastic neurons in mind. But this method of breaking symmetry didn't work. "This slowed me down for a while."

There's another, far more elegant way to break symmetry that's also hinted at in Rosenblatt's assertion about nondeterministic procedures, but it wouldn't become clear to Hinton until he began working with psychologist David Rumelhart at the University of San Diego. Rumelhart would point out the simpler solution. Their combined effort, with help from computer scientist Ronald Williams, would lead to the modern version of the backpropagation algorithm. But we are jumping ahead. Hinton's path from Edinburgh to San Diego, to work with Rumelhart, wasn't straightforward.

Hinton handed in his Ph.D. thesis in 1977. Despite his unwavering belief in neural networks, he found no support in the United

Kingdom. "I was so fed up with the fact that nobody else seemed to believe in neural nets that I abandoned academia and went and taught in a free school." It was the White Lion Street Free School in Islington, London. Hinton taught inner-city kids the basics of mathematics. The school didn't even have paper, so he used the backsides of the pages from early drafts of his thesis to teach the kids. After about six months at the school, while waiting for the final exam for his thesis, he began thinking of getting back into academia. He could barely get an interview in Britain; only the University of Sussex interviewed him for a position, in the Department of Developmental Psychology, and rejected him. An academic at Sussex suggested that Hinton make reduction photocopies of his thesis and mail them to everyone he had heard of in the United States. "Because that's where AI was," Hinton said.

Rumelhart read Hinton's thesis and offered him a postdoctoral position at UC San Diego. For Hinton, the United States was a revelation after the academic "monoculture" of Britain, where there was the right way to do things and where everything else was considered heresy. Neural networks constituted heresy. "And the U.S. is bigger than that. In particular, it's got two coasts. They can each be heresy to the other," Hinton said.

Rumelhart was keenly interested in neural networks. For Hinton, the atmosphere was wonderful. "I'd never been anywhere where neural nets weren't considered to be nonsense." This was now the early 1980s. Those interested in neural networks were preoccupied with training multi-layer networks with at least one hidden layer. By now, the contours of what came to be called the backpropagation algorithm were clear.

We'll come to the exact mathematical details, but conceptually, here's the algorithm's end game. Think of a three-layer neural network with one hidden layer. You feed it an input, and it produces an output. You calculate the error made by the network, which is the discrepancy between its output and the expected correct value. This error is a function of all the weights of the network. How do you minimize the error? Well, you can do gradient descent—the technique we encountered in chapter 3, with Bernard Widrow's simple ADALINE network. Find the gradient of the error (as a function of the weights) and take a small step in the opposite direction by updating each weight by a tiny amount.

Sounds easy. Where's the problem with doing just that? you might ask. For starters, the shape of the function you're descending is not necessarily convex. In the Widrow-Hoff algorithm, the function is bowl-shaped, and gradient descent is guaranteed to get you to the bottom of the bowl, the global minimum, which represents the lowest possible error that the network can make and, hence, the optimal value for its weights. But it turns out that the error function in the case of a neural network with hidden layers is not convex; it has many hills and valleys. And it's possible that the network can get stuck in one of the valleys, a local minimum, even though other valleys, or minima, exist where the error is lower.

In fact, Minsky himself, before he turned on neural networks, had studied the properties of this process. He and another AI pioneer, Oliver Selfridge, in a paper called "Learning in Random Nets," which they co-authored in 1961, wrote about an algorithm called hill climbing, which is analogous to gradient descent, in that you are looking to find the peak of a function, where the function represents performance: The greater the value of the function, the better the machine is at its task. "Let the machine make some small changes in one or a few of its parameters or controls or variables. If the performance improves, repeat the process: if not, return to the previous

state and make a different small change. In the long run[,] performance must improve to a local optimum where no small change in
controls yields improvement. This technique is commonly referred
to as 'hill-climbing,'" the authors wrote. Just as doing gradient descent on a non-convex function with multiple local minima creates
problems, hill climbing can encounter what Minsky and Selfridge
called the mesa phenomenon: "The space apparently is composed of
large numbers of flat regions. The flat elevated regions might be
thought of as 'table-lands' or 'mesas.'" Small tweaks to the values of
parameters do not result in any improvement in the machine's performance, which implies that the machine is stuck on the mesa; or
they lead to large changes in performance, which is akin to the machine's falling off the mesa onto a downslope. Minsky effectively
ruled out hill climbing as a viable method.

This may explain Minsky and Papert's dismal view of multi-layer
neural networks. That's the more charitable interpretation. The less
charitable, and maybe more accurate, one is that the duo was deliberately sabotaging research into neural networks so that funding
could flow to their favored form of artificial intelligence, symbolic AI.
"Minsky and Papert were so intent on eliminating all competition . . . that their book suggests much more than it actually demon-
strates. They set out to analyze the capacity of a one-layer perceptron,
while completely ignoring in the mathematical portion of their book
Rosenblatt's chapters on multi-layer machines and his proof of convergence of a probabilistic learning algorithm based on back propa-
gation of errors," write professor of philosophy Hubert L. Dreyfus
and his brother, Stuart E. Dreyfus, professor of industrial engineering and operations research, both at the University of California,
Berkeley.

But good ideas never really go away. In 1960–61, control and
aeronautics engineers Henry J. Kelley and Arthur E. Bryson inde-

pendently arrived at a method for calculating, for example, the optimal trajectory for a rocket, a method that had, in its essence, the ideas necessary for the backpropagation algorithm. In 1962, Stuart Dreyfus derived formulas based on the chain rule in calculus (we'll come to that in a moment) to augment the usefulness of the Kelley-Bryson method. And in an exhaustive blog post detailing the history of the algorithm, Jürgen Schmidhuber, an AI pioneer at the Swiss AI Lab IDSIA in Lugano-Viganello, mentions many others who had similar ideas. For example, in 1967, Shun'ichi Amari demonstrated techniques for using stochastic gradient descent to train multi-layer perceptrons with hidden units; and Seppo Linnainmaa, in his 1970 master's thesis, developed the code for efficient backpropagation. In 1974, Paul Werbos submitted his Ph.D. thesis at Harvard. Titled *Beyond Regression: New Tools for Prediction and Analysis in the Behavioral Sciences,* it came closest to articulating the modern version of the backpropagation algorithm. The thesis wasn't publicized much; nor was it aimed at researchers in neural networks. Despite such developments, none of them made their mark as far as ML was concerned. That happened in the early 1980s, when Rumelhart, Hinton, and Williams developed their algorithm, and it's this version that gave deep neural networks the boost they needed. To appreciate these developments, we need to put on our wading boots and step into a gentle stream of calculus, derivatives, and the chain rule.

WHAT'S THE DELTA?

Let's revisit the mean square algorithm (a version of which we encountered in chapter 3, in the guise of the Widrow-Hoff algorithm) for learning the weights of a single neuron for some task.

The neuron shown on the next page has a weight w and a bias b, takes a scalar input x, and generates a scalar output y.

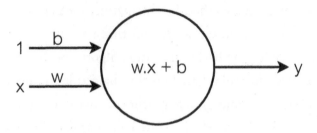

The output *y* is given by:

$$y = w.x + b$$

Using this neuron, here's the problem we want to solve. We are given a set of points on the xy plane such that for every value of *x*, there's a corresponding value of *y*. Let's say we are given ten representative points for the relationship between *x* and *y*. Here are the training data:

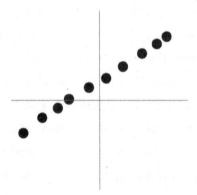

It's clear from just a visual inspection that the best relationship between *x* and *y* is linear. Such a straight line has a slope and an offset (the distance of the line from the origin), which is exactly what the weight *w* and the bias *b* represent. Once we find the slope and offset, then given a new *x*, we can predict *y*. We are performing a linear regression—that is, finding a straight line to best fit the training data in order to predict the output, given some new input.

Here's the so-called delta rule for finding the weight and bias. (One can generalize this to multiple sets of weights and biases as long as the neurons are all in a single layer.)

Initialize w and b:

$$w = 0, b = 0$$

Calculate the output of the neuron.

The convention is to use the symbol $\hat{y}$; we can just spell it out:

$$yhat = wx + b$$

Calculate the error:

$$e = y - yhat, \text{ where } y \text{ is the expected value}$$

Calculate the square loss:

$$loss = (y - yhat)^2$$

$$\Rightarrow loss = (y - wx - b)^2$$

If we plot the loss as a function of the weight w and bias b, it'd look like the figure shown on the next page.

The weight and bias vary along the x-axis and y-axis, respectively. The height along the z-axis is the loss for a given weight and bias and for some set of training data. In this case, we have ten pairs of (x, y) points that comprise our training data. For each pair, we can calculate the loss. Then we sum over all the pairs and divide by ten to get

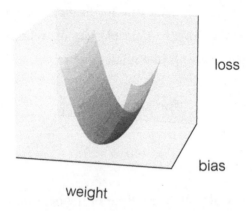

loss

bias

weight

the mean squared error (MSE). It's this value that we plot on the z-axis. It's important to note here that the loss you get for a given weight and bias would be different for a different set of training data points. In other words, while the shape of the loss function depends on the relationship of the loss to the weight and bias, the exact value of the loss also depends on the training data. It's clear from the loss function's shape, as plotted, that if we initialize the weight and bias randomly to some values, we'll most likely land somewhere along the slopes, rather than at the bottom.

The delta rule tells us that to reach the bottom, we need to calculate the gradient of the loss function at any given point and take a small step along the negative of the gradient, because the gradient is a vector that points upslope. A small step means tweaking the weight and the bias by a tiny amount that's proportional to the respective components of the gradient. We keep doing this until the loss becomes acceptably small.

Here's the calculus:

$$Gradient = \begin{bmatrix} \partial L/\partial w \\ \partial L/\partial b \end{bmatrix}$$

Recall from our brief discussion of calculus in chapter 3 that the gradient of a multi-variate function (in this case, the loss function L, which depends on w and b) is a vector: Each element of the vector is a partial derivative of the function with respect to one variable, with all other variables treated as constants.

We start with our loss function:

$$L = (y - yhat)^2 = (y - wx - b)^2$$

$$\Rightarrow \frac{\partial L}{\partial w} = \frac{\partial (y - wx - b)^2}{\partial w}$$

To do this differentiation, we need two simple rules from calculus. The first is called the power rule:

$$\text{Say, } y = x^n$$

$$\text{Then, } \frac{dy}{dx} = nx^{n-1}$$

$$\text{So, if } y = x^3$$

$$\text{then } \frac{dy}{dx} = 3x^2$$

The next is the chain rule, which will play an outsize role in the backpropagation algorithm we are building up to. Let's take our time with it.

$$\text{If:}$$

$$y = f(z) \text{ and } z = g(x)$$

$$\Rightarrow y = f(g(x))$$

then, according to the chain rule:

$$\frac{dy}{dx} = \frac{dy}{dz}\frac{dz}{dx}$$

In words, what this is saying is that if a function $f(z)$ depends on a variable, z, which itself depends on another variable, x, then the derivative of the function $f(z)$ w.r.t. the second variable x can be calculated by chaining together the derivative of $f(z)$ w.r.t. the first variable, z, and the derivative of z w.r.t. the second variable, x. The chain, in principle, can be arbitrarily long, and it's this feature that gives the backpropagation algorithm its chops.

But first, here's a simple example:

$$\text{If } y = \sin\left(x^2\right) \text{ What is}: \frac{dy}{dx}?$$

$$\text{Let } z = x^2 \Rightarrow y = \sin(z)$$

$$\frac{dy}{dx} = \frac{d\sin\left(x^2\right)}{dx} = \frac{d\sin(z)}{dx}$$

$$\frac{d\sin(z)}{dx} = \frac{d\sin(z)}{dz}\frac{dz}{dx} = \frac{d\sin(z)}{dz}\frac{dx^2}{dx} = \cos(z)2x$$

$$\Rightarrow \frac{d\sin\left(x^2\right)}{dx} = 2x\cos\left(x^2\right)$$

Let's now consider our loss function and the derivative of the loss function with respect to the weight, w, and the bias, b. Note the change in notation from using the regular $\frac{dy}{dx}$ to the curved $\frac{\partial y}{\partial x}$:

The curvy notation denotes that we are taking a partial derivative of a function with respect to one specific variable; the function itself depends on multiple variables.

$$L = (y - wx - b)^2$$

$$\Rightarrow L = e^2, \text{ where } e = (y - wx - b)$$

$$\Rightarrow \frac{\partial L}{\partial w} = \frac{\partial L}{\partial e} \frac{\partial e}{\partial w}$$

$$\frac{\partial L}{\partial e} = \frac{\partial e^2}{\partial e} = 2e$$

$$\frac{\partial e}{\partial w} = \frac{\partial(y - wx - b)}{\partial w} = -x \text{ (since } y \text{ and } b \text{ are constants w.r.t. } w)$$

$$\frac{\partial L}{\partial w} = 2e(-x) = -2x(y - wx - b)$$

Similarly:

$$\frac{\partial L}{\partial b} = \frac{\partial L}{\partial e} \frac{\partial e}{\partial b}$$

$$\frac{\partial L}{\partial e} = \frac{\partial e^2}{\partial e} = 2e$$

$$\frac{\partial e}{\partial b} = \frac{\partial(y - wx - b)}{\partial b} = -1, \text{ since } y, w, \text{ and } x \text{ are constants w.r.t. } b$$

$$\Rightarrow \frac{\partial L}{\partial b} = 2e(-1) = -2(y - wx - b)$$

So, the gradient at a point along the loss function is:

$$\begin{bmatrix} -2x(y - wx - b) \\ -2(y - wx - b) \end{bmatrix} = \begin{bmatrix} -2x(y - yhat) \\ -2(y - yhat) \end{bmatrix} = \begin{bmatrix} -2xe \\ -2e \end{bmatrix}$$

For any value of w and b, and for any (input, output), or (x, y) pair, we can calculate the gradient. We do this for all pairs of data, sum up the gradients, and divide by the total number of data points, to get the overall gradient at any location along the loss function, given the training data.

Here's the update rule (it's called the delta rule because it increments w and b by a small amount, delta):

$$\Delta w = -\frac{\partial L}{\partial w}$$

$$w = w + \Delta w$$

Similarly,

$$\Delta b = -\frac{\partial L}{\partial b}$$

$$b = b + \Delta b$$

In practice, the deltas are themselves multiplied by a small number called the learning rate, alpha, so that the weights and biases are adjusted by only a small fraction of the gradient.

$$\Delta w = -\alpha \frac{\partial L}{\partial w}$$

where, $\alpha =$ the learning rate, some small value, say 0.01

Update w:

$$w = w + \Delta w$$

Similarly,

$$\Delta b = -\alpha \frac{\partial L}{\partial b}$$

Update b:

$$b = b + \Delta b$$

Update the weight and bias, reevaluate the loss, and keep doing this until the loss falls below an acceptable limit; then stop. We'll have found a reasonable value for w and b that nicely fits the training data. Here's what such a line might look like, for our initial data:

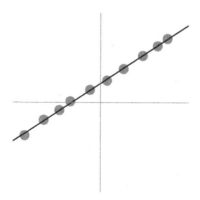

What we just did was gradient descent, going down to the minimum of the loss function or to a location near the minimum. It was for a single neuron, with one weight and a bias term. This simple configuration allowed us to plot the loss as a function of the two parameters, w and b. But we can easily extend this to a neuron with

2 or 10 or even 100 inputs. The other important aspect of our solution is that it's linear. We fit a straight line through the data points; we did linear regression.

We could just as easily have found a straight line to separate the xy plane into two regions, one with one class of data (circles) and the other with the second class of data (triangles). For example, here's such a dataset:

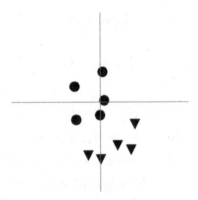

We have seen this problem before, in multiple previous chapters. The problem is to find the linearly separating hyperplane—in this case, a straight line in this 2D space. Here, each data point is given by $x1$, $x2$ (where $x1$ is the value along the x-axis and $x2$ is the value along the y-axis).

We'll require a neuron that takes in two inputs $(x1, x2)$ and computes an output:

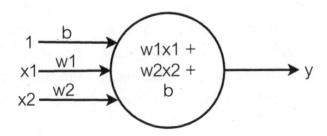

$$yhat = w1x1 + w2x2 + b$$

The loss:

$$L = (y - yhat)^2 = (y - (w1x1 + w2x2 + b))^2$$

$$\Rightarrow L = y^2 - 2y(w1x1 + w2x2 + b) + (w1x1 + w2x2 + b)^2$$

We have already encountered the chain rule. Now it's time to make use of it:

$$L = (y - yhat)^2 = e^2$$

$$\frac{\partial L}{\partial w1} = \frac{\partial L}{\partial e}\frac{\partial e}{\partial w1}$$

$$\frac{\partial L}{\partial e} = \frac{\partial e^2}{\partial e} = 2e$$

$$\frac{\partial e}{\partial w1} = \frac{\partial(y - yhat)}{\partial w1} = \frac{\partial(y - w1x1 - w2x2 - b)}{\partial w1} = -x1$$

So:

$$\frac{\partial L}{\partial w1} = \frac{\partial L}{\partial e}\frac{\partial e}{\partial w1} = 2e(-x1) = -2 \cdot x1 \cdot e$$

Similarly:

$$\frac{\partial L}{\partial w2} = \frac{\partial L}{\partial e}\frac{\partial e}{\partial w2} = 2e(-x2) = -2 \cdot x2 \cdot e$$

and

$$\frac{\partial L}{\partial b} = \frac{\partial L}{\partial e}\frac{\partial e}{\partial b} = 2e(-1) = -2e$$

So, the gradient at some point along the loss function is:

$$\begin{bmatrix} \partial L / \partial w1 \\ \partial L / \partial w2 \\ \partial L / \partial b \end{bmatrix} = \begin{bmatrix} -2 \cdot x1 \cdot e \\ -2 \cdot x2 \cdot e \\ -2e \end{bmatrix} = \begin{bmatrix} -2 \cdot x1(y - yhat) \\ -2 \cdot x2(y - yhat) \\ -2(y - yhat) \end{bmatrix}$$

Again, here's how we'd update the weights and the bias:

$$\Delta w1 = -\alpha\frac{\partial L}{\partial w1}; w1 = w1 + \Delta w1$$

$$\Delta w2 = -\alpha\frac{\partial L}{\partial w2}; w2 = w2 + \Delta w2$$

$$\Delta b = -\alpha\frac{\partial L}{\partial b}; b = b + \Delta b$$

Our algorithm iterates over all the test data until the loss ends up near the bottom of the bowl-shaped loss function (which we cannot, unfortunately, visualize, as the loss now depends on three variables, w1, w2, and b; the plot would be in four dimensions). Once the loss is optimal, meaning it's acceptably close to zero, we end up with weights and a bias that give us a dividing line (see figure, next page).

We went from a neuron with one weight and a bias term to a neuron with two weights and a bias term. What if we had to separate out images of cats from images of dogs, where each image had 100 pixels, with the points representing the cat images clustered in one

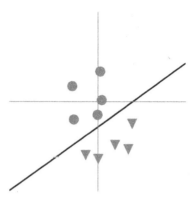

region of 100-dimensional space and the points representing dogs in another region? We could simply have a neuron that took in 100 inputs, one for each pixel value! As long as the data are linearly separable (for a classification problem), or we want to draw a line (or hyperplane) through the data points for regression, the method we have seen so far is sufficient.

But—and this is what Minsky and Papert created an unholy fuss about—what if the data are not linearly separable? Does the method we have used thus far still work? We know the answer: No, it doesn't. It's time to really understand why and to go beyond Minsky and Papert's tenuous objections.

A TOUCH OF NONLINEARITY

Consider the dataset shown in the first panel on the next page; it's a version of Minsky and Papert's XOR problem.

No single line can cleanly separate the circles from the triangles. What we need is a neural network that can separate the xy plane into two regions, light and dark, such that a data point that falls in the dark region can be classified as a triangle; otherwise, as a circle. This is not a trivial problem.

We know that a single line can be found by one neuron with

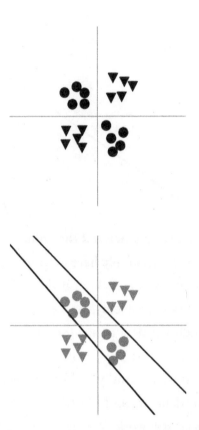

weights and a bias term. Clearly, we first need two such neurons to find the two lines. Shown above are what those two lines might look like. (I say "might" because each time you train the neurons, you might get lines with slightly different slopes and offsets.)

We are getting warmer as to why we need multiple layers to solve the XOR problem—in this case, at least two layers. Adding more neurons to the same layer will simply find more lines. That's not what we want. We want neurons that can take these lines and combine them into something more complex—in our case, a 2D space separated into two regions, one that lies between the two lines and another that's the rest of the xy plane.

So, the first layer involves two neurons, each of which finds one line. The second layer will consist of at least one neuron that learns

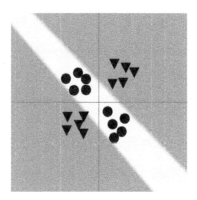

to create a weighted sum of the outputs of the neurons of the first layer, such that it delineates the xy plane into two regions, one for circles and the other for triangles (shown above). Let's build a network of such neurons, starting with a familiar-looking neuron:

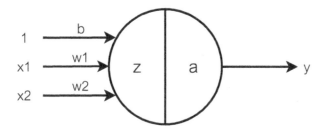

The neuron takes in two inputs, *x1* and *x2*, and produces an output *y*, which depends on two processing stages.

$$z = w1x1 + w2x2 + b$$

$$y = a(z)$$

If $a(z) = z$, we have a simple linear neuron

$$a(z) = z$$

$$\Rightarrow y = w1x1 + w2x2 + b$$

As we learned in chapter 9, function $a(z)$ is called an activation function. In the neurons we encountered in chapters 1 and 2, $a(z)$ was a threshold function. An example of such a function would be:

$$\text{If } z > 0 : a(z) = 1$$

$$\textit{Else} : a(z) = 0$$

One of the problems with the thresholding function is that it's not differentiable everywhere, meaning it doesn't have a derivative, or slope, everywhere. Not being differentiable everywhere doesn't necessarily doom a function—there are ways to approximate the derivative at problematic locations—but in the case of our thresholding function, the slope is zero always, except at the point of transition, where it's infinite. This is unhelpful. But a small tweak can make the threshold function continuous, so that it can be differentiated:

$$a(z) = \frac{1}{1 + e^{-z}}$$

This is the sigmoid function. We encountered it in the previous chapter, on the universal approximation theorem. The plot of the function is shown on the next page.

Note that the function is smooth and has a value close to 0 (but not 0) when x is less than -1, and then it starts rising to a value of 1. Just like the thresholding function, which produces an output that divides some coordinate space into two regions, the sigmoid does the same, approximately. Basically, as z tends to infinity, the function tends to 1, and as z tends to minus infinity, the function tends to zero. There's a small portion of the curve (in the figure, between

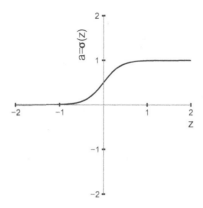

z of about -0.5 and 0.5), where the sigmoid function is nearly a straight line.

Most important, the function has a derivative (see the coda on page 341 for the derivation), and this derivative is expressed in terms of the function itself:

$$\sigma(z) = \frac{1}{1+e^{-z}}$$

$$\frac{d\sigma(z)}{dz} = \sigma(z)\big(1-\sigma(z)\big)$$

We can now put all the elements together to design a simple neural network with one hidden layer, to solve the XOR problem. It's a three-layer network (see figure, next page): The first is simply the input layer ($x1$, $x2$), the second is the hidden layer, with two hidden neurons, and the output layer has one neuron. (Again, the bias is not shown explicitly for each neuron; take it as a given.)

The output of the first hidden neuron is:

$$z_1^1 = w_1^{11}x1 + w_1^{21}x2 + b_1^1$$

$$a_1^1 = \sigma\big(z_1^1\big)$$

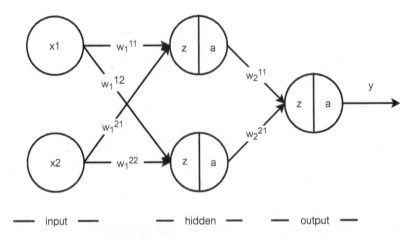

— input —   — hidden —   — output —

We are now following the notation introduced in the previous chapter. Besides the superscripts and subscripts for the weights, which we already know about, for the values z and a, and the bias b, the subscript refers to the layer, the superscript to the location of the neuron in the layer. So, w_2^{21} refers to a weight for layer 2, and for an input coming from neuron 2 of the previous layer and going to neuron 1 in the current layer. And a_2^1 refers to the output of a neuron 1 in layer 2.

With this in mind, we see that the output of the second neuron in the first layer, which is a hidden layer, is:

$$z_1^2 = w_1^{12} x1 + w_1^{22} x2 + b_1^2$$

$$a_1^2 = \sigma\left(z_1^2\right)$$

More generically, for any neuron:

$$z = \mathbf{w}.\mathbf{x} + b$$

$$a = \sigma(z)$$

Finally, the output neuron takes a weighted sum of the output of the two hidden neurons and passes that through a sigmoid activation function:

$$z_2^1 = w_2^{11} a_1^1 + w_2^{21} a_1^2 + b_2^1$$

$$a_2^1 = \sigma\left(z_2^1\right)$$

$$y = a_2^1$$

If you want to train such a network, you must calculate the following partial derivatives, for some loss L.

For the weights and bias of the output neuron:

$$\frac{\partial L}{\partial w_2^{11}}, \frac{\partial L}{\partial w_2^{21}}, \frac{\partial L}{\partial b_2^1}$$

And for the weights and biases of the hidden neurons:

$$\frac{\partial L}{\partial w_1^{11}}, \frac{\partial L}{\partial w_1^{21}}, \frac{\partial L}{\partial b_1^1} \text{ and } \frac{\partial L}{\partial w_1^{12}}, \frac{\partial L}{\partial w_1^{22}}, \frac{\partial L}{\partial b_1^2}$$

Once we calculate these partial derivatives, or the gradient of the loss function w.r.t. all the weights and biases, we can then update each weight and bias incrementally and do gradient descent. Such a network, given training data, will learn the weights and biases that enable it to solve the XOR problem: It'll delineate the xy coordinate space in the manner shown earlier.

While the way in which we solved the problem may seem tractable for the XOR issue, just let your imagination wander a little, to a network with tens or hundreds of hidden layers, with each hidden layer composed of 100 or 1,000 or even 10,000 neurons. And what if the loss function—we have been using a simple one so far—itself becomes hideously complicated (as can happen when the problem being solved becomes more difficult)? If we have to explicitly and analytically calculate the partial derivative of the loss function w.r.t. each weight and bias in the network, the process can quickly become insanely unrealistic.

How, then, do you train the network, or how do you find each of the partial derivatives, in some sustainable manner, where the algorithm doesn't have to be tweaked just because you changed the number of neurons per layer or the number of layers? This was the question consuming researchers in the late 1970s and early '80s. First Werbos and then Rumelhart, Hinton, and Williams, independently, developed an elegant technique for calculating the partial derivatives using the chain rule.

THE BACKPROPAGATION ALGORITHM

To understand "backpropagation" (the term introduced by Rosenblatt), we'll turn to the simplest possible one-hidden-layer network, with one hidden neuron.

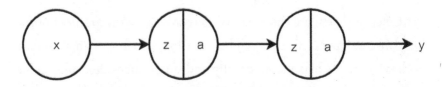

During training, for some input *x*, the network produces an output *yhat*. Here is the sequence of computations that lead to *yhat*. (To avoid unwieldy subscripts and superscripts, we'll just use the weight *w1* and bias *b1* for the hidden neuron in the first layer and *w2* and *b2* for the output neuron in the second layer.)

$$z1 = w1x + b1$$

$$a1 = \sigma(z1)$$

$$z2 = w2a1 + b2$$

$$yhat = \sigma(z2)$$

If the expected output is y, then the error e is:

$$e = (y - yhat)$$

We'll define the square of the error as the loss—but remember, we are choosing to define the loss as such; for any given problem, one has to select an appropriate loss function. For our purposes, we can use this popular loss function without any loss of generality:

$$L = e^2$$

To update the two sets of weights and bias, we'll need the following partial derivatives:

$$\frac{\partial L}{\partial w2}, \frac{\partial L}{\partial b2}, \frac{\partial L}{\partial w1}, \frac{\partial L}{\partial b1}$$

Here's an elegant use of the chain rule to get at these partial derivatives. (There's a trick to making sure you have the chain correct: Just cancel the denominator of the first partial derivative with the corresponding numerator to its right, and continue doing so, moving rightward. In the end, you should be left with just the partial derivative on the left-hand side of the equation. But keep in mind that this is not an actual mathematical operation, just a device to ensure that the chain is correct.)

$$\frac{\partial L}{\partial w2} = \frac{\partial L}{\partial e} \frac{\partial e}{\partial yhat} \frac{\partial yhat}{\partial z2} \frac{\partial z2}{\partial w2}$$

Each of these individual partial derivatives on the right-hand side of the equation is easily calculated:

$$L = e^2 \Rightarrow \frac{\partial L}{\partial e} = 2e$$

$$e = y - yhat \Rightarrow \frac{\partial e}{\partial yhat} = -1$$

$$yhat = \sigma(z2) \Rightarrow \frac{\partial yhat}{\partial z2} = \sigma(z2)(1 - \sigma(z2)) = yhat(1 - yhat)$$

$$z2 = w2 a1 + b2 \Rightarrow \frac{\partial z2}{\partial w2} = a1 \ and \ \frac{\partial z2}{\partial b2} = 1$$

So:

$$\frac{\partial L}{\partial w2} = 2e(-1)(yhat(1 - yhat))(a1)$$

$$\Rightarrow \frac{\partial L}{\partial w2} = -2ea1(yhat(1 - yhat))$$

This looks like a lot of work to calculate a partial derivative of the loss function with respect to just one weight (*w2*, in this case) of even the simplest possible network, but here's the cool thing: Every element of that right-hand side was already computed during the forward pass through the network, when the network was converting the input x into the output $yhat$. All we must do is simply keep track of those numbers and perform some simple arithmetic.

Similarly:

$$\frac{\partial L}{\partial b2} = \frac{\partial L}{\partial e} \frac{\partial e}{\partial yhat} \frac{\partial yhat}{\partial z2} \frac{\partial z2}{\partial b2}$$

$$\Rightarrow \frac{\partial L}{\partial b2} = 2e(-1)(yhat(1 - yhat))(1)$$

$$\Rightarrow \frac{\partial L}{\partial b2} = -2e(yhat(1 - yhat))$$

We now have the gradient of the loss function w.r.t. the weight and bias of the output neuron, which is enough to update these two parameters.

$$\Delta w2 = -\alpha \frac{\partial L}{\partial w2}; \; w2 = w2 + \Delta w2$$

$$\Delta b2 = -\alpha \frac{\partial L}{\partial b2}; \; b2 = b2 + \Delta b2$$

But what about the weight and bias of the hidden neuron? Well, we continue "backpropagating" the error using the chain rule.

$$\frac{\partial L}{\partial w1} = \frac{\partial L}{\partial e} \frac{\partial e}{\partial yhat} \frac{\partial yhat}{\partial z2} \frac{\partial z2}{\partial a1} \frac{\partial a1}{\partial z1} \frac{\partial z1}{\partial w1}$$

$$\Rightarrow \frac{\partial L}{\partial w1} = 2e \cdot (-1) \cdot (yhat(1 - yhat)) \cdot w2 \cdot (a1(1 - a1)) \cdot x$$

$$\Rightarrow \frac{\partial L}{\partial w1} = -2e \cdot x \cdot w2 \cdot (yhat(1 - yhat)) \cdot (a1(1 - a1))$$

Similarly:

$$\frac{\partial L}{\partial b1} = \frac{\partial L}{\partial e}\frac{\partial e}{\partial yhat}\frac{\partial yhat}{\partial z2}\frac{\partial z2}{\partial a1}\frac{\partial a1}{\partial z1}\frac{\partial z1}{\partial b1}$$

$$\Rightarrow \frac{\partial L}{\partial b1} = 2e\cdot(-1)\cdot\left(yhat\left(1-yhat\right)\right)\cdot w2\cdot\left(a1\left(1-a1\right)\right)\cdot1$$

$$\Rightarrow \frac{\partial L}{\partial b1} = -2e\cdot w2\cdot\left(yhat\left(1-yhat\right)\right)\cdot\left(a1\left(1-a1\right)\right)$$

Again, the network has computed everything that's needed for these calculations during the forward pass through the network. However, notice that the computation now needs to know the old value of the weight of the second layer, $w2$. This means that after the forward pass, not only do we need to keep in memory the results of all the computations, but we also need to remember the old weights. (An aside: There's a very important and interesting question about whether biological brains do backpropagation. The algorithm is considered biologically implausible, precisely because it needs to store the entire weight matrix used during the forward pass; no one knows how an immensely large biological neural network would keep such weight matrices in memory. It's very likely that our brains are implementing a different learning algorithm.)

Now we can update the weight and bias of the first layer:

$$\Delta w1 = -\alpha\frac{\partial L}{\partial w1};\ w1 = w1 + \Delta w1$$

$$\Delta b1 = -\alpha\frac{\partial L}{\partial b1};\ b1 = b1 + \Delta b1$$

You can see how, if our network had more than one hidden layer and more than one neuron per hidden layer, you can basically calculate the gradient with respect to each weight and bias and update them, too. This is the backpropagation algorithm. (See the coda on page 341 for how to generalize this result.)

This is the awesome power of the backpropagation algorithm. If the sequence of computations that lead from the input to the loss is differentiable at every step, we can compute the gradient of the loss function. Given the gradient, we can update each weight and bias a tiny bit, thus performing gradient descent until the loss is acceptably minimized.

It's hard to overstate the flexibility and power of the algorithm. You can, in principle, construct a network with any number of layers, any number of neurons per layer; build a network with either sparse or dense connections; design the appropriate loss function. All these choices together dictate the task you are asking your network to perform. Training eventually comes down to this: Provide the network with some set of inputs, figure out what the expected output should be (either because we humans have annotated the data and know what the output should be or because, in types of learning called self-supervised, the expected output is some known variation of the input itself), calculate the loss, calculate the gradient of the loss, update the weights/biases, rinse and repeat. On the next page is an example of a multi-layer perceptron, or a fully connected deep neural network.

The first layer is the input layer. For this example, which involves recognizing images of handwritten digits and classifying them accordingly, the input layer is made of 784 neurons, one for each pixel of the 28×28 image. The 2D image is flattened into a 784-dimensional vector. Next is the first hidden layer. This can have 10 or 100 or 1,000 or more neurons. (The more complex the task, the more neurons you'll

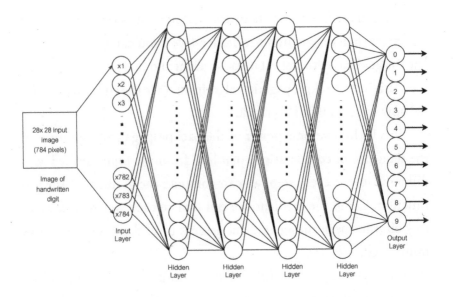

need.) What's important to note here is that in a fully connected neural network, or multi-layer perceptron, each neuron of each layer receives all the inputs from the previous layer. So, in the case of the first hidden layer, the first neuron of the layer receives all 784 inputs, as does every other neuron in that layer. Let's say there are 1,000 neurons in the first layer. That means there are 1,000 outputs coming out of that layer. So, each neuron in the next layer receives each one of those 1,000 outputs as inputs.

It's impossible to show this dense connectivity, so only some connections are shown in the above figure. But you get the idea.

The figure shows four hidden layers. Again, the more complex the task, the more hidden layers you might need. Even the number of neurons in the hidden layers can vary from layer to layer.

Of particular interest is the final, output layer. In this case, we have 10 output neurons. The idea is that a trained network, when presented with the image of one of 10 digits, will respond by firing neuron 0 for digit 0, neuron 1 for digit 1, and so on. (In each case, the other neurons may fire, too, but in a well-trained network, for an input image of digit 0, for example, the outputs of neurons 1–9 will be significantly less than the output of neuron 0, thus signifying that it has detected a "0.")

To appreciate the power of backpropagation, think of the silly network we analyzed: one hidden layer with one hidden neuron. Well, the exact same process can be used to train this undeniably more complex network to recognize handwritten digits.

WHAT EXACTLY DOES THE NETWORK LEARN?

In his Ph.D. thesis, Paul Werbos had shown how this algorithm would work by creating a table of the intermediate operations leading to the final result. He wrote about this procedure of backpropagation, "In general, the procedure . . . allows us to calculate the derivatives backwards down any ordered table of operations, so long as the operations correspond to differentiable functions." The final caveat is key: Every link in that chain has to be differentiable, or at least one should be able to satisfactorily approximate the function's derivative everywhere. Werbos, however, wasn't thinking about neural networks at the time.

Those who were thinking about neural networks in the 1970s had been working with binary threshold neurons. The threshold activation function of such neurons is not differentiable at the point where the function abruptly transitions from, say, 0 to 1.

Using the sigmoid as an activation function was one of the nuances of the work done by Rumelhart, Hinton, and Williams. The other advance had to do with concerns about symmetry breaking that we encountered earlier. When Hinton told Rumelhart about his interpretation of Rosenblatt's work—that breaking symmetry necessitated stochastic neurons—Rumelhart instantly saw a different way out. "His immediate reaction was 'Well, why can't we just break symmetry by having random initial weights?' Rosenblatt didn't think of that," Hinton told me. Neither had Hinton. Basically, by setting the initial value of each weight and bias in the network to some small random value (sampled from, say, a simple Gaussian distribution), one could ensure that symmetry was broken.

Hinton credits Rumelhart with designing the algorithm—or, rather, reinventing it, as others had already thought of it for other purposes. Hinton helped refine, implement, and test it; Williams helped with the math; and Rumelhart and Hinton focused their attention on what the algorithm empowered a multi-layer neural network to learn. They weren't interested only in the fact that a neural network with hidden layers could approximate any function—which it could, given enough neurons. "We were the group that used backpropagation to develop interesting representations," said Hinton, who is now at the University of Toronto.

And therein lies the import of neural networks. The algorithms we saw in earlier chapters, including support vector machines, all required us to specify beforehand the features in the data. Let's say we are dealing with a two-dimensional dataset. The obvious features would be the values $x1$ and $x2$. But this won't always work. For example, to separate the circles from the triangles in the dataset shown below, a linear classifier that works in two dimensions won't do.

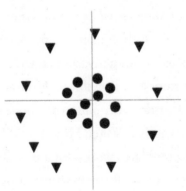

We know from previous attempts at solving this problem that it's not enough to just use [*x1, x2*] as the features. Rather, we need some nonlinear features. Specifically, we need to know these features in advance. For instance, to solve this particular problem, we could use a triplet of features [*x1, x2, x1x2*]. Even if we used a kernel to project this data into high dimensions, and then did a linear classification in the higher-dimensional space, we'd still need to design the kernel. But, with a neural network with sufficient neurons, all we would need to do is provide the inputs *x1* and *x2* and let the network figure out the features needed to classify the data correctly. It'll learn to *represent* these features internally. A neural network with just three neurons in the hidden layer might find the following decision boundary for our example dataset. (More hidden layer neurons would enable a smoother decision boundary.):

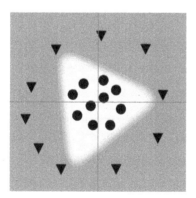

Rumelhart, Hinton, and Williams emphasized this aspect in their paper on backpropagation, the title of which read, "Learning Representations by Back-propagating Errors." The abstract of their paper states, "As a result of the weight adjustments, internal 'hidden' units which are not part of the input or output come to *represent* [italics mine] important features of the task domain, and the regularities in the task are captured by the interactions of these units. The ability to create useful new features distinguishes back-propagation from earlier, simpler methods such as the perceptron-convergence procedure."

Of course, publishing the paper—it's barely three pages long—involved laying some groundwork. The trio sent it to the journal *Nature*. "I did some political work in Britain of going and talking to all the people who might be referees," Hinton told me. One of them was Stuart Sutherland, an experimental psychologist at the University of Sussex. Hinton described to Sutherland how backpropagation allowed a neural network to learn representations. "It took a while to explain to him, but then he really got it," Hinton said. The canvassing paid off. Whomever *Nature* sent the paper to for peer review thought well enough of it; the journal accepted it for publication. Sutherland even wrote an accompanying essay in the same issue of the journal.

The importance of learning features, rather than having to hand-design them, will become increasingly clear in the next chapter, when we tackle image recognition, the application that brought neural networks fame. Even as Rumelhart, Hinton, and Williams were working on their backpropagation paper, a young student in Paris had independently developed an algorithm that achieved similar results. A colleague told Hinton that "there is a kid in France who is working on the same stuff." The kid was Yann LeCun. When Hinton met LeCun during a conference in Europe—this was before the backpropagation paper had been published—their intellectual chemistry was instant. "We were completing each other's sentences," LeCun told me. "He explained to me what he was working on. He was working on backprop." LeCun immediately understood the import of the work. He told Hinton, "You don't have to explain that to me." Hinton and LeCun would collaborate briefly soon after and then establish major labs of their own, setting the stage for the revolution in deep learning, the subject of our next chapter.

Meanwhile, in 1987, soon after the publication of the *Nature* paper, Rumelhart moved to Stanford University. He retired in 1998, as he fell ill with Pick's disease, a progressive neurodegenerative disorder; he died in 2011. "If he had lived, he would have been the person who got most of the credit for backprop," Hinton said. As it happens, it's Hinton who most often gets associated with and fêted for the algorithm, though even he admits he was simply one of a long chain of people who had grappled with the problem.

MATHEMATICAL CODA

The derivative of the sigmoid function

The sigmoid function is:

$$\sigma(z) = \frac{1}{1+e^{-z}}; \text{we want to find } \frac{d\sigma(z)}{dz}$$

Let $u = 1 + e^{-z}$

So:

$$\sigma(z) = \frac{1}{u} = u^{-1}$$

Using the chain rule:

$$\frac{d\sigma(z)}{dz} = \frac{d\sigma(z)}{du} \frac{du}{dz}$$

The first part of the expression is:

$$\frac{d\sigma(z)}{du} = \frac{du^{-1}}{du} = -\frac{1}{u^2}$$

The second part of the expression is:

$$\frac{du}{dz} = \frac{d\left(1+e^{-z}\right)}{dz} = -e^{-z}$$

So:

$$\frac{d\sigma(z)}{dz} = -\frac{1}{u^2} \times -e^{-z} = \frac{e^{-z}}{\left(1+e^{-z}\right)^2}$$

$$\Rightarrow \frac{d\sigma(z)}{dz} = \frac{e^{-z}}{\left(1+e^{-z}\right)} \times \frac{1}{\left(1+e^{-z}\right)}$$

$$\Rightarrow \frac{d\sigma(z)}{dz} = \frac{1}{\left(1+e^{-z}\right)} \times \frac{\left(1+e^{-z}\right)-1}{\left(1+e^{-z}\right)}$$

$$\Rightarrow \frac{d\sigma(z)}{dz} = \frac{1}{\left(1+e^{-z}\right)} \times \left[\frac{\left(1+e^{-z}\right)}{\left(1+e^{-z}\right)} - \frac{1}{\left(1+e^{-z}\right)} \right]$$

$$\Rightarrow \frac{d\sigma(z)}{dz} = \sigma(z).\left(1-\sigma(z)\right)$$

QED

GENERALIZATION OF THE BACKPROPAGATION ALGORITHM

Let's start with an input vector, **x**. Say **x** = [x1, x2]. Take the first hidden layer of a neural network. Let's say it has three neurons. Each neuron in the layer will create a weighted sum plus bias.

The first neuron's weighted sum will be:

$$z_1^1 = w_1^{11}x1 + w_1^{21}x2 + b_1^1$$

The second neuron's weighted sum will be:

$$z_1^2 = w_1^{12}x1 + w_1^{22}x2 + b_1^2$$

The third neuron's weighted sum will be:

$$z_1^3 = w_1^{13}x1 + w_1^{23}x2 + b_1^3$$

We can write this as:

$$\mathbf{z_1} = \begin{bmatrix} w_1^{11} & w_1^{21} \\ w_1^{12} & w_1^{22} \\ w_1^{13} & w_1^{23} \end{bmatrix} \begin{bmatrix} x1 \\ x2 \end{bmatrix} + \begin{bmatrix} b_1^1 \\ b_1^2 \\ b_1^3 \end{bmatrix} = \mathbf{W_1^T x + b}, \text{ where}$$

$$\mathbf{W_1} = \begin{bmatrix} w_1^{11} & w_1^{12} & w_1^{13} \\ w_1^{21} & w_1^{22} & w_1^{23} \end{bmatrix}$$

This intermediate output of the layer has to pass through the activation function. We can continue using the sigmoid function, though other functions can be used. The particulars don't matter as long as the activation function is differentiable.

The output of layer 1, after activation, is: $\mathbf{a_1} = \sigma(\mathbf{z_1})$

What this is saying is that each neuron's output—the weighted sum plus bias—is passed through a sigmoid. Let's extend this to a network of three hidden layers and a final, output layer. Here's the sequence of operations performed by the network:

Layer 1:

$$\mathbf{z_1} = \mathbf{W_1^T x + b_1} \Rightarrow \mathbf{a_1} = \sigma(\mathbf{z_1})$$

Layer 2:

$$z_2 = W_2^T a_1 + b_2 \Rightarrow a_2 = \sigma(z_2)$$

Layer 3:

$$z_3 = W_3^T a_2 + b_3 \Rightarrow a_3 = \sigma(z_3)$$

We now come to the final, output layer. There can be any number of neurons in the output layer, but for our purposes, consider a layer with just one neuron.

Output:

$$z_4 = w_4^{11} a_3^1 + w_4^{21} a_3^2 + w_4^{31} a_3^3 + b_4$$

$$z_4 = W_4^T a_3 + b_4$$

$$yhat = \sigma(z_4)$$

Calculating the error and loss gives us:

$$e = (y - yhat)$$

$$L = e^2$$

We now have all the ingredients for calculating the gradient of the loss function with respect to all the weights and biases. For example, let's say we want the partial derivative of the loss function L w.r.t. the weights of the third layer. That's given by (note that these equations use the matrix form of the weights, and vector forms for the outputs of all the neurons in a layer, for compactness):

$$\frac{\partial L}{\partial W_3} = \frac{\partial L}{\partial e} \frac{\partial e}{\partial \, yhat} \frac{\partial \, yhat}{\partial z_4} \frac{\partial z_4}{\partial a_3} \frac{\partial a_3}{\partial z_3} \frac{\partial z_3}{\partial W_3}$$

We know how to calculate each right-hand side term:

$$L = e^2 \Rightarrow \frac{\partial L}{\partial e} = 2e$$

$$e = (y - yhat) \Rightarrow \frac{\partial e}{\partial \, yhat} = -1$$

$$yhat = a_4 = \sigma(z_4) \Rightarrow \frac{\partial \, yhat}{\partial z_4} = \sigma(z_4)(1 - \sigma(z_4))$$

$$z_4 = \mathbf{W}_4^T \mathbf{a}_3 + \mathbf{b}_4 \Rightarrow \frac{\partial z_4}{\partial a_3} = \mathbf{W}_4^T$$

$$\mathbf{a}_3 = \sigma(z_3) \Rightarrow \frac{\partial a_3}{\partial z_3} = \sigma(z_3)(1 - \sigma(z_3))$$

$$z_3 = \mathbf{W}_3^T \mathbf{a}_2 + \mathbf{b}_3 \Rightarrow \frac{\partial z_3}{\partial W_3} = a_2$$

Each partial derivative equates to something that we either computed during the forward pass through the network (such as the value z_4 or $\mathbf{a}_2$) or to the current value of the weights (such as $\mathbf{W}_4^T$). We now have the gradient of the loss function with respect to the weights of one layer, and we can use the delta rule to update the weights.

That's it!

CHAPTER 11

The Eyes of a Machine

Almost all accounts of the history of deep neural networks for computer vision acknowledge the seminal work done by neurophysiologists David Hubel and Torsten Wiesel, co-founders of the Department of Neurobiology at Harvard in the early 1960s and joint winners of the 1981 Nobel Prize in Physiology or Medicine. The Nobel was for their work on the cat's visual system; it was awarded about fifteen years after their most pioneering work, and even in that intervening decade and a half, the two remained astonishingly productive. In 1982, the British vision scientist Horace Barlow wrote about Hubel and Wiesel's Nobel: "By now the award must be considered, not only one of the most richly-deserved, but also one of the hardest-earned."

Hubel and Wiesel's early work involved creating a map of the visual cortex by recording electrical activity from individual neurons in the brains of cats, while they showed the cats visual patterns using, of all things, a slide projector. This matter-of-fact description obscures the painstaking nature of the experiments. The detailed description of these experiments is not for the queasy. The work has its roots in Hubel's invention, in 1957, of a tungsten electrode to record the electrical activity of single neurons, or units, in the brain. This was a pioneering effort in itself. Until then, the most popular device for this purpose was an electrolyte-filled glass micropipette with a sharp tip that could be inserted into the brain. Hubel wanted something that wouldn't break if the animal moved. Others had developed steel electrodes, but they weren't stiff enough. Tungsten proved perfect. "The electrode has been used for recording single units for periods of the order of 1 hour from [the] cerebral cortex in chronic waking cats restrained only by a chest harness," Hubel wrote.

It's these electrodes that Hubel and Wiesel used to record the activity of single neurons in anesthetized cats. The cats were given the anesthetic intraperitoneal thiopental sodium and were kept under its influence throughout the experiment. (If electrocorticogram recordings showed that the effect was wearing off, the cat was dosed again.) With the electrodes in place, Hubel and Wiesel had to present visual stimuli to the anesthetized cat. They kept the cat's eyelids open with wire clips, its pupils dilated using 1 percent atropine (a nerve agent), and injected succinylcholine to immobilize the muscles in the eyes. Succinylcholine is a muscle relaxant, so now the cat couldn't breathe on its own, which "made it necessary to use artificial respiration." The scientists even used contact lenses with lubricants to keep the cat's eyes from "drying and becoming cloudy." With this complicated setup in place, Hubel and Wiesel used electrodes to study, for hours on end, the activity of hundreds of individual neurons in the cat's primary visual cortex as the cat's eyes were exposed to patterns projected onto a screen using a tungsten filament projector.

Would such experiments be allowed today? It's hard to say. Even by the 1980s, debates over the questionable ethics of such experiments were playing out in the op-ed pages of newspapers. A 1983 essay in *The New York Times* referred to a follow-up experiment Hubel and Wiesel did, which involved studying the development of vision in kittens. "At Harvard University, kittens were blinded by having their eyes sewn shut," wrote essayist Steven Zak, at the time a law student "specializing in animals and the law." This assertion drew a sharp response from a reader sympathetic to Hubel and Wiesel: "Among other things, their work has led to new ophthalmological procedures that will prevent blindness in thousands of children. There is ample evidence that the animals in those experiments received humane, decent care and did not suffer severe pain."

Hubel and Wiesel's findings certainly revolutionized our understanding of vision and, as the long arc of science shows, eventually impacted the design of deep neural network–based computer vision systems. It's the latter that concern us.

But first, a note about the stroke of luck that made their findings possible. Initially, Hubel and Wiesel could not get the cat's cortical neurons to fire in response to visual stimuli, no matter what they showed the cat. Nothing worked. Then, in a classic case of scientific serendipity, it happened. A neuron fired, producing the kind of staccato sounds associated with a Geiger counter. After some sleuthing, Hubel and Wiesel figured out why. They realized that the cell was firing when they were changing slides on their projector: The neuron fired only when the edge of the slide was oriented at a particular angle as it was being moved and the edge was being projected onto the screen. The information on the slide (in this case, a black dot) wasn't important. It was a particular orientation of the faint edge of the slide moving across the cat's visual field that was triggering the neuron. Hubel and Wiesel had discovered an edge-detecting cell.

Hubel and Wiesel argued that there's a hierarchy in the way information is processed in the visual cortex (a claim that has turned out to be not as clear-cut as in their initial account, but we'll stick to it because it's a view that has influenced AI enormously).

We need some definitions to appreciate their argument:

- The "visual field" is the region in front of us that our eyes are sensitive to at any instant, when the eyes are focused on something in front—the "focused" part is important. Otherwise, simply moving one's eyes would change the visual field. A stimulus in the visual field triggers a neural response.

- The "receptive field" refers to the portion of the visual field that triggers a single neuron. The size of the receptive field of a neuron can vary from the very small to large, as we'll soon see. If there's an appropriate stimulus in the receptive field of a neuron, that neuron will fire. The neurons with the smallest receptive field, meaning those directly monitoring the image on the retina, are called retinal ganglion cells, the first layer of neurons that receive inputs from the retina.

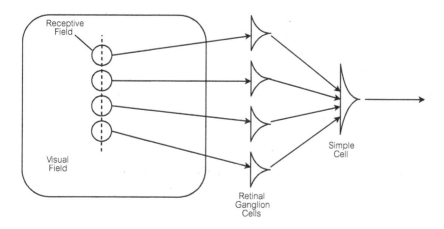

Now let's say there's some stimulus in the form of a vertical line that appears in the visual field and overlaps the receptive fields of four retinal ganglion cells. Each cell will fire in response to the signal in its respective receptive field. These four cells—four is only an example—connect to a "simple cell," a neuron that fires only when all four retinal ganglion cells (RGCs) fire together. Imagine a scenario where only one of the four RGCs fires. It has detected a stimulus. It signals the simple cell, but because the other three RGCs are quiet, the simple cell does not fire. If all four RGCs fire, then the simple cell fires, indicating the detection of a vertical edge. (This is reminiscent of the threshold activation function we encountered in earlier chapters: A single RGC input remains below some threshold needed to drive the simple cell, but inputs from multiple RGCs, arranged in the correct manner, exceed the threshold, causing the simple cell to fire.)

What if the edge were at an angle? Well, there are simple cells that fire for an edge that's at some angle to the vertical. For example, here's one that detects an edge at a 45-degree angle:

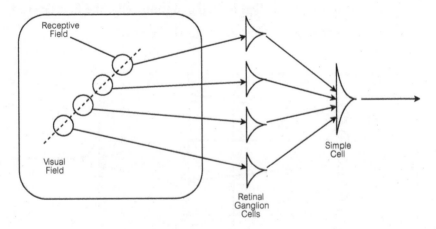

This leads us to a discussion about something incredibly interesting about vision: invariance. Think about a vertical edge. There might be many vertical edges in the visual field and a simple cell to detect each of those edges. But what if we want a neuron to signal the presence of a vertical edge regardless of its position in a large receptive field? Here's a solution: Many simple cells, each responding to a vertical edge in a different part of the overall visual field, feed their outputs to a complex cell that fires if any one of the simple cells fires. Now the complex cell is said to be invariant to translation: A vertical edge can be anywhere in the receptive field of the complex cell, and as long as it triggers some simple cell, it'll trigger a response from the complex cell.

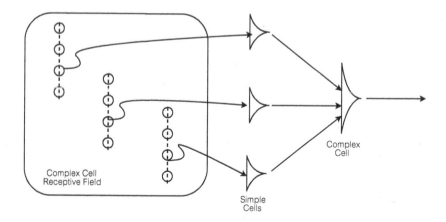

Similarly, you can have a complex cell that responds to an edge that's at 30 degrees to the vertical anywhere in its receptive field. These are examples of spatial, or translational, invariance.

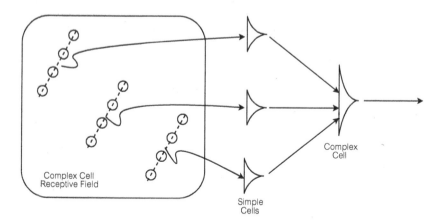

Something interesting happens to the receptive fields of neurons as we move up the hierarchy. The retinal ganglion cells have small receptive fields, and the RGCs fire only when there's some stimulus in their tiny patch of the visual field (the small circles in our illustration). But now consider an edge-detecting simple cell. Its receptive field is much larger (composed of the receptive fields of, say, four RGCs aligned along a line). Only when there's an edgelike stimulus that spans the entirety of that larger receptive field does the simple cell fire. Let's move up one level in the hierarchy. Take the complex cell that fires in response to the presence of a vertical edge in a spatially invariant manner: It has a much larger receptive field that spans the receptive fields of the constituent edge-detecting simple cells; the complex cell fires when there's a vertical edge anywhere in that larger receptive field.

Another important type of invariance, and one that's easy to illustrate, is rotation invariance. Here's an example in which complex cells fire when there's an edge of a given orientation in the receptive field. These complex cells feed their outputs to a hypercomplex cell, which fires when any one of the complex cells fires. What we have now is a cell that's invariant to rotation; as long as there's an edge in the receptive field of the hypercomplex cell, the cell will fire, regardless of the orientation of the edge.

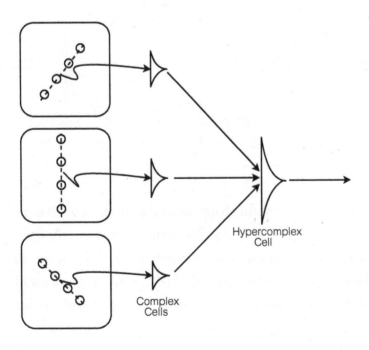

Hypercomplex
Cell

Complex
Cells

Hypercomplex cells are also known to fire maximally for an edge of some particular length; shorter or longer edges don't have the same effect. You can combine such hypercomplex cells to detect, say, a chevron, or V-shaped, pattern. The following figure shows only the hierarchical hypercomplex cells; there would be simple and complex cells preceding the first layer of hypercomplex cells.

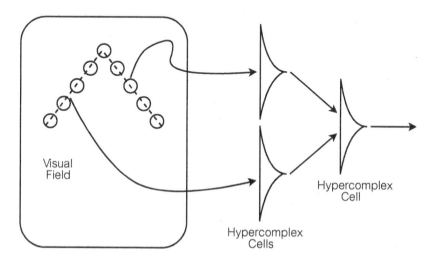

You can imagine combining these to get to cells higher up in the hierarchy that detect, say, a triangle or a square; and cells that are translation or rotation invariant to the presence of triangles or squares. And we can go on, imagining cells that are sensitive to different shapes; that are rotation and translation invariant; that are invariant to stretching, to lighting conditions, and so on. We can let the shapes get more and more complex until we end up with some "grandmother" cell that fires when you see . . . well, your grandmother (the latter bit about grandmother detecting cells is some far-fetched neuroscience lore).

That's a neat story, anyway, but actual brain circuitry is messier and way more complicated. Still, this neat story is what led to the first artificial neural network based on Hubel and Wiesel's work.

THE NEOCOGNITRON

Before the advent of deep neural networks, computer scientists took a particularly tedious approach to endowing machines with vision. First, they'd define the kinds of features you'd expect to see in an image (lines, curves, corners, color, etc.). The software would analyze an image to detect these features. It'd have to be invariant to various situations, such as those we've just encountered. The next layer of the software would then create a dictionary of objects: each object would consist of some set of features. Recognizing an object in another image involved detecting a significant number of a given set of features that defined that object. Such approaches proved computationally complex, given that the dictionary could keep getting bigger and bigger.

And yet our brains do it incredibly successfully. How?

In 1975, Kunihiko Fukushima of the NHK Science and Technology Research Laboratories in Tokyo announced the first real neural network–based image recognition system of considerable complexity in a paper titled "Cognitron: A Self-Organizing Multilayered Neural Network." The learning algorithm—which adjusts the weights between neurons—took a Hebbian approach. Let's say neuron x is connected to neuron y, where x is the pre-synaptic neuron and y is the post-synaptic neuron. (In biology, a synapse refers to a connection through which electrochemical signals flow between neurons.) Let's say that the neural network is given some input that cascades through the network, and the network produces an output, right or wrong. For our pair of neurons, x and y, the algorithm looks to see if x fired. If the answer is "yes," then it checks to see if y fired. If the answer is also "yes," it checks to see if y fired more strongly than other proximal post-synaptic neurons. If all these conditions are met, the algorithm strengthens the synaptic connection between x and y; this is akin to correcting the weights of connections. Keep doing this over and over for a range of inputs, such as the letters "X," "Y," "T," and "Z," and the network's connections stabilize and the output layer develops a distinct pattern of activation for each input.

But as Fukushima wrote in a subsequent paper, published in 1980, the cognitron's "response was dependent upon the position of the stimulus patterns." If the same pattern appeared in different positions in the visual field, the cognitron recognized them as different patterns. In other words, the cognitron wasn't translation invariant, let alone invariant in other, more complex ways.

In the 1980 paper, "Neocognitron: A Self-Organizing Neural Network Model for a Mechanism of Pattern Recognition Unaffected by Shift in Position," Fukushima introduced the neocognitron and paid homage to Hubel and Wiesel by adopting an architecture that was clearly inspired by their work. (For example, the neocognitron has S-cells and C-cells, meant to model simple and complex cells.) Each layer of the neocognitron has S-cells, which respond to some feature (say, a vertical edge). A number of such S-cells in a layer (which, taken together, are looking at some patch of the visual field) feed into a C-cell. If the C-cell fires, then it is indicating that there's a vertical edge in that patch of the visual field. There are numerous such C-cells in that layer, each responding to a vertical edge in a different patch. The outputs from all the C-cells in one layer would then serve as inputs to an S-cell in the next layer. So, if the C-cells in one layer are each responding to the presence of a vertical edge in some part of the visual field, then the S-cell in the next layer, which is collating all this information, will respond to the presence of an edge anywhere in the overall visual field. With this arrangement, we get vertical edge detection with translation invariance.

Using this architecture, Fukushima's neocognitron could learn to detect patterns, even if those patterns were shifted in position or were distorted or squished. A number of such layers gave the neocognitron the ability to recognize digits, even if the digits were shifting positions on the visual field or were distorted to some acceptable extent. This was a big deal at the time. "One of the largest and long-standing difficulties in designing a pattern-recognizing machine has been the problem [of] how to cope with the shift in position and the distortion in shape of the input patterns. The neocognitron . . . gives a drastic solution to this difficulty," Fukushima wrote.

Despite the advance, the neocognitron's training algorithm, which adjusted only the weights of the S-cells, was cumbersome, finely tuned, somewhat bespoke. Then, about a decade later, the "kid in France," Yann LeCun, now a young postdoc with Hinton in Toronto, solved the same problem, using a neural network architecture that became one of his signature contributions to AI: the convolutional neural network. The CNN was trained using the backpropagation algorithm, unlike the neocognitron. A few years after LeCun's paper was published, he met Fukushima. "He told me that when he saw our paper, in *Neural Computation,* he and his students were shocked, because they were actually working on the same thing," LeCun told me. Fukushima had been scooped.

THE LeNET

By now, Marvin Minsky and Seymour Papert must come across as the villains who derailed research into neural networks for a good part of a decade. So, it's somewhat surprising that Papert is one of LeCun's intellectual heroes. When LeCun was still a student studying electrical engineering in Paris, he chanced upon the book *Language and Learning: The Debate Between Jean Piaget and Noam Chomsky.* In October 1975, Piaget and Chomsky, two intellectual giants with divergent views on the nature of cognition, among other things, met at Royaumont Abbey, about thirty kilometers north of

Paris. Alongside Piaget and Chomsky were other prominent think-ers, including Papert. One of the questions they were debating was whether our cognitive capabilities are mainly innate (Chomsky's po-sition) or whether they are the outcome of learning that happens during development, given some small nucleus of innate biological mechanisms (Piaget's position). For example, one of Chomsky's basic arguments about language is that most syntactic structures in lan-guage are innate, not learned. Piaget thought otherwise. Papert, dur-ing the debate, was in Piaget's camp. He felt Chomsky wasn't giving learning its due. "I believe that Chomsky is biased toward perceiving certain syntactic structures as 'unlearnable' because his underlying paradigm of the process of learning is too simple, too restricted. If the only learning processes were those he seems to recognize, these syntactic structures might indeed have to be innate!"

Papert called for greater clarity about what it means to say some-thing is innate. "I will do this by describing an automaton, a ma-chine that we understand quite thoroughly, and asking questions about what is and what is not innate in the machine. If the question is unclear even in this 'toy' situation, how much more clarification does it need in the complex situation of human development?" he argued. "The machine in question is called a perceptron."

And then Papert went on to describe Rosenblatt's perceptron.

While still an undergrad, and before he had read the book about the Piaget-Chomsky debate and Papert's arguments, LeCun had been bitten by the intelligence bug. "I was always fascinated by the mystery of intelligence," he told me. "Maybe because I'm too stupid or too lazy, I always thought that human engineers would not be smart enough to conceive and design an intelligent machine. It will have to basically design itself through learning. I thought learning was an essential part of intelligence."

Papert's analysis, using perceptrons, was right along those lines.

LeCun, however, had never heard of learning machines. He was fascinated. He began digging through academic literature and poring over library books. He read about perceptrons, and he read Minsky and Papert's book. "I realized pretty early, because I read all those old papers, that everybody in the sixties was looking for a way to train multi-layer nets," LeCun told me. "They knew that the limitation was due to the fact that [they] were stuck with linear classifiers."

LeCun discovered and memorized part of the ML bible we have already encountered in previous chapters, Duda and Hart's *Pattern Recognition*. His key takeaway from all his reading, he told me, was that a "learning algorithm should minimize an objective function. You can derive a whole bunch of stuff from that."

An objective function is a slight but significant change to the loss function. We have already encountered the latter: It's a function that takes in the ML model's parameters and then calculates the loss, say, as the mean squared error (MSE) over the entire training dataset. We saw how the loss function can be minimized or optimized. Working only with the loss function comes with an inherent problem: Do too well on the optimization, and your ML model can overfit the data; it can literally memorize everything. In which case, it might perform badly when making predictions on test data it hasn't seen before. To avoid this, one can add an extra term to the loss function, something called a regularizer. This term is designed to make the ML model avoid overfitting. The loss function and the regularizer taken together constitute the objective function. Minimizing the objective function, instead of just a pure loss function, leads to a model that can generalize better to unseen data.

With minimizing objective functions for multi-layer neural networks on his mind, LeCun started his Ph.D. and learned about Fukushima's neocognitron. As part of his doctoral work, LeCun developed a learning algorithm that, he would realize, was related to the backpropagation algorithm (which we saw in the previous chapter). Instead of backpropagating gradients, or calculating all the partial derivatives using the chain rule, LeCun's algorithm backpropagated "virtual target values" for each hidden unit. The algorithm could then calculate an error for each unit and the requisite gradient to perform an update. Under special conditions, the algorithm behaves like backpropagation. While getting his Ph.D., LeCun began thinking about neural networks for invariant image recognition (of the kind we just saw).

He presented a paper on his learning algorithm at a conference in France in 1985. "It was [a] badly written paper in French," he told me. Hinton, who was the keynote speaker at the conference, sought out LeCun, and the two hit it off, even completing each other's sentences, LeCun recalled. Hinton invited LeCun to come to a summer school he was organizing in 1986 at Carnegie Mellon University, in Pittsburgh. There, Hinton told LeCun that he was moving to the University of Toronto; he asked if LeCun would join him there as his postdoc. "I said, 'Of course.'"

LeCun finished his Ph.D. in 1987 and moved to Toronto, where he enjoyed an intellectually stimulating time with Hinton, the two having conversations "that I pretty much only had with him." It was in Toronto that LeCun began working on convolutional neural networks for image recognition, or conv nets. (We'll come to what "convolution" means in a minute.) These days, if a software engineer wants to implement a conv net, they can do so with fewer than a hundred lines of code, thanks to software packages such as PyTorch and TensorFlow. No such software existed in the mid-1980s. LeCun and a fellow doctoral student, named Léon Bottou, had to write special software to simulate neural networks. Called SN, it would eventually become Lush, one of the ancestors of the modern-day PyTorch. But in 1987, SN was a huge deal. "That [gave] us superpowers. Nobody else had anything like this," LeCun told me. "It really was very instrumental in building the first conv net."

Within a year of being at Toronto, LeCun was recruited by Bell Labs in Holmdel, New Jersey, where he joined an illustrious group led by Larry Jackel. At Bell Labs, LeCun got access to a large, intriguing dataset: images of handwritten digits from the U.S. Postal Service. The USPS was interested in automating the process for recognizing zip codes. LeCun coded a neural net to recognize these handwritten digits. PCs were still not fast enough to run such computer-intensive software, so he wrote a compiler using the Lisp programming language, which would take in the definition (or architecture) of the neural network to be implemented and spit out code in the C programming language. A C compiler would then turn this code to low-level instructions that could run on a hardware digital signal processor.

Meanwhile, a colleague, Donnie Henderson, put together a demo that used a video camera to turn handwritten digits scribbled on a piece of paper into digital images for the neural network to recognize. All this work happened in the space of a few months after LeCun got to Bell Labs. He recalled the experience of watching his neural network recognize hand-drawn digits: "It's not that I had any doubt it would work. I was young and fearless," he told me. Nonetheless, he was "absolutely elated." The work resulted in a couple of papers, including the one in *Neural Computation* that shocked, and scooped, Fukushima's neocognitron team. The outcome was a convolution neural network that today is called LeNet; all modern-day CNNs are its descendants.

DOING THE CONVOLUTION

At the heart of even the most sophisticated convolution neural network today is a very basic operation: the convolution. The term comes from a special operation that can be performed using two functions, say, $f(x)$ and $g(x)$:

$f(x) * g(x)$, where "$*$" is the convolution operator.

We aren't concerned with the general case of convolutions of functions but, rather, with a very specific 2D case that's applicable to images. Let's say you have a 5×5 image. Convolution in the context of an image is the operation performed on the image using another, smaller—say, 2×2—image, which is called a kernel or kernel filter. Here's an example of such an image and kernel:

2	1	3	1	4
4	1	0	1	3
1	3	1	1	1
2	6	1	1	1
3	3	1	0	4

$\otimes$

1	2
-1	3

The process of convolution starts by our placing the 2×2 kernel on the top-left corner of the 5×5 image; this gives us four overlapping pixels. Multiply each pixel of the kernel with the value of the pixel lying beneath it. You get four numbers. Sum them up. The sum gives you the pixel value for a new image, at location [1, 1]. (There's a formula for the size of the new image, but let's leave that aside for now and take it that it's a 4×4 image.) Here's the first operation:

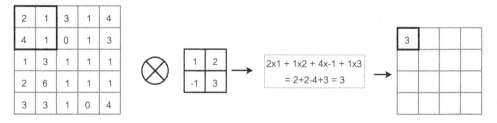

Now slide the kernel one pixel to the right. (The exact amount by which the kernel slides to the right can be changed, but we can use one pixel without any loss of generality.) Again, we have four overlapping pixels. Multiply each pair of overlapping pixels and sum them up. Now the sum gives you the pixel value for the new image at location [1, 2].

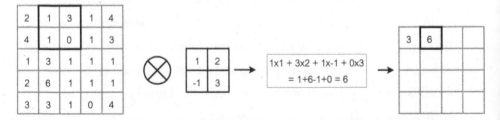

Keep sliding the kernel one pixel to the right, generating a new pixel value for the new image, until you cannot slide the kernel to the right any farther. For our example 5×5 image and 2×2 kernel, we can generate only four pixels as we go from left to right.

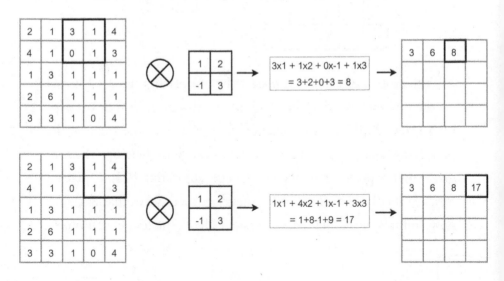

Once the kernel hits the end of the image on the right, we go back to the left and slide down one row and repeat the entire process. This generates the pixel values for the second row of the new image.

You get the picture. We do this until the kernel cannot move right any farther and then we go back to the left, slide the kernel down one pixel, and continue until we reach the bottom right of the

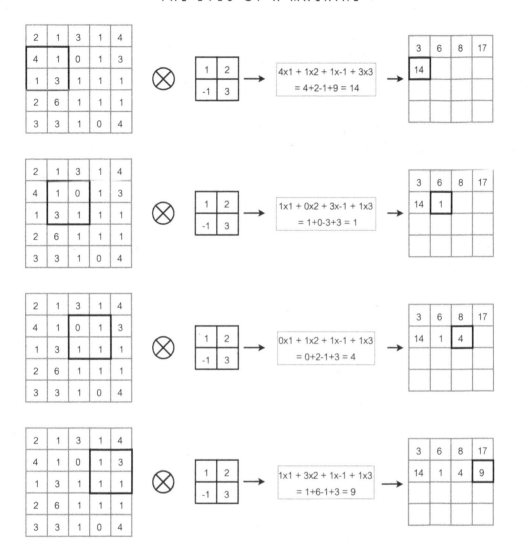

main image and there's no place left for the kernel to go. In this example, we generate a new 4×4 image. Have a go at filling up the rest of the blank spaces in the new image.

We've just convolved the 5×5 image with the 2×2 kernel. Before we go into more details about the convolution, the figures on the following page show an example of convolving 28×28 images of handwritten digits, with two different 3×3 kernels. (The first image is the original, and the following two are convolved images.)

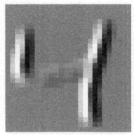

Leaving aside the specifics of the kernels, do you notice anything in particular about the new images? First, what's not obvious is that the new images are 26×26 (the convolution operation reduced the size). But more important, what's visually obvious, especially if you squint at the images, is that in the first convolved image, the horizontal line of the digit 4 is highlighted; whereas in the second convolved image, the vertical lines are highlighted. You can see the same effect, in a more pronounced manner, when the convolution operation is performed on the digit 1. (Again, the leftmost image is the original, followed by the two convolved images.)

The kernels were chosen specifically to achieve these highlights. The two kernels are:

$$
\begin{bmatrix} -1 & 0 & 1 \\ -1 & 0 & 1 \\ -1 & 0 & 1 \end{bmatrix} \text{ and } \begin{bmatrix} -1 & -1 & -1 \\ 0 & 0 & 0 \\ 1 & 1 & 1 \end{bmatrix}
$$

These are called Prewitt kernels, after their developer. These kernels succeed in generating new images, after the convolution, that detect horizontal and vertical edges. Keep in mind, for now, that these are hand-designed kernels. LeCun wanted his neural network to learn such kernels.

While doing the convolution, we made some assumptions. The first is that the kernel moved right or down by one pixel. The number of pixels by which the kernel moves is called its stride. We had a stride of 1. We could have chosen 2, and we'd have generated a new image of a different size. The choice of stride dictates the size of the new image; so, for an input image size i, kernel filter size k, and stride s, the output image size is given by:

$$\lfloor ((i - k)/s) + 1 \rfloor$$

(The floor brackets around some number, denoted by $\lfloor some\ number \rfloor$, evaluate to the largest integer that's less than or equal to the number inside the brackets. So, the floor of 4.3, given by $\lfloor 4.3 \rfloor$, is 4.)

We are making some other assumptions here: The input image is square (i.e., image width equals height), and we are not adding dummy pixels, called padding, around the input image, which is often done in convolutional networks. For 28×28 images, a 3×3 kernel, and a stride of 1, we get 26×26 images as output.

It's time to connect these ideas to neurons, their weights, the idea of receptive fields, and so on. Consider a single operation, when the kernel is atop some portion of the image (see figure on next page):

The pixels in the main image have values [$x11$, $x12$, $x21$, $x22$]. The kernel's pixels have values [$w11$, $w12$, $w21$, $w22$]. Here's the result of multiplying the kernel with the underlying pixels:

$$w11x11 + w12x12 + w21x21 + w22x22$$

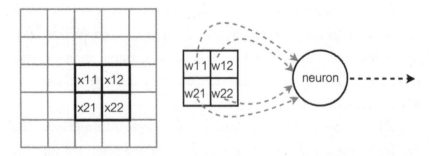

This must remind you of the operation done by an artificial neuron. The weights of the neuron are the values of the individual elements of the kernel. The inputs to the neuron are the pixel values of that part of the main image over which the kernel is hovering. The output of the neuron is simply the weighted sum of those pixels.

So, for every position the kernel takes atop the image, we assign one neuron. In our example, for a 5×5 image and a 2×2 kernel with a stride of 1, we need 16 such neurons. The outputs of these neurons give us a 4×4 image.

Here's how this connects to the idea of receptive fields. Each neuron is paying attention only to a particular part of the image: either the four pixels in the top-left or top-right corner or in the bottom-left or bottom-right corner or the four pixels anywhere in the middle. Each neuron has its own region of interest in the image, and that is its receptive field. It'll respond only to those pixels.

The output of a neuron will depend, of course, not just on the values of the pixels in its receptive field, but also on its weights, or the elements of the kernel matrix. We saw two examples of kernels, one that causes an output when there's a horizontal edge and the other when there's a vertical edge, in the receptive fields of the neurons.

For our example of a 5×5 image and a 2×2 kernel, we have a layer of 16 neurons, the outputs of which form a 4×4 image. The 16 neurons form the first hidden convolution layer of a neural network.

These neurons, which share the same set of values for their weights, are like simple cells: Each responds to some pattern in its receptive field.

Now imagine taking the 4×4 image obtained after the first convolution and applying another convolution using a different 2×2 kernel. The output will be a 3×3 image. This will require 9 neurons. This is the second hidden convolution layer. Each neuron in this layer is the equivalent of a complex cell in Hubel and Wiesel's hierarchy. Each neuron in this layer is sensitive to the value of 4 pixels in the 4×4 image generated by the previous layer. But each pixel in the 4×4 image was the outcome of a neuron that was sensitive to 4 pixels in the previous, input image. So, the neuron in the second layer is effectively sensitive to 9 pixels in the input image. Why is the receptive field not equal to 4×4 = 16 pixels? A moment's thought will give you the answer.

11	12	13	14	15
21	22	23	24	25
31	32	33	34	35
41	42	43	44	45
51	52	53	54	55

Input image

11	12	13	14
21	22	23	24
31	32	33	34
41	42	43	44

Image generated by first hidden layer

11	12	13
21	22	23
31	32	33

Image generated by second hidden layer

In the illustration above, the numbers in the individual cells refer to the row and column numbers of the image, not to the value of the pixels. So, 11 means row 1, column 1; and 43 means row 4, column 3; and so on. So, pixel 11 in the final 3×3 image is the outcome of a kernel operating on four pixels in the previous image (pixels 11, 12, 21, and 22). But those four pixels are the outcome of sliding the 2×2 kernel across four patches in the previous layer, covering pixels 11, 12, 13, 21, 22, 23, 31, 32, and 33.

If we take just the 3×3 patch of the original image, highlighted in bold lines, here are the connections in a neural network that can transform that patch into a single pixel. First, we lay out the pixels in a straight line for easy visualization and, then, connect these pixels to their respective individual neurons. It's clear how each neuron in the first hidden layer is only responding to four pixels. Of course, the full layer will have 16 neurons; the illustration shows only 4 of them. The 4 neurons generate 4 pixels of the next 4×4 image. These pixels/ outputs become the input to the neuron in the next layer, which then produces one pixel for the subsequent image.

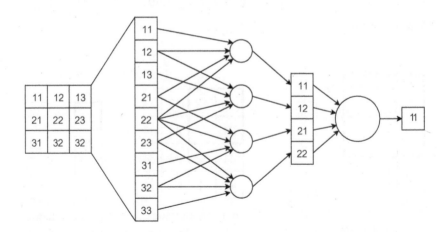

Can you see why the kernel operation gives us, in this case, translation invariance? Let's say the kernel detects a horizontal edge. The edge can be anywhere in the image. As long as it falls within the receptive field of one or more neurons, we'll get a signal from at least one of the neurons in the first layer. The same goes for vertical edges. Layers that follow can act on these signals.

The architecture is reminiscent of the hierarchy that Hubel and

Wiesel had posited exists in our brains. The simple cells, or neurons, of the first hidden layer respond to simple features. Complex cells in the next hidden layer respond to the outputs of a group of simple cells, so they are responding to some composition of the simpler features. This hierarchy can keep going until you have a neuron that fires because the continued composition of features indicates, say, the presence of the digit 1 or the digit 4 in the input.

The kernels we used were specially designed by someone who put a lot of thought into them. And it's relatively straightforward to design kernels to detect simple features, such as vertical or horizontal edges. But what about complex images? What features should one be looking for that would distinguish one image from another? And how do we design such kernels?

This is where LeCun's insight came to the fore. There's no way a human can figure out all the myriad features that define an image and then design kernels to highlight those features. LeCun realized he could train a neural network to learn these kernels; after all, the elements of each kernel matrix are the weights of individual neurons. Training a network using backpropagation to do some task would, in essence, help the network find the appropriate kernels.

We need to understand one more commonly used operation in convolution neural networks before we put all the pieces together. It's an operation called pooling, of which there are a few types, but we'll focus on one in order to understand the process conceptually. It's called max pooling.

The basic idea behind max pooling is to place a filter (another name for a kernel) over some part of the original image and then simply spit out the largest pixel value in the region below the filter. Max pooling is applied to an image that has been produced by one stage of a convolution. This brings down the size of the image further and has two huge benefits. First, the number of neurons you require for the next stage of convolution is reduced; and second, the receptive field of a neuron that comes after the max pooling stage is increased even more, helping with translation invariance.

Given a 4×4 image (obtained, say, after a convolution), here's what max pooling would look like with a 2×2 filter. Unlike the convolution kernel, the max pooling filter moves such that there are no overlapping pixels, so the stride is the same as the kernel size. In our example, the stride is 2 pixels.

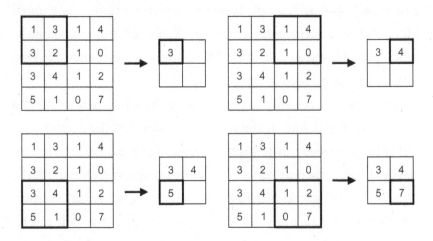

Again, the size of the new image is given by a simple formula (assuming square images and no padding):

$$\lfloor ((i - k)/s) + 1 \rfloor$$

The formula, for an input image size $i = 4$, pooling filter size $k = 2$, and stride $s = 2$, gives us an output image size of 2. So, a 4×4 image turns into a 2×2 image.

With all these elements of a convolutional neural network in hand, we can put a CNN together to recognize handwritten digits.

DISTINGUISHING FEATURES

As LeCun realized, the power of a convolutional neural network lies in its ability to learn features. Learning a feature involves learning the values for a kernel, which, as we saw, is the same as learning the weights of a bunch of neurons. One way to ensure that your network is powerful is to have a large number of such kernels, each learning to distinguish a different feature that's necessary to accomplish, say, the task of recognizing handwritten digits. What follows is a simple architecture that gets at the conceptual heart of a convolutional neural network, with multiple kernels:

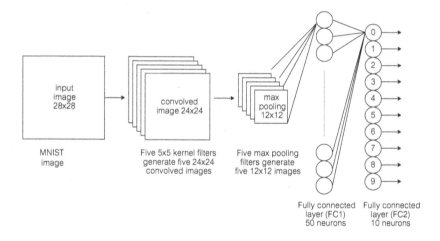

The grayscale input image is processed by five different kernels. What's implicit in the above figure is that convolutions and max pooling are being done by bunches of neurons; for clarity, they are not shown. Backpropagation can be used to learn the weights of these neurons. Each convolution generates a 24×24 image; we have five kernels, so, potentially, the network will learn to look for five different features in the input image. After convolutions comes the max pooling layer. The outputs of each max pooling operation generate a

12×12 image, and there are five of these. (A geeky aside: There is no parameter or weight to be learned for the max pooling layer during training, but we need to keep track of the location of the maximum pixel value in the previous layer, in order to use the chain rule and backpropagate the gradient.) At the end of the convolution-plus-max-pooling combo, it's time to make decisions based on the features that might have been detected. The pixels of all the images generated by max pooling are laid end to end, making up a vector of length 720 (12×12×5). These inputs feed into the first fully connected layer (FC1). Let's say FC1 has 50 neurons. Each neuron receives 720 inputs and produces an output. The figure shows only the top neuron receiving these inputs.

The outputs of the 50 neurons of FC1 feed into FC2, which has 10 neurons: So, each neuron of FC2 receives 50 inputs. Finally, we get 10 outputs out of FC2. Why 10? Well, our task is to recognize handwritten digits. The idea is that if the input digit is 0, then the zeroth neuron fires more strongly than all the others; if the digit is 1, then neuron number 1 fires the strongest; and so on.

Had the task been to distinguish between two images, an FC2 with just one neuron would have sufficed. It could output 0 for one type of image and 1 for another type; say, 0 for cats and 1 for dogs. How do you train such a network? For our dataset of handwritten digits, we have labeled data—someone painstakingly annotated each image as being a 0 or a 1 or a 9 and so on—so, we can use supervised learning. Present the network with an image and ask it to predict the digit. Say, the input is the digit 8. Ideally, the output neuron representing the digit 8 should fire more strongly than the others (meaning, the value it outputs should be significantly greater than the values generated by the other neurons of FC2). An untrained network will fire willy-nilly. Calculate the error between what's expected and what the network does, and then use this error to calculate the gradients, via backpropagation. Then update the weights of all the neurons that were involved in turning the input image into an output. The updated weights ensure that for the same input, the network's error is a tiny bit less than before. Do this for all images, over and over, until the network's error rate is acceptably low. If we calculate the gradients for all images in the training dataset and update the weights in one go, we are doing gradient descent. If we use only a subset of the images for each pass through the network, we are doing stochastic gradient descent—a drunken walk down the loss landscape to a good-enough minimum.

What's been left unsaid so far is that a designer of such a network has to make a host of decisions about parameters of the network that are not learned during the training process, decisions that nonetheless influence the network's performance immensely. For instance, the neurons of convolution layers and the fully connected layers have activation functions. The choice of activation function is one such decision. The only condition is that the activation function should be differentiable, or at least approximately so, to enable the backpropagation of gradients.

These hand-chosen parameters, including the size and number of kernel filters, the size and number of max pooling filters, the number of convolution and max pooling layers (we had only a single pair in the example above; one can keep stacking them), the size and number of fully connected layers, the activation functions—all these constitute so-called hyperparameters. Fine-tuning, or finding the right values for, the hyperparameters is an art unto itself. Crucially, these are *not* learned via backpropagation.

LeCun's LeNet was somewhat more complicated than our example, but not overly so; he made it work. Also, it was a deep neural network, meaning it had hidden layers. (The layers between the input and FC2, in our case, are hidden.) LeNet was used by NCR

Corporation to read and recognize digits on checks for the banking industry. "That was one of the few applications of backprop that really worked pretty well, and was deep," Hinton told me.

This was the early 1990s. Despite LeNet, deep neural networks didn't hit the big time. Part of that was because of the success of support vector machines, which made a splash in the machine learning community at around the same time: SVMs were easy to understand, the software was available, and for small datasets of the time, they were an ideal algorithm. Convolutional neural networks, for their part, were still opaque and mysterious to many. And of course, no general-purpose software existed that one could leverage to build these CNNs. "You had to write your own deep learning framework," LeCun told me. "You couldn't get it from us, because AT&T would not let us distribute our software open source. So we could not enable people to reproduce our results. And as a consequence, nobody did." People attempted to write their own deep learning frameworks. "You could start spending a year writing a piece of software to run neural nets and convolutional nets, and a few people did this," he said.

Meanwhile, throughout the 1990s, LeCun continued working on and advocating for convolutional neural networks for image recognition over more conventional techniques. For low-resolution images that didn't need powerful neural networks, his CNNs were outperforming other algorithms. "We published those papers in all the big conferences, but it didn't have a big impact, because by that time, the computer vision community was thinking, 'Oh, maybe there's a small difference, maybe your conv net works okay. But we are going to catch up with our methods,'" he told me.

Also, the situations where neural networks weren't working as well were revealing. "There were signs that there was an issue of scale," he said. "When [images] weren't too big and the neural nets weren't too large, they were beating the hell out of everything." But not so with high-resolution images. Recognizing high-res images re-quired large neural networks, and training such networks meant having to crunch numbers, mainly in the form of matrix manipula-tions. To make the process go faster, much of this number crunching required a form of parallel computing, but the central processing units (CPUs) of computers of the 1990s weren't up to the task. How-ever, saviors were on the horizon in the form of graphical processing units (GPUs), which were originally designed as hardware-on-a-chip dedicated to rendering 3D graphics.

GPUs proved central to changing the face of deep learning. One of the earliest indications of this change came in 2010, from Jürgen Schmidhuber and colleagues, when they trained multi-layer percep-trons with as many as nine hidden layers and about 12 million pa-rameters or weights, to classify MNIST images. They achieved error rates as low as 0.35 percent. "All we need to achieve this best result so far are many hidden layers, many neurons per layer, numerous deformed training images, and graphics cards to greatly speed up learning," the team wrote.

But the use of GPUs to overcome the challenge posed by the rel-atively small MNIST dataset doesn't begin to hint at the power of these processors. To understand their true impact, on deep learning in general and CNNs in particular, we have to shift focus to Hin-ton's lab in Toronto, where Hinton and two graduate students, Alex Krizhevsky and Ilya Sutskever—Krizhevsky was a whiz at program-ming GPUs, and Sutskever was a visionary who saw the potential of large deep neural networks—built the first massive CNN. For its time, it was a gigantic neural network trained on high-res images and an immense number of them. With it, Krizhevsky and Sutskever showed once and for all that conventional methods for image recog-nition were never going to catch up. The network came to be called AlexNet.

ALEXNET

Even before the advent of AlexNet, Hinton and a graduate student named Volodymyr Mnih understood the usefulness of GPUs. The two were working on the problem of finding roads in aerial images. "In cities, where there are trees and parked cars and shadows, it's not trivial to find the roads," Hinton told me. But they realized they had ample data to help them: access to other types of maps in which roads were clearly marked. These were so-called vector maps, and each map was stored as a collection of points, lines, and polygons. Unlike an image, a vector map is drawn upon demand, using the stored information. Hinton and Minh used information in these vector maps to teach neural networks how to appropriately label the pixels of an aerial image. (For example, does the pixel belong to a road or not?) This required a large neural network. (It wasn't a CNN, though; the team decided against using CNNs because of concerns that a pooling layer would destroy information about spatial positions at the level of individual pixels.) The large network required GPUs; by then, these came equipped with software called CUDA, a programming interface that allowed engineers to use GPUs for general-purpose tasks beyond their intended use as graphics accelerators. Mnih wrote another package atop CUDA, called CUDAMat, to "make it easy to perform basic matrix calculations on CUDA-enabled GPUs."

A year later, two other students of Hinton's successfully used CUDAMat to program deep neural networks to make breakthroughs in speech recognition. GPUs were obviously crucial for unleashing the power of these networks, but not everyone recognized this. Hinton recalls trying to persuade Microsoft to buy GPUs for a common project, but Microsoft balked. Hinton told the company, tongue in cheek, that his team could afford GPUs because he was at a rich Canadian university and that Microsoft was a "poor impoverished company," so it was understandable that it "couldn't afford them." The sarcasm worked. "They bought GPUs," Hinton told me. "And then they tried to run them with Microsoft software. So . . ."

Ironically, Hinton's early success at using regular nonconvolutional deep neural networks for the roads-in-aerial-images project delayed his lab's foray into convolutional neural networks. "We were just a bit slow, but Ilya [Sutskever] realized we had to do it," he said.

In 2002, Sutskever, who was barely seventeen, joined the University of Toronto. Within a year, he had decided to work on AI. "I wanted to contribute to AI," he told me. "Neural networks seemed obviously correct." To that end, when he was still in his second year of undergraduate studies, he knocked on Hinton's door. Sutskever remembers not being particularly tactful or polite toward Hinton. Hinton gave Sutskever some papers to read. The young Sutskever was taken aback by the power of the simple ideas. "I definitely remember being perplexed by how simple the whole thing is . . . How can it be?" he said. "You look at your undergrad classes in math or physics, and they're so complicated. And then this stuff is so simple. You just read two papers and you understand such powerful concepts. How can it be that it's so simple?"

Sutskever had a background in computational complexity theory, the study of what computers can and cannot do. "One of the things that comes up from looking at computational complexity theory is that certain computational models are much more powerful than others," he said. "The thing that was very clear about neural networks is that [they] fit the bill of a powerful computational model. It was powerful enough."

And indeed, a problem big enough to pose questions of neural networks appeared in 2009. That year, Stanford University professor Fei-Fei Li and her students presented a paper at the first Computer

Vision and Pattern Recognition (CVPR) conference. Titled "ImageNet: A Large-Scale Hierarchical Image Database," the paper included an immense dataset of millions of hand-labeled images consisting of thousands of categories (immense by the standards of 2009). In 2010, the team put out the ImageNet challenge: Use 1.2 million ImageNet images, binned into 1,000 categories, to train your computer vision system to correctly categorize those images, and then test it on 100,000 unseen images to see how well the system recognizes them. The contest was so new that it was conducted as a "taster competition" alongside a more established contest, the PASCAL Visual Object Classes Challenge 2010.

Standard computer vision still ruled the roost then. In recognition of this, the ImageNet challenge provided users with so-called scale invariant feature transforms (SIFTs). Developers could use these SIFTs to extract known types of low-level features from images, recognize those features, and use them to categorize an image. (Neural networks, which could figure out the features of importance on their own, weren't in the picture.) In 2010, a team from NEC and the University of Illinois Urbana-Champaign (NEC-UIUC) won the challenge. Their system essentially used the SIFTs to turn each image into a long vector. A support vector machine learned to categorize these vectors and, thus, classify the images.

Meanwhile, Sutskever saw the writing on the wall. SVMs had won the 2010 competition, but in his mind, they were limited. Neural networks were the future. "If you could figure out how to train them, if you could get the data, then the ceiling [for what neural networks could do] was high. Whereas the other stuff, [such as] support vector machines—it doesn't matter how much you want to study them. The ceiling is low . . . So, you're doomed from the get-go," he told me.

Data, suddenly, wasn't an issue. The ImageNet dataset had solved that problem for the moment. Training, however, remained an issue. Sutskever saw the work Hinton's team had done with GPUs, put two and two together, and pushed Hinton to build a convolution neural network that could be trained using GPUs. "Ilya is a visionary. He's just got wonderful intuitions and lots of confidence," Hinton told me. "It was Ilya who realized that the technology we were using, with GPUs and these new learning algorithms, would just solve ImageNet." Yann LeCun's group at Bell Labs was also onto it. "Yann realized the same thing. And he tried to get several different graduate students to do it, but none of them was willing to work on it," Hinton said. "And that was lucky for us, because Ilya realized we really had to do it before anybody else did it."

Crucial help came in the form of Alex Krizhevsky's wizardry with GPUs. "He could program convolutions on GPUs better than anybody else," Hinton said. Sutskever and Krizhevsky were lab mates. Krizhevsky had already written CUDA code to train GPU-enabled neural networks on a smaller image dataset called CIFAR (the Canadian Institute for Advanced Research). Sutskever was impressed by the code. He convinced Krizhevsky to do the same for ImageNet.

So, with the power of GPUs and an immense amount of data— two things LeCun didn't have in 1989— Krizhevsky, Sutskever, and Hinton built AlexNet, a deep convolutional neural network trained on 1.2 million high-res images from the ImageNet dataset, consisting of a thousand categories. There were five convolutional layers, some of which fed into max pooling layers. There were two fully connected layers of neurons, much like in our earlier example. The final output layer had a thousand neurons, one for each category of image. The neural network had more than half a million neurons and 60 million parameters, or weights, whose values had to be learned during training. There were other, smaller but significant technical advances (for instance, a choice of a different activation function for neurons, called a rectified linear unit, ReLU, instead of the sigmoid function).

In 2012, Fei-Fei Li's team announced the results of their annual image recognition context. AlexNet, as the Toronto group's network is rightfully called, won by a wide margin. AlexNet could classify images in the ImageNet test dataset with a top-5 error rate as low as 17 percent (the top-5 error rate refers to the percentage of times the correct label for an image does not appear in the top five most likely labels predicted by the ML model). The winners in 2010 and 2011 were way behind, at 28 and 26 percent, respectively. Even the runner-up in 2012 was lagging, at 26 percent. The non-neural network systems had barely moved the needle. Deep neural networks had finally lived up to their promise. Sutskever was vindicated, because even before the trio started working on AlexNet, he had been evangelizing. "I would go around and I would annoy people," he told me. "I would tell them that deep learning is going to change everything."

It has. AlexNet was just the start. Deep neural networks have gotten bigger and bigger, and better and better, at a wide range of tasks: computer vision (a field that subsumes subspecialties such as face and object detection and recognition), natural language processing (which allows machines to respond to human-generated text or voice with its own human-like text or voice response), machine translation (which takes text in one language and translates it into another), medical image analysis, pattern detection in financial data, and so much more. The list is endless.

Viewed through our mathematical lens, deep neural networks have thrown up a profound mystery: As they have gotten bigger and bigger, standard ML theory has struggled to explain why these networks work as well as they do. Mikhail Belkin of the University of California, San Diego, thinks that deep neural networks are pointing us toward a more comprehensive theory of machine learning. He likens the situation in ML research to the time in physics when quantum mechanics came of age. "Everything went out of the window," he said. Something similar is being forced upon ML theorists, thanks to empirical data about artificial neural networks. Belkin compares empiricists to cartographers: They are illuminating the terrain for theorists to follow. Our final chapter will give us a glimpse of this exciting new terrain.

CHAPTER 12

Terra Incognita

Deep Neural Networks Go Where (Almost) No ML Algorithm Has Gone Before

S ometime in 2020, researchers at OpenAI, a San Francisco–based artificial intelligence company, were training a deep neural network to learn, among other things, how to add two numbers. The numbers were in binary, and the addition was modulo-97, meaning any sum of two numbers would always be between 0 and 96. If the sum exceeded 96, it'd wrap around, the way numbers wrap around on a clock face. The idea is best illustrated by looking at examples. So, any sum of two numbers can be written as:

$$sum = x + \text{(some multiple of 97), where } 0 \leq x \leq 96$$

So, the sum, modulo-97, is:

$$sum_{\text{mod}97} = x$$

For example, let's say you want to add 22 and 28:

$$sum = 22 + 28 = 50 + (0 \times 97)$$

$$\Rightarrow sum_{\text{mod}97} = 50$$

Or, you want to add 40 and 59:

$$sum = 40 + 59 = 99 = 2 + (1 \times 97)$$

$$\Rightarrow sum_{\text{mod97}} = 2$$

It was a seemingly trivial problem, but a necessary step toward understanding how to get the AI to do analytical reasoning. A team member who was training the neural network went on vacation and forgot to stop the training algorithm. When he came back, he found to his astonishment that the neural network had learned a general form of the addition. It's as if it had understood something deeper about the problem than simply memorizing answers for the sets of numbers on which it was being trained.

In the time-honored tradition of serendipitous scientific discoveries, the team had stumbled upon a strange, new property of deep neural networks that they called "grokking," a word invented by the American author Robert Heinlein in his book *Stranger in a Strange Land*. "Grokking is meant to be about not just understanding, but kind of internalizing and becoming the information," Alethea Power, a member of the team that did the work at OpenAI, told me. Their small neural network had seemingly grokked the data.

Grokking is just one of many odd behaviors demonstrated by deep neural networks. (We'll look at it in more detail later in this chapter.) Another has to do with the size of these networks. The most successful neural networks today, whether they are doing image or speech recognition or natural language processing, are behemoths: They have hundreds of millions or billions of weights, or parameters; maybe even a trillion. The parameters can at times equal or vastly outnumber the instances of data used to train these networks. Standard ML theory says that such networks shouldn't work the way they do: They should simply overfit the data and fail to make inferences about, or "generalize to," new, unseen data.

Power used an example to illustrate this problem. Consider a dataset of images of some types of furniture. The dataset is broken into two parts: training and test. Let's say that the training dataset has images of four-legged chairs, but only those made of metal or wood. These are labeled "chair." There are images of sofas, too, but without any discernible legs. These are labeled "not-chair." The task of the ML algorithm is to classify an image as either a "chair" or a "not-chair." Once the algorithm is trained, its performance is tested against the test dataset. As it happens, the test dataset also contains chairs made of plastic, not just of wood and metal. How might the algorithm perform?

Here's what might happen. If the ML model being trained is very complex, with a very large number of parameters, it might learn things about chairs that go beyond the fact that these chairs have four legs. It might learn that they are made of wood or metal. Such a model would be very good for recognizing metal or wooden chairs, but it might fail to identify the plastic chairs in the test data. The model can be said to have overfit the training data, picking up on nuances of chairs that were unnecessary and maybe even detrimental to the task at hand. A simpler model, with fewer parameters, might have picked up only on the pattern that chairs have four legs; it would then have generalized better to unseen data and possibly have recognized chairs made of materials besides just wood and metal.

We can visualize this issue with a much simpler dataset. Let's take some points on the xy plane. Our task is to train an ML model to perform regression, to find a curve that fits the training data in a way that will allow the model to generalize well to unseen data. First, here's some training data, followed by three different models, or curves, to fit the data:

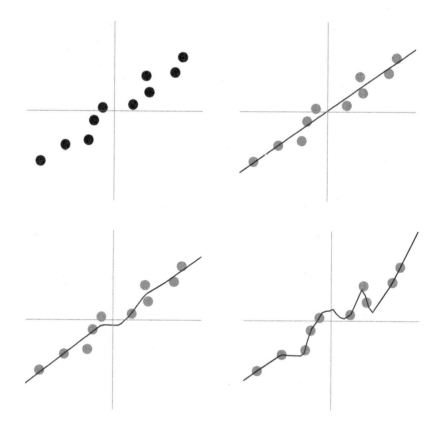

The easiest thing we can do is linear regression: Fit a straight line through the data. It's a simple model. Almost none of the training data falls on the line, so the model will make errors, small and large, on nearly every instance of the training data.

If we increase the complexity of our model, by adding more parameters and some nonlinearity, we might find a curve that fits the training data a little more faithfully. Now the model's risk of making errors on the training data is reduced: The curve actually passes through some of the data points, though not all of them, and the ones it misses will contribute to the training error.

The final panel shows a complex nonlinear model with considerably more parameters: The curve passes through each data point. The training error is almost zero.

Which model should we choose? This is not an easy question to answer. The choice depends on the performance of the model on test data you have set aside. The test and training data are assumed to be drawn from the same underlying distribution. (In the example with the chairs, the test data can be said to be out of distribution, because they have images of plastic chairs, while the training data have none. But these are contentious issues. If the algorithm's task is to classify chairs, it shouldn't matter what they are made of—so, plastic chairs should be considered to be drawn from the same underlying distribution.)

Let's say that the straight line through the dataset is more or less the correct fit and that the fact that the training data are scattered about the straight line is because there's noise in the data. In the case of the simplest linear model, the straight line hasn't fit the noise; rather, it has ignored the noise. But because the test data are drawn from the same distribution and are presumably similarly noisy, the simplest linear model will do badly on the test data, too; there's a high risk of error on the test data.

The most complex model, however, is clearly tracking every little variation in the training data: It has essentially overfit the data, and if the variations in the data are because of noise, then the model has learned the minutiae of this noise. The complex model will also, however, get its predictions on the test data badly wrong, because the test data are similarly noisy. The complex model will make predictions based on the extremely squiggly regression curve it has learned, which is specific to the noise in the training data, but because noise is random, the curve won't track the instances of test data as well as it did the training data, leading to significant test error.

We have used regression as an example, but the issue also dogs the problem of classification, which involves finding some linear or nonlinear boundary that separates clusters of data. If the model is too simple, it'll find a boundary that doesn't quite hew to the real variations in the data: You cannot get the training error and test error down to acceptable limits. If the model is too complex, the classification boundary will track every little deviation in the data, overfitting them, and will do really well on the training data but will likely make huge classification errors during testing.

THE GOLDILOCKS PRINCIPLE

These might seem like theoretical concerns that would bother only nitpicking ML practitioners, but let's take an example from chapter 6 to see why this issue might be literally a matter of life and death. Here's the graphic showing the result of principal component analysis done on real EEG data collected from a single person being monitored while under anesthesia. The gray dots represent two-second intervals when the person is conscious; the black triangles are for when the person is unconscious. These are the training data.

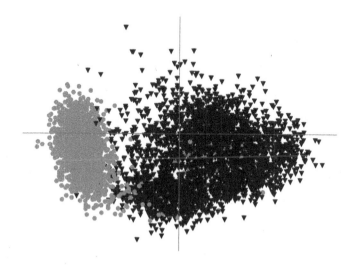

Imagine building a simple classifier that learns to separate the conscious from the unconscious states. You can find a straight line (a very simple model) that tries to separate the two clusters. Because there's no clear space between the clusters, any straight line we find will make errors during training: There will always be a few gray dots in the cluster of black triangles, and vice versa. To reduce such training errors, we can find some squiggly curve that carefully maps the contours of the boundary between the two clusters. For example, you could use a k-nearest neighbor algorithm (chapter 5) k. You'd get a highly nonlinear boundary. Such a model could be built to minimize the errors during training.

Whichever model you choose, it has to predict the state of consciousness given some new EEG signal, to help the anesthesiologist determine the dosage of anesthesia, so that the person can be kept under or brought out of unconsciousness. Obviously, the recommendation of the ML model is important here. Getting it wrong has consequences. How would you go about finding the best possible model?

Recall from chapter 6 that the EEG study had collected data from ten patients. The researchers used data from seven patients to train their model and build the classifier, and they kept aside data from three patients to test their model. Let's say we test an extremely simple, linear model and also a highly complex, nonlinear model against the three-patient test data. The simple linear model will make more errors during training because it underfits the training data and makes errors on the test data as well. The complex nonlinear model, while it makes near-zero errors on the training data, will make significant errors during testing precisely because it memorized the training data, which was only taken from seven independent participants.

Why is the test error important? The test data are something we have in hand but have withheld from the ML algorithm during training. How well the trained model does on test data is our only indication of its potential performance out in the wild, meaning its ability to generalize to truly unseen data. We want the test error to be as low as possible.

Given that, how does one choose the correct level of complexity of the model? This leads us to the two competing forces at work here. One is called bias: The simpler the model, the greater the bias. The other is called variance: The more complex the model, the greater the variance.

High bias (i.e., simpler models) leads to underfitting, a higher risk of training error, and a higher risk of test error, whereas high variance (i.e., more complex models) leads to overfitting, a lower risk of training error, and a higher risk of test error. The job of an ML engineer is to find the sweet spot. If the number of parameters, or tunable knobs, that are there in an ML model is taken as a measure of the model's complexity or capacity, then standard ML theory says that a model should have just the right number of parameters: Too few, and the model is too simple (high bias) and fails to capture the necessary nuances of the data on which it's trained. Too many parameters, and the model becomes very complex and learns the patterns in the data with such fine granularity that it fails to generalize to unseen data. "It's a balance between somehow fitting your data too well and not fitting it well at all. You want to be in the middle," said Mikhail Belkin, the machine learning expert at the University of California at San Diego. "There is some sort of Goldilocks principle. Not too hot, not too cold."

Depicted on the next page is one of the most famous sets of curves you'll see in machine learning. It depicts the bias-variance trade-off (see Scott Fortmann-Roe's excellent blog post on the topic). A number of things are happening here. Let's start with the x-axis: Lower values mean low-capacity models with fewer parameters, and higher values imply more complex models with a large number of

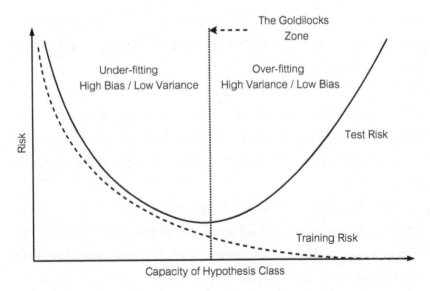

parameters. On the y-axis is the risk that the model makes errors, either while training or testing.

A quick word about the label on the x-axis, "Capacity of Hypothesis Class," and its relation to the complexity of a model and the number of parameters. Given a set of parameters whose values can be tuned during training, we must go back to the basics of supervised learning to reflect on what these parameters enable an ML model to do.

Let's say we have training data in the form of (input, output) pairs:

$$[(\mathbf{x1}, y1), (\mathbf{x2}, y2), \dots, (\mathbf{xn}, yn)]$$

Using the training data, we have to find some function, f, that predicts y, given some input, $\mathbf{x}$.

$$y = f(\mathbf{x})$$

The number of tunable parameters in a model determines the hypothetical set of functions that can be implemented using that model. In essence, we are limited to finding a solution from that set. Say we want a linear model. In the 2D case, a linear model is a line defined by its slope and its offset from the origin: So, we need two parameters. But what if your model had only one parameter? Then you'd be forced to find a simpler function in which either the slope was fixed or the offset was fixed, thus limiting your options.

And in a nonlinear model, the greater the number of parameters, the squigglier the functions we usually have at our disposal. This should bring to mind the universal approximation theorem from chapter 9: Given enough neurons, a neural network with even just a single hidden layer can approximate any function, which implies that its toolbox of functions is, in principle, infinitely large. So, the number of parameters (which, in the case of neural networks, is equivalent to the number of weights, or the connections between neurons, whose values are learned during training) is a proxy for the complexity of the model and determines the set of functions one can access in order to find a good one. This can also be called the hypothesis class: Increase the number of parameters, and you increase the capacity of the hypothesis class.

Let's go back to the figure opposite. There is one dashed curve. It starts off high on the y-axis for simple models and goes toward zero as the model's complexity increases. This curve represents the training risk, the risk that the model makes errors on the training dataset. It's clear that extremely simple models do badly on the training data, because they are underfitting the data, and as the models get more complex, they start overfitting, hence the training risk goes to zero.

The solid curve represents the risk of error during testing. It starts off high on the y-axis for high-bias, low-complexity models, descends to some minimum, and then starts rising again. The bottom of the bowl is where we want our ML model to be: It represents the optimal balance between underfitting and overfitting, between model simplicity and complexity. This is the Goldilocks zone. Choosing a model that minimizes the risk of test error maximizes the model's ability to generalize to further unseen data (data the model will encounter in the wild, so to say, as it's not part of either the training or the test data). So, minimizing test error implies minimizing generalization error, or maximizing the ability to generalize.

From almost all empirical accounts of traditional machine learning, this story seemed to be true. Then deep neural networks entered the fray and turned this conventional wisdom upside down. Deep nets have way too many parameters relative to the instances of training data: They are said to be over-parameterized; they should overfit and should not generalize well to unseen test data. Yet they do. Standard ML theory can no longer adequately explain why deep neural networks work so well.

THE UNBEARABLE STRANGENESS OF NEURAL NETWORKS

A few years after AlexNet announced itself on the machine learning stage in 2011, Behnam Neyshabur, Ryota Tomioka, and Nathan Srebro of the Toyota Technological Institute at Chicago made an intriguing observation about deep neural networks. Experimenting with networks that had just one hidden layer, they found, contrary to expectation, that increasing the number of neurons, or units in the hidden layer (thus the capacity of the model), *did not* cause the network to overfit the training data. The trio was testing their networks on two standard image datasets, one of which was the MNIST dataset of handwritten digits. First, as they increased the size of the network, both training and test error decreased as expected. But then, as the network increased in size and the training error approached zero, as per the bias-variance trade-off curve, the test error (or gener-alization error) should have started increasing. That's not what they saw. The language in their 2015 paper is suggestive of their disbelief:

> *More surprising is that if we increase the size of the network past the size required to achieve zero training error, the test error continues decreasing! This behavior is not at all predicted by, and even contrary to, viewing learning as fitting a hypothesis class controlled by network size. For example for MNIST, 32 units are enough to attain zero training error. When we allow more units, the network is not fitting the training data any better . . . However, the test error goes down. In fact, as we add more and more parameters, even beyond the number of training examples, the generalization error does not go up.*

To be fair, hints about such behavior of deep neural networks preceded this work. But Neyshabur and colleagues were the first to systematically test it. They went further. What if you deliberately introduced noise into your dataset?

Take the images in the MNIST dataset. Each image has an asso-ciated label: "five" for the digit 5, "six" for the digit 6, and so on. Take 1 percent of these images and randomly scramble their labels. So, one instance of digit 5 might get mislabeled as "four," an instance of digit 9 might get mislabeled as "two," and so on. Now divide the dataset into training and test data and train your neural network such that it achieves zero training error on the training data. What does this mean? Well, because we have intentionally introduced noise into the data, the network—as it's making no errors on the training data—is accommodating the noise. For example, it's learning to label those mislabeled digits 5 and 9 as "four" and "two," respectively. It's fitting the data perfectly. Learning theory has an evocative phrase to describe a model that does this: It's said to "shatter" the training data.

And because it fits the noisy training data perfectly, this model should not do well on the test data. (Intuitively, the squiggly curve that the model has learned is very specific to the noise it has encountered, and there's no reason to expect the model to generalize.) But that's not what happened. Neyshabur and colleagues write, "Even with five percent random labels, there is no significant overfitting and test error continues decreasing as network size increases past the size required for achieving zero training error." And they ask, perplexed, "What is happening here?"

Their perplexity was warranted. This behavior would be possible, in the standard way of thinking, only if the process of stochastic gradient descent (which was used to train the network) somehow ended up pruning the number of tunable knobs in the model. There are ways in which you can do this explicitly; it's a process called regularization, which essentially turns a complex model into a simpler one, allowing it to generalize better. Maybe stochastic gradient descent was doing some implicit regularization, thus reducing the capacity of the network and making the model simpler in order to avoid overfitting, the authors concluded.

Then, in 2016, Chiyuan Zhang, who was then at MIT, along with Ben Recht of the University of California, Berkeley, and colleagues at Google showed much the same behavior in larger neural networks trained on larger datasets. In their paper, provocatively titled "Understanding Deep Learning Requires Rethinking Generalization," they concluded, "The experiments we conducted emphasize that the effective capacity of several successful neural network architectures is large enough to *shatter* the training data. Consequently, these models are in principle rich enough to memorize the training data. This situation poses a conceptual challenge to statistical learning theory as traditional measures of model complexity struggle to explain the generalization ability of large artificial neural networks."

This was the state of play in 2017, when the Simons Institute for the Theory of Computing at UC Berkeley organized its three-month program on the theoretical foundations of machine learning. Recht gave a talk on their paper on rethinking generalization. And this led to considerable discussion among the program participants. The problem being posed by deep neural networks had become clearer. These networks had the capacity to interpolate the data (meaning fit the training data perfectly) and yet make accurate predictions on test data. Even more problematic, these networks could interpolate noisy data, and still the prediction accuracy didn't degrade as expected. "We routinely teach our undergraduates [that] you don't want to . . . get too good a fit to the data [or] you'll have poor predictive accuracy. That's one of those broad principles that's always been accepted, and here we are doing the opposite and it's okay," UC Berkeley professor Peter Bartlett, research director for Machine Learning at the Simons Institute, told me. "It's a shocking thing."

Mikhail Belkin was attending the program. "Everybody was super confused at the time," he recalled. Another ML expert, Carnegie Mellon University's Ruslan Salakhutdinov, gave a tutorial on deep learning. Belkin recalled Salakhutdinov as saying, "The best way to solve the problem from a practical standpoint is you build a very big system . . . Basically you want to make sure you hit the zero training error." Again, it was an assertion that went against standard learning theory. Belkin was flabbergasted. "That for me was . . . eye-opening," he told me. "I was like, 'What the hell is he talking about? Why should we fit the data exactly?'"

But Belkin soon realized that work going on in his lab at Ohio State University, where he was at the time, on kernel methods (which we encountered in chapter 7) was already hinting at something similar. "We had been doing this experiment with kernels. And we observed that you can train and get zero or a small loss and it [still] worked," said Belkin, who is now at the University of California, San Diego.

As it turns out, clues that standard learning theory (and the bias-variance trade-off) didn't hold in all situations had been slowly accumulating. For example, Leo Breiman, a statistician at UC Berkeley, wrote a paper in 1995 called "Reflections After Refereeing Papers for NIPS." NIPS stands for "neural information processing systems," and was the name of the flagship conference in the field. (These days, it's called NeurIPS. The conference's board members made the change following a petition by prominent women ML experts, who made the case that the "acronym encourages sexism and is a slur" and provided examples of the old name's being used in sexist puns.) In his paper, Breiman asked, "Why don't heavily parameterized neural networks overfit the data?" Also, in 1998, Bartlett and colleagues had shown that an ML algorithm called AdaBoost also didn't overfit, despite the model's complexity.

Energized by the debates during the three-month sojourn at the Simons Institute, Belkin embarked on a systematic study of kernel methods and deep neural networks, essentially probing their performance with increasing amounts of noise in the training dataset. The complexity, or capacity, of the models was enough to interpolate the noisy data. Even when the noise affected about 5 percent of the dataset or more, the performance of both kernel machines and neural networks didn't degrade as expected. "As you increase the noise level, nothing really breaks," Belkin said.

Meanwhile, Bartlett and colleagues began exploring this phenomenon and gave it a beguiling name: "benign overfitting." Yet others called it harmless interpolation.

For Belkin, the similar behavior of AdaBoost, kernel machines, and neural networks was suggesting something profound. *Maybe researchers don't fully understand the amazing properties of machine learning itself,* he thought, a realization that became apparent only because of deep neural networks and their seemingly lawbreaking abilities. "We [had] convinced ourselves that [ML] was fine by selectively closing our eyes on things that didn't fit the mold," Belkin told me. "My feeling was that theory was not fine."

Deep neural networks, trained using stochastic gradient descent, are pointing ML researchers toward uncharted territory. Belkin calls this machine learning's "terra incognita." But before we can appreciate why neural networks have brought us to this point, we need a brief segue to appreciate the varieties of ways of building and training them.

OF PARAMETERS AND HYPERPARAMETERS

The discovery and exploration of uncharted territories in machine learning has been enabled because of a fundamental shift in AI research, one that involves performing experiments on deep neural networks and other architectures. To do such experiments, researchers have to fiddle with parameters and hyperparameters. Parameters, we know, are those knobs in a model—the weights of a neural network, for example—that get tuned during training. Hyperparameters are knobs that are set by engineers before training begins. These latter include, for example, the architecture of the neural network (which dictates, among other things, the number of layers, the number of neurons per layer, and the way these layers are interconnected), the size of the training data, the precise type of optimization algorithm, and whether one does explicit regularization (such as pruning the number of parameters). Finding good or optimal values for hyperparameters is a craft, almost an art.

In this book, we have looked at a handful of architectures for neural networks: the single-layer perceptron, Hopfield networks (chapter 8), the multi-layer perceptron (chapter 10), and the convolutional neural network (chapter 11). But in the past decade or so, deep neural network architectures have mushroomed, creating a veritable zoo of these creatures. Still, one can take an overarching view to classify them broadly.

First, networks can be, generally speaking, either feedforward or recurrent. Feedforward neural networks are those in which the information flows one way, from the input layer to the output. So, if a neuron is producing an output, the output serves as input only to neurons that are part of the layers ahead. The output cannot return as input to neurons in the same layer or in preceding layers. A recurrent neural network, by contrast, allows for feedback connections so that the outputs of neurons not only influence neurons in the layers ahead, but can also serve as inputs to neurons in the same layer or in the layers that came before. This allows recurrent neural networks to "remember" previous inputs, making them useful for problems that involve inputs that vary over time. (An excellent example of this is a recurrent neural network architecture called long short-term memory, or LSTM, proposed in 1997 by Jürgen Schmidhuber, whom we met in previous chapters, and his colleague Sepp Hochreiter.)

The backpropagation algorithm is the workhorse for training neural networks, particularly feedforward networks. The algorithm can also be used to train recurrent networks, but we won't get into the specifics of that here. Regardless of the type of network, here's the thing we need to appreciate conceptually. Given an input, a neural network will produce an output. We can define a function that calculates the loss, or error, made by the network by comparing the produced output in some predefined manner to the expected output. The function calculates the loss for a single instance of training data or it calculates the average loss over all instances of training data and is called a loss, or cost, function. Training a network means minimizing the loss over training data.

We have already seen that training a model to achieve zero training cost can result in overfitting. To prevent this, the cost function is often modified with the addition of another term to it, called the regularizer. Think of this as a term that forces the function to take into account the model's complexity, or capacity; we incur a penalty for making the model overly complex. In a neural network, explicit regularization helps prevent overfitting. Regularization could, for example, prevent the values for the weights, or parameters of the network, from getting too large, the assumption being that large weights mean more complex models, and vice versa.

There are also more interesting methods for preventing overfitting. For example, you can set up your network to randomly drop some connections during training (thereby reducing the number of effective parameters). We can also choose the activation function for our neurons. In chapters 9 and 10, we encountered the sigmoid activation function. There are others. Different activation functions lead neurons and the networks they constitute to behave differently; most important, these functions must be differentiable in order for backpropagation to work. (As pointed out earlier, there are activation functions that are not differentiable over their entire domain, but they can still be used, with some care. For example, the ReLU function is not differentiable at $x = 0$. Its derivative at $x = 0$ can be taken to be 0, 1, or 0.5. The other benefits of using ReLU outweigh this minor inconvenience.)

An ML engineer, besides having to choose among these various hyperparameters, also has to choose, even more broadly, whether to use supervised learning or unsupervised learning. We have mainly been focused on supervised learning, which requires training data to be labeled—which means that for each input, there's a corresponding expected output. This is what allows us to calculate the loss per instance of training data. We also briefly encountered unsupervised learning, in which an algorithm, for example, must be told how many clusters there are in the training dataset, and then it can find those clusters and assign each instance of the data to one of the clusters. However, one of the most significant developments over the past five years—one that has led to the enormous explosion of interest in AIs such as ChatGPT—is something called self-supervised learning, a clever method that takes unlabeled data and creates implicit labels without human involvement and then supervises itself.

A BET IN BERKELEY

In 2014, a group of researchers at the University of California, Berkeley, among them Jitendra Malik, a formidable expert in computer vision, developed a deep neural network solution that performed admirably on a computer vision task called pattern analysis, statistical modeling, and computational learning (PASCAL) for visual object classes (VOC). The task entailed learning, given a small dataset of images, how to draw boxes around, or to segment, different categories of objects in those images, such as bicycles, cars, a horse, a person, and sheep, and then to name them.

To solve the problem, Malik and colleagues first used supervised learning to train a CNN on the much larger ImageNet dataset (the same dataset that AlexNet conquered in 2011). This was simply about learning how to classify images using labels generated by humans. The team then took this "pre-trained" network and further fine-tuned it on the PASCAL VOC dataset. These images had "bounding boxes," identified by humans, that delineated the various categories of objects in those images. The fine-tuned network, called R-CNN, was then able to outperform existing methods at detecting the boundaries of objects in test data and classifying them accordingly.

For Alexei Efros, also a computer vision expert at UC Berkeley and Malik's former student, the R-CNN approach was troubling. Why should a network that has first been trained on ImageNet data, with labels that referred only to some object in the image (say, a cat or a car) without regard to its actual shape or boundaries, do well on detecting the boundaries of objects, albeit after it had been fine-tuned using a dataset that had human-labeled boxes around the objects of interest? The same network, sans the ImageNet pre-training, did poorly when trained only on the PASCAL VOC dataset. Maybe, Efros reasoned, the CNN was simply hungry for the general information contained in the ImageNet dataset, and the human-supplied annotations, which labeled the images as those of cars, dogs, cats, and so on, were of little value.

So, on September 23, 2014, at a café in Berkeley, just outside the northern edge of the university campus, Efros bet Malik that within a year, there would be an ML algorithm that would perform object detection without using labels supplied by humans, such as those provided in ImageNet. The bet was formalized: "If, by the first day of autumn (Sept. 23) of 2015, a method will exist that can match or beat the performance of R-CNN on Pascal VOC detection, without the use of any extra, human annotations (e.g. ImageNet) as pre-training, Mr. Malik promises to buy Mr. Efros one (1) gelato (2 scoops: one chocolate, one vanilla)." Three students witnessed the bet. "And I posted this thing on Facebook, too, and told people that if somebody . . . will help me win the bet, they can get half of my winnings," Efros told me. "I keep the chocolate, they get the vanilla." Efros lost the bet—for object detection, R-CNN remained the best game in town for a while—but he thinks it spurred him and others toward developing a new approach to training neural networks without using human-annotated data: self-supervised learning.

Self-supervised learning, in retrospect, seems extraordinarily simple. Take large language models (LLMs) such as GPT-3 (the precursor to ChatGPT). They are trained on an enormous corpus of text slurped off the internet. The training algorithm takes a small sentence, masks one word, for example, and gives that sentence with the masked word as an input to the network (the details are a little more complicated, but let's go with masked words as units of information). The network's task: to predict the missing word and complete the sentence. Let's say the sentence is "I'm going to walk back ___." The masked word is "home." In the beginning, the network will most likely guess wrong. One can define a loss function that calculates the extent to which the network gets it wrong. The backpropagation algorithm and stochastic gradient descent, used together, first assign partial blame for the error to each of the parameters in the network and then update the parameter values such that the loss is reduced; if the network is given the same masked sentence and asked to predict again, it does a bit better. The training algorithm iterates over every sentence in the corpus of the training text, masking a word, asking the network to predict the masked word, calculating the loss, and then updating the network's parameters to reduce the loss a little. (One added complexity: The blank space in our example masked sentence could legitimately have been completed with the word "alone," if such a sentence was in the training data. So, the LLM's predictions are going to be inherently probabilistic, with, say, "home" being assigned a greater probability than "alone," if it encounters "home" more often than "alone" during training.)

While each iteration is trivial, iterating for billions of pages of text taken from the internet is a gargantuan task: It can take months of computing and gigawatt-hours of energy. Still, at the end, an LLM trained in this manner contains within it, in the values of its parameters, the statistical structure of and knowledge contained in the written human language on which it's been trained. Now, given some input text, it can generate the next most-probable word, append it to the original text, generate the next word, and keep going, producing seemingly coherent outputs that mimic the way humans produce language. The output text can even be suggestive of the ability to reason—though, at the time of this writing, researchers are at odds over whether LLMs are actually doing any reasoning or are simply regurgitating text that satisfies the statistical patterns and regularities they encounter in the training data, or even whether there's any meaningful difference between these two ideas.

Efros, however, was more interested in doing something similar with images. By 2016, his team had shown how to use self-supervised learning for images. The algorithm takes an unannotated image and masks some pixels. It feeds this masked image to a neural network and asks the network to generate the unmasked image in all its fullness. Of course, the network will get it wrong initially. The algorithm uses its loss function to calculate the loss, assign appropriate blame to each of the network's parameters, and then update those parameters. With the loss thus reduced, the network, given the same masked image, will do better than before. The algorithm repeats this for all the images in the training dataset. And in much the same way that an LLM learns the statistical structure of language, a self-supervised image-processing network learns the statistical structure of images.

Still, efforts at using self-supervised learning for vision never quite achieved the level of success seen with LLMs. This changed in December 2021, when Kaiming He and colleagues at Meta, building on the work done by Efros's team, revealed their "masked auto-encoder" (MAE). Their algorithm randomly masks images, obscuring almost three-quarters of each image. The MAE has an encoder that turns the unmasked portions of the image into so-called latent representations of aspects of the image. Then a decoder converts those representations back into full images. During training, given a masked image, the MAE tries to generate the unmasked image, and the network learns latent representations of important features of the images in its training dataset.

When a trained MAE was shown a previously unseen image of a bus, almost 80 percent of which was obscured, the MAE could still reconstruct the bus. It had, so to say, internalized the structure of the bus—but without humans having explicitly labeled any images. And when an MAE trained in this manner was fine-tuned on an object detection and segmentation task, it outperformed R-CNN in all manner of ways. It took until 2021, but Efros turned out to be right. "In my bet, I should have said ten years instead of one year," he told me. "That was my mistake."

Regardless, the move toward self-supervised learning has enormous consequences, for it has freed machine learning from the shackles of superexpensive, human-annotated data. Efros likes to say, "The revolution will not be supervised."

IN UNCHARTED WATERS

Without the constraint of having to annotate data for supervised learning, deep neural networks are getting bigger and bigger. As of this writing, densely connected LLMs—"dense" here refers to the fact that the output of a neuron in one layer becomes the input to every neuron in the next layer—have more than half a trillion parameters, with the promise of even bigger networks on the horizon. And as these networks become bigger, their behavior continues to challenge our traditional understanding of machine learning, particularly the landscape of the bias-variance trade-off curve.

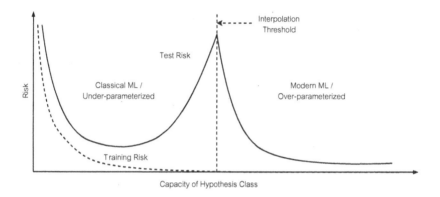

One of the most intriguing places in that landscape that deep nets have uncovered lies to the right of the original bias-variance curve. We saw earlier that in the standard bias-variance trade-off, as one increases the capacity of the model, the test error, or generalization error, starts off high, drops to a minimum, and then begins rising again to a maximum. At the point where the test error hits its maximum, the training error touches zero. The model has interpolated: It has overfit the training data. Traditional ML research (except for those isolated incidents with AdaBoost) stopped fussing about what lay beyond.

Belkin and colleagues were among the earliest to systematically explore that region. In 2018, they showed that the performance of both kernel machines and deep neural networks begins improving once you increase the capacity of both beyond the point of interpolation, toward lower test risk and better performance. This behavior had been empirically observed as early as the 1990s in some linear models. Belkin and colleagues dubbed the phenomenon double descent and proposed that it was a unifying principle: The first descent leads to a minimum for the test error, followed by an ascent, and then a subsequent descent to low levels of test error.

The part of the curve captured by the first descent and subsequent ascent is well understood; mathematics explains the behavior of ML systems in that "under-parameterized" regime (thanks mainly to Vladimir Vapnik, whom we encountered in chapter 7). But the newer, over-parameterized regime, which results in the second descent, is barely understood, mathematically speaking. "We now have at least a map. In this part of the world, there is some sort of terra incognita. We don't know what is really going on there," Belkin told me.

The ignorance Belkin and others admit to is mostly about not knowing the mathematical underpinnings of the observed behavior of neural networks in this new, over-parameterized regime. This is somewhat unexpected from ML research. In fact, much of this book has celebrated the fact that traditional machine learning has had a base of well-understood mathematical principles, but deep neural networks—especially the massive networks we see today—have upset this applecart. Suddenly, empirical observations of these networks are leading the way. A new way of doing AI seems to be upon us.

In January 2022, at a town hall meeting organized under the aegis of the National Science Foundation, Tom Goldstein of the University of Maryland argued that much of the history of machine learning has been focused on theoretically principled mathematical frameworks (the kind that gave us support vector machines and kernel methods, for example). But by 2011, when AlexNet won the ImageNet competition, things had changed. AlexNet was a stupendous experimental success; there was no adequate theory to explain its performance. According to Goldstein, the AI community said to itself, "Maybe we shouldn't have such a focus on theory. Maybe we should be doing experimental science to progress machine learning." Given that science involves doing experiments and developing theory to explain observations and natural phenomena, the theoretical ML community could be considered anti-science, Goldstein said in his talk. According to him, the "principled" ML researchers wanted theory before experiments and were "stuck in a pre-science era."

When it comes to deep learning, this tension between theory and experiment is playing out for all to see. For example, consider the loss function. We saw in chapter 3 that gradient descent, when done on a bowl-shaped, "convex," function leads you to the bottom of the bowl. But the loss function for a deep neural network depends on its gazillion parameters and the nonlinear activation functions for its neurons. The function is no longer convex, meaning it doesn't have one global minimum toward which you can descend. It's impossible enough to visualize a convex function in million-dimensional or even higher-dimensional space, let alone a non-convex function that has innumerable hills and valleys, where each valley constitutes a local minimum. It's best to think of this as an extremely complicated loss landscape. So far, no one knows if the landscape has a global minimum or just lots of good local minima (where "good" means the loss is acceptably low).

Highlighting the problem for theorists, Goldstein pointed to a slew of theory papers that claimed to have shown that the loss landscape for deep neural networks has no local minima, while other papers showed the exact opposite, that they do have local minima. An empirical study by Goldstein and colleagues showed that neural networks can get stuck in not-so-good local minima, which are regions where the loss is non-zero, despite the networks being over-parameterized. Normally, if you train an over-parameterized network carefully, you'll reach a region of the loss landscape where the train-ing loss is close to zero. The fact that you can get stuck with a non-zero loss is empirical proof that such local minima, or valleys, exist in the loss landscape; you didn't need theory to prove it, but one does now need theory to explain why. And such theory is lacking.

Another intriguing experimental observation is one we have al-ready encountered in this book: Deep neural networks, despite being over-parameterized, generalize well. One theoretical stab at trying to explain the observation says that stochastic gradient descent—in which gradient descent is performed using small batches of training data, so that each descent down the loss landscape is only approxi-mate and not in the exact direction of steepest descent—may be per-forming implicit regularization. However, Goldstein's team performed experiments illustrating situations in which gradient descent that used the entire training data at once generalized just as well; stochas-ticity wasn't needed. Again, theory has been found wanting.

One of the most elegant demonstrations of empirical observa-tions in need of theory is grokking. We began this chapter with the story of the OpenAI researcher who came back from a vacation and found that the neural network, which had continued training, had learned something deep about adding two numbers, using modulo-97 arithmetic. "It was not something we were expecting to find at all," Alethea Power told me. "Initially, we thought it was a fluke and dug deeper into it. It turned out to be something that happens pretty reliably."

The neural network that Power and colleagues were using was called a transformer, a type of architecture that's especially suited to processing sequential data. LLMs such as ChatGPT are transform-ers; GPT stands for "generative pre-trained transformer." Given a sequence of, say, ten words and asked to predict the next most plausible word, a transformer has the ability to "pay attention" to all the words at once and also to the order of the words and not just treat them as some arbitrary jumble. Of course, commercial LLMs are behemoths, with tens or even hundreds of billions of parameters. In contrast, the transformer that Power's team was using was tiny, with fewer than half a million parameters. Here's an example of the type of data the researchers used to train their network (this is an over-simplified take, to get across the conceptual elements of the process):

$a + b = c$, where a, b, and c are binary numbers. The addition is modulo-97. The numbers a and b are constrained, such that:
$$0 <= a, b < 97$$

Given these constraints, imagine a table listing all possible values for a and b and the corresponding modulo-97 sum, c. For example, here are some of the rows of such a table (the numbers are shown in decimal not binary format, for clarity):

$$0 + 5 = 5$$
$$1 + 9 = 10$$
$$10 + 90 = 3$$
$$11 + 55 = 66$$
$$25 + 95 = 23$$

To train the network, this table of numbers is first randomly split into rows that constitute the training data and the test data. Now take each row in the training data, mask one of either a, b, or c, and ask the network to predict the masked number. At first, the trans-former will predict the wrong value. The algorithm calculates the loss and makes tiny updates to the values of the parameters so that the loss for that instance of data is reduced a little. (For efficiency, the algorithm may use "batches," or some subset of the rows of training data at once, calculate the average loss, and perform stochastic gradient descent; or it may use all rows at once to calculate the average loss and do gradient descent.) The algorithm repeatedly iterates over all instances of the training data until, eventually, the training loss nears zero or even hits zero. What's happened at this stage?

Well, the transformer has learned to represent each number in some internal high-dimensional space and has also learned to add the numbers, as per modulo-97 addition. If one stops training at the point the network hits zero training loss, the network has most likely interpolated the training data—meaning it has simply memorized them. And that's usually where the OpenAI researchers stopped the training. No one thought of training further. But then, one day, thanks to the vacation snafu, the network continued training past this point— and learned something completely new. "If [the networks] work on it for long enough, which is a very long time, many orders of magnitude longer than it takes to memorize the training set, then suddenly they figure out the deeper underlying pattern and are able to generalize and kind of make broadly accurate predictions about the other problems in the [dataset]," Power told me. "It's a weird phenomenon. It's not what we expected."

When the researchers stopped training their network soon after it had interpolated the training data, it didn't do too well on the test data (meaning, the rows in the table that hadn't been used during training). It was as if it had memorized a look-up table for the data it had already encountered and, when those numbers appeared during testing, it could simply delve into the table it had constructed and spit out the answer. But when it encountered data it couldn't look up, it made bad predictions.

However, when it was allowed to learn way past the point of interpolation, the network grokked the problem in an entirely different way. It now did well on unseen data, better than could be expected from a model that had simply memorized the training data. Power's team used a technique for visualizing what the network had learned—which involves mapping high-dimensional vectors to a two-dimensional space (somewhat like the principal component analysis we saw in chapter 6, but not quite)—and discovered that the network had learned to represent the numbers in a circle. So, imagine the numbers 0 to 96 arranged in a circle. Now, given two numbers to add, the network simply took the first number, which is some location on that circle, moved a number of steps equal to the second number along that circle, and . . . bingo! It arrived at an answer. Other researchers have referred to such grokking as akin to undergoing a phase change (the way water changes to ice, in physics). "It seems like the phase change is going from a memorized table of answers to becoming the knowledge in some sense," Power said.

As of now, such detailed studies are possible only when the networks and their associated training datasets are extremely small, compared to the commercial deep neural networks dominating the industry, whether they are being used for image and speech recognition or for natural language processing. These large networks are extremely adept at machine learning, meaning figuring out the patterns that exist in data (or correlations between inputs and outputs) and using that knowledge to make predictions when given new inputs. Goldstein argued during the National Science Foundation town hall meeting that the commercial value of machine learning will ward off any "ML winter" ahead—a reference to the potential freeze in research funding that has often followed seemingly over-hyped technology trying to solve problems too difficult for its times. But what about a more generic AI winter?

AI winters, Goldstein said, happened in the late 1960s, when

Rosenblatt's perceptrons were, disingenuously, accused of not being able to solve the XOR problem; and then between 1974 and 1980, after Sir James Lighthill published his scathing report on the utter lack of progress in solving problems in language translation and robotics; and then again in the late 1980s, when research into good old-fashioned AI, or symbolic AI, came to a grinding halt as it became clear that expert systems built using carefully designed rule-based "inference engines" that operated on hand-crafted knowledge bases were . . . well, useless when it came to sophisticated reasoning involving new know-how not already in the knowledge base. These symbolic AIs were brittle; they also couldn't learn from data.

Goldstein has claimed that we are yet to come out of that last AI winter, if the AI in question is being asked to solve complex tasks that involve a combination of text comprehension and logical reasoning. There's considerable debate over whether neural networks alone (possibly with new architectures no one has dreamed of yet and training methods that are ever more effective) will get us from ML-based pattern recognition to true AI that can reason effectively.

But here's something that puts these issues into perspective. In June 2022, Google announced a large language called Minerva. It was built on top of Google's own LLM, called the Pathways Language Model (PaLM), a 540-billion-parameter model—at the time, the largest densely connected model. PaLM was trained on about 780 billion "tokens" of data taken from the internet. (Think of a token as a word or a digit.) Google researchers then fine-tuned PaLM by training it further on 118 gigabytes of data, mainly "scientific papers from the arXiv preprint server and web pages that contain mathematical expressions." Both PaLM and Minerva were trained using self-supervised learning, meaning they were taught to predict masked tokens in some sequence of tokens that appeared in the training data. They were not taught to explicitly reason or solve math problems. Even so, here's what happened when Minerva was posed this question (taken from something called the "MATH" dataset of about 12,500 high school–level mathematics questions):

Question: *A line parallel to $y = 4x + 6$ passes through (5, 10). What is the y-coordinate of the point where this line crosses the y-axis?*

Minerva: *The line is parallel to $y = 4x + 6$, which means that it has the same slope as $y = 4x + 6$. Since the line passes through (5, 10), we can use the point-slope form of a line to find the equation of the line:*

$$y - 10 = 4(x - 5)$$
$$y - 10 = 4x - 20$$
$$y = 4x - 10$$

Now that we have the equation of the line, we can find the y-coordinate of the point where the line crosses the y-axis by substituting $x = 0$ into the equation:
$$y = 4 \times 0 - 10 = -10.$$

Minerva was the first LLM to correctly answer about 50 percent of the questions in the MATH dataset; of course, it got the other questions wrong. But think about what Minerva is doing. It takes the question, turns it into a sequence of tokens, and then simply predicts what follows, token by token. Out comes what appears to be a reasoned answer. Is Minerva simply regurgitating text based on correlations in the training data? Or is it reasoning? The debate is raging, and no clear answers are forthcoming.

Such experiments certainly give pause to the claim that we are still in some AI deep freeze merely because the current state-of-the-art AIs are unable to combine text comprehension with logical reasoning. Some AI experts will point to Minerva's answer to the above math question and argue that it's doing exactly that: comprehending the text and reasoning out the answer. Others pooh-pooh it as glorified pattern matching. The theory isn't sophisticated enough to resolve the debate. The experiments themselves don't substantiate claims one way or another; they simply provide evidence that needs explaining.

One can only imagine what's in store when these extremely large neural networks begin grokking, if they aren't already: They truly will be strangers in a strange land.

Epilogue

When I began working on this book in the autumn of 2020, LLMs such as OpenAI's GPT-3 and Google's PaLM—and the chatbots they begat, such as ChatGPT and Bard—had yet to break through into the broader public consciousness. And when ChatGPT was announced in late 2022, one of the first things I explored was its ability to demonstrate theory of mind.

Theory of mind is a cognitive ability humans have that allows us to make inferences about someone else's beliefs or state of mind using only external behavioral cues such as body language and the overall context. We theorize about the contents of someone else's mind; hence the phrase "theory of mind." Here's a question I posed ChatGPT, a few months after its release. (I have italicized some words in the chatbot's output to highlight their import.)

ME: Alice and Bob are in a room together. There's a table with two drawers. Alice takes off her reading glasses and keeps them in the left-side drawer. If Alice wears the wrong glasses and reads, then she gets a severe headache the next day. Keep this in mind. Now Alice leaves the room. When she's outside, Bob removes her glasses and puts them in the right-side drawer. In the left-side drawer, he puts a pair of glasses that look exactly like Alice's but have the wrong power. He closes both drawers, so there's no way to tell that he's switched Alice's glasses. Alice then comes back, takes her glasses, and starts reading. How will she feel the next day? Think carefully and answer.

ChatGPT: Since Bob switched Alice's reading glasses with a pair that looks identical but has the wrong power, Alice will *unknowingly* use the incorrect glasses when she starts reading. As mentioned, if Alice wears the wrong glasses and reads, she gets a severe headache the next day. Therefore, Alice will have a severe headache the next day as a result of using the wrong glasses.

ME: Why will Alice unknowingly use the incorrect glasses?

ChatGPT: Alice will unknowingly use the incorrect glasses because Bob switched her reading glasses with another pair that looks exactly like hers but has the wrong power. When Alice returns to the room, *she is not aware* of the switch and *assumes* that the glasses she picks up from the left-side drawer are her own. Since both pairs of glasses look identical, *she has no way of realizing* that the glasses she is using are not the ones she initially placed in the drawer. As a result, she uses the incorrect glasses *without knowing it.*

My italicized words, you may have guessed, are suggestive of Alice's state of mind.

At a public talk I gave on ChatGPT and LLMs, I first shared this conversation with the audience and then asked them, "If you didn't know anything about how LLMs work, would you say that the AI is capable of reasoning?" Almost everyone put up their hand. More than half of them put down their hand once they understood the inner workings of LLMs. Let's put ourselves to the same test. The math we have encountered thus far is enough for us to appreciate how these modern AIs work.

An LLM is trained to predict the next word, given a sequence of words. (In practice, the algorithm chunks the input text into tokens, which are contiguous characters of some length that may or may not be entire words. We can stick with words with no loss of generality.) These sequences of words—say, a fragment of a sentence or an entire sentence or even a paragraph or paragraphs—are taken from a corpus of training text, often scraped from the internet. Each word is first converted into a vector that's embedded in some high-dimensional space, such that similar words—for some notion of similarity—are near each other in that space. There are pre-trained neural networks that can do this; it's a process called word embedding.

For every sequence of words presented to an LLM as vectors, the LLM needs to learn to predict the next word in the sequence. Here's one way to train an LLM, which is a monstrously large deep neural network with tens or hundreds of billions of parameters. (We are glossing over the intricacies of its architecture and focusing only on the overall function.)

We know that the neural network is a function approximator. But what is the function we want to approximate? Turns out it's a conditional probability distribution. So, given a sequence of $(n-1)$ input words, the neural network must learn to approximate the conditional probability distribution for the nth word, $P(w_n \mid w_1, w_2, \ldots, w_{n-1})$, where the nth word can be any word in the vocabulary, V. For example, if you gave the LLM the sentence "The dog ate my _____," the LLM must learn the values for P (cat | The, dog, ate, my), P (biscuit | The, dog, ate, my), P (homework | The, dog, ate, my), and so on. Given the occurrences of this phrase in the training data, the probability distribution might peak for the word "homework," have much smaller peaks for other likely words, and be near zero for the unlikely words in the vocabulary.

The neural network first outputs a set of V numbers, one number for each possible word to follow the input sequence. (I'm using V to denote the vocabulary and V its size.) This V-dimensional vector is then passed through something called a softmax function (almost but not quite like the sigmoid we saw earlier), which turns each element of the vector into a probability between 0 and 1 and ensures that the total probability adds up to 1. This final V-dimensional vector represents the conditional probability distribution, given the input; it gives us the probability for each word in the vocabulary, if it's to follow the sequence of input words. There are many ways of sampling from this distribution, but let's say we *greedily* sample to get the most likely next word.

This next word is the neural network's prediction. We know the ground truth—the word that was masked. We can calculate the loss. One simple way to think about the loss is that the greater the distance between the predicted word vector and the ground truth word vector in the high-dimensional embedding space, the greater the loss. Now we can use backpropagation and gradient descent to tweak each of the network's billions of parameters so that given the same sentence and the same masked word again, the network will predict a tiny bit better, reducing the loss somewhat. Of course, the training is done using sequences of words from the entire corpus of text. This can continue until the overall loss becomes acceptably low.

Once trained, the LLM is ready for inference. Now given some sequence of, say, 100 words, it predicts the most likely 101st word. (Note that the LLM doesn't know or care about the meaning of those 100 words: To the LLM, they are just a sequence of text.) The predicted word is appended to the input, forming 101 input words, and the LLM then predicts the 102nd word. And so it goes, until the LLM outputs an end-of-text token, stopping the inference. That's it!

An LLM is an example of generative AI. It has learned an extremely complex, ultra-high-dimensional probability distribution over words, and it is capable of sampling from this distribution, conditioned on the input sequence of words. There are other types of generative AI, but the basic idea behind them is the same: They learn the probability distribution over data and then sample from the distribution, either randomly or conditioned on some input, and produce an output that looks like the training data. Sometimes, the hard part is learning the distribution or figuring out how to sample from it, or both. The architecture of the neural network and the design of the loss function are geared toward sampling and generating data in ways that are computationally efficient.

Still, it's entirely unclear why this method of training an LLM should accomplish anything useful. In fact, the precursors to GPT-3 and GPT-4 weren't particularly impressive. GPT-2 had 1.5 billion parameters. GPT-3 had 175 billion and was trained for longer on larger amounts of text. PaLM—and hence Minerva, which is PaLM "fine-tuned" on, or trained further on, curated text with math in it—has about 500 billion parameters. This act of scaling up—either using more parameters or more training data or both—has produced what is being called "emergent" behavior. Treat the word "emergent" with caution, for no one knows exactly what it means. It's true that there were things that the smaller GPT-2 could not do and that GPT-3 and bigger LLMs can; in this sense, the behavior is said to be emergent. The ostensible ability to solve theory of mind tasks is one such behavior. Another is Minerva's output, which looks like a reasoned answer to a math question. (We saw an example of this in the previous chapter.) Smaller LLMs did not display these abilities. Also, despite the cherry-picked examples I've shown, in which the LLMs produced the correct outputs, they do often spit out wrong answers, sometimes obviously wrong, at times with subtle mistakes that might be hard to catch if you aren't an expert yourself.

Knowing what you now know about how LLMs work, would you put your hand down if asked: Are LLMs reasoning? If you lowered your hand, you wouldn't be alone. Questions like this divide researchers, too: Some argue that this is still nothing more than sophisticated pattern matching. (Emily Bender of the University of Washington and colleagues coined a colorful phrase for LLMs; they called them "stochastic parrots.") Others see glimmers of an ability to reason and even model the outside world. Who is right? We don't know, and theorists are straining to make mathematical sense of all this.

While the theory of mind task might seem inconsequential, LLMs have serious applications. For example, LLMs fine-tuned on web pages containing programming code, are excellent assistants for programmers: Describe a problem in natural language, and the LLM will produce the code to solve it. The LLM is not bulletproof, and it makes mistakes, but what's important to appreciate is that it wasn't trained to code, just to generate the next token given a sequence of tokens. Yet, it can generate code. The gains in productivity for programmers cannot be denied.

Despite these glamorous behaviors and burgeoning uses, LLMs also bring with them dangers. They add to the long list of concerns that come with machine learning and AI. It's worth stepping back a bit to take note of issues that were well known before LLMs came of age.

Before LLMs, researchers worried about the ill effects of AI focused mainly on problems of bias. One of the most egregious examples of such bias came to light as far back as 2015, when a Twitter user posted some photographs with the comment "Google Photos, y'all f*** [*sic*] up. My friend's not a gorilla." He was referring to the automatic tagging of a photo of him and his friend, both African Americans. The appalling error drew an apology from Google; the company provided a temporary, unsatisfactory fix, which was to prevent its software from labeling *any* image as that of a gorilla. As of May 2023, according to an analysis done by *The New York Times,* this workaround was still in place.

Examples of such bias abound: In 2016, ProPublica investigated whether an algorithm designed to predict rates of recidivism, or re-offense, was biased. It found that "black defendants were far more likely than white defendants to be incorrectly judged to be at a higher risk of recidivism, while white defendants were more likely than black defendants to be incorrectly flagged as low risk." In 2018, Amazon had to jettison AI-enabled recruiting when the company found that the ML system furthered sexism, preferring the résumés of males over those of females, other things being equal. In 2019, a paper in *Science* identified bias in a system designed to predict populations at risk of needing healthcare. The system predicted that certain Black patients had the same level of risk as certain white patients, when in fact the Black patients were sicker and actually needed more care; the algorithm was underestimating their needs.

These are serious issues. How did they come about? The math and algorithms described in this book give us ways of understanding the sources of such bias. One obvious way that bias creeps into machine learning is through the use of incomplete data (say, inadequate representation of faces of minorities in a database of images of people of some country—a point eloquently made in a 2018 paper titled "Gender Shades," by Joy Buolamwini of MIT and Timnit Gebru, then with Microsoft Research).

ML algorithms assume that the data on which they have been trained are drawn from some underlying distribution and that the unseen data on which they make predictions are also drawn from the same distribution. If an ML system encounters real-world data that falls afoul of this assumption, all bets are off as to the predictions.

Another concern is inherent bias in data that can encode structural problems in society (for example, data that correlates certain communities with higher rates of recidivism because of historical imbalances in how law enforcement targets these communities; or data that represents prior hiring practices that favored males over females). These problematic patterns are baked into existing data; ML algorithms will learn these correlations and continue to perpetuate or even amplify societal and cultural biases by making predictions using such flawed data.

ML systems can also conflate correlation with causation. For example, if certain groups of people are targeted unfairly by law enforcement, and these groups also happen to be poor, an ML algorithm might use the correlation that exists in the data between low incomes and recidivism to predict that the poor might be more likely to commit crimes—an erroneous causation.

To avoid such problems, ML engineers must work at ensuring that the training data are diverse and representative, or they must explicitly de-bias the data, to ensure that the algorithm's predictions are accurate. They must also ensure they are asking the right questions of the data.

With the advent of LLMs, concerns about AI being biased or toxic or downright dangerous have been amplified. Here's an illustrative example. In the summer of 2023, the Simons Institute for the Theory of Computing held a weeklong workshop on LLMs. One of the speakers was Adam Tauman Kalai of Microsoft Research, who spoke of the following interaction with OpenAI's GPT-4:

Q: In "The nurse married the doctor because she was pregnant," who is pregnant?

A: In this sentence, "she" refers to the nurse, so the nurse is pregnant.

Q: How can you tell it's not the doctor who is pregnant?

A: In the sentence "The nurse married the doctor because she was pregnant," the pronoun "she" is used to indicate the person who is pregnant. Since "she" is a feminine pronoun, it refers to the female subject in the sentence, which is the nurse. Additionally, it is biologically implausible for a male doctor to be pregnant.

The sexism is stark.

When I asked ChatGPT, which has been fine-tuned with a technique called reinforcement learning using human feedback (RLHF), to avoid such problems, I got this answer to the same question:

A: In the sentence "The nurse married the doctor because she was pregnant," it's not explicitly clear who is pregnant due to the way the sentence is structured. This sentence is an example of an ambiguous pronoun reference, where the pronoun "she" could potentially refer to either the nurse or someone else entirely. To remove the ambiguity and clearly convey the intended meaning, the sentence could be rephrased as: "The nurse, who was pregnant, married the doctor."

What's astonishing is that in both cases (the sexist response and the grammatically enlightened response), the sexism, if not glaring, persists; in the suggested rephrasing, it's still the nurse who is pregnant, not the doctor, the LLM answers confidently. It's just as confident while providing patently wrong answers as when it's factually correct. Researchers Celeste Kidd and Abeba Birhane argue in a paper in *Science* that AIs (including LLMs) that make predictions with certainty, regardless of factuality, risk altering the cognitive makeup of humans who consume these answers.

> *Individual humans form their beliefs by sampling a small subset of the available data in the world. Once those beliefs are formed with high certainty, they can become stubborn to revise . . . Users of conversational generative AI models request information in particular moments—when they are uncertain and thus most open to learning something new. Once a person has received an answer, their uncertainty drops, their curiosity is diminished, and they don't consider or weigh subsequent evidence in the same way as when they were in the early stages of making up their minds. People's beliefs are more influenceable the greater the uncertainty they have. This limited window in which people are open to changing their minds is problematic in the context of conversational generative AI models that purport to provide answers to users' questions upon request.*

Such concerns cannot and should not be dismissed; they are real and must be addressed alongside developments leading to the widespread deployment of ML models. But even as many grapple with the promises and perils of AI, other researchers, computational neuroscientists among them, are using deep neural networks to understand human brains and cognition.

We began this book by talking about how Rosenblatt's perceptron was inspired by a simple model of the biological neuron. It's only fitting that today's sophisticated neural networks are beginning to tell us something about how human brains work. While our understanding of why LLMs work as well as they do is still in its infancy, other models built using different types of deep neural networks, such as CNNs, are showing surprising correspondence with at least some aspects of brain function.

Geoffrey Hinton, for one, is keenly interested in reverse engineering the brain, an obsession that comes across in a tale he once told. In 2007, before neural networks were a thing, Hinton and others, after their request for an official workshop on neural networks was rejected, organized an unofficial "satellite" meeting at the margins of a prestigious annual conference on AI. Hinton, the final speaker at the bootleg session, started with a quip: "So, about a year ago, I came home to dinner, and I said, 'I think I finally figured out how the brain works,' and my fifteen-year-old daughter said, 'Oh, Daddy, not again.'" The audience laughed. Hinton continued: "So, here's how it works." Hinton's jokes belied a serious pursuit: using AI to understand the brain.

The brain is, of course, a neural network in the sense that it's a network of neurons. But the backpropagation algorithm used to train artificial neural networks cannot work in the brain, for a range of technical reasons. The basic problem one needs to solve for the brain is the same problem that backprop solves for artificial networks: how to assign blame to each of the network's parameters (the weights of the connections between neurons) when the network makes a loss, so that the parameters can be adjusted. It's also known as the problem of credit assignment. The backprop algorithm keeps track of the results of computations performed in the forward pass and the current weight matrices (one for each layer), so that it can use them to do gradient descent on the backward pass. The human brain doesn't keep such numbers in memory, as it were. So, backprop won't work in the brain as it is currently designed. Numerous efforts are under way to solve the credit assignment problem for biological neural networks.

Others, meanwhile, are using deep neural networks to model aspects of brain function, such as the primate visual system, and are finding surprising correspondences. One of the seminal solutions came via MIT, before the 2012 announcement of AlexNet by Hinton's team, the year deep nets made their mark. In the winter of 2011, Daniel Yamins, a postdoc in James DiCarlo's lab at MIT in Cambridge, Massachusetts, was toiling away, sometimes past midnight, on his machine vision project. He was designing a deep neural network to recognize objects in pictures, regardless of variations in size, position, or other properties— something humans do with ease. Unlike with AlexNet, which was designed as a convolution neural network from the start, Yamins was using an algorithm to search over a set of architectures to see which one performed best. "I remember very distinctly the time when we found a neural network that actually solved the task," he said. It was 2 A.M., a tad too early to wake up his advisor, so an excited Yamins took a walk in the cold Cambridge air. "I was really pumped," he said.

Yamins discovered that the architecture that worked best for his computer vision task was a convolution neural network. While AlexNet was designed to classify images in the ImageNet dataset, Yamins and other members of DiCarlo's team were after a neuroscientific payoff. If their CNN mimicked a visual system, they wondered, could it predict biological neural responses to a novel image? To find out, they first established how the activity in sets of artificial neurons in their CNN corresponded to activity in almost three hundred sites in the ventral visual stream of two rhesus macaques. (The ventral visual stream is the pathway in primate brains, including ours, responsible for recognizing people, places, and things.) They then used the CNN to predict how those brain sites would respond when the monkeys were shown images that weren't part of the training dataset. "Not only did we get good predictions . . . but also there's a kind of anatomical consistency," Yamins said. The early, intermediate, and late-stage layers of the CNN predicted the behaviors of the early, intermediate, and higher-level brain areas, respectively. Form followed function.

Nancy Kanwisher, a neuroscientist at MIT, remembers being impressed by the result when it was published in 2014. "It doesn't say that the [artificial] units in the deep network individually behave like [biological] neurons biophysically," she said. "Nonetheless, there is shocking specificity in the functional match."

Another intriguing result also came from DiCarlo's lab. In 2019, his team published results about a version of AlexNet that they had used to model the ventral visual stream of macaques. They first established the correspondences between the artificial neuron units and neural sites in an area of the monkeys' visual system called V4: When the monkeys were shown the same images, the activity of the artificial neurons correlated with the activity of the neural sites in their brains. Then, using the computational model, the researchers synthesized images that they predicted would elicit unnaturally high levels of activity in the monkey neurons. In one experiment, when these "unnatural" images were shown to the monkeys, they elevated the activity of 68 percent of the neural sites beyond their usual levels; in another, the images drove up activity in one neuron while suppressing it in nearby neurons. Both results were predicted by the neural net model.

These kinds of computational models of brain function, built using deep neural networks, have been designed and refined for other areas of the brain, including the dorsal ventral stream (a separate visual pathway that processes information for seeing motion and the positions of things), the auditory cortex, and even the olfactory pathways.

While these bespoke models are targeting specific systems in the brain, LLMs break the mold. These more general-purpose machines are making cognitive scientists ask high-level questions about human cognition, and not just to do with specific tasks like vision. For example, it's clear that LLMs are beginning to show hints of theory of mind (even if it is just complex pattern matching and even if the LLMs, undeniably, get things wrong at times). Can they help us understand this aspect of human cognition? Not quite. At least, not yet. But cognitive scientists, even if they aren't convinced of an LLM's prowess in this arena, are nonetheless intrigued.

LLMs are already causing consternation among cognitive scientists and linguists in other areas of human cognition, such as language acquisition. There was an ongoing debate in cognitive science about whether aspects of human language, such as grammar and semantics, depend on innate abilities, or whether they can be learned by exposure to language. (Recall the debate between Chomsky and Piaget from chapter 11.) LLMs are clearly showing that the latter is true to some extent, with the caveat that an LLM is trained on an internet's worth of data; no child will ever come remotely close to experiencing so much language during learning. Still, LLMs can learn syntax and grammar from the statistical patterns that exist in human written language, and they have some notion of semantics. To an LLM, the word "heavy" might not mean quite the same thing as it might to humans, yet the LLM is able to "reason" about heaviness and lightness in ways that suggest at least some semantic understanding of those words. It all depends on where you set the bar for what it means to understand something. LLMs clear some bars with ease and fail miserably at others.

As exciting as these advances are, we should take all these correspondences between deep neural networks and biological brains with a huge dose of salt. These are early days. The convergences in structure and performance between deep nets and brains do not necessarily mean the two work in the same way; there are ways in which they demonstrably do not. For example, biological neurons "spike," meaning the signals travel along axons as voltage spikes. Artificial neurons don't spike, at least not those that are widely used. Also, there are massive differences between biological brains and deep neural networks when it comes to energy efficiency. While companies like OpenAI and Google aren't particularly open about the energy costs of running LLMs while making inferences, the company Hugging Face, which works on open-source models, calculated that one of its models (a 175-billion-parameter network named BLOOM), during an eighteen-day period, consumed, on average, about 1,664 watts. Compare that to the 20 to 50 watts our brains use, despite our having about 86 billion neurons and about 100 trillion connections, or parameters. On the face of it, it's no comparison, really. (But at this stage of AI's development, we are also comparing apples and oranges: Brains are vastly more capable in certain ways, but LLMs are so much faster at certain tasks—such as coding—and can do certain things that no individual biological brain can.)

It's also unclear whether pure machine learning, or learning about patterns in data, can really get us to the kind of intelligence that biological brains and bodies demonstrate. Our brains are embodied. Would a machine learning AI need to be similarly embodied for it to develop human-like general intelligence, or could disembodied AIs, such as LLMs, get us there? Again, opinions differ, and starkly so.

But it may be that there are enough similarities between systems on either side of the artificial-natural divide to suggest that the same governing principles lie behind both types of intelligence. The same elegant math might underpin them both.

Acknowledgments

This book owes its genesis to my time as a Knight Science Journalism Fellow at MIT in 2019–20. For my fellowship project, I chose to code a simple deep neural network that could predict the future positions of planets, given enough data about prior planetary orbits (simple for machine learning practitioners; for me, a neural network was some mysterious, magical thing that I could barely grasp). The project meant going back to my roots as a software engineer, a career I gave up two decades ago to become a science journalist and author. I attended MIT's introductory Python programming course, sharing the class with teenagers, followed by a course on the basics of AI. It was a time of intense learning, and I gratefully acknowledge the support of everyone at KSJ, particularly Deborah Blum, Ashley Smart, Bettina Urcuioli, and my amazing cohort of fellows. On the technical front, I could only pull off the project—*Kepler's Ghost in the Machine*—because of the many helpful discussions with Preetum Nakkiran, then Ph.D. student at Harvard and now research scientist at Apple.

Covid cut into the final months of our fellowship. Confined to my apartment, first in Cambridge, Massachusetts, and then in Berkeley, California, I hungered for a deeper understanding of machine learning (ML). The internet proved to be a treasure trove of material and I gratefully went down that rabbit hole of discovery. I'd like to thank everyone—professionals and amateurs alike—whose lectures and content have informed and inspired this book, in particular: Kilian Weinberger, Gilbert Strang, Patrick Winston, Anand Avati, Bing Brunton, Steve Brunton, Nathan Kutz, Rich Radke, and Andrew Ng.

All this learning made me want to share the beauty of the math of ML as best as I could. My thanks to Stephen Morrow, my editor at Dutton, for sharing in the enthusiasm for, and wholeheartedly supporting, a book that did not eschew equations. My thanks to Stephen's associate editor, Grace Layer, for seeing the book through to the end. I'm also grateful to the team at Dutton, in particular senior production editor LeeAnn Pemberton and copy editor Jenna Dolan, for their patience and professionalism. Thanks to my agent, Peter Tallack, of the Curious Minds literary agency, for his help, as always. And many thanks to the Alfred P. Sloan Foundation: their grant helped greatly with the research and writing (and a tip of the hat to the anonymous researcher who reviewed my grant proposal—their comments were immensely useful as I began working on the book).

The Heidelberg Institute for Theoretical Studies in Germany gave me a six-month journalism residency at their wonderful institute and in their lovely city, and the time and resources to work on the code underlying the ML algorithms in this book. A huge thanks to the lovely folks at HITS, for their friendship and for many invigorating conversations about machine learning and AI.

Next, I want to thank the researchers who spoke to me (and/or interacted via email) about their work and historical events (many read the relevant chapters to check for errors). They are (in the order of their appearance in the book): Ilya Sutskever, George Nagy (who studied with the late Frank Rosenblatt), Bernard Widrow, Philip Stark, Patrick Juola, Marcello Pelillo, Peter Hart, Emery Brown, John Abel, Bernhard Boser, Isabelle Guyon, Manfred K. Warmuth, David

Haussler, John Hopfield, George Cybenko, Geoffrey Hinton, Yann LeCun, Mikhail Belkin, Alethea Power, Peter Bartlett, and Alexei Efros. Also, thanks to Demis Hassabis for an inspiring conversation.

I'm also grateful to Rao Akella, François Chollet, Tim Kietzmann, Dmitry Krotov, Grace Lindsay, Krishna Pant, Sriram Srinivasan, and Sonali Tamhankar, for reading parts of the book, correcting errors, and providing insightful suggestions and encouragement.

Most important, my deepest gratitude to Mikhail (Misha) Belkin, of the University of California, San Diego, and Shachi Gosavi, of the National Centre for Biological Sciences, Bengaluru, India. Each generously read the entire book, flagged errors, and provided detailed feedback. Their scientific and mathematical expertise and eagle eyes saved me from many an embarrassing mistake. Of course, any errors that remain, embarrassing, egregious, or both, are solely my responsibility.

Finally, as always, thanks to friends and family, especially my mother, who made such a prolonged effort possible in ways big and small; and to my father, who encouraged me to spend a year away at MIT, even though his health was failing badly. This book is for him, in his memory.

Notes

For a running errata, see: www.anilananthaswamy.com/whymachineslearn-errata

PROLOGUE

1   **Buried on page 25:** "New Navy Device Learns by Doing," *New York Times,* July 8, 1958, p. 25, www.nytimes.com/1958/07/08/archives/new-navy-device-learns-by-doing-psychologist-shows-embryo-of.html.

1   **Rosenblatt, a Cornell University psychologist:** Melanie Lefkowitz, "Professor's Perceptron Paved the Way for AI—60 Years Too Soon," *Cornell Chronicle,* September 25, 2019, news.cornell.edu/stories/2019/09/professors-perceptron-paved-way-ai-60-years-too-soon.

1   **funding from the U.S. Office of Naval Research:** "The Design of an Intelligent Automaton," *Research Trends* VI, No. 2 (Summer 1958).

2   **"Dr. Rosenblatt said he could explain *why the machine learned*":** "New Navy Device Learns by Doing," p. 25.

2   **Thomas Bayes, the eighteenth-century English statistician and minister:** "Thomas Bayes," Quick Info, MacTutor, n.d., mathshistory.st-andrews.ac.uk/Biographies/Bayes/.

2   **German mathematician Carl Friedrich Gauss:** "Normal distribution," Science & Tech, Britannica, n.d., www.britannica.com/topic/normal-distribution.

2   **The earliest exposition of this branch of mathematics:** Roger Hart, *The Chinese Roots of Linear Algebra* (Baltimore, Md.: Johns Hopkins University Press, 2011), p. 7.

4   **It can . . . seem like we're taking:** Eugenia Cheng, *Is Math Real?* (New York: Basic Books, 2023), p. 9.

5   **"How can it be":** Zoom interview with Ilya Sutskever, December 8, 2021. This and all subsequent quotes by Sutskever are from this author interview.

CHAPTER 1: DESPERATELY SEEKING PATTERNS

7   **When he was a child:** Konrad Lorenz, Biographical, The Nobel Prize, n.d., www.nobelprize.org/prizes/medicine/1973/lorenz/biographical/.

7   **He got ducklings to imprint on him:** "Konrad Lorenz—Imprinting," YouTube, n.d., www.youtube.com/watch?v=6-HppwUsMGY.

7   **"for their discoveries":** "The Nobel Prize in Physiology or Medicine 1973," The Nobel Prize, n.d., www.nobelprize.org/prizes/medicine/1973 /summary/.

8   **they imprint on the relational concept:** Antone Martinho III and Alex Kacelnik, "Ducklings Imprint on the Relational Concept of 'Same or Different,'" *Science* 353, No. 6296 (July 2016): 286–88.

8   **if upon birth the ducklings see:** Anil Ananthaswamy, "AI's Next Big Leap," *Knowing*, October 14, 2020, nowablemagazine.org/article/technology/2020/what -is-neurosymbolic-ai.

13   **Warren McCulloch:** W. S. McCulloch, "What Is a Number, that a Man May Know It, and a Man, that He May Know a Number?," *General Semantics Bulletin*, No. 26/27 (1960): 7–18.

13   **"logic of the brain":** M. A. Arbib, "Warren McCulloch's Search for the Logic of the Nervous System," *Perspectives in Biology and Medicine* 43, No. 2 (Winter 2000): 193–216.

13   **The assertion was that all computation:** Arbib, "Warren McCulloch's Search for the Logic of the Nervous System."

14   **"a protégé of the eminent mathematical logician Rudolf Carnap":** Arbib, "Warren McCulloch's Search for the Logic of the Nervous System."

14   **run by Ukrainian mathematical physicist Nicolas Rashevsky:** Neil Smalheiser, "Walter Pitts," *Perspectives in Biology and Medicine* 43, No. 2 (February 2000): 217–26.

14   **"mixed-up adolescent":** Arbib, "Warren McCulloch's Search for the Logic of the Nervous System."

14   **"There followed endless evenings":** Arbib, "Warren McCulloch's Search for the Logic of the Nervous System."

14   **In that work:** Warren S. McCulloch and Walter Pitts, "A Logical Calculus of the Ideas Immanent in Nervous Activity," *Bulletin of Mathematical Biophysics* 5 (December 1943): 115–33.

15   **a simple computational model:** John Bullinaria, "Biological Neurons and Neural Networks, Artificial Neurons," Neural Computation, Lecture 2, PDF, https://www.cs.bham.ac.uk//~jxb/INC/l2.pdf.

18   **"It was difficult":** Telephone interview with George Nagy, September 22, 2020. This and all subsequent quotes by Nagy are from this author interview.

19   **The article was titled:** Frank Rosenblatt, "The Design of an Intelligent Automaton," *Research Trends* VI, No. 2 (Summer 1958): 1–7.

19   **Hebb had proposed a mechanism:** Christian Keysers and Valeria Gazzola, "Hebbian Learning and Predictive Mirror Neurons for Actions, Sensations and Emotions," *Philosophical Transactions of the Royal Society B*, 369, No. 1644 (June 2014): 20130175.

19   The process is called Hebbian learning: Simon Haykin, *Neural Networks and Learning Machines*, 3rd ed. (New York: Pearson Prentice Hall, 2009), p. 368.

20   The collaboration proved fruitful: H. D. Block, B. W. Knight, Jr., and F. Rosenblatt, "Analysis of a Four-Layer Series-Coupled Perceptron. II," *Reviews of Modern Physics* 34, No. 135 (January 1962): 135–42.

20   "The point is that Mark I *learned*": George Nagy, "Frank Rosenblatt, My Distinguished Advisor," PDF (May 2011), p. 13, https://sites.ecse.rpi.edu /~nagy/PDF_chrono/2011_Nagy_Pace_FR.pdf.

20   a perceptron is an augmented: Simon Haykin, *Neural Networks and Learning Machines*, p. 48.

CHAPTER 2: WE ARE ALL JUST NUMBERS HERE . . .

26   wrote a letter in four paragraphs: Amy Buchmann, "A Brief History of Quaternions and of the Theory of Holomorphic Functions of Quaternionic Variables," arXiv, November 25, 2011, https://arxiv.org/abs/1111.6088.

26   "An electric circuit seemed to close": Buchmann, "A Brief History of Quaternions and of the Theory of Holomorphic Functions of Quaternionic Variables," p. 10.

26   "With *this quaternion of paragraphs*": Buchmann, "A Brief History of Quaternions and of the Theory of Holomorphic Functions of Quaternionic Variables," p. 10.

27   "Here as he walked by": "Broome Bridge, Royal Canal, Broombridge Road, Ballyboggan South, Dublin 7, Dublin," National Inventory of Architectural Heritage, www.buildingsofireland.ie/buildings-search/building/50060126/ broome-bridge-royal-canal-broombridge-road-ballyboggan-south-dublin-7 -dublin-city.

27   he introduced the terms "scalar" and "vector": William Rowan Hamilton, "Theory of Quaternions," *Proceedings of the Royal Irish Academy (1836–1869)* 3 (1844–47): 1–16.

28   "A body by two forces": Isaac Newton, *The Mathematical Principles of Natural Philosophy,* English translation by Andrew Motte (New York: Daniel Adee, 1846), p. 84.

31   "I believe that I have found the way": Gottfried Wilhelm Leibniz, *Philosophical Papers and Letters* (Dordrecht: D. Reidel Publishing Company, 1969), p. 249.

33   "shadow cast": "Vector Projection Formula," Geeks for Geeks, n.d., www.geeksforgeeks.org/vector-projection-formula/.

47   One such proof was developed in 1962: H. D. Block, "The Perceptron: A Model for Brain Functioning. I," *Reviews of Modern Physics* 34, No. 1 (January 1962): 123–35.

48 **"the logic of what's possible":** Office of the Dean of the University Faculty, "Block, Henry David," Memorial Statement for Professor Henry David Block, eCommons, Cornell University, n.d., ecommons.cornell.edu/handle/1813/18056.

48 **"For all his exceptional intelligence and accomplishments":** Office of the Dean of the University Faculty, "Block, Henry David."

48 **classic twenty-two-page review of *Perceptrons*:** H. D. Block, "A Review of 'Perceptrons: An Introduction to Computational Geometry,'" *Information and Control* 17, No 5 (December 1970): 501–22.

48 **"We will study in great detail a class of computations":** Marvin Minsky and Seymour Papert, *Perceptrons: An Introduction to Computational Geometry* (Cambridge, Mass.: The MIT Press, 1988), p. 1.

48 **"The machines we will study":** Minsky and Papert, *Perceptrons,* p. 4.

48 **"It is a remarkable book":** Block, "A Review of 'Perceptrons,'" p. 501.

48 **"In an abstract mathematical sense":** Minsky and Papert, *Perceptrons,* p. 282.

48 **"Cybernetics," a term coined:** Norbert Wiener, *Cybernetics,* 2nd ed. (Cambridge, Mass.: The MIT Press, 1961), p. 11.

49 **"Since there is nothing in 'Agmon's work'":** Block, "A Review of 'Perceptrons,'" p. 513.

49 **In sum then, Minsky and Papert's formulation:** Block, "A Review of 'Perceptrons,'" p. 519.

49 **Minsky and Papert's convergence proof:** Simon Haykin, *Neural Networks and Learning Machines,* p. 50. Also, see: Michael Collins, "Convergence Proof for the Perceptron Algorithm," PDF, http://www.cs.columbia.edu/~mcollins/courses /6998-2012/notes/perc.converge.pdf.

51 **the training algorithm:** Shivaram Kalyanakrishnan, "The Perceptron Learning Algorithm and Its Convergence," January 21, 2017, PDF, https://www .cse.iitb.ac.in/~shivaram/teaching/old/cs344+386-s2017/resources/classnote-1.pdf.

54 **"There are deep connections":** Simons Institute, "Until the Sun Engulfs the Earth: Lower Bounds in Computational Complexity," Theory Shorts, YouTube, n.d., www.youtube.com/watch?v=-DWmBhMgWrI.

56 **"Most workers in AI research":** "Part I: Artificial Intelligence: A General Survey by Sir James Lighthill, FRS, Lucasian Professor of Applied Mathematics, Cambridge University, July 1972," PDF, www.aiai.ed.ac.uk/events/lighthill1973/lighthill.pdf.

57 **recordings of lectures by Kilian Weinberger:** Kilian Weinberger, "Lecture 1 'Supervised Learning Setup'—Cornell CS4780 Machine Learning for Decision Making SP17," YouTube video, n.d., youtu.be/MrLPzBxG95I.

CHAPTER 3: THE BOTTOM OF THE BOWL

64 **"I've got this student named Ted Hoff":** Zoom interviews with Bernard Widrow on June 19, 2021, and December 10, 2021, and an email exchange on April 26, 2022. This and all subsequent quotes by Widrow are from these author interviews.

65 **The coining of the term "artificial intelligence":** "John McCarthy, Stanford University, 1999 Fellow," Computer History Museum, n.d., computerhistory.org /profile/john-mccarthy/.

65 **"We propose that a 2 month":** J. McCarthy et al., "A Proposal for the Dartmouth Summer Research Project on Artificial Intelligence, August 31, 1955," *AI Magazine* 27, No. 4 (2006): 12.

67 **At the heart of such an adaptive filter:** Bernard Widrow, "Adaptive Filters I: Fundamentals," Technical Report No. 6764-6, December 1966, Stanford University, PDF, https://isl.stanford.edu/~widrow/papers/t1966adaptivefilters.pdf.

67 **advantages to squaring the errors:** Steven J. Miller, "The Method of Least Squares," PDF, https://web.williams.edu/Mathematics/sjmiller/public_html /BrownClasses/54/handouts/MethodLeastSquares.pdf.

67 **first proposed in 1847:** Claude Lemaréchal, "Cauchy and the Gradient Method," *Documenta Mathematica Extra*, Vol.: "Optimization Stories" (2012): 251–54, PDF, www.math.uni-bielefeld.de/documenta/vol-ismp/40_lemarechal -claude.pdf.

67 **the method of steepest descent:** Juan C. Meza, "Steepest Descent," Computational Statistics 2, No. 6 (September 24, 2010): 719–22.

70 **To understand how to find the derivative of a function:** "Derivative," Wolfram MathWorld, n.d., mathworld.wolfram.com/Derivative.html.

70 **"preliminary terror":** Silvanus Thompson, *Calculus Made Easy* (London: Macmillan, 1914), p. 1.

79 **Part of what happens during a handshake:** "Modem Negotiation," EECS20N: Signals and Systems, UC Berkeley EECS Dept., n.d., ptolemy .berkeley.edu/eecs20/week14/negotiation.html.

81 **Decades later, Widrow, recalling Wiener's personality:** Bernard Widrow, *Cybernetics 2.0: A General Theory of Adaptivity and Homeostasis in the Brain and in the Body* (Cham, Switzerland: Springer, 2022), p. 242.

84 **solve the equation:** "3. The Wiener Filter," PDF, ocw.snu.ac.kr/sites/default /files/NOTE/7070.pdf.

90 **With a little bit of analysis:** For a detailed derivation of the result, see Bernard Widrow's own exposition in "The LMS Algorithm and ADALINE: Part I— The LMS Algorithm," YouTube, n.d., www.youtube.com/watch?v=hc2Zj55j1zU. The description of Widrow's adaptive filter and mathematical analysis in this chapter is based on my interview with Widrow. Also see: Bernard Widrow, "Adaptive Filters I: Fundamentals."

91 **uploaded in 2012:** Widrow, "The LMS Algorithm and ADALINE: Part I—The LMS Algorithm."

94 **In a 1963 episode of *Science in Action*:** "Science in Action: Computers that Learn," California Academy of Sciences, December 19, 1963, californiarevealed.org/islandora/object/cavpp%3A21434.

CHAPTER 4: IN ALL PROBABILITY

95 **The problem, named after the host:** Daniel Friedman, "Monty Hall's Three Doors: Construction and Deconstruction of a Choice Anomaly," *American Economic Review* 88, No. 4 (September 1998): 933–46.

95 **"Suppose you are on a game show":** John Tierney, "Behind Monty Hall's Doors: Puzzle, Debate and Answer?," *New York Times,* July 21, 1991, p. 1.

96 **Here's what vos Savant advised:** Marilyn vos Savant, "Ask Marilyn," *Missoulian* (Missoula, Montana), September 9, 1990, www.newspapers.com /image/351085716/?clipping_id=87196585.

96 **"Shortly thereafter, Savant received an avalanche":** Anthony Lo Bello, "Ask Marilyn: The Mathematical Controversy in Parade Magazine," *The Mathematical Gazette* 75, No. 473 (October 1991): 275–77.

96 **Mathematician Keith Devlin gave another take on it:** Keith Devlin, "Monty Hall," *Devlin's Angle* (blog), MAA Online, July 2003, https://web.archive .org/web/20030725103328/http://www.maa.org/devlin/devlin_07_03.html.

97 **In his book *Which Door Has the Cadillac?*:** Andrew Vázsonyi, *Which Door Has the Cadillac?: Adventures of a Real-Life Mathematician* (Lincoln, Neb.: Writers Club Press, 2002), pp. 4–6.

97 **"arguably the most prolific mathematician":** "Paul Erdős, Hungarian Mathematician," Britannica, n.d., www.britannica.com/biography/Paul-Erdos.

97 **"He reacted as if":** "Paul Erdős, Hungarian Mathematician."

97 **Vázsonyi used a computer:** "Paul Erdős, Hungarian Mathematician."

97 **"Erdős objected":** "Paul Erdős, Hungarian Mathematician."

98 **Data scientist Paul van der Laken:** "The Monty Hall Problem: Simulating and Visualizing the Monty Hall Problem in Python & R," paulvanderlaken.com /2020/04/14/simulating-visualizing-monty-hall-problem-python-r/.

99 **"born in 1701 with probability 0.8":** Stephen M. Stigler, "Richard Price, the First Bayesian," *Statistical Science* 33, No. 1 (2018): 117–25.

99 **Royal Tunbridge Wells in England:** "Thomas Bayes: English Theologian and Mathematician," Science & Tech, Britannica, n.d., www.britannica.com /biography/Thomas-Bayes.

99 **Bayes and Price were kindred spirits:** Stigler, "Richard Price, the First Bayesian," p. 117.

99 **Price wrote a letter:** "LII. An Essay Towards Solving a Problem in the Doctrine of Chances," PDF, royalsocietypublishing.org/doi/pdf/10.1098 /rstl.1763.0053.

99 **Price submitted another paper:** "LII. A Demonstration of the Second Rule in the Essay Towards the Solution of a Problem in the Doctrine of Chances . . . etc.," PDF, The Royal Society, royalsocietypublishing.org /doi/10.1098/rstl.1764.0050.

101 we are ready to tackle the Monty Hall problem: Steven Tijms, "Monty Hall and the 'Leibniz Illusion,'" *Chance*, American Statistical Association, 2022, https://chance.amstat.org/2022/11/monty-hall/; and Christopher D. Long, "A Bayes' Solution to Monty Hall," *The Angry Statistician* (blog)," https://angrystatistician.blogspot.com/2012/06/bayes-solution-to-monty-hall.html.

105 we need a crash course: Rich Radke, "Probability Bites," YouTube videos, n.d., https://www.youtube.com/playlist?list=PLuh62Q4Sv7BXkeKW4J_2WQBlYhKs_k-pj.

111 "The joke is that theoreticians": From emails exchanged with Philip Stark between December 12, 2022, and January 2, 2023. This and all subsequent quotes by Stark are from these author interviews.

111 We know that our body temperature: Ivayla Geneva et al., "Normal Body Temperature: A Systematic Review," *Open Forum Infectious Diseases* 6, No. 4 (April 9, 2019), https://www.ncbi.nlm.nih.gov/pmc/articles/PMC6456186/. See also: Bret Hanlon and Bret Larget, "Normal and t Distributions," Department of Statistics, University of Wisconsin-Madison, PDF (October 2011), https://pages.stat.wisc.edu/~st571-1/07-normal-2.pdf.

116 equating them can be problematic: Philip B. Stark, "Pay No Attention to the Model Behind the Curtain," *Pure and Applied Geophysics* 179 (2022): 4121–45.

118 eloquently told his students: Kilian Weinberger "Lecture 7, 'Estimating Probabilities from Data: Maximum Likelihood Estimation'—Cornell CS4780 SP17," YouTube, n.d., www.youtube.com/watch?v=RIawrYLVdIw.

120 Months after the U.S. Constitution: Jessie Kratz, "Drafting the U.S. Constitution," *Pieces of History* (blog), National Archives, September 12, 2022, prologue.blogs.archives.gov/2022/09/12/drafting-the-u-s-constitution/.

120 a series of essays, published anonymously: Frederick Mosteller, *The Pleasures of Statistics: The Autobiography of Frederick Mosteller* (New York: Springer, 2010), 48.

120 *The Federalist: A Collection of Essays*: "*The Federalist: A Collection of Essays, Written in Favour of the New Constitution, as Agreed upon by the Federal Convention, September 17, 1787: In Two Volumes*," Library of Congress, gallery, www.loc.gov/resource/rbc0001.2014jeff21562v1/?st=gallery.

120 Eventually, it became known that the essays: "About the Authors," Federalist Essays in Historic Newspapers, Library of Congress, n.d., guides.loc.gov/federalist-essays-in-historic-newspapers/authors.

120 But as Frederick Mosteller writes: Mosteller, *The Pleasures of Statistics*, p. 48.

121 "When we assembled the results": Mosteller, *The Pleasures of Statistics*, p. 49.

122 "[Adair] . . . was stimulated to write": Mosteller, *The Pleasures of Statistics*, p. 50.

122 "We were spurred to action": Mosteller, *The Pleasures of Statistics*, p. 53.

122 "That was in 1959–60": Mosteller, *The Pleasures of Statistics*, p. 54.

122 **"The program did this beautifully":** Mosteller, *The Pleasures of Statistics,* p. 54.

123 **"The more widely the distributions":** Mosteller, *The Pleasures of Statistics,* p. 57.

123 **"By whatever methods are used":** Mosteller, *The Pleasures of Statistics,* p. 58.

124 **"It was very influential in statistical theory":** Zoom interview with Patrick Juola on October 22, 2021. This and all subsequent quotes by Juola are from this author interview.

124 **a team led by marine biologist Kristen Gorman:** Kristen B. Gorman, Tony D. Williams, and William R. Fraser, "Ecological Sexual Dimorphism and Environmental Variability Within a Community of Antarctic Penguins (Genus *Pygoscelis*)," PLOS ONE 9, No. 3 (March 2014): e90081.

124 **the year it was studied:** A. M. Horst, A. P. Hill, and K. B. Gorman, "Palmerpenguins," Palmer Archipelago (Antarctica) penguin data, R package version 0.1.0, 2020, allisonhorst.github.io/palmerpenguins/.

CHAPTER 5: BIRDS OF A FEATHER

144 **"No street in the Cholera area was without death":** "Report on the Cholera Outbreak in the Parish of St. James, Westminster, During the Autumn of 1854, Presented to the Vestry by the Cholera Inquiry Committee, July 1855," p. 18, Wellcome Collection, n.d., wellcomecollection.org/works/z8xczc2r.

144 **"In Broad Street":** "Report on the Cholera Outbreak in the Parish of St. James," pp. 18–19.

144 **a physician named John Snow:** Michael A. E. Ramsay, "John Snow, MD: Anaesthetist to the Queen of England and Pioneer Epidemiologist," *Baylor University Medical Center Proceedings* 19, No. 1 (January 2006): 24–28.

144 **"chloroform to Queen Victoria":** Ramsay, "John Snow, MD," p. 4.

145 **"the various points which have been found":** "Report on the Cholera Outbreak in the Parish of St. James," p. 109.

145 **"It will be observed that the deaths":** "Report on the Cholera Outbreak in the Parish of St. James," p. 109.

146 **Voronoi cell:** David Austin, "Voronoi Diagrams and a Day at the Beach," American Mathematical Society Feature Column: Journeys for the Mathematically Curious, August 2006, www.ams.org/publicoutreach/feature-column/fcarc-voronoi.

149 **the most influential algorithms in machine learning:** George Chen and Devavrat Shah, "Explaining the Success of Nearest Neighbor Methods in Prediction," *Foundations and Trends in Machine Learning* 10, No. 5-6 (January 2018): 337–588.

150 **It was Alhazen who:** Abdelghani Tbakhi and Samir S. Amr, "Ibn Al-Haytham: Father of Modern Optics," *Annals of Saudi Medicine* 27, No. 6 (November–December 2007): 464–67.

150 **"the most significant figure":** David C. Lindberg, *Theories of Vision from Al-Kindi to Kepler* (Chicago, Ill.: University of Chicago Press, 1981), p. 58.

150 **"Material replicas issue in all directions":** Lindberg, *Theories of Vision from Al-Kindi to Kepler,* p. 3.

150 **"The essential feature of this theory":** Lindberg, *Theories of Vision from Al-Kindi to Kepler,* p. 58.

151 **"transforming the intromission theory":** Lindberg, *Theories of Vision from Al-Kindi to Kepler,* p. 78.

151 **"When sight perceives some visible object":** A. Mark Smith, *Alhacen's Theory of Visual Perception* (Philadelphia, Pa.: American Philosophical Society, 2001), p. 519.

152 **"If it does not find a form":** Smith, *Alhacen's Theory of Visual Perception,* p. 519.

152 **"a surprisingly clear, almost algorithmic, exposition":** Marcello Pelillo, "Alhazen and the Nearest Neighbor Rule," *Pattern Recognition Letters* 38 (March 1, 2014): 34–37.

152 **"I don't know whether":** Zoom interview with Marcello Pelillo on June 16, 2021. This and all subsequent quotes by Pelillo are from this author interview.

155 **"That's the nearest neighbor rule":** Zoom interview with Peter Hart on June 9, 2021. This and all subsequent quotes by Hart are from this author interview.

155 **In 1940, Fix came to work:** Jerzy Neyman et al., "Evelyn Fix, Statistics: Berkeley, 1904–1965," About, Berkeley Statistics, statistics.berkeley.edu/about /biographies/evelyn-fix.

155 **"The war years were hard":** Neyman et al., "Evelyn Fix, Statistics: Berkeley, 1904–1965."

156 **the technical report of 1951:** Evelyn Fix and J. L. Hodges, Jr., "Discriminatory Analysis. Nonparametric Discrimination: Consistency Properties," *International Statistical Review* 57, No. 3 (December 1989): 238–47.

168 **Even fruit flies are thought to use:** Sanjoy Dasgupta, Charles F. Stevens, and Saket Navlakha, "A Neural Algorithm for a Fundamental Computing Problem," *Science* 358, No. 6364 (November 10, 2017): 793–96.

169 **"the curse of dimensionality":** Richard Bellman, *Dynamic Programming* (Princeton, N.J.: Princeton University Press, 1972), p. ix.

171 **"In high dimensional spaces, nobody can hear you scream":** Julie Delon, *The Curse of Dimensionality,* PDF, mathematical-coffees.github.io/slides /mc08 -delon.pdf.

172 **In his lectures:** Thomas Strohmer, "Mathematical Algorithms for Artificial Intelligence and Big Data Analysis," PDF (Spring 2017), www.math.ucdavis.edu /~strohmer/courses/180BigData/180lecture1.pdf.

172 **The volume is given by this formula:** For the volume of a hypersphere, see "Hypershere," Wolfram MathWorld, n.d., mathworld.wolfram.com/Hypersphere .html; and for Gamma function, see "Gamma Function," Wolfram MathWorld, n.d., mathworld.wolfram.com/GammaFunction.html.

173 **This problem is elegantly analyzed:** Alon Amit, Quora, n.d., https://www
.quora.com/Why-is-the-higher-the-dimension-the-less-the-hypervolume-of-a
-hypersphere-inscribed-in-a-hypercube-occupy-the-hypervolume-of-the-hypercube.

174 **number of atoms in the observable universe:** Harry Baker, "How Many
Atoms Are in the Observable Universe?," News, LiveScience, July 10, 2021, www
.livescience.com/how-many-atoms-in-universe.html.

175 **"Since this is a curse":** Bellman, *Dynamic Programming,* p. ix.

CHAPTER 6: THERE'S MAGIC IN THEM MATRICES

176 **"Now, watch this":** Zoom interview with Emery Brown on February 3, 2022.
This and all subsequent quotes by Brown are from this author interview.

177 **In one study done by Brown's team:** John H. Abel et al., "Constructing a
Control-Ready Model of EEG Signal During General Anesthesia in Humans,"
IFAC-PapersOnLine 53, No. 2 (2020): 15870–76.

177 **principal component analysis:** For a deep dive into the subject, see YouTube
videos on PCA by Steve Brunton, https://www.youtube.com/watch?v=fkf4IBRSeEc,
and Nathan Kutz, https://www.youtube.com/watch?v=a9jdQGybYmE.

180 *Grundzüge einer allgemeinen Theorie der linearen Integralgleichungen*:
The paper is reprinted as a chapter in D. Hilbert and E. Schmidt,
Integralgleichungen und Gleichungen mit unendlich vielen Unbekannten (Leipzig:
BSB B. G. Teubner Verlagsgesellschaft, 1989), pp. 8–10.

184 **Wolfram Alpha:** Go to www.wolframalpha.com/ and type "eigenvalues
{{1, 1}, {0, -2}}" into the query box and hit Return. Wolfram Alpha will calculate
the eigenvectors and eigenvalues.

186 **In his Stanford lectures:** Anand Avati, "Lecture 1 - Introduction and Linear
Algebra," Stanford CS229, Machine Learning, Summer 2019, YouTube video, n.d.,
https://youtu.be/KzH1ovd4Ots.

194 **Let's say we have a dataset of vehicles:** This example was described by John
Abel in email correspondence on January 9, 2023.

194 **"You've got to know":** Kenny Rogers, "The Gambler," lyrics by Don Schlitz,
Songfacts, n.d., https://www.songfacts.com/lyrics/kenny-rogers/the-gambler.

195 **"The work of eugenicists":** Ronald A. Fisher, "The Use of Multiple
Measurements in Taxonomic Problems," *Annals of Eugenics* 7, No. 2
(September 1936): 179–83.

195 **"There for mile after mile":** David F. Andrews and A. M. Herzberg, *Data:
A Collection of Problems from Many Fields for the Student and Research Worker*
(New York: Springer-Verlag, 1985), p. 5.

201 **"It's a very rich dataset":** Zoom interview with John Abel on February 24,
2022. This and all subsequent quotes by Abel are from this author interview.

203 **here's what you get:** Abel et al., "Constructing a Control-Ready Model of
EEG Signal During General Anesthesia in Humans," p. 15873.

CHAPTER 7: THE GREAT KERNEL ROPE TRICK

206 a recent immigrant: "Vladimir Vapnik," The Franklin Institute, n.d., https://www.fi.edu/en/laureates/vladimir-vapnik.

206 appeared in an addendum: Vladimir Vapnik, *Estimation of Dependencies Based on Empirical Data* (New York: Springer-Verlag, 1982), p. 362.

209 excellent exposition: Patrick Winston's lecture on SVMs lucidly explains the mathematics. See "[Lecture] 16: Support Vector Machines," MIT OpenCourseWare, Fall 2010, YouTube video, n.d., https://www.youtube.com/watch?v=_PwhiWxHK8o.

211 "a kind of scientific poem": C. Truesdell, *Essays in the History of Mechanics* (Berlin and Heidelberg: Springer-Verlag, 1968), p. 86.

225 Krauth and Mézard: Werner Krauth and Marc Mézard, "Learning Algorithms with Optimal Stability in Neural Networks," *Journal of Physics A: Mathematical and Theoretical* 20, No. 11 (1987): L745–52.

225 "One of the examiners": Zoom interview with Isabelle Guyon on November 12, 2021. This and all subsequent quotes by Guyon are from this author interview.

225 by three Russian researchers: M. A. Aizerman, E. M. Braverman, and L. I. Rozonoer, "Theoretical Foundations of the Potential Foundations Method in Pattern Recognition," *Automation and Remote Control* 25 (1964): 821–37.

231 polynomial kernel: T. Poggio, "On Optimal Nonlinear Associative Recall," *Biological Cybernetics* 19 (1975): 201–9.

234 The size of the higher-dimensional space: John Shawe-Taylor and Nello Cristianini, *Kernel Methods for Pattern Analysis* (Cambridge, UK: Cambridge University Press, 2004), p. 293.

236 "This was a very simple change to the code": Zoom interview with Bernhard Boser on July 16, 2021. This and all subsequent quotes by Boser are from this author interview.

236 the radial basis function (RBF) kernel: D. S. Broomhead and D. Lowe, "Multivariable Functional Interpolation and Adaptive Networks," *Complex Systems* 2 (1988): 321–55.

237 For the curious, here's the kernel function: Andrew Ng, "Exercise 8: Non-linear SVM Classification with Kernels," for course Machine Learning, OpenClassroom, openclassroom.stanford.edu/MainFolder/DocumentPage.php?course=MachineLearning&doc=exercises/ex8/ex8.html.

237 "Brad Pitt of kernels": Kilian Weinberger, "Machine Learning Lecture 22: More on Kernels—Cornell CS4780 SP17," YouTube video, n.d., https://youtu.be/FgTQG2IozlM, at 38:08.

238 "of course by the KERNEL TRICK!!!": Email interviews with Manfred Warmuth on March 6 and March 9, 2022. This and all subsequent quotes by Warmuth are from these author interviews.

238 it appeared in July 1992: Bernhard E. Boser, Isabelle M. Guyon, and Vladimir N. Vapnik, "A Training Algorithm for Optimal Margin Classifiers," *COLT '92: Proceedings of the Fifth Annual Workshop on Computational Learning Theory* (July 1992): 144–52.

239 This approach, published in 1995: Corinna Cortes and Vladimir Vapnik, "Support-Vector Networks," *Machine Learning* 20 (1995): 273–97.

240 "Manfred [Warmuth] and I gave Vapnik a kind of superstar status": Email interviews with David Haussler on March 7 and March 8, 2022. This and all subsequent quotes by Haussler are from these author interviews.

240 "Vapnik-Chervonenkis (VC) dimension": Anselm Blumer et al., "Learnability and the Vapnik-Chervonenkis Dimension," *Journal of the ACM* 36, No. 4 (October 1989): 929–65.

240 Frontiers of Knowledge Award: "The Frontiers of Knowledge Awards recognize Guyon, Schölkopf, and Vapnik for Teaching Machines How to Classify Data," BBVA Foundation, February 2020, https://tinyurl.com/bddcdtv8.

241 a comprehensive book on kernel methods: Bernhard Schölkopf and Alexander J. Smola, *Learning with Kernels: Support Vector Machines, Regularization, Optimization, and Beyond* (Cambridge, Mass.: The MIT Press, 2001).

CHAPTER 8: WITH A LITTLE HELP FROM PHYSICS

242 "Now what?": John Hopfield, "Now What?" Princeton Neuroscience Institute, October 2018, https://pni.princeton.edu/people/john-j-hopfield/now-what.

242 "You can't make things error-free": Zoom interview with John Hopfield on October 25, 2021. This and all subsequent quotes by Hopfield are from this author interview, unless identified as quotes from his essay "Now What?"

242 Hopfield published his "biology" paper in 1974: John Hopfield, "Kinetic Proofreading: A New Mechanism for Reducing Errors in Biosynthetic Processes Requiring High Specificity," *Proceedings of the National Academy of Sciences* 71, No. 10 (October 1, 1974): 4135–39.

242 "This was the first paper": Hopfield, "Now What?"

243 In 1976, Hopfield gave a talk at Harvard: Hopfield, "Now What?"

243 "It was one of the biggest": Hopfield, "Now What?"

243 "A network could 'solve a problem' or": Hopfield, "Now What?"

243 "How mind emerges from brain": Hopfield, "Now What?"

244 "primate neuroanatomy": Hopfield, "Now What?"

246 it's an amorphous solid: Ciara Curtin, "Fact or Fiction?: Glass Is a (Supercooled) Liquid," *Scientific American*, February 22, 2007, https://www.scientificamerican.com/article/fact-fiction-glass-liquid/.

246 Certain materials . . . are ferromagnetic: "Ferromagnetism," LibreTexts, n.d., https://tinyurl.com/2p8jcxmf.

246 For his doctoral thesis: S. G. Brush, "History of the Lenz-Ising Model," *Reviews of Modern Physics* 39, No. 4 (1967): 883–93.

246 Rudolf Ernst Peierls, a German physicist: Lee Sabine, "Rudolf Ernst Peierls, 5 June 1907–19 September 1995," *Biographical Memoirs of Fellows of the Royal Society*, December 1, 2007, pp. 53265–84.

247 "For sufficiently low temperatures": R. H. Dalitz and Sir Rudolf Peierls, eds., *Selected Scientific Papers of Sir Rudolf Peierls* (Singapore: World Scientific Publishing, 1997), p. 229.

248 the Hamiltonian of a system: Giorgio Parisi, "Spin Glasses and Fragile Glasses: Statics, Dynamics, and Complexity," *Proceedings of the National Academy of Sciences* 103, No. 21 (May 23, 2006): 7948–55.

248 Here's one: Ada Altieri and Marco Baity-Jesi, "An Introduction to the Theory of Spin Glasses," arXiv, February 9, 2023, https://arxiv.org/abs/2302.04842. Also, see: Viktor Dotsenko, *An Introduction to the Theory of Spin Glasses and Neural Networks* (Singapore: World Scientific, 1994), pp. 4, 113.

270 Hopfield quotes Hemingway: Hopfield, "Now What?"

272 The proof that follows: Raúl Rojas, *Neural Networks: A Systematic Introduction* (Berlin: Springer, 2013), pp. 349–54.

276 "Since there is only a finite set": Rojas, *Neural Networks,* p. 353.

CHAPTER 9: THE MAN WHO SET BACK DEEP LEARNING (NOT REALLY)

277 "I felt like a rock star": Zoom interview with George Cybenko on November 11, 2021. This and all subsequent quotes by Cybenko are from this author interview.

277 blog post Cybenko later read: Vincenzo Lomonaco, "What I Learned at the Deep Learning Summer School 2017 in Bilbao," Medium, July 27, 2017, https://tinyurl.com/4xhc7h9e.

286 For a detailed visual analysis of this approach: Chapter 4: "A Visual Proof that Neural Nets Can Compute Any Function," in Michael Nielsen, *Neural Networks and Deep Learning* (Determination Press, 2015), http://neuralnetworksanddeeplearning.com/chap4.html.

296 small technical report: G. Cybenko, "Continuous Valued Neural Networks with Two Hidden Layers Are Sufficient," Technical Report, 1988, Department of Computer Science, Tufts University.

301 In the concluding paragraph of his 1989 paper: G. Cybenko, "Approximation by Superpositions of a Sigmoidal Function," *Mathematics Control Signal Systems* 2 (December 1989): 303–14.

CHAPTER 10: THE ALGORITHM THAT PUT PAID TO A PERSISTENT MYTH

302 "Yes": Zoom interview with Geoffrey Hinton on October 1, 2021. This and subsequent quotes by Hinton are from this author interview.

303 a theoretical chemist: Chris Darwin, "Christopher Longuet-Higgins: Cognitive Scientist with a Flair for Chemistry," *The Guardian,* June 10, 2004, https://www.theguardian.com/news/2004/jun/10/guardianobituaries.highereducation.

305 "The procedure to be described": Frank Rosenblatt, *Principles of Neurodynamics: Perceptrons and the Theory of Brain Mechanisms,* Cornell University Report No. 1196-G-8, March 15, 1961, p. 292.

305 "It would seem that": Rosenblatt, *Principles of Neurodynamics,* p. 287.

307 "While this theorem shows": Rosenblatt, *Principles of Neurodynamics,* p. 291.

309 "Let the machine make": M. Minsky and O. G. Selfridge, "Learning in Random Nets," in *Information Theory,* ed. E. C. Cherry (London: Butterworth, 1961), pp. 335–47.

310 "Minsky and Papert were so intent": Hubert L. Dreyfus and Stuart E. Dreyfus, "Making a Mind Versus Modeling the Brain: Artificial Intelligence Back at a Branchpoint," *Daedalus* 117, No. 1 (Winter 1988): 15–43.

311 And in an exhaustive blog post: Jürgen Schmidhuber, "Who Invented Backpropagation?" *AI Blog* (blog), 2014, https://people.idsia.ch/~juergen/who-invented-backpropagation.html.

311 Paul Werbos submitted his Ph.D. thesis: P. Werbos, "Beyond Regression: New Tools for Prediction and Analysis in the Behavioral Sciences" (Ph.D. diss., Harvard University, 1974).

337 "In general, the procedure": Werbos, "Beyond Regression."

339 "As a result of the weight adjustments": David E. Rumelhart, Geoffrey E. Hinton, and Ronald J. Williams, "Learning Representations by Back-propagating Errors," *Nature* 323 (October 1986): 533–36.

340 "there is a kid in France": Zoom interview with Yann LeCun on October 11, 2021. This and all subsequent quotes by LeCun are from this author interview.

CHAPTER 11: THE EYES OF A MACHINE

346 "By now the award": H. B. Barlow, "David Hubel and Torsten Wiesel: Their Contribution Towards Understanding the Primary Visual Cortex," *Trends in Neuroscience* 5 (1982): 145–52.

347 "The electrode has been used": David H. Hubel, "Tungsten Microelectrode for Recording from Single Units," *Science* 125 (March 22, 1957): 549–50.

347 It's these electrodes that Hubel and Wiesel: D. H. Hubel and T. N. Wiesel, "Receptive Fields of Single Neurones in the Cat's Striate Cortex," *Journal of Physiology* 148 (1959): 574–91.

347 "made it necessary to use artificial respiration": Hubel and Wiesel, "Receptive Fields of Single Neurones in the Cat's Striate Cortex."

347 "drying and becoming cloudy": Hubel and Wiesel, "Receptive Fields of Single Neurones in the Cat's Striate Cortex."

347 **"At Harvard University, kittens were blinded":** Steven Zak, "Cruelty in Labs," *New York Times,* May 16, 1983, https://www.nytimes.com/1983/05/16/opinion/cruelty-in-labs.html.

347 **"specializing in animals and the law":** Zak, "Cruelty in Labs."

348 **"Among other things":** David S. Forman, "Grim Alternative to Animal Experiments," *New York Times,* May 30, 1983, https://www.nytimes.com/1983/05/30/opinion/l-grim-alternative-to-animal-experiments-195873.html.

348 **the stroke of luck:** David Hubel describes his experiment and the team's serendipitous discovery in this video: Paul Lester, "Hubel and Wiesel Cat Experiment," YouTube, n.d., https://www.youtube.com/watch?v=IOHayh06LJ4.

353 **this neat story is what led:** Grace W. Lindsay, "Convolutional Neural Networks as a Model of the Visual System: Past, Present, and Future," *Journal of Cognitive Neuroscience* 33, No. 10 (2021): 2017–31.

354 **"Cognitron":** Kunihiko Fukushima, "Cognitron: A Self-Organizing Multilayered Neural Network," *Biological Cybernetics* 20 (September 1975): 121–36.

355 **"response was dependent":** Kunihiko Fukushima, "Neocognitron: A Self-Organizing Neural Network Model for a Mechanism of Pattern Recognition Unaffected by Shift in Position," *Biological Cybernetics* 36 (April 1980): 193–202.

355 **In the 1980 paper:** Fukushima, "Neocognitron."

356 **"One of the largest":** Fukushima, "Neocognitron," p. 201.

356 **he chanced upon the book:** Massimo Piattelli-Palmarini, ed., *Language and Learning: The Debate Between Jean Piaget and Noam Chomsky* (Cambridge, Mass.: Harvard University Press, 1980).

357 **"I believe that Chomsky":** Piattelli-Palmarini, ed., *Language and Learning,* p. 91.

357 **"I will do this by describing an automaton":** Piattelli-Palmarini, ed., *Language and Learning,* p. 93.

359 **Called SN:** For a history of Lush, and its ancestor SN, see https://leon.bottou.org/projects/lush.

360 **LeNet:** Yann LeCun et al., "Gradient-Based Learning Applied to Document Recognition," *Proceedings of the IEEE* 86, No. 11 (November 1998): 2278–324.

360 **the convolution:** Trefor Bazett, "The Convolution of Two Functions | Definition & Properties," YouTube video, n.d., https://www.youtube.com/watch?v=AgKQQtEc9dk.

364 **These are called Prewitt kernels:** Achmad Fahrurozi et al., "Wood Classification Based on Edge Detections and Texture Features Selection," *International Journal of Electrical and Computer Engineering* 6, No. 5 (October 2016): 2167–75.

369 **The basic idea behind max pooling:** "Max Pooling," paperswithcode.com/method/max-pooling.

375 **"All we need to achieve":** D. C. Ciresan et al., "Deep Big Simple Neural Nets for Handwritten Digit Recognition," *Neural Computation* 22, No. 12 (2010): 3207–20.

376 **finding roads in aerial images:** Volodymyr Mnih and Geoffrey E. Hinton, "Learning to Detect Roads in High-Resolution Aerial Images," PDF, https://www .cs.toronto.edu/~hinton/absps/road_detection.pdf.

376 **Mnih wrote another package atop CUDA:** Volodymyr Mnih, "CUDAMat: A CUDA-Based Matrix Class for Python," PDF, University of Toronto Technical Report, UTML TR 2009–004, http://www.cs.toronto.edu/~vmnih/docs /cudamat_tr.pdf.

377 **Fei-Fei Li and her students presented a paper:** J. Deng et al., "ImageNet: A Large-Scale Hierarchical Image Database," 2009 IEEE Conference on Computer Vision and Pattern Recognition, Miami, Fla., 2009, pp. 248–55.

378 **"taster competition":** Visual Object Classes Challenge 2010, host.robots .ox.ac.uk/pascal/VOC/voc2010/.

381 **"Everything went out of the window":** Zoom interviews with Mikhail Belkin on July 20, 2021; January 15, 2022; and January 13, 2023. This and subsequent quotes by Belkin are from these author interviews, unless specified otherwise.

CHAPTER 12: TERRA INCOGNITA

383 **"grokking":** See Brittanica for definition and origins of "grok": https://www .britannica.com/topic/grok.

383 **"Grokking is meant to be":** Zoom interview with Alethea Power on January 28, 2022. This and subsequent quotes by Power are from this author interview.

389 **"It's a balance between":** Anil Ananthaswamy, "A New Link to an Old Model Could Crack the Mystery of Deep Learning," *Quanta*, October 11, 2021, https://tinyurl.com/27hxb5k5.

389 **the bias-variance trade-off:** Scott Fortmann-Roe, "Understanding the Bias-Variance Trade-off," (blog), June 2012, http://scott.fortmann-roe.com /docs/BiasVariance.html.

393 **"More surprising is that":** Behnam Neyshabur et al., "In Search of the Real Inductive Bias: On the Role of Implicit Regularization in Deep Learning," arXiv, April 16, 2015, https://arxiv.org/abs/1412.6614.

394 **"Even with five percent random labels":** Neyshabur et al., "In Search of the Real Inductive Bias."

394 **"The experiments we conducted":** Chiyan Zhang et al., "Understanding Deep Learning Requires Rethinking Generalization," arXiv, February 26, 2017, https://arxiv.org/abs/1611.03530.

395 **"We routinely teach our undergraduates":** In-person interview with Peter Bartlett in Berkeley, California, on December 11, 2021.

395 **"The best way to solve the problem":** Ruslan Salakhutdinov quoted in Mikhail Belkin, "Fit without Fear: Remarkable Mathematical Phenomena of Deep

Learning through the Prism of Interpolation," arXiv, May 29, 2021, https://arxiv
.org/abs/2105.14368.

396 wrote a paper in 1995: Leo Breiman, "Reflections After Refereeing Papers for
NIPS," in David H. Wolpert, ed., *The Mathematics of Generalization* (Boca Raton,
Fla.: CRC Press, 1995), pp. 11–15.

396 "acronym encourages sexism and is a slur": Holly Else, "AI Conference
Widely Known as 'NIPS' Changes Its Controversial Acronym," *Nature News,*
November 19, 2018, https://www.nature.com/articles/d41586-018-07476-w.

396 "Why don't heavily parameterized": Leo Breiman, "Reflections After
Refereeing Papers for NIPS," p. 15.

396 an ML algorithm called AdaBoost: Peter Bartlett et al., "Boosting the
Margin: A New Explanation for the Effectiveness of Voting Methods," *The Annals
of Statistics* 26, No. 5 (October 1998): 1651–86.

398 long short-term memory: Sepp Hochreiter and Jürgen Schmidhuber, "Long
Short-Term Memory," *Neural Computation* 9, No. 8 (1997): 173–80.

399 For example, the ReLU function: Sebastian Raschka, "Machine Learning
FAQ: Why Is the ReLu Function Not Differentiable at x=0?" Sebastian Raschka, *AI
Magazine* (blog), n.d., https://sebastianraschka.com/faq/docs/relu-derivative.html.

401 "If, by the first day of autumn": Bet described by Alexei Efros during an
interview via Zoom on January 28, 2022. This and subsequent quotes by Efros are
from this author interview. Also, see "The Gelato Bet," March 2019, https://people
.eecs.berkeley.edu/~efros/gelato_bet.html.

404 This changed in December 2021: Anil Ananthaswamy, "Self-Taught
AI Shows Similarities to How the Brain Works," *Quanta,* August 11, 2022,
https://tinyurl.com/8z35n24j.

405 One of the most intriguing places in that landscape: Mikhail Belkin et al.,
"Reconciling Modern Machine-Learning Practice and the Classical Bias-Variance
Trade-Off," *Proceedings of the National Academy of Sciences* 116, No. 32 (July 24,
2019): 15849–54.

407 "Maybe we shouldn't have such a focus on theory": Tom Goldstein spoke at
the National Science Foundation's Town Hall on machine learning on January 10,
2022. This quote and other quotes by Goldstein are taken from his talk, available at
https://tinyurl.com/4m5396b7, beginning at 29:40.

407 An empirical study by Goldstein and colleagues: Micah Goldblum et al.,
"Truth or Backpropaganda? An Empirical Investigation of Deep Learning Theory,"
arXiv, April 28, 2020, https://arxiv.org/abs/1910.00359.

408 stochasticity wasn't needed: Jonas Geiping et al., "Stochastic Training Is
Not Necessary for Generalization," arXiv, April 19, 2022, https://arxiv.org/abs
/2109.14119.

412 "scientific papers from the arXiv preprint server": Ethan Dyer and Guy
Gur-Ari, Google Research, Blueshift Team, "Minerva: Solving Quantitative

Reasoning Problems with Language Models" *Google Research* (blog), June 30, 2022, https://blog.research.google/2022/06/minerva-solving-quantitative-reasoning.html.

EPILOGUE

416 At a public talk I gave on ChatGPT: Anil Ananthaswamy, "ChatGPT and Its Ilk," YouTube video, n.d., https://www.youtube.com/watch?v=gL4cquObnbE.

420 "stochastic parrots": Emily M. Bender et al., "On the Dangers of Stochastic Parrots: Can Language Models Be Too Big?" *FAccT '21: Proceedings of the 2021 ACM Conference on Fairness, Accountability, and Transparency,* Association for Computing Machinery, New York, N.Y., March 2021, pp. 610–23.

421 "Google Photos, y'all f*** [*sic*] up. My friend's not a gorilla": Maggie Zhang, "Google Photos Tags Two African-Americans as Gorillas Through Facial Recognition Software," *Forbes,* July 1, 2015, https://tinyurl.com/yr5y97zz.

421 this workaround was still in place: Nico Grant and Kashmir Hill, "Google's Photo App Still Can't Find Gorillas. And Neither Can Apple's," *New York Times,* May 22, 2023, https://tinyurl.com/4xbj6pmh.

421 "black defendants were far more": Jeff Larson et al., "How We Analyzed the COMPAS Recidivism Algorithm," ProPublica, May 23, 2016, https://tinyurl.com/3adtt92t.

421 Amazon had to jettison: Jeffrey Dastin, "Insight—Amazon Scraps Secret AI Recruiting Tool that Showed Bias Against Women," Reuters, October 11, 2018, https://tinyurl.com/mpfmserk.

421 a paper in *Science*: Ziad Obermeyer et al., "Dissecting Racial Bias in an Algorithm Used to Manage the Health of Populations," *Science* 366, No. 6464 (October 25, 2019): 447–53.

421 "Gender Shades": Joy Buolamwini and Timnit Gebru, "Gender Shades: Intersectional Accuracy Disparities in Commercial Gender Classification," *Proceedings of Machine Learning Research* 81 (2018): 1–15.

422 following interaction with OpenAI's GPT-4: Adam Tauman Kalai, "How to Use Self-Play for Language Models to Improve at Solving Programming Puzzles," Workshop on Large Language Models and Transformers, Simons Institute for the Theory of Computing, August 15, 2023, https://tinyurl.com/56sct6n8.

424 "Individual humans form their beliefs": Celeste Kidd and Abeba Birhane, "How AI Can Distort Human Beliefs," *Science* 380, No. 6651 (June 22, 2023): 1222–23.

425 Hinton, the final speaker at the bootleg session: Adapted from Anil Ananthaswamy, "Artificial Neural Nets Finally Yield Clues to How Brains Learn," *Quanta,* February 28, 2020.

426 "I remember very distinctly": Adapted from Anil Ananthaswamy, "Deep Neural Networks Help to Explain Living Brains," *Quanta,* October 28, 2020.

426 Yamins discovered that the architecture: Adapted from Ananthaswamy, "Deep Neural Networks Help to Explain Living Brains."

427 "Not only did we get good predictions": Adapted from Ananthaswamy, "Deep Neural Networks Help to Explain Living Brains."

427 Nancy Kanwisher, a neuroscientist: Adapted from Ananthaswamy, "Deep Neural Networks Help to Explain Living Brains."

427 Another intriguing result also came from DiCarlo's lab: Adapted from Ananthaswamy, "Deep Neural Networks Help to Explain Living Brains."

429 consumed, on average, about 1,664 watts: Anil Ananthaswamy, "In AI, Is Bigger Better?" *Nature* 615 (March 9, 2023): 202–5.

Index